ANNETTE FLAVEL

SPEAK YOUR MIND

TEACHER'S EDITION
+ access to Teacher's App

1

macmillan education

Macmillan Education
4 Crinan Street
London N1 9XW
A division of Macmillan Education Limited

Companies and representatives throughout the world

Speak Your Mind Level 1 Teacher's Edition
ISBN 978-1-380-03112-9
Speak Your Mind Level 1 Teacher's Edition + access to Teacher's App ISBN 978-1-380-03104-4

Written by Annette Flavel
Additional material by Mickey Rogers and Spencer Kagan

First published 2020

Teacher's Edition credits:
Designed by QBS Learning
Original cover design by therestless.co.uk
Cover adaptation by Roberto Martínez
Cover background by **Getty Images**/Chatuporn Sornlampoo/EyeEm.

The publishers would like to thank all the teachers that piloted and reviewed the series, and a special thanks to Dr. Spencer Kagan for sharing his expertise in the article included in the Introduction.

The authors and publishers would like to thank the following for permission to reproduce their photographs:
Kagan Publishing and Professional Development pp. xxviii, xxx; **Khristian Snyder** p. xxviii; **Shutterstock**/davooda p. xxx, Shutterstock/vasabii pp. xxix, xxxi; **Macmillan Education Limited**/Getty Images/iStockphoto/zentilia p. xxv, Macmillan Education Limited/iStockphoto/alexsl p. xxvi–xxvii.

The authors and publishers are grateful for permission to reprint the following copyright material (pp. xxviii-xxxi): "Thinking Skills" by Spencer Kagan. Copied with permission from Kagan Publishing and Professional Development, Kagan Online website.

Student's Book credits:

Written by Mickey Rogers, Joanne Taylore-Knowles, and Steve Taylore-Knowles

Designed by QBS Learning
Illustrated by Jerome Brasseur (Beehive Illustration) p. 68 (t), p. 110; Lon Eric Craven (Wendy Lynn & Co.) p. 42; Daniel Deamo (Lemonade Illustration) pp. 21, 81, 90, 153; Keith Favazza (Wendy Lynn & Co.) pp. 70, 75; Bunky Hurter (Mendola Artists) pp. 82, 92; QBS Learning pp. 41, 52, 68(c), 80, 140.
Picture research by Fernanda Rocha/Ikonia LLC

Full acknowledgements for photographs in the facsimile pages can be found in the Student's Book ISBN 978-1-380-01306-4.

Additional sources:
p. 26 – Bradley Barth, "Malicious bot traffic climbs 9.5 percent in 2017, says report," *SC Magazine*, 2018, Tweak Library, "27 Interesting Facts about Computer Virus," 2018.
p. 56 – UNESCO, *UNESCO Science Report*, 2019; Drew DeSilver, "Few Students Likely to Use Print Books for Research," Pew Research Center, 2013; Dan Ackman, "For 53% Reliable Information, Click Here," *Forbes*, 2003.
p. 66 – Vincent Wee, "101 Interesting Facts about Digital Marketing," Tech Edt, 2016; "The 25 Best Cities for Marketing Jobs in 2017," Best Marketing Degrees website, 2017.
p. 106 – Sandra Choron, Harry Choron, *Wedding Planning: A Nuptial-pedia*, 2010; PaperStyle, "Fun Facts About Birthdays," 2017; Stefania Sainato, "12 Fun Facts About Wedding Planning," *Bridal Guide Magazine*, 2012.
p. 126 – Paul Sims, *Daily Mail*, 2012; Mental Floss, "11 Scientific Benefits of Being Outdoors," 2019.

Printed and bound in Brazil
2025
32

Table of Contents

Speak Your Mind Philosophy

In the 21st century, it is no longer enough just to teach subject matter. Teachers need to help their students develop important skills that can lead to success in whatever they choose to do.

The core objective of ***Speak Your Mind*** is to help students become confident communicators. The focus is on using English to communicate in both local and global contexts. Most students may not live in an English-speaking country, but it is probable they will need to use English in the course of their academic and professional lives. Being a confident and competent communicator involves going beyond language skills. Students need to analyze ideas, work effectively in teams, and solve problems.

Job readiness consists of more than just a strong academic performance. The ability to communicate effectively in English and to use 21st-century skills is essential in order for young adults to enter successfully into or advance within the complex, global world in which they live. ***Speak Your Mind*** is designed to help students achieve their goals.

Speak Your Mind has a number of features that help students in their academic, professional, and everyday lives:

- Every lesson in ***Speak Your Mind*** ends with a specific communicative outcome. Students do a collaborative task in which they use target language from the lesson to communicate their ideas and express their opinions on a topic related to the subject of the lesson.
- Students learn skills that transfer from the classroom to real life. The lessons contain thinking questions that help improve their thinking skills as they learn English. The last lesson in every unit (Language and Life) develops problem-solving and teamwork skills by taking students through a step-by-step process in which they work together to solve a problem or produce a proposal in a real-life scenario.
- Young-adult students already have a great deal of knowledge about the world, and they are encouraged to transfer their real-life knowledge to the classroom. The topics in ***Speak Your Mind*** allow students to express their opinions on real-world events and issues and to learn more about those topics. Students are often asked to give opinions or to say what they already know about a topic before listening to or reading a text on the subject.
- Most young adults will have at least some previous knowledge of English. They are encouraged to share that knowledge and to build on it according to their personal needs and interests. Unit Openers help them be aware of how many words they already know in English and to share their knowledge with their classmates. *Make It Yours* boxes allow them to build their own personal vocabulary lists.
- Videos further help students connect their language learning to real life. For each unit, there is a video that focuses on the Unit Opener topic and acts as a prompt for discussion. For even-numbered units, there are documentary-style Follow A Pro videos that follow a day in the life of a person in a particular profession.

Unit Structure

***Speak Your Mind* Student's Books 1–3** consist of 12 units of 10 pages each. Every unit begins with a one-page Unit Opener designed to introduce the unit topic and to elicit vocabulary and other language that students are already familiar with. Each Unit Opener features a *Video* that can be used to prompt a discussion.

The Unit Opener is followed by four double-page lessons. Lessons 1–3 contain the core GRAMMAR, VOCABULARY, READING, SPEAKING, LISTENING, PRONUNCIATION, and WRITING sections for the unit. Lesson 4 is called Language and Life. It also includes a reading, but its purpose is to provide students with a task that will help them develop key 21st-century skills.

At the end of each unit, there is a REVIEW page with additional practice of the target grammar and vocabulary. This page also contains a section to introduce a study skill (in odd-numbered units) or a profession related to the topic of the unit (in even-numbered units).

At the end of each **Student's Book**, there are lessons connected to the study skills and the professions introduced on the *Review* pages. There is also a list of common irregular verbs, as well as further practice of the target grammar in the book.

Apart from the **Student's Book**, there is a **Workbook** available in print or digital form. The **Student's Resource Center** contains *Reading Worksheets* for extra reading practice, as well as lesson plans adapted from Macmillan's *OneStopEnglish* website. The **Teacher's Resource Center** contains printable tests for unit, mid-course, and end-of-course assessment.

For more information on each feature mentioned in this Introduction, please see the relevant sections that follow.

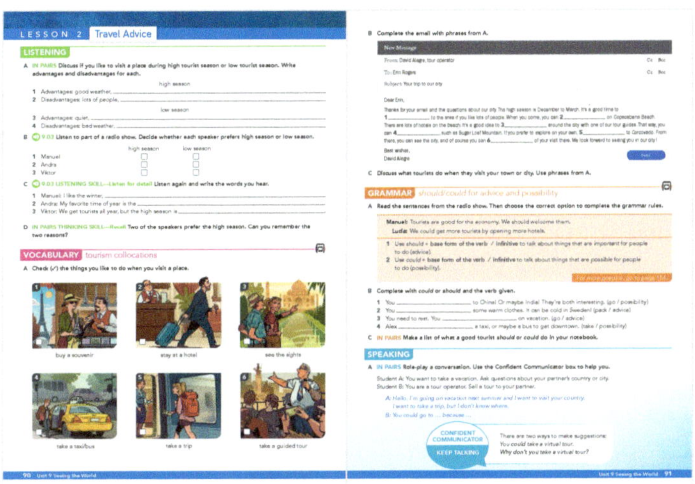

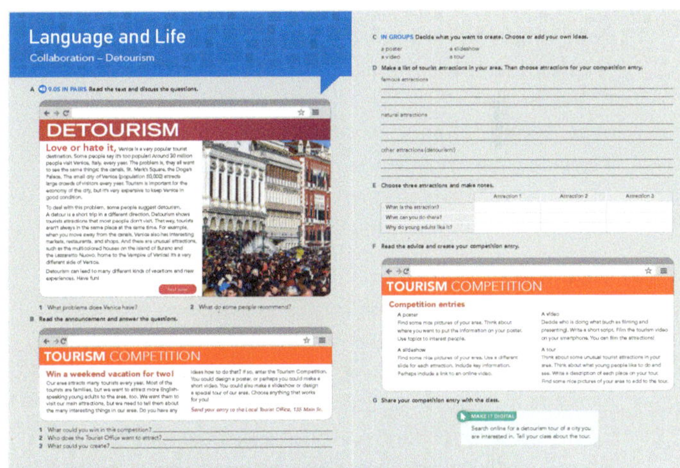

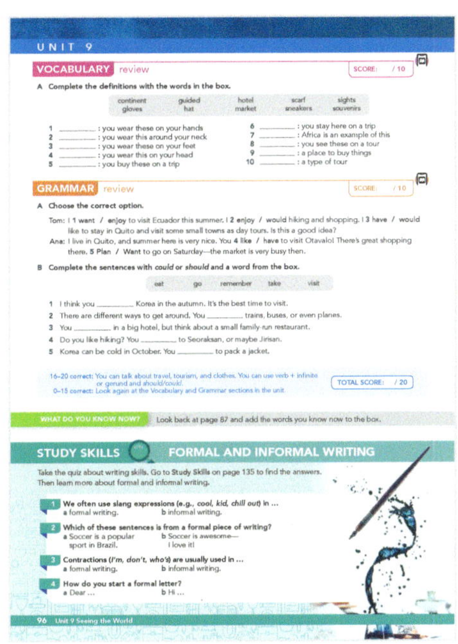

Unit Opener

Each Unit Opener introduces the general topic of the unit in a way that will stimulate the interest and curiosity of young adults. The Unit Openers give students the opportunity to think about topic-related words and phrases they already know and to discuss a question they can think about as they work through the unit. Each Unit Opener features a video to support this discussion.

The ability to use prior knowledge to support the acquisition of new knowledge is an important learning strategy. Having students think about language they already know or knowledge they already have helps them approach new material with greater confidence.

Another important concept in today's classrooms is cooperative learning. Students begin by thinking about something or doing a task individually, then work in pairs to share and build on their individual work. Finally, they work in groups to apply what they have learned individually and in pairs.

PROCEDURE: Teaching the **Unit Opener** in *Speak Your Mind*

① **Individual work.** Have students work individually to list familiar words and phrases related to the unit topic. This helps build their confidence by highlighting the fact that they already know a lot of English. This section also gives them the chance to think about how the unit topic relates to their own lives.

② **Peer teaching and learning.** Put students in pairs and ask them to share the words and phrases they wrote. At the beginning of the course, explain that working together and sharing what they know allows them to increase their knowledge. Note that at the end of the unit, they will be asked to come back to the Unit Opener and add new words they have learned in the unit.

③ **Video.** A short, optional video accompanies each DISCUSS & SHARE section. The purpose of these videos is to provide input that can support students in their discussion of the ***Speak Your Mind*** Question. Note that the videos are intended to provide information and context for the discussion, but the ***Speak Your Mind*** Question can easily be discussed without viewing them. Teachers are strongly encouraged to use them, as they provide fun and interesting contexts for the discussion, as well as input from both sides of the issue to help students form opinions.

④ **Speak Your Mind Question.** Ask students to work in groups to discuss the ***Speak Your Mind*** Question. Explain that the questions do not have specific right or wrong answers because the purpose is to make students think and allow them to express their opinions. Note that these questions are part of the critical-thinking thread in ***Speak Your Mind***. Students should think in terms of a continuum. For example, in Unit 2 Work/Life Balance, some students may think that it's best to work a great deal in order to be successful, some students may think that it's best to have a lot of personal time in order to be happy, while other students may think that the best work/life balance is something in between those two extremes.

⑤ **Unit Summary.** At the bottom of the Unit Opener page, there is a summary of what students will learn in the unit. You may want to go over this so students know what they will learn in the unit.

Vocabulary

Vocabulary plays a very prominent role in ***Speak Your Mind***. Every unit begins with a focus on vocabulary through Unit Opener activities that elicit familiar vocabulary related to the unit topic. Students build on that knowledge through peer sharing. In Lessons 1–3, there is a VOCABULARY section to present and practice new vocabulary related to the specific lesson topic. In Lesson 4, there are opportunities for students to use vocabulary from the unit in the context of the tasks in the lesson.

In ***Speak Your Mind***, vocabulary is presented within the context of the reading or listening text in the lesson. Sometimes the vocabulary is pre-taught in order to help students understand it when they encounter it as they read or listen. Other times, the VOCABULARY section follows the READING or LISTENING section, and students are encouraged to use the context of the text to help them figure out the meaning of the words.

PROCEDURE: Teaching **Vocabulary** in *Speak Your Mind*

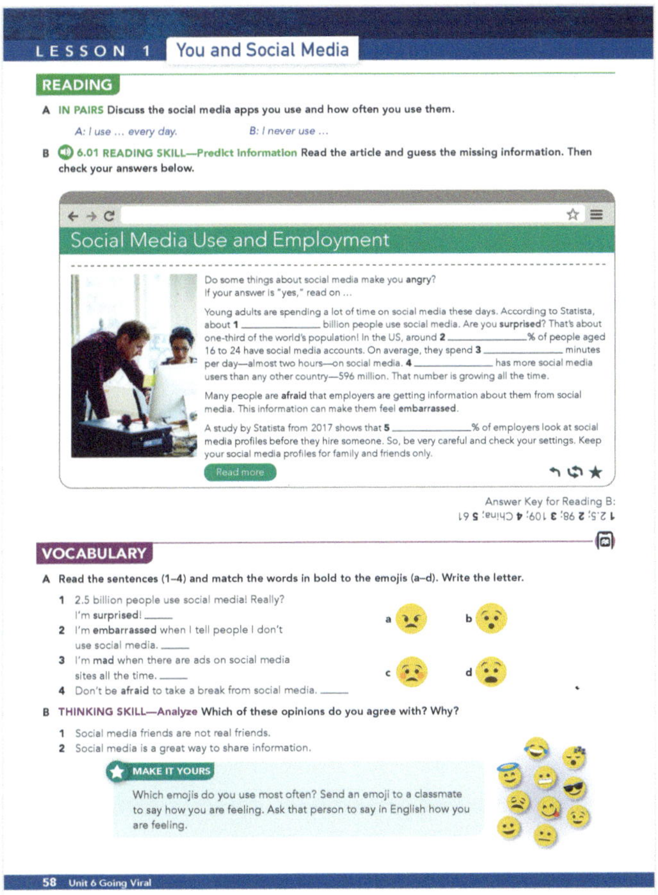
LESSON 1 You and Social Media

READING

A IN PAIRS Discuss the social media apps you use and how often you use them.

A: I use … every day. *B: I never use …*

B 6.01 READING SKILL—Predict Information Read the article and guess the missing information. Then check your answers below.

Social Media Use and Employment

Do some things about social media make you **angry**?
If your answer is "yes," read on …

Young adults are spending a lot of time on social media these days. According to Statista, about **1** ______ billion people use social media. Are you **surprised**? That's about one-third of the world's population! In the US, around **2** ______% of people aged 16 to 24 have social media accounts. On average, they spend **3** ______ minutes per day—almost two hours—on social media. **4** ______ has more social media users than any other country—596 million. That number is growing all the time.

Many people are **afraid** that employers are getting information about them from social media. This information can make them feel **embarrassed**.

A study by Statista from 2017 shows that **5** ______% of employers look at social media profiles before they hire someone. So, be very careful and check your settings. Keep your social media profiles for family and friends only.

Read more

Answer Key for Reading B:
1 2.5; **2** 98; **3** 109; **4** China; **5** 61

VOCABULARY

A Read the sentences (1–4) and match the words in bold to the emojis (a–d). Write the letter.

1 2.5 billion people use social media! Really? I'm **surprised**! ___
2 I'm **embarrassed** when I tell people I don't use social media. ___
3 I'm **mad** when there are ads on social media sites all the time. ___
4 Don't be **afraid** to take a break from social media. ___

a b c d

B THINKING SKILL—Analyze Which of these opinions do you agree with? Why?

1 Social media friends are not real friends.
2 Social media is a great way to share information.

MAKE IT YOURS

Which emojis do you use most often? Send an emoji to a classmate to say how you are feeling. Ask that person to say in English how you are feeling.

58 Unit 6 Going Viral

Lexical sets. These are particularly relevant at lower levels, when students need a great deal of basic vocabulary related to topics such as food or sports. The lexical sets are often presented through visuals, and students are asked to match the words to the pictures.

When a lexical set is presented, ask students if they know or want to know any other words related to the set. This is a good way to utilize peer teaching, to make students feel that they are participating in the learning process, and to expand the target vocabulary to include words that students are interested in knowing.

Remember to have students practice saying vocabulary words that are intended for active use. It is also important for them to learn how to spell the words.

Topic-related vocabulary. Words or phrases that are related to the topic of the reading or listening are frequently presented by asking students to look at sentences from the text and match the target words to their definitions, or use them to complete sentences or a short text.

When the VOCABULARY section comes after a reading text, encourage students to go back to the text and look at the words in context to help them confirm their answers to the vocabulary activity.

When the vocabulary is presented before a LISTENING section, encourage students to listen for the words during the listening activity. Either before or after students listen, you may want to write the sentences with the vocabulary words on the board and check that they understand how each word is used.

Word formation. Students learn to use prefixes and suffixes to change the meaning or the part of speech of a word.

It is a good idea to have students make a word-formation chart in their notebooks that they can add to as they learn different prefixes and suffixes. Organize the chart into columns by parts of speech: noun, verb, adjective, and adverb. If there are equivalents to the affixes in their own language, you may want to include those in the chart to help students relate the English forms to elements in their own language.

Synonyms and antonyms. Learning synonyms and antonyms helps students expand the range and variety of their vocabulary.

There are vocabulary lessons on synonyms and antonyms in ***Speak Your Mind***, but you can teach synonyms or antonyms appropriate to the level as an extension to any vocabulary lesson. For example, if students learn *delicious*, also teach *tasty* or the slang word *yummy*. If they see *shiny* in a text, you can teach them that the opposite is *dull*.

Grammar

Grammar in ***Speak Your Mind*** is taught through an inductive approach in which students are encouraged to observe grammatical structures in context and to go through an analytical process that allows them to figure out rules of structure and function. At the beginning of the course, explain to students that they will be asked to actively participate in their own learning by using observation and thinking skills to figure out grammar rules about form and function. Point out that we tend to learn more effectively when we figure something out for ourselves rather than just being told. Each unit has two GRAMMAR sections: one in Lesson 1 and one in Lesson 2. In Lessons 3 and 4, students have opportunities to use the grammar they have just learned.

PROCEDURE: Teaching **Grammar** in *Speak Your Mind*

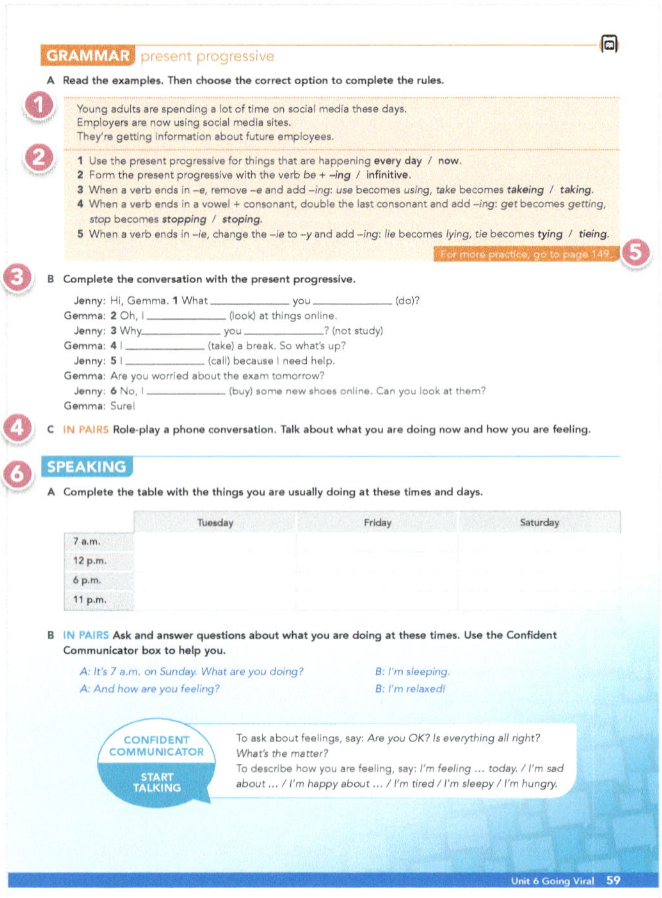

GRAMMAR present progressive

A Read the examples. Then choose the correct option to complete the rules.

1 Young adults are spending a lot of time on social media these days.
Employers are now using social media sites.
They're getting information about future employees.

2
1 Use the present progressive for things that are happening **every day** / **now**.
2 Form the present progressive with the verb *be* + **–*ing*** / **infinitive**.
3 When a verb ends in –*e*, remove –*e* and add –*ing*: *use* becomes *using*, *take* becomes ***takeing*** / ***taking***.
4 When a verb ends in a vowel + consonant, double the last consonant and add –*ing*: *get* becomes *getting*, *stop* becomes ***stopping*** / ***stoping***.
5 When a verb ends in –*ie*, change the –*ie* to –*y* and add –*ing*: *lie* becomes *lying*, *tie* becomes ***tying*** / ***tieing***.

For more practice, go to page 149. 5

3 B Complete the conversation with the present progressive.

Jenny: Hi, Gemma. **1** What ______ you ______ (do)?
Gemma: **2** Oh, I ______ (look) at things online.
Jenny: **3** Why ______ you ______? (not study)
Gemma: **4** I ______ (take) a break. So what's up?
Jenny: **5** I ______ (call) because I need help.
Gemma: Are you worried about the exam tomorrow?
Jenny: **6** No, I ______ (buy) some new shoes online. Can you look at them?
Gemma: Sure!

4 C IN PAIRS Role-play a phone conversation. Talk about what you are doing now and how you are feeling.

6 SPEAKING

A Complete the table with the things you are usually doing at these times and days.

	Tuesday	Friday	Saturday
7 a.m.			
12 p.m.			
6 p.m.			
11 p.m.			

B IN PAIRS Ask and answer questions about what you are doing at these times. Use the Confident Communicator box to help you.

A: It's 7 a.m. on Sunday. What are you doing? *B: I'm sleeping.*
A: And how are you feeling? *B: I'm relaxed!*

CONFIDENT COMMUNICATOR
START TALKING
To ask about feelings, say: *Are you OK? Is everything all right? What's the matter?*
To describe how you are feeling, say: *I'm feeling … today. / I'm sad about … / I'm happy about … / I'm tired / I'm sleepy / I'm hungry.*

Unit 6 Going Viral 59

(1) **Notice the grammar in context.** Students are exposed to the new grammar structure in the context of a reading or listening text before they are asked to study and work with the grammar itself. You may want to point out one or two examples of the new structure in a reading text or explain that students will hear examples of new grammar in a listening text. It is not necessary to pre-teach the grammar in order for them to understand the text. Part of learning a new language is learning to use context to understand the meaning of new grammar or vocabulary.

(2) **Complete the rule.** Ask students to look at examples of the grammar from the reading or listening text. The examples are usually included in the GRAMMAR section, but sometimes students are asked to look for examples in the text. Explain that they should notice the form of the grammar and also think about the meaning, or the function, of the grammatical structure. Then ask them to do the activity that follows the examples. The activity asks them to complete grammar rules or answer questions about the grammar in order to show that they have understood it. When going over the rules, have students point out the grammar structures in the example sentences that confirm the rules.

(3) **Practice.** The analysis of the grammar rules is followed by one or more written activities to practice the new structure. You may want to let students compare their answers in pairs before checking answers as a class. This will provide an opportunity for cooperative learning.

If students have had trouble with an activity, refer back to the grammar rules as you go over each answer to make sure that students understand why the answer is what it is.

(4) **Oral practice.** The GRAMMAR sections often include a short pair or group communicative activity to practice the new grammar. Make sure that everyone has an opportunity to use several examples of all forms of the new grammar. For example, if they are learning questions and answers with a verb tense, make sure that students are practicing both the question forms and the answer forms.

(5) **Further practice.** In the highlighted boxes, there is a reference to further practice in the *Grammar Reference* section at the back of the book. These activities could be done in class if you feel that students need more practice right away to help them understand the grammar, or they could be done as homework or as review before an exam. At the end of this section, there is a list of suggestions for further grammar practice.

(6) **Further oral practice.** The grammar is also used in the SPEAKING section at the end of each lesson, which gives students communicative practice with the target structure. Remind them that they should use the grammar as much as possible in the speaking activities in order to become comfortable with it. You may want to elicit some examples of how they can use the grammar before they start the speaking activity.

Speak Your Mind provides a number of opportunities for further practice of the grammar:

- The *Grammar Quiz* before Unit 1 is a quick test of what students should have learned before beginning the course.
- The *Grammar Review* after Unit 12 is a review of what students should have learned in prior levels. The *Grammar Review* of Level 1 (A1) reviews language at the pre-A1 level.
- The **Student's App** contains grammar practice. An [app icon] indicates where there is practice in the app.
- A *Grammar Reference* section at the end of the **Student's Book** gives further explanations and practice activities for the grammar points in each unit.
- Grammar practice activities in the **Workbook** reinforce the GRAMMAR sections in the lessons.

Pronunciation

In ***Speak Your Mind***, pronunciation is taught through a combination of observation and practice. There is a PRONUNCIATION section in each unit, and four main areas are emphasized: specific sounds, specific words, stress and intonation, and juncture and reduction.

Students are first asked to listen to examples and to notice a pattern or confirm a rule. It is important to allow them to listen and understand the pronunciation point before asking them to try to produce it.

The noticing activity is followed by practice of the pronunciation point, sometimes as a whole class and other times in pairs.

PROCEDURE: Teaching **Pronunciation** in *Speak Your Mind*

1 **PRONUNCIATION** /ju/

A 12.03 **Listen and notice. The long *u* sound /u/ sometimes has a *y* sound /ju/.**

beautiful communicate cute document music popular

B **Practice saying the words with the correct pronunciation.**

2 **PRONUNCIATION** *can/can't*

A 7.02 **Listen. Choose the words you hear.**

1 Can / Can't you swim?
2 I can / can't.
3 Can / Can't you come to a new water polo class with me?
4 Sorry, I can / can't. I play tennis then.

B IN PAIRS **Practice saying the conversation. Notice the /t/ sound in *can't*.**

3 **PRONUNCIATION** word stress in information questions

A 4.02 **Listen and underline the stressed words.**

1 What do you do?
2 Where do you live?
3 Why do you like your job?
4 When do you go on vacation?
5 How do you get to class?

B 4.02 **Listen again. Practice reading the questions with the correct word stress.**

4 **PRONUNCIATION** *an* + vowel

A 2.02 **Listen and notice how phrases with *an* sound like /æ/ + a word beginning with *n*. Practice saying the words. Draw a line to connect *an* to the vowel of the next word.**

an architect an art teacher an economist an engineer an interior designer an interpreter an office manager an optometrist

① **Specific sounds:** Make sure students understand the rule and can distinguish the sound. Model the sound for them, first with the sound only and then using the sound in a word. Allow them to practice the sound a number of times until they feel comfortable with it.

② **Specific words:** When students have to recognize specific words in a sentence, you may want to let them listen to the sentences more than once. If they are asked to notice a sound within a word, make sure they can all distinguish it.

③ **Stress and intonation:** You may want to read the sentences yourself before students practice them. In this way, you can exaggerate the stressed words or the intonation pattern to make sure students can recognize the pattern.

④ **Juncture or reduction:** Many languages do not have juncture or reduction features similar to the ones in English, so this can be a difficult concept for students. It is very important to make sure that they understand the explanations of these features. However, especially at beginning levels, it is more important for students to be able to understand native speakers when they reduce unstressed vowels or combine words (as in this example) than for them to be able to produce them perfectly.

Reading

Good readers unconsciously use a number of different skills when they read in their own language. When people learn a second language, they often need to become aware of those skills and learn how to use them when reading in the second language. Reading is considered a receptive skill, but that does not mean that it is a passive activity. Reading involves interacting with a text by reading it with questions in mind, comparing one's own knowledge or opinions to the information in the text, and applying skills to help one understand and interpret the text.

In the classroom, reading is usually done to develop reading skills or as a vehicle for language study. However, a text will be more effective for academic purposes if students find it interesting. In ***Speak Your Mind***, reading texts on a wide variety of topics in a number of different genres are designed to engage students' interest while providing work on key reading skills and general reading comprehension.

PROCEDURE: Teaching **Reading** in *Speak Your Mind*

① **Pre-reading.** Every READING section begins with a pre-reading activity to remind students of knowledge they already have about the topic or to raise their interest in the topic. Before students read the text, have them discuss what they know, or would like to know, about the topic, have them predict what information they think will be in the text, or have them give their opinions about the topic.

② **Reading.** The ***Speak Your Mind*** reading texts introduce vocabulary words in bold to help students focus on them. As students read, they should circle words they don't know and keep reading, then go back to unknown words and guess their meaning. Audio recordings are available for reading texts.

③ **Comprehension.** There are two types of comprehension activities that accompany reading texts: activities for general comprehension and activities to develop specific reading skills. For general comprehension activities, it is a good idea to have students read the questions before reading the text in order to help them quickly identify key information while reading. Good readers usually have an idea of what information they want to get from a text before they begin reading. You may want to ask students to underline key words and information as they read, or to make notes or write questions in the margin next to the text.

④ **Reading Skill.** For READING SKILL activities, check that students understand what the skill is and why it is useful before asking them to do the activity. Each unit of the **Workbook** has an explanation of the skill presented in the **Student's Book**, as well as further practice of the skill. You may want to direct students to the explanation in the **Workbook** before having them do the activity in the **Student's Book**.

⑤ **Thinking Skill.** Reading should cause us to think. In some cases, we may agree or disagree with a text. A text may raise further questions about a topic, or it may excite and motivate us to share information with others or to take some kind of action. While young adult students of a foreign language, especially at lower levels, do not have great ability with the language, they nevertheless possess adult-level thinking skills. It is more motivating for them to read texts if they know that they will be able to interact with the texts or the topics in a way that takes into account their cognitive abilities. For more on thinking skills, see *Thinking Skills* by Dr. Spencer Kagan on pages xxviii-xxxi of this book.

Further Reading. For further practice of reading skills and general reading comprehension, there are *Reading Worksheets* available in the **Student's Resource Center**.

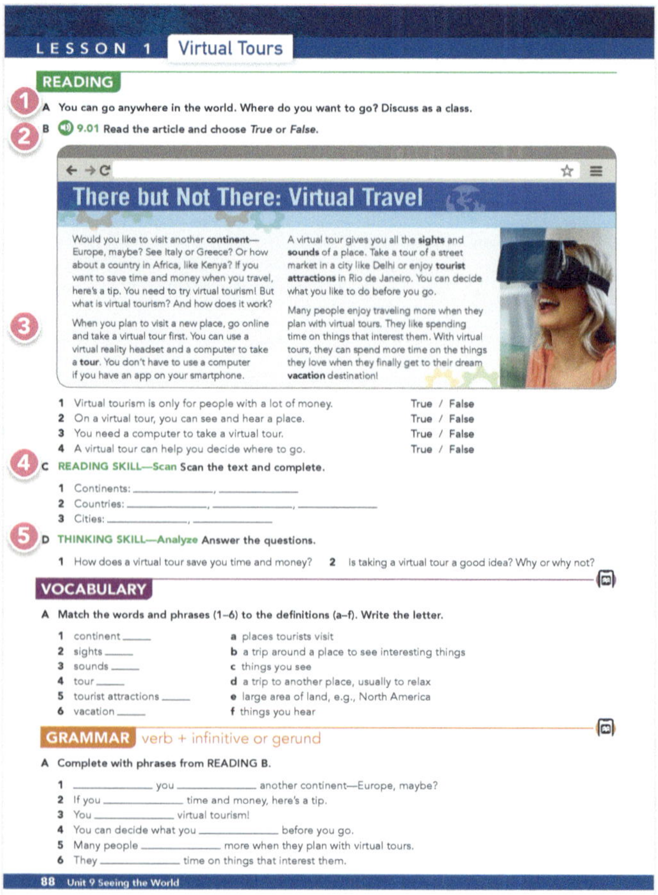
LESSON 1 Virtual Tours

READING

① A You can go anywhere in the world. Where do you want to go? Discuss as a class.

② B 9.01 Read the article and choose *True* or *False*.

There but Not There: Virtual Travel

Would you like to visit another **continent**—Europe, maybe? See Italy or Greece? Or how about a country in Africa, like Kenya? If you want to save time and money when you travel, here's a tip. You need to try virtual tourism! But what is virtual tourism? And how does it work?

When you plan to visit a new place, go online and take a virtual tour first. You can use a virtual reality headset and a computer to take a **tour**. You don't have to use a computer if you have an app on your smartphone.

A virtual tour gives you all the **sights** and **sounds** of a place. Take a tour of a street market in a city like Delhi or enjoy **tourist attractions** in Rio de Janeiro. You can decide what you like to do before you go.

Many people enjoy traveling more when they plan with virtual tours. They like spending time on things that interest them. With virtual tours, they can spend more time on the things they love when they finally get to their dream **vacation** destination!

③
1 Virtual tourism is only for people with a lot of money. True / False
2 On a virtual tour, you can see and hear a place. True / False
3 You need a computer to take a virtual tour. True / False
4 A virtual tour can help you decide where to go. True / False

④ C READING SKILL—Scan Scan the text and complete.

1 Continents: ______, ______
2 Countries: ______, ______, ______
3 Cities: ______, ______

⑤ D THINKING SKILL—Analyze Answer the questions.

1 How does a virtual tour save you time and money? 2 Is taking a virtual tour a good idea? Why or why not?

VOCABULARY

A Match the words and phrases (1–6) to the definitions (a–f). Write the letter.

1 continent ______ a places tourists visit
2 sights ______ b a trip around a place to see interesting things
3 sounds ______ c things you see
4 tour ______ d a trip to another place, usually to relax
5 tourist attractions ______ e large area of land, e.g., North America
6 vacation ______ f things you hear

GRAMMAR verb + infinitive or gerund

A Complete with phrases from READING B.

1 ______ you ______ another continent—Europe, maybe?
2 If you ______ time and money, here's a tip.
3 You ______ virtual tourism!
4 You can decide what you ______ before you go.
5 Many people ______ more when they plan with virtual tours.
6 They ______ time on things that interest them.

88 Unit 9 Seeing the World

Listening

The importance of good listening skills cannot be over-emphasized, as listening represents 45% of adult communication. In ***Speak Your Mind***, there are listening comprehension sections in two of the four lessons in each unit. These sections are designed to help students develop key listening skills as well as general comprehension skills. The listening texts represent a variety of genres, including conversations, lectures, radio broadcasts, and podcasts, to give students exposure to as many different listening situations as possible.

Like reading, listening is a receptive skill, but it is not a passive activity. Listeners rely on their own prior knowledge of a topic, their expectations about what a speaker will say, as well as contextual clues like body language to help them predict what will be said. Listeners also employ a variety of skills while listening, such as identifying key words to help them understand the gist of a conversation as well as important details.

There are a number of things that teachers can do to help students improve their listening comprehension:

- Do not speak too slowly or enunciate too perfectly. This will make it easier for students to understand in the classroom, but much more difficult when they encounter English outside the classroom. You may want to slow down a word or a sentence occasionally, but in general you should use normal speech.
- Remind students not to worry if they do not understand every word in a listening text. Point out that we often miss words even when listening in our own language. Encourage them to identify key words to help them understand the gist of a listening text as well as important details.
- As students develop specific listening skills, remind them to use those skills when they are listening to the teacher or to their classmates. Point out that they get listening practice not only in the listening sections of their textbook, but also during speaking activities and classroom interactions.

PROCEDURE: Teaching **Listening** in *Speak Your Mind*

LESSON 2 Natural Features

VOCABULARY natural features

A Check (✓) the natural features you can find less than 100 kilometers (60 miles) from where you live.

desert · forest · hill · lake · mountain · river · volcano · waterfall

B IN PAIRS Name examples of each natural feature in your country.

An example of a waterfall here in Chile is the Laja Falls.

LISTENING

1 **A** Look at the picture. Where do you think this place is?

MAKE IT YOURS
Can you think of more natural features in your country? Find out what they are called.

2 **B** 12.02 Listen and choose *True* or *False*.

1 Kerry is a student. True / False
2 The Iguazu River starts in Argentina. True / False
3 Niagara Falls is just one waterfall. True / False
4 The speaker went to Angel Falls last year. True / False

3 **C** 12.02 LISTENING SKILL—Listen for specific information Listen again and complete the table.

	Country	Height	Number of waterfalls	Good time to visit
Iguazu Falls			300	
Niagara Falls	Canada/US	50 meters		
Angel Falls				May–October

4 **D** THINKING SKILL—Induce Answer the questions.

1 Which of the waterfalls do you want to see? Why?
2 How do you think people feel when they visit places like Iguazu Falls?

120 Unit 12 The Great Outdoors

1. **Pre-Listening**. Pre-listening activities help students prepare for listening by asking them to predict what speakers will say or talk about what they already know about a topic.
2. **Listening comprehension**. Especially at beginning levels, students often need a lot of support for listening comprehension. It is a good idea to allow them to read through a comprehension activity before listening in order to give them an idea of what to listen for. You may want to ask students to listen to the recording once before attempting to do the activity. After they listen, give them a few minutes to do the activity and then play the recording again for them to check their work.
3. **Listening Skill**. As with reading, every *Listening* section of ***Speak Your Mind*** includes the development of a listening skill. Check that students understand what the skill is and why it is useful. You may want to refer students to the explanation of the listening skill in the relevant unit of the **Workbook**.
4. **Thinking Skill.** In each listening section of ***Speak Your Mind***, there is a thinking activity which encourages students to further analyze what they've heard and to express their opinions or to extend and apply the ideas in the listening text to their own context. For more on thinking skills, see *Thinking Skills* by Dr. Spencer Kagan on pages xxviii-xxxi of this book.

Speaking

Foreign-language teachers often comment that students just don't want to speak. There are a number of reasons for this. Sometimes they are afraid of making mistakes. This is especially true of young-adult and adult students who are used to thinking of themselves as competent. Other times students are just not prepared when asked to speak. It can be very difficult for them to think of what to say and how to say it if they are not able to prepare beforehand, especially at lower levels. It is important to create a classroom environment in which students feel confident and motivated to communicate in English.

It it is important to provide frequent opportunities for students to speak. In ***Speak Your Mind***, there is a strong emphasis on speaking, and students are given many opportunities throughout the lessons to voice their ideas and to practice the language that they are learning:

- Unit Openers have cooperative learning opportunities and group discussion questions.
- Pre-reading and pre-listening activities often involve class discussions.
- Thinking skills sections have questions for group or class discussions.
- GRAMMAR and VOCABULARY sections frequently include group or pair speaking activities.
- Lessons 1–3 end with a SPEAKING section, which allows students to use the grammar and vocabulary of the lesson to talk about a related topic.
- Language and Life lessons (Lesson 4 in every unit) are designed as collaborative tasks that involve a variety of interactive pair, group, and class activities.

PROCEDURE: Teaching **Speaking** in *Speak Your Mind*

1. **Preparation.** SPEAKING sections are scaffolded in order to give students the support they need when they speak. They first think about the topic and make notes, fill in a form, or in some other way prepare for what they are going to say. It is important to give them enough time to do this so that they feel confident when they start speaking. You may want to add a class preparation stage before asking students to work on their own—have a class brainstorming session to help them come up with ideas, or you could elicit vocabulary and grammar structures that they may need for the speaking activity.
2. **Practice.** Once students have had a chance to prepare, they work in pairs or groups to share their ideas. Make sure that students understand what they are going to do and exactly what their roles are before you put them in their groups or pairs. You may want to model the activity with a student or ask two students to model it.
3. **Present.** Be sure to allow plenty of time for the speaking activities, as this is the communicative outcome of the lesson. The SPEAKING section frequently takes up less space on the page than other sections in the lesson, so it is easy to make the mistake of thinking that the activity is very short. In fact, it may require the most time. It is important to allow enough time for preparation and for each student to have the chance to speak.

   When students are working in groups or pairs, listen for common errors, especially in the target language of the lesson. Have a short review session after the speaking activity. This generally works better than interrupting students while they are speaking. If you have a large class, you may not be able to listen to every pair or group, but you can get a good idea of things they may need more practice with by listening to as many of them as possible.

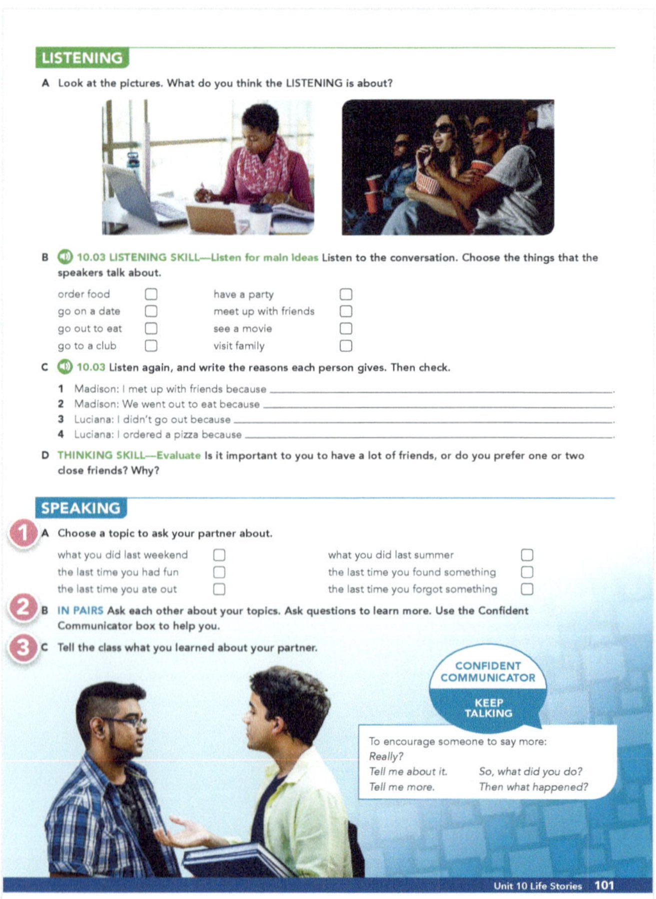

LISTENING

A Look at the pictures. What do you think the LISTENING is about?

B 10.03 LISTENING SKILL—Listen for main ideas Listen to the conversation. Choose the things that the speakers talk about.

order food	☐	have a party	☐
go on a date	☐	meet up with friends	☐
go out to eat	☐	see a movie	☐
go to a club	☐	visit family	☐

C 10.03 Listen again, and write the reasons each person gives. Then check.

1 Madison: I met up with friends because ________.
2 Madison: We went out to eat because ________.
3 Luciana: I didn't go out because ________.
4 Luciana: I ordered a pizza because ________.

D THINKING SKILL—Evaluate Is it important to you to have a lot of friends, or do you prefer one or two close friends? Why?

SPEAKING

1 A Choose a topic to ask your partner about.

what you did last weekend	☐	what you did last summer	☐
the last time you had fun	☐	the last time you found something	☐
the last time you ate out	☐	the last time you forgot something	☐

2 B IN PAIRS Ask each other about your topics. Ask questions to learn more. Use the Confident Communicator box to help you.

3 C Tell the class what you learned about your partner.

CONFIDENT COMMUNICATOR
KEEP TALKING

To encourage someone to say more:
Really?
Tell me about it. *So, what did you do?*
Tell me more. *Then what happened?*

Unit 10 Life Stories 101

Confident Communicator

One of the core objectives of ***Speak Your Mind*** is that students should become confident users of English—that is, Confident Communicators. Every SPEAKING section in ***Speak Your Mind*** includes a *Confident Communicator* box that gives students tips on what to say and how to say it. Some of the tips focus on functional language, which includes words and phrases used in specific situations, such as greeting someone or asking directions. Others focus on speaking strategies, such as taking time to think or explaining what you mean. The subheadings *Start Talking*, *Keep Talking*, and *Repair It* indicate how the language in the *Confident Communicator* box functions in a conversation.

Before students get into pairs or groups to do the interactive part of the SPEAKING section, go over the language in the *Confident Communicator* box to make sure they understand how to use it. You may want to practice a few short interactions with some or all of the phrases before they start working together.

When applied to language learning, the old saying "Practice makes perfect" should probably be changed to "Practice makes perfectly adequate." Wanting students to be confident communicators does not mean that everything they say should be perfectly constructed. In our own languages, we often communicate with incomplete sentences or even just facial expressions or gestures. The goal is to give students the confidence to express their ideas in English, and the best way to do that is through a combination of frequent opportunities to speak and support with the language.

Confident Communicator feature in *Speak Your Mind*

Start Talking. With the *Start Talking* boxes, students learn phrases for initiating a conversation or topic.

CONFIDENT COMMUNICATOR
START TALKING

There are different ways to ask about preferences.
Do you like Thai food? Yes, I do. / No, I don't.
Which do you prefer, chicken or fish?
I prefer chicken (to fish).
Do you prefer pasta or rice? I prefer pasta.

Keep Talking. With the *Keep Talking* boxes, students learn strategies and phrases to keep a conversation going even when they are not yet very proficient in the language.

CONFIDENT COMMUNICATOR
KEEP TALKING

Take time to think about what you want to say and how you want to say it. Use words and sounds like:
Um …
Uh …
Let me think …

Repair It. With the *Repair It* boxes, students learn phrases to use when there is a problem in communication.

CONFIDENT COMMUNICATOR
REPAIR IT

Sometimes you need to ask someone to say something again to check your understanding. There are polite ways to say this:
Can you say that again, please?
Can you repeat that?
Can you say that more slowly, please?

Writing

The ability to communicate effectively in writing is more important than ever for professional success. In the past, a great deal of business communication was conducted on the phone, but now most business communication is done via email. Email is no longer considered just an informal mode of written communication. Emails, like letters in the past, can have varying degrees of informality or formality, and young adults who are about to enter a very competitive professional world will have to be able to communicate competently in writing.

Teaching students to communicate in written English is complicated by the fact that many students do not have good writing skills, even in their own language. In ***Speak Your Mind***, students are taught basic writing skills like planning before starting to write, reviewing and editing their work after they write, and how to construct different genres of written communication. Learning to write short texts in different genres gives students practice in skills such as describing a situation or event, persuading the reader to agree with a point of view, giving instructions, or presenting a proposal. While the topics they write about may not be directly related to a profession, the skills they learn can be applied later on in business communications, both in English and in their own language. There is a WRITING section in Lesson 3 of every unit in ***Speak Your Mind***.

Remember that the purpose of writing is to communicate ideas, so it is always a good idea to have students share their finished work. You could have them read their texts aloud in small groups and then have a discussion, or you could have them work with a partner and read each other's texts. They can then get together to discuss their ideas or report on each other's texts to different partners.

There is further practice in writing mechanics and editing skills in the **Workbook**. In ***Speak Your Mind***, students are given the support and the practice they need in order for them to become competent writers in English.

PROCEDURE: Teaching **Writing** in *Speak Your Mind*

① **Read the model.** A model text is provided, either in the WRITING section or in another section in the lesson. Students read the text and do an activity that asks them to notice elements of content, organization, or language commonly used in a specific genre. You may want to have students read the text and then ask some general comprehension questions before having them do the activity.

② **Organize [Pre-writing].** After students have worked with the model text, they are given a framework to provide them with cues and help them organize their ideas for their own text. You may want to start with a class brainstorming session to help generate ideas. As they work, give individual help with ideas and vocabulary as needed.

③ **Write and share.** Once students have written their texts, give them time to review and correct their work. This may be done individually or in pairs. If it is done in pairs, it is a good opportunity for cooperative learning. You may want to go over some common grammar or spelling errors before they start editing their work in order to help them spot their own errors.

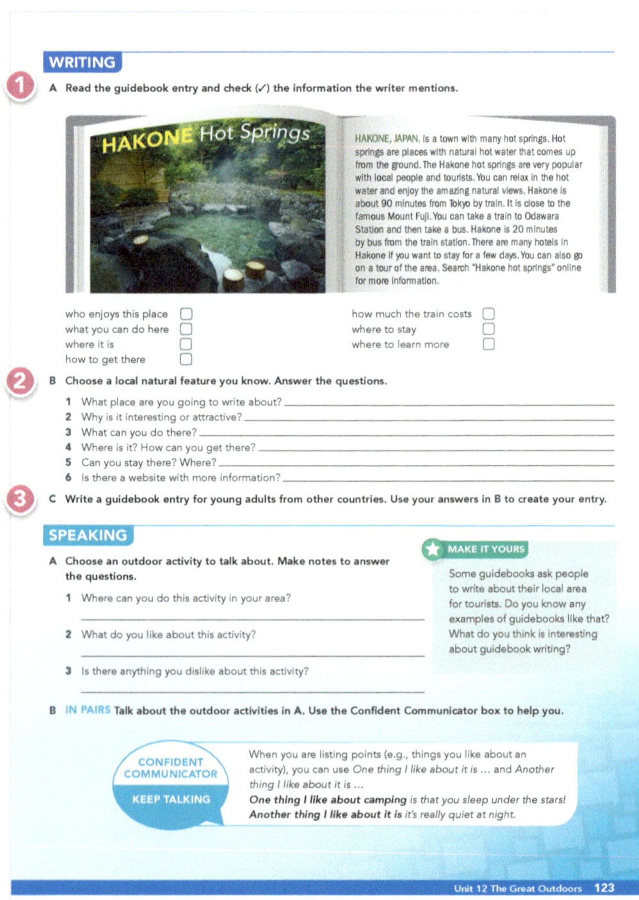
WRITING

① A Read the guidebook entry and check (✓) the information the writer mentions.

HAKONE Hot Springs

HAKONE, JAPAN, is a town with many hot springs. Hot springs are places with natural hot water that comes up from the ground. The Hakone hot springs are very popular with local people and tourists. You can relax in the hot water and enjoy the amazing natural views. Hakone is about 90 minutes from Tokyo by train. It is close to the famous Mount Fuji. You can take a train to Odawara Station and then take a bus. Hakone is 20 minutes by bus from the train station. There are many hotels in Hakone if you want to stay for a few days. You can also go on a tour of the area. Search "Hakone hot springs" online for more information.

who enjoys this place ☐
what you can do here ☐
where it is ☐
how to get there ☐
how much the train costs ☐
where to stay ☐
where to learn more ☐

② B Choose a local natural feature you know. Answer the questions.

1 What place are you going to write about? ____
2 Why is it interesting or attractive? ____
3 What can you do there? ____
4 Where is it? How can you get there? ____
5 Can you stay there? Where? ____
6 Is there a website with more information? ____

③ C Write a guidebook entry for young adults from other countries. Use your answers in B to create your entry.

SPEAKING

A Choose an outdoor activity to talk about. Make notes to answer the questions.

1 Where can you do this activity in your area?
____
2 What do you like about this activity?
____
3 Is there anything you dislike about this activity?
____

MAKE IT YOURS

Some guidebooks ask people to write about their local area for tourists. Do you know any examples of guidebooks like that? What do you think is interesting about guidebook writing?

B IN PAIRS Talk about the outdoor activities in A. Use the Confident Communicator box to help you.

CONFIDENT COMMUNICATOR
KEEP TALKING

When you are listing points (e.g., things you like about an activity), you can use *One thing I like about it is …* and *Another thing I like about it is …*
One thing I like about camping *is that you sleep under the stars!*
Another thing I like about it is *it's really quiet at night.*

Unit 12 The Great Outdoors 123

Language and Life

In the 21st century, the teaching of academic subjects is accompanied by the development of the types of skills that are necessary for success in academics, work, and life. These skills for success include communication, collaboration, problem-solving, creativity, self-direction, critical thinking, and media literacy.

In ***Speak Your Mind***, these skills are developed throughout each unit through collaborative activities, training in effective communication, and tasks that require critical thinking and problem-solving. The last lesson in each unit is specifically designed to focus on the development of 21st-century skills while recycling key grammar and vocabulary from the unit.

Every unit in ***Speak Your Mind*** includes a suggestion for online work outside of class. *Make It Digital* often occurs in Lesson 4 because the Language and Life tasks tend to lend themselves to further investigations or to a product that can be posted on a school website. You could have students do the research for homework and then report back to the class.

Sometimes, the lesson ends with questions that encourage students to reflect on the process they followed to achieve the outcome of the lesson and to think about what they might do better in a similar situation in the future. It is a good idea to discuss these questions as a class.

PROCEDURE: Teaching **Language and Life** in *Speak Your Mind*

1. **Present the life skill.** The heading is in two parts. The first part indicates the target 21st-century skill. The second part indicates the outcome of the task sequence in the lesson. Check that students understand both the skill that they will be using and the objective of the task.
2. **Read the text.** The lesson begins with a text that introduces students to the topic of the lesson. The topic is directly related to the overall unit topic. After students have read the text and done the activity, you may want to ask some further questions to check comprehension.
3. **Read the task.** Students are then given a problem or a task, and they have to work through a series of steps in order to achieve an outcome. They work individually to decide how they would solve the problem or carry out the task. Make sure they understand exactly what to do at this stage because everyone's input will be needed for the subsequent activities.
4. **Collaborate.** In the next stage, students work in pairs or in groups, to share the ideas from the previous stage. Depending on the topic and task type, you may want to organize students in different ways:
   - Pair a more confident student with a less confident student.
   - Pair or group students according to their academic majors or interest areas.
   - Let students choose who they want to work with.

   The pairs or groups discuss and combine their ideas and then produce a proposal or set of recommendations in the form of a concrete outcome such as a guide, a presentation, a poster, or an online post. If the final product is a written document, have students write it in the correct format in their notebooks. If it is a presentation, have them write notes on notecards for use during their presentation.
5. **Present.** In the final stage, students share their proposals or recommendations. They frequently finish the task sequence by discussing their ideas as a whole class and reaching a consensus on the best ideas. Have them work in pairs or small groups so that everyone will have plenty of time to talk, as this is the communicative outcome of the lesson.

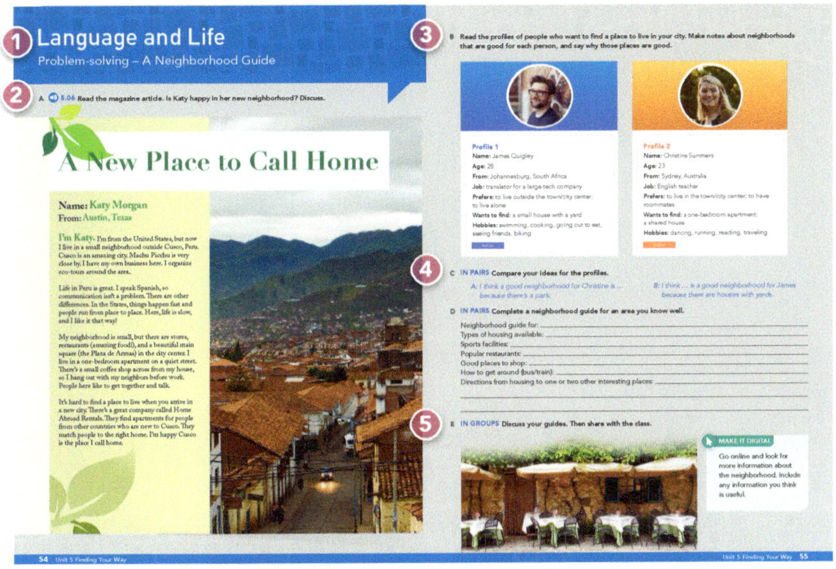
1 Language and Life
Problem-solving – A Neighborhood Guide

2 A 5.06 Read the magazine article. Is Katy happy in her new neighborhood? Discuss.

A New Place to Call Home

Name: Katy Morgan
From: Austin, Texas

I'm Katy. I'm from the United States, but now I live in a small neighborhood outside Cusco, Peru. Cusco is an amazing city. Machu Picchu is very close by. I have my own business here. I organize eco-tours around the area.

Life in Peru is great. I speak Spanish, so communication isn't a problem. There are other differences. In the States, things happen fast and people run from place to place. Here, life is slow, and I like it that way!

My neighborhood is small, but there are stores, restaurants (amazing food!), and a beautiful main square (the Plaza de Armas) in the city center. I live in a one-bedroom apartment on a quiet street. There's a small coffee shop across from my house, so I hang out with my neighbors before work. People here like to get together and talk.

It's hard to find a place to live when you arrive in a new city. There's a great company called Home Abroad Rentals. They find apartments for people from other countries who are new to Cusco. They match people to the right home. I'm happy Cusco is the place I call home.

54 Unit 5 Finding Your Way

3 B Read the profiles of people who want to find a place to live in your city. Make notes about neighborhoods that are good for each person, and say why those places are good.

Profile 1
Name: James Quigley
Age: 28
From: Johannesburg, South Africa
Job: translator for a large tech company
Prefers: to live outside the town/city center; to live alone
Wants to find: a small house with a yard
Hobbies: swimming, cooking, going out to eat, seeing friends, biking

Profile 2
Name: Christine Summers
Age: 23
From: Sydney, Australia
Job: English teacher
Prefers: to live in the town/city center; to have roommates
Wants to find: a one-bedroom apartment; a shared house
Hobbies: dancing, running, reading, traveling

4 C IN PAIRS Compare your ideas for the profiles.
A: I think a good neighborhood for Christine is ... because there's a park.
B: I think ... is a good neighborhood for James because there are houses with yards.

D IN PAIRS Complete a neighborhood guide for an area you know well.
Neighborhood guide for:
Types of housing available:
Sports facilities:
Popular restaurants:
Good places to shop:
How to get around (bus/train):
Directions from housing to one or two other interesting places:

5 E IN GROUPS Discuss your guides. Then share with the class.

MAKE IT DIGITAL
Go online and look for more information about the neighborhood. Include any information you think is useful.

Unit 5 Finding Your Way 55

Make It ...

Personalization is an important part of building vocabulary for English language learners. The *Make It ...* features in ***Speak Your Mind*** show students where they should add the words and phrases they need to use for work or study. Students should be encouraged to build a list of words, phrases, or expressions that are meaningful to them.

PROCEDURE: Using the **Make It ...** features in *Speak Your Mind*

Make It Yours. *Make It Yours* boxes encourage students to expand their vocabulary by making a list of words that are useful for them personally or by using target vocabulary in a personalized way. Go over the information in the boxes and elicit words from the class, or ask them to do the task suggested in the box for homework.

> **MAKE IT YOURS**
>
> Make a list of the jobs your family members have. Include your job or the job you want to have in the future. Use your dictionary if necessary.

Make It Happen. The Study Skills page ends with a *Make It Happen* box that has a suggestion for an activity in which students would use the skill they have just learned. These could work well as homework assignments or even short projects.

> **MAKE IT HAPPEN**
>
> Choose 10 new words you want to learn. Use three of the memory strategies to help you learn them. With a partner, talk about the three memory strategies. Use the phrases to help you.
>
> *A: I think that it's a good idea to study with friends.*
>
> *B: I agree. And I want to use colors for my notes. It's easy to remember the new words that way.*

Make It Real. GRAMMAR and VOCABULARY sections are often accompanied by a *Make It Real* box. The purpose of this feature is to provide students with examples of language that they may not be formally taught but which is commonly used by native speakers. This helps them understand more easily when they listen to a native speaker, and it can help them sound more natural when they speak English.

> **MAKE IT REAL**
>
> To "hit the gym" is a phrase people use when they decide to go to the gym regularly.
>
> *I need to get some exercise. I'm going to hit the gym.*

Make It Digital. Every unit in ***Speak Your Mind*** includes a suggestion for online work outside of class. The *Make It Digital* box always appears in Lesson 4 because the Language and Life tasks lend themselves to further investigations or to a product that can be posted on a school website. You could have students do the research for homework and then report back to the class.

> **MAKE IT DIGITAL**
>
> Go online to look for a new dish for the restaurant to serve. Include pictures, prices, and some information about the dish to make people want to try it!

Unit Review

Every unit in ***Speak Your Mind*** includes an end-of-unit review of the target grammar and vocabulary from the unit. The activities are designed as a general review to help students and teachers identify areas of strength and weakness so that students know what to focus on when studying for their exams.

PROCEDURE: Teaching the **Unit Review** in *Speak Your Mind*

1. **Review.** The VOCABULARY and GRAMMAR *Review* sections each have one or two activities for a total of 10 items per section. The activities are written in a variety of formats that reflect the different activity types that students may encounter on an exam.

   For Unit Tests, Mid-Course Tests, and End-of-Course Tests, use the Ready to Go tests or make customized tests with the ***Speak Your Mind* Test Generator**. If possible, it is a good idea to have students do the *Review* section a couple of days before a unit exam so that they have plenty of time to study their weak areas before the exam. The *Review* may be assigned as homework or done in class as a practice test.

2. **Score.** There are 10 points per section for a combined total of 20 points for the two sections. Students should write the number of correct answers in the blank in each section and the total number of correct answers in the *Total Score* box. Point out the score interpretations under the *Total Score* box. Remind students that they will be tested on the grammar and vocabulary of the unit, and if they have a low score on the *Review*, they need to go back to the relevant sections in the unit and study the material.

   When you go over the answers to the *Review* section, make sure that students understand their errors and that they know which section of their **Student's Book** to study for each incorrect item. Remind them that they need to study all of the vocabulary items in the three VOCABULARY sections in the unit, not just the items that were included in the *Review* activities.

3. **Further review.** Every *Review* section ends with the question WHAT DO YOU KNOW NOW? Students are asked to go back to the vocabulary activity in the Unit Opener and add words that they have learned in the unit. This is useful both as a reflection activity and as a review tool. It raises students' awareness that they are increasing their vocabulary in English. Also, by looking back at the words they listed in the Unit Opener, they are reviewing vocabulary related to the unit topic.

4. **Study Skill / Follow a Pro.** Please see the following pages for explanations of the Study Skills and Follow A Pro sections on the *Review* page.

UNIT 5

① VOCABULARY review ② SCORE: / 10

A Complete the sentences with words from the box.

across, apartment, boring, difficult, expensive, gym, on, popular, square, tiny

Jasper: I live near the university. There are many students here, so it's not an expensive part of town. I live in an old **1** ________ with only one room. It's **2** ________ , but it's OK for me.
Kate: I live with my parents. It's a big house near the main **3** ________ in town, but there is nothing fun to do in the neighborhood. It's **4** ________ .
Ed: I have a new apartment **5** ________ the corner of Main and First. I like it, but I pay a lot—about $1,300 a month. It's a very **6** ________ neighborhood.
Kim: I love my neighborhood. There are fun coffee shops, great restaurants, and a new **7** ________ to work out in. The neighborhood is **8** ________ with students and families.
Neil: My new house is on Third Street. From here, cross the bridge and then turn left. It's **9** ________ from the park. It's not **10** ________ to find.

GRAMMAR review SCORE: / 10

A Combine the two sentences into one.
1 Cusco is a city. Cusco is exciting.
2 It's a place. It's friendly.
3 There are many neighborhoods. They're lively.
4 There's a market. It's very interesting.
5 Cusco has some buildings. They're very old.

B Match the sentence beginning (1–5) to the sentence end (a–e). Write the letter.
1 There are ____ a many Cuban restaurants?
2 There is ____ b an airport near the city?
3 There's no ____ c people from all over the world.
4 Is there ____ d train to Everglades National Park.
5 Are there ____ e a zoo with lots of different animals.

16–20 correct: You can talk about places in a neighborhood and give directions. You can use adjectives and *there is/there are*.
0–15 correct: Look again at the Vocabulary and Grammar sections in the unit.
TOTAL SCORE: / 20

③ WHAT DO YOU KNOW NOW? Look back at page 47 and add the words you know now to the boxes.

④ STUDY SKILLS RESEARCH SKILLS

Take the quiz about research skills. Go to **Study Skills** on page 131 to find the answers. Then learn more about research skills.

1 About ... people around the world work full-time as researchers.
a 5.3 million b 7.8 million c 10 million
2 It takes the average person ... to read one page.
a one minute b two minutes c three minutes
3 Only 12% of teachers say their students use books for research.
a true b false
4 About 95% of internet users believe that most or all of the information they find online is true.
a true b false

56 Unit 5 Finding Your Way

UNIT 2

VOCABULARY review SCORE: / 10

A Choose the correct option to complete the sentences about Elena's family.

My **1 mother / father** is very creative. She's an art **2 engineer / teacher**. My mother's sister Ana is my **3 aunt / cousin**. Her house is beautiful. She's an **4 accountant / interior designer**. Nina is Ana's daughter. She's my **5 sister / cousin**. When I have a laptop problem, I call her. She's a **6 computer technician / marketer**. My **7 father / daughter** works for a large company. His name is Ricardo. He speaks English and Portuguese. He's an **8 interpreter / office manager**. My **9 grandfather / uncle** is my father's father. He sells computers. He's a small business **10 owner / optometrist**.

GRAMMAR review SCORE: / 10

A Complete the job ad with *a*, *an*, or *X* (no article).

Do you want **1** ____ interesting job? Think about a job as **2** ____ social media manager. **3** ____ social media manager writes **4** ____ comments and connects with **5** ____ customers. Contact us at our website to apply.

B Complete the sentences with words from the box.

'*s*, *s'*, his, her, their

1 My parent ________ names are Mark and Cindy.
2 My sister is named Kathy, but ________ nickname is Kat.
3 My brother ________ name is Jeff.
4 He's married to ________ wife, Ann.
5 ________ daughter's name is Barbara.

16–20 correct: You can talk about family and jobs. You can use *a/an* and the verb *be*.
0–15 correct: Look again at the Vocabulary and Grammar sections in the unit.
TOTAL SCORE: / 20

WHAT DO YOU KNOW NOW? Look back at page 17 and add the words you know now to the boxes.

④ FOLLOW A PRO INFORMATION TECHNOLOGY (IT)

Take the quiz about IT (information technology). Go to **Follow A Pro** on page 128 to find the answers. Then learn more about the IT industry.

1 Which country has the most internet users?
a China b the UK c the US
2 How many new viruses go into the internet every month?
a 360 b 6,000 c 10,000
3 Why is November 30 a special day? It's ...
a clean your computer day. b internet safety day. c computer security day.
4 What percentage of internet traffic is web robots?
a 8% b 55% c 21%

26 Unit 2 Work/Life Balance

Study Skills

In order to be successful, not only in learning English but also in academics in general, students must develop good study skills, such as how to do efficient research, how to give presentations, and how to improve their memory. In ***Speak Your Mind***, there is a study skills syllabus that is based on universal needs regardless of the subject but modified when appropriate to focus on skills specific to learning a new language.

In each level of ***Speak Your Mind***, study skills are presented and practiced in every other unit. To raise students' interest in the study skill and to give them an idea of what they already know about the skill, there is a short quiz at the end of the *Review* page in odd-numbered units.

PROCEDURE: Teaching Study Skills in *Speak Your Mind*

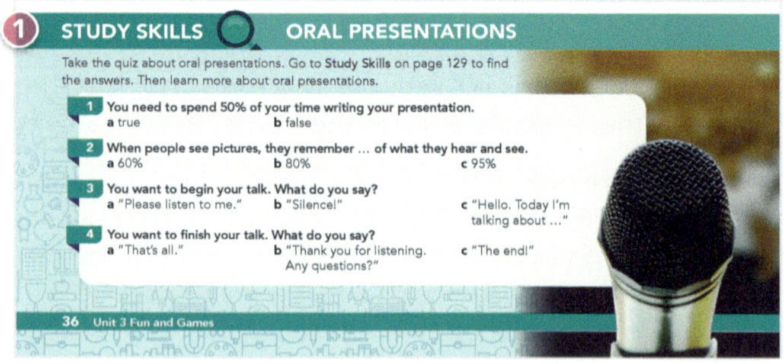

1 STUDY SKILLS — ORAL PRESENTATIONS

Take the quiz about oral presentations. Go to **Study Skills** on page 129 to find the answers. Then learn more about oral presentations.

1 **You need to spend 50% of your time writing your presentation.**
a true **b** false

2 **When people see pictures, they remember … of what they hear and see.**
a 60% **b** 80% **c** 95%

3 **You want to begin your talk. What do you say?**
a "Please listen to me." **b** "Silence!" **c** "Hello. Today I'm talking about …"

4 **You want to finish your talk. What do you say?**
a "That's all." **b** "Thank you for listening. Any questions?" **c** "The end!"

36 Unit 3 Fun and Games

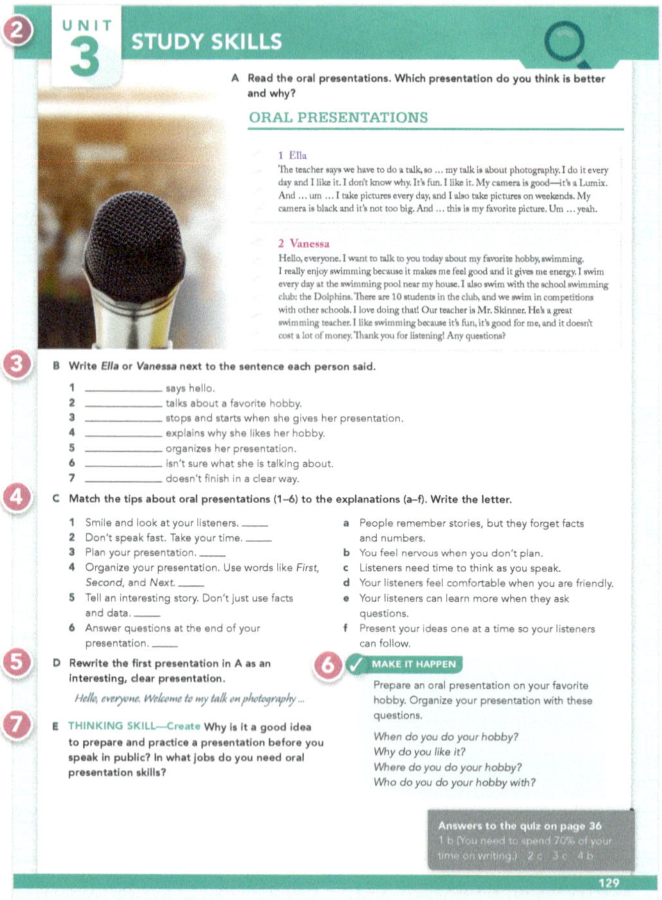

2 UNIT 3 STUDY SKILLS

A Read the oral presentations. Which presentation do you think is better and why?

ORAL PRESENTATIONS

1 Ella
The teacher says we have to do a talk, so … my talk is about photography. I do it every day and I like it. I don't know why. It's fun. I like it. My camera is good—it's a Lumix. And … um … I take pictures every day, and I also take pictures on weekends. My camera is black and it's not too big. And … this is my favorite picture. Um … yeah.

2 Vanessa
Hello, everyone. I want to talk to you today about my favorite hobby, swimming. I really enjoy swimming because it makes me feel good and it gives me energy. I swim every day at the swimming pool near my house. I also swim with the school swimming club: the Dolphins. There are 10 students in the club, and we swim in competitions with other schools. I love doing that! Our teacher is Mr. Skinner. He's a great swimming teacher. I like swimming because it's fun, it's good for me, and it doesn't cost a lot of money. Thank you for listening! Any questions?

3 **B Write *Ella* or *Vanessa* next to the sentence each person said.**

1 ______ says hello.
2 ______ talks about a favorite hobby.
3 ______ stops and starts when she gives her presentation.
4 ______ explains why she likes her hobby.
5 ______ organizes her presentation.
6 ______ isn't sure what she is talking about.
7 ______ doesn't finish in a clear way.

4 **C Match the tips about oral presentations (1–6) to the explanations (a–f). Write the letter.**

1 Smile and look at your listeners. ___
2 Don't speak fast. Take your time. ___
3 Plan your presentation. ___
4 Organize your presentation. Use words like *First*, *Second*, and *Next*. ___
5 Tell an interesting story. Don't just use facts and data. ___
6 Answer questions at the end of your presentation. ___

a People remember stories, but they forget facts and numbers.
b You feel nervous when you don't plan.
c Listeners need time to think as you speak.
d Your listeners feel comfortable when you are friendly.
e Your listeners can learn more when they ask questions.
f Present your ideas one at a time so your listeners can follow.

5 **D Rewrite the first presentation in A as an interesting, clear presentation.**

Hello, everyone. Welcome to my talk on photography …

6 MAKE IT HAPPEN

Prepare an oral presentation on your favorite hobby. Organize your presentation with these questions.

When do you do your hobby?
Why do you like it?
Where do you do your hobby?
Who do you do your hobby with?

7 **E THINKING SKILL—Create Why is it a good idea to prepare and practice a presentation before you speak in public? In what jobs do you need oral presentation skills?**

Answers to the quiz on page 36
1 b (You need to spend 70% of your time on writing.) 2 c 3 c 4 b

129

① **Take the quiz.** Direct students' attention to the skill in the heading and make sure they understand what the skill is. Have them take the quiz. You may want to let them do the quiz in pairs or check their answers with a partner before going to the *STUDY SKILLS* page at the back of the **Student's Book** to check their answers. The answers are at the bottom of the *STUDY SKILLS* page.

② **Present the study skill.** The quiz on the Unit Review page leads students to the Study Skills page at the back of the book. In the first activity, students are asked to apply critical-thinking skills to do a broad analysis of a text in relation to the target study skill. The topic of the text is often related to the topic of the unit. Have students read the text and then answer the question or do the task as a whole-class activity.

③ **Do the task.** The second activity goes into more detail about the study skill. After students have done the activity, go over it as a class to make sure they have understood the skill.

④ **Read the tips or rules.** The third activity is usually focused on tips and rules for carrying out the study skill effectively. Encourage students to refer back to these from time to time to help them remember the skill.

⑤ **Apply the skill.** In the fourth activity, students apply what they have learned and use the study skill to do an academic task or discuss how they can use the skill in their own studies. This is the productive outcome of the lesson, so be sure to allow enough time for the activity.

⑥ **Transfer the skill.** The *Make It Happen* box suggests a task that allows students to apply the skill they have just learned. These could work well as homework assignments or even short projects.

⑦ **Reflect.** The last activity develops a thinking skill. Students are asked to discuss how the study skill can be applied in real-life academic or professional situations. These often work well as class discussions.

Follow A Pro

Speak Your Mind has a strong emphasis on professional readiness, and in every other unit, a job is highlighted in a section called Follow A Pro. As with the Study Skills section, there is a short quiz at the end of the *Review* page in even-numbered units to generate interest in and highlight previous knowledge of a particular job or professional field.

PROCEDURE: Teaching **Follow A Pro** in *Speak Your Mind*

① **Take the quiz.** Ask students to take the quiz about a specific job or a general professional area, and then go to the corresponding page at the back of the **Student's Book** to check their answers. Answers are at the bottom of the page.

② **Read about a professional.** Ask students to read the text about a person who does a particular job or about a job in general. The topic of the text is related to an aspect of the topic of the unit. When students have finished reading, have them answer the comprehension questions individually. Check the answers as a class.

③ **Discuss the job.** Have students discuss different aspects of the job in the text and whether they would be good at or enjoy doing that job themselves. If you have a large class, you may prefer to do the discussion in small groups so that all students will have an opportunity to talk.

④ **Watch the video.** A video follows a professional in a job that is related to or in the same general field as the job in the text. There is an option to view the video script, if desired. Have students answer comprehension questions about the video. For this activity, students work in small groups. It is a good idea to have students read the questions before they watch the video so that they can more easily pick out the information that they need to remember. You may want to play the video once without the video script and ask students to answer the questions as well as they can, and then play it again with the video script in view to reinforce their comprehension. They can then go back and complete or revise their answers to the questions.

⑤ **Talk about the industry or field.** The final set of discussion questions asks students to think about the job and industry in general. Have students work in pairs or small groups to explain what they know about the job and the skills it requires. Because these questions do not refer specifically to the video, the discussion can be done even if the video is not used.

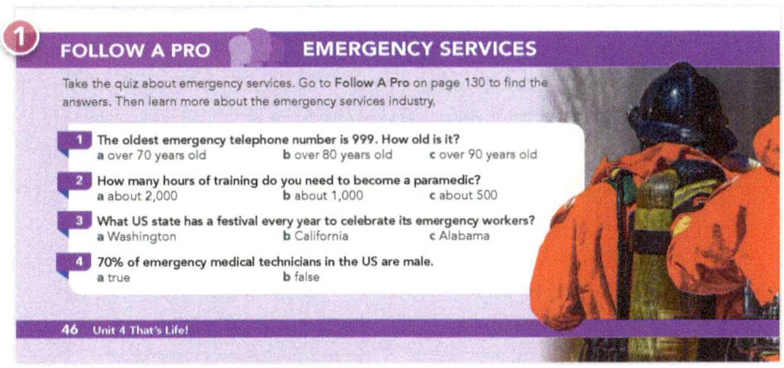

①

FOLLOW A PRO — EMERGENCY SERVICES

Take the quiz about emergency services. Go to **Follow A Pro** on page 130 to find the answers. Then learn more about the emergency services industry.

1 **The oldest emergency telephone number is 999. How old is it?**
a over 70 years old **b** over 80 years old **c** over 90 years old

2 **How many hours of training do you need to become a paramedic?**
a about 2,000 **b** about 1,000 **c** about 500

3 **What US state has a festival every year to celebrate its emergency workers?**
a Washington **b** California **c** Alabama

4 **70% of emergency medical technicians in the US are male.**
a true **b** false

46 Unit 4 That's Life!

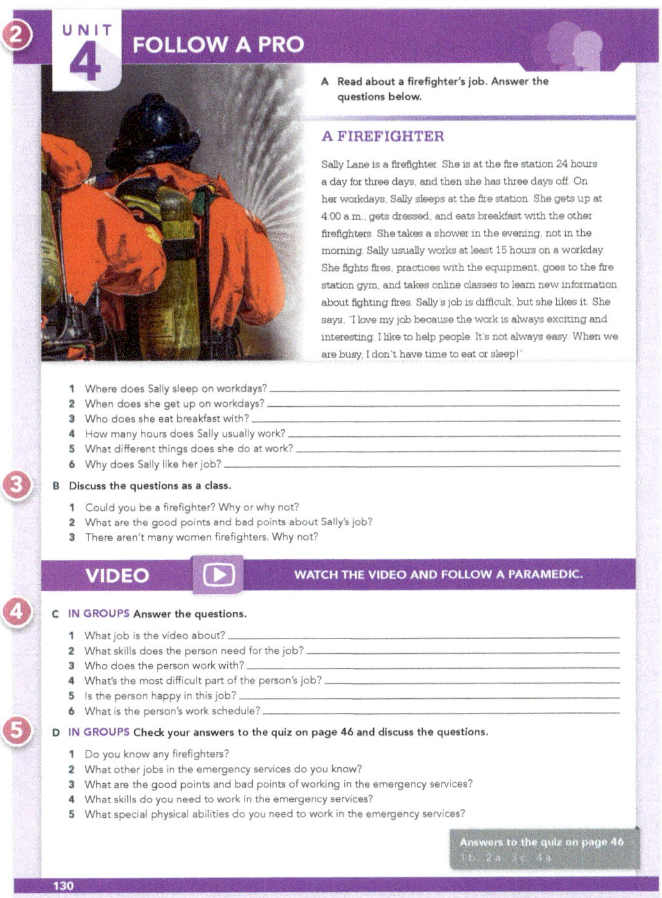

②

UNIT 4 FOLLOW A PRO

A Read about a firefighter's job. Answer the questions below.

A FIREFIGHTER

Sally Lane is a firefighter. She is at the fire station 24 hours a day for three days, and then she has three days off. On her workdays, Sally sleeps at the fire station. She gets up at 4:00 a.m., gets dressed, and eats breakfast with the other firefighters. She takes a shower in the evening, not in the morning. Sally usually works at least 15 hours on a workday. She fights fires, practices with the equipment, goes to the fire station gym, and takes online classes to learn new information about fighting fires. Sally's job is difficult, but she likes it. She says, "I love my job because the work is always exciting and interesting. I like to help people. It's not always easy. When we are busy, I don't have time to eat or sleep!"

1 Where does Sally sleep on workdays? ______
2 When does she get up on workdays? ______
3 Who does she eat breakfast with? ______
4 How many hours does Sally usually work? ______
5 What different things does she do at work? ______
6 Why does Sally like her job? ______

③ **B Discuss the questions as a class.**

1 Could you be a firefighter? Why or why not?
2 What are the good points and bad points about Sally's job?
3 There aren't many women firefighters. Why not?

VIDEO — WATCH THE VIDEO AND FOLLOW A PARAMEDIC.

④ **C IN GROUPS Answer the questions.**

1 What job is the video about? ______
2 What skills does the person need for the job? ______
3 Who does the person work with? ______
4 What's the most difficult part of the person's job? ______
5 Is the person happy in this job? ______
6 What is the person's work schedule? ______

⑤ **D IN GROUPS Check your answers to the quiz on page 46 and discuss the questions.**

1 Do you know any firefighters?
2 What other jobs in the emergency services do you know?
3 What are the good points and bad points of working in the emergency services?
4 What skills do you need to work in the emergency services?
5 What special physical abilities do you need to work in the emergency services?

Answers to the quiz on page 46
1 b 2 a 3 c 4 a

130

Unit Opener Videos

The Discuss & Share section of the Unit Opener features an optional ***Speak Your Mind*** video. The video provides information and context for the discussion of the question. In each video, two vloggers answer the ***Speak Your Mind*** SYM **question**. One vlogger expresses one point of view, while the other one answers with the opposite point of view. The video ends with the vloggers posing the question to the students. The two opposing answers provide a model for the students' own responses. In most cases, the students' opinions will fall somewhere between the two opposing points of view. You should encourage students to state their opinion and explain where they are on the continuum of the two opposite points of view.

PROCEDURE: Using the **Unit Opener Videos** in *Speak Your Mind*

① ***Speak Your Mind*** **question.** Make sure students understand the two points of view. You may want to draw a line with the opposing views at either end to show the continuum.

typical ——————————— different

② **Before viewing.** The teacher's page provides a question or questions to ask students before they watch the video. Use the question(s) to focus the students' attention on the differing points of view.

③ **Mark the continuum.** After viewing the video, have students mark where they are on the continuum by placing an X on the line between the points of view. Alternatively, ask students to form a line in the classroom, placing themselves between the two ends of the line, according to their opinion.

④ **Discuss & Share**. Ask students to explain why they have placed themselves at their selected point on the continuum. Encourage them to use the words they wrote in the What Do You Already Know? word list.

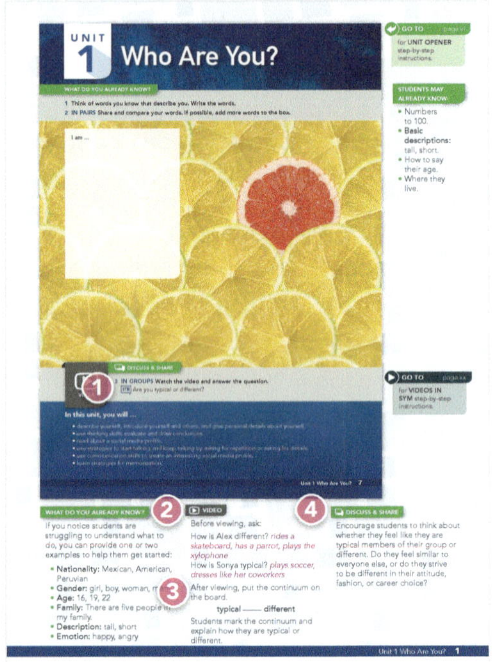
UNIT 1 Who Are You?

WHAT DO YOU ALREADY KNOW?

1 Think of words you know that describe you. Write the words.

2 IN PAIRS Share and compare your words. If possible, add more words to the box.

I am ...

DISCUSS & SHARE

3 IN GROUPS Watch the video and answer the question.

SYM Are you typical or different?

In this unit, you will ...

Unit 1 Who Are You? 7

GO TO for UNIT OPENER step-by-step instructions.

STUDENTS MAY ALREADY KNOW:
- Numbers to 100.
- **Basic descriptions:** tall, short.
- How to say their age.
- Where they live.

GO TO for VIDEOS IN SYM step-by-step instructions.

WHAT DO YOU ALREADY KNOW?

If you notice students are struggling to understand what to do, you can provide one or two examples to help them get started:
- **Nationality:** Mexican, American, Peruvian
- **Gender:** girl, boy, woman, m...
- **Age:** 16, 19, 22
- **Family:** There are five people in my family.
- **Description:** tall, short
- **Emotion:** happy, angry

VIDEO

Before viewing, ask:

How is Alex different? *rides a skateboard, has a parrot, plays the xylophone*

How is Sonya typical? *plays soccer, dresses like her coworkers*

After viewing, put the continuum on the board.

typical —— different

Students mark the continuum and explain how they are typical or different.

DISCUSS & SHARE

Encourage students to think about whether they feel like they are typical members of their group or different. Do they feel similar to everyone else, or do they strive to be different in their attitude, fashion, or career choice?

Unit 1 Who Are You? 1

Follow A Pro Videos

The Follow A Pro videos follow professionals through their daily work lives. The job in the video is in the same industry or field as the job on the Follow A Pro page. Students should be able to recycle some of the vocabulary from the text and discussion in activities **A** and **B** as they answer the questions about the video in **C**. There are many ways to maximize learning when using videos. These suggestions support vocabulary acquisition and listening comprehension.

PROCEDURE: Using the **Follow A Pro Videos** in *Speak Your Mind*

① **Look for images.** Tell students they are going to watch the video with the sound off. Give them the list of words to look for, provided on the **Teacher's Edition** page. If they see any of the things on the list, they should circle the words. For further challenge, ask students to predict what the professional will say about his or her life based on the images in the video.

② **Listen for words.** Play the video with the sound on. Provide the list of words or phrases from the Teacher's Edition page. Ask students to circle any words or phrases they hear. Have students answer the questions in activity **C**. A challenge question is provided on the **Teacher's Edition** page to check students' comprehension of the video.

③ **Watch again.** Play the video again with or without the video script visible. Students can check or correct their answers to the questions in activity **C** and the challenge question.

Grammar Quiz

Before students begin their course, have them take the Grammar Quiz on page 6. This quiz is a quick review of language from the Starter level of ***Speak Your Mind***. For a longer review, go to the Grammar Review on page 140.

Grammar Review

At the back of the ***Speak Your Mind*** **Student's Book**, there is a *Grammar Review* section. The section starts with a page containing a list of common irregular verbs.

The *Grammar Review* pages review language that was taught in the previous level of ***Speak Your Mind***. You can use the *Grammar Review* when students begin their level to test what they have retained from previous classes.

Grammar Reference

Following the *Grammar Review* are the *Grammar Reference* pages. They provide an expanded explanation of the function of the grammar points. The form of the grammar is shown in a table. Practice activities follow the explanation. Note that the *Reference* section is in the **Student's Book** only, but the *Answer Key* for the practice activities in this section is at the back of this **Teacher's Edition**. Grammar points are labeled clearly with a heading.

The *Grammar Reference* pages can be used in several ways:

- **Further practice.** When a new grammar point is introduced in a unit, you may want to refer students to the relevant section in the *Grammar Reference* and go over the explanations of form and function with them, pointing out the examples in the table(s). You could do this before or after doing the grammar presentation in the unit.
- **Homework.** You may want to do the grammar practice activity in the unit in class and assign the activities in the *Grammar Reference* section for homework, along with or instead of the activities in the **Workbook**.
- **Review.** The *Grammar Reference* activities can be used for review before an exam.

Grammar Reference

UNIT 9 — verb + infinitive or gerund

Function

Some verbs (e.g., *want*, *need*, and *plan*) are followed by an infinitive (*to* + verb). Some verbs (e.g., *enjoy*) are followed by a gerund (verb + *–ing*). Some verbs (e.g., *like*) are followed by either an infinitive or a gerund, with no change in meaning.

Form

Verb + infinitive	Verb + gerund
I want to travel to Mexico. He would like to take a guided tour. She needs to get a passport. We have to buy some souvenirs. They plan to take a vacation soon.	I enjoy traveling by boat. **Verb + infinitive or gerund** They like to visit new cities. They like visiting new cities.

A Find and correct one error in each sentence.

1 She wants get a hotel near the city center. ______
2 Do you need get a new backpack for your trip? ______
3 I don't enjoy to travel in a large group. ______
4 They plan spending two weeks in Thailand. ______
5 He doesn't like to eating in hotel restaurants. ______
6 Would you like visit Europe or Asia? ______

B Read the travel blog. Complete the sentences with the infinitive or gerund form of the verb in parentheses.

I'm here in Oaxaca, Mexico! This city is great. I am enjoying **1** ______ (walk) around the city very much, but tomorrow I plan **2** ______ (take) a guided tour of the market. I want **3** ______ (try) some local food. I like **4** ______ (meet) the local people, but my Spanish is not very good. I really need **5** ______ (study) the language more. I have **6** ______ (buy) some cool souvenirs for my family, and I would like **7** ______ (get) a good price.

UNIT 9 — *should/could* for advice and possibility

Function

We use *should* to give advice to others and *could* to say what is possible for people to do. Both are followed by the base form of a verb (e.g., *should stay, could visit*).

Form

***should* + verb (advice)**
Everyone needs a passport to go overseas. You should get one right away. It's very cold and snowy there right now. You should pack a warm coat.
***could* + verb (possibility)**
There are lots of places to stay. You could stay in a hotel, at a hostel, or with a local family. All the islands in Hawaii are popular. You could visit Oahu, Maui, Kauai, or the Big Island.

154 Grammar Reference

A Match the sentence beginning (1–6) to the sentence end (a–f). Write the letter.

1 Don't take a suitcase on your trip. You should ____
2 I hear you like cold weather. You could ____
3 It's very hot there right now. You should ____
4 I want to follow you on your trip. You should ____
5 You don't drive? You could ____
6 Not many people speak English. You should ____

a post updates every few days.
b plan to stay out of the sun.
c take a taxi or a bus to the airport.
d learn some of the local language.
e visit Iceland, Alaska, or even Siberia!
f bring just a small backpack.

UNIT 10 — simple past (affirmative statements)

Function

We use the simple past to talk about states, events, and actions in the past.

Form

We generally add *–ed* to regular verbs (e.g., *walk–walked, live–lived, stop–stopped*).

Regular verbs	Add *–ed.*	listen–listened
Verbs ending in *e*	Add *–d.*	love–loved
Verbs ending in vowel + consonant	Double the last consonant and add *–ed.*	hop–hopped
Verbs ending in consonant + *y*	Change *y* to *i* and add *–ed.*	copy–copied

There are many irregular simple past forms (e.g., *speak–spoke, take–took, eat–ate*). See the irregular verbs chart on page 139. Notice spelling patterns on the list of irregular verbs.

Affirmative statements	
I You He She It We They	inspired many people. had an interesting life.

A Write the simple past forms of the verbs.

1 eat ______
2 learn ______
3 play ______
4 speak ______
5 talk ______
6 become ______
7 do ______
8 have ______
9 cry ______
10 shop ______
11 make ______
12 go ______

Grammar Reference 155

The following features are accessible via the ***Speak Your Mind*** Resource Centers.

Student's Resource Center

- **Reading Worksheets**
- **Student's Book** and **Workbook** audio files
- **Student's Book** videos
- **Word Lists**

Teacher's Resource Center

- **Reading Worksheets**
- ***OneStopEnglish*** **Worksheets**
- **Student's Book** and **Workbook** audio files
- **Student's Book** videos
- **Printable Ready-to-Go Tests**
- **CEFR Correlations**
- **Word Lists**

Reading Worksheets

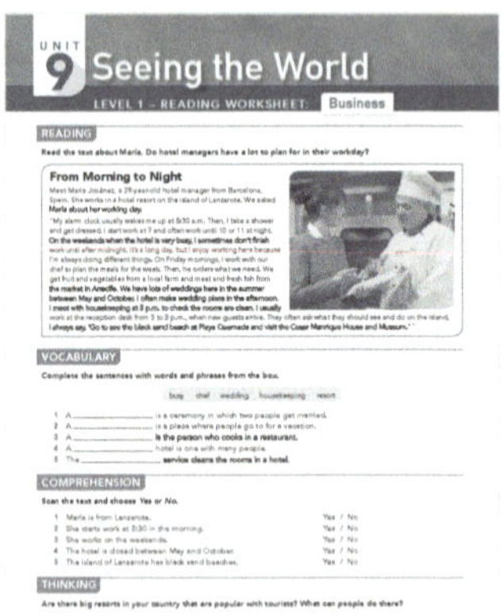

Each unit of ***Speak Your Mind*** has three extensive **Reading Worksheets**, for a total of 36. The topics of the worksheets extend the themes and vocabulary sets of the units in the areas of General English, Business, Science, and Services. They are designed to appeal to students who are studying academic subjects and young adults who are already working in their careers.

The **Reading Worksheets** have a text with a VOCABULARY activity and COMPREHENSION questions. A THINKING question at the end of the worksheet can be used as a departure for discussion in the classroom or a writing assignment for homework.

OneStopEnglish Worksheets

The ***OneStopEnglish*** **Worksheets** give students further speaking practice in a fun and engaging way. Speak Your Mind has chosen select worksheets from the OneStopEnglish website, the world's number one teacher resource site for English Language teachers. The ***OneStopEnglish*** **Worksheets** have been adapted for the course, with one worksheet for each unit. The worksheets consist of one page of teacher's notes, which includes the aim, procedure, and estimated activity time, and one page with the student's activity.

Printable Ready-to-Go Tests

All the tests for ***Speak Your Mind*** can be found in the **Teacher's Resource Center**. This includes a Placement Test, Unit Tests, a Mid-Course Test, and an End-of-Course Test. All tests are available as ready-to-print PDFs. Tests can be customized using the **Test Generator** (see the **How to Use the Digital Components** section, page xxvii).

- The Placement Test places students in a ***Speak Your Mind*** level.
- The Unit Tests include vocabulary, grammar, listening, reading, writing, and speaking items for each unit.
- The Mid-Course Test include vocabulary, grammar, listening, reading, writing, and speaking items for units 1–6.
- The End-of-Course Test includes vocabulary, grammar, listening, reading, writing, and speaking items for units 7–12.

CEFR Correlations

The Common European Framework of Reference for Languages (CEFR) is an international standard that aims to provide a transparent, coherent, and comprehensive means of describing language ability. It describes what language learners can do in different skills across six broad levels, from A1 to C2, and consists of a set of scales containing descriptors indicating what a learner can do in that context. The **CEFR Correlations** document is a map is organized unit by unit, which allows you to browse the course learning outcomes chronologically. These are mapped to the relevant CEFR descriptors, levels, and scales.

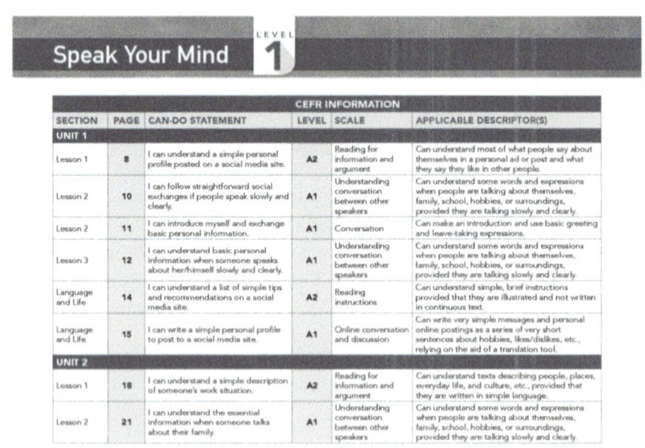

Word Lists

The **Word Lists** are a list of the main vocabulary that appears in ***Speak Your Mind***. These include words that appear in the **Student's Book** and **Student's App** VOCABULARY sections, as well as the glossaries of the **Student's Book** READING sections. The word lists include the word, part of speech, IPA pronunciation, definition, and frequency, as well as an example sentence using the word.

How to Use the Teacher's Edition

The up-to-date, innovative approach to the ***Speak Your Mind*** **Teacher's Edition** takes into account that teachers have very busy lives and want the class-planning process to be as streamlined as possible. The introductory pages of the **Teacher's Edition** are designed to provide general explanations and instructions that are needed to teach each section of the unit and use the special features.

The introductory pages also include information on how to use the special features, the **Workbook**, the *Videos*, and the digital material included in the ***Speak Your Mind*** series. The *Answer Keys* for the **Workbook** activities and the **Student's Book** *Grammar Reference* activities are at the back of this book, as are the *Audio Scripts* for the listening activities in the **Student's Book** and **Workbook**.

The core pages of the **Teacher's Edition** include:

1. ***GO TO***. Teachers can read the introductory information once for guidelines on how to teach these sections throughout the book. *GO TO* pointers help teachers find the procedure pages they need quickly.
2. **Answer Key.** The core pages have the detailed information a teacher needs to teach specific activities. The **Teacher's Edition** has reduced **Student's Book** pages with answers in place or in the margin next to the Student's Book pages.
3. **Specific notes.** Notes below the **Student's Book** reduced page include relevant background information for texts, tips for dealing with specific language issues, common errors to watch out for, cultural information, classroom management ideas, and suggestions for extra or alternative activities.

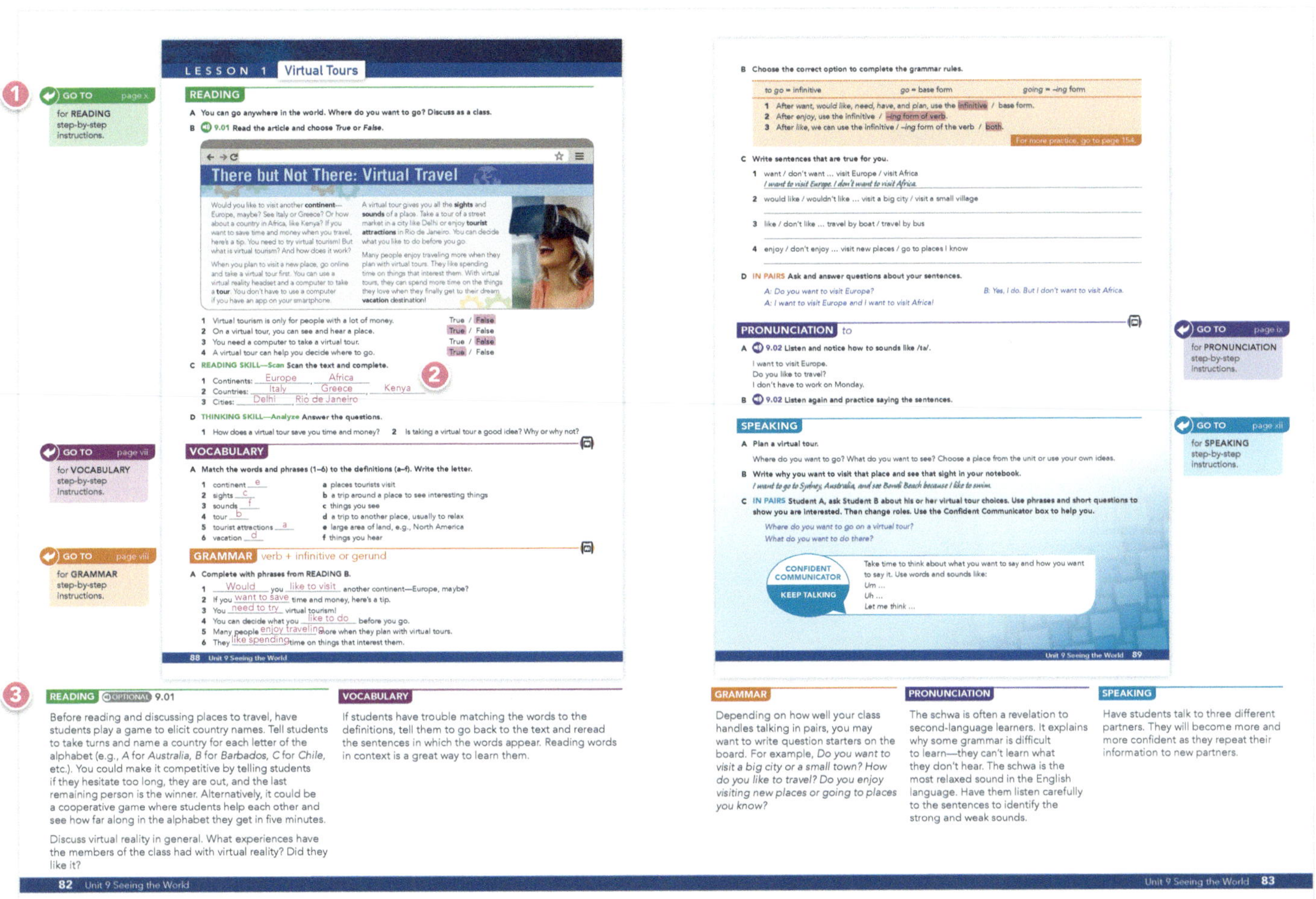

How to Use the Workbook

The ***Speak Your Mind* Workbook** is designed to give students further practice in grammar and vocabulary, as well as the listening, reading, and writing skills taught in the **Student's Book**. The **Workbook** is available in both print and digital form. The **Digital Workbook** can be accessed through the **Student's App**. At the end of the **Workbook**, there are five pages of activities designed to familiarize students with the most common exam formats (Cambridge suite, TOEFL, and IELTS).

The **Workbook** activities can be used in several ways:

- As homework or further classroom practice after teaching a section in the **Student's Book**.
- As a review of a whole lesson after finishing the lesson.
- As a review session before a unit exam.

① **Reading and listening skills expansion.** Skills boxes give explanations of the reading and listening skills taught in the **Student's Book**. You may want to refer students to the explanation in the **Workbook** before asking them to do the skill activity in the **Student's Book**. Following each skill box, there is an activity to practice the skill.

② **Vocabulary practice.** There is additional practice of the target vocabulary of the lesson.

③ **Grammar practice.** The grammar of the lesson is practiced in a variety of ways.

④ **Writing skills.** In the WRITING section, there is practice in the mechanics of writing.

⑤ **Progress check.** Students check the areas they feel competent in. If they feel that they need to review a particular point, they are directed to the relevant section in the **Student's Book**.

How to Use the Digital Components

Teacher's App

The ***Speak Your Mind*** **Teacher's Edition** comes with an innovative **Teacher's App**, which gives access to the **Classroom Presentation Kit**, **Homework Manager**, **Progress Tracker**, **Test Generator**, and **Teacher's Resource Center**.

Classroom Presentation Kit

The **Classroom Presentation Kit** is a page-faithful view of the **Student's Book** and **Workbook**. It is designed to be displayed on an interactive whiteboard (IWB) or using a projector. It is user-friendly for teachers and students, with activities clearly visible for the whole class.

The **Classroom Presentation Kit** allows teachers to play the audio tracks, show the course videos, and present the interactive versions of the book activities from the page. Teachers can zoom in on each activity with one click, then move smoothly through the activities or zoom out to see the whole page. Answer reveal enables teachers to elicit students' responses and check answers one by one or all together.

Embedded tools make it possible to highlight and annotate texts to prompt noticing or self-correction. Teachers also have the option to show scripts when listening to audio or watching video for easy clarification. There is also the option to create a whiteboard area for additional notes.

Homework Manager

Using the practice activities available in the **Student's App**, teachers can assign homework by selecting and publishing content directly to their students' devices. Students will then be alerted by a push notification telling them they have activities to complete. This enables teachers to personalize the amount and kind of practice students have each week and to track their progress using the **Progress Tracker**.

Progress Tracker

The **Progress Tracker** gives teachers an overview of students' progress, allowing teachers to monitor scores and see at a glance that students are performing well or that they may need additional support. Student data is presented in a way that is clear and easy to understand.

Test Generator

Ready-to-Go print tests are available in the **Teacher's Resource Center** for teachers who want to give a test on every skill. If you prefer to customize tests for your students, you can do so through the **Test Generator** in the **Teacher's App**. The **Test Generator** allows you to create tests by selecting only the activities you want from a menu. You can save and print out the tests from the **Test Generator**. You may also use a randomized function to create different tests for the same unit.

Student's App

Each **Student's Book** includes a code for the **Student's App**, which gives access to new **On-the-Go Practice** activities, **Progress Tracker**, **eBook**, **Digital Workbook**, and the **Student's Resource Center**.

On-the-Go Practice

Through the **Student's App**, students will have access to new grammar, vocabulary, and pronunciation activities that have been mapped to the course scope and sequence. These bite-sized activities have been specifically designed for use on smartphones. They include game-like elements to encourage repetition and deeper retention of key language. Questions are shown in random order to increase interest and ensure a thorough understanding of each language point. Students are able to complete activities in a standard practice mode or in a more difficult challenge mode, where they can earn medals based on their performance.

Each **Student's App** unit also contains a new speaking activity that recycles the Unit Opener video, providing an opportunity to review the Unit Opener topic and the language encountered throughout the unit. These activities have been designed to increase students' confidence as they see how their language competence has developed over the course of each unit, while reinforcing what they have learned.

Progress Tracker

The **Student's App** gives a clear overview of students' progress, clearly highlighting areas of strength and areas for improvement. Students have the opportunity to review their weakest activities and repeat them to improve their scores.

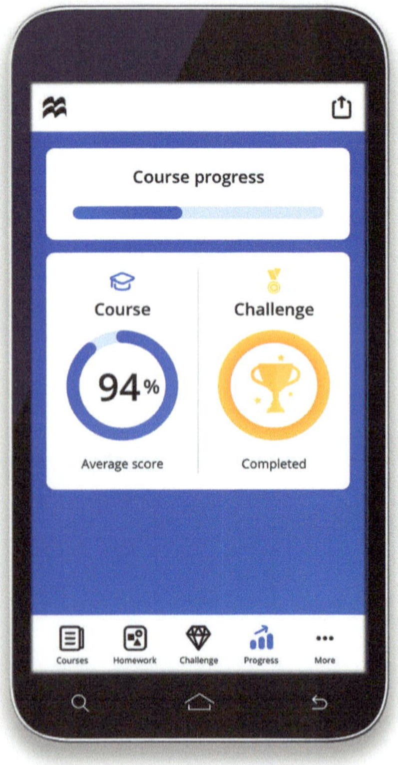

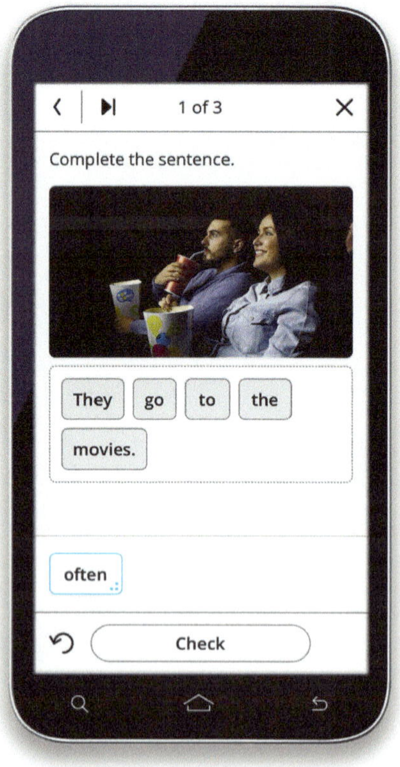

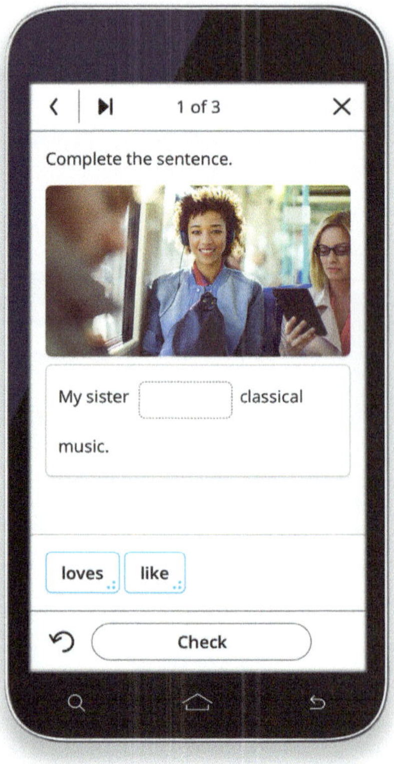

eBook

The **eBook** is a digital version of the **Student's Book** with embedded audio and video files, so students can access the book and its media on their desktop, in their classroom, or at home.

Digital Workbook

The **Digital Workbook** is a new, digital version of the students' **Workbook** designed to be accessible on students' devices. The **Digital Workbook** contains digital versions of the **Workbook** activities designed to work across mobile, tablet, and desktop to provide a rich interactive experience. The **Workbook** audio and video files can be accessed from the page so students have everything they need in one place. Built-in answer keys give instant feedback, while students' scores feed to the **Progress Tracker** for easy monitoring.

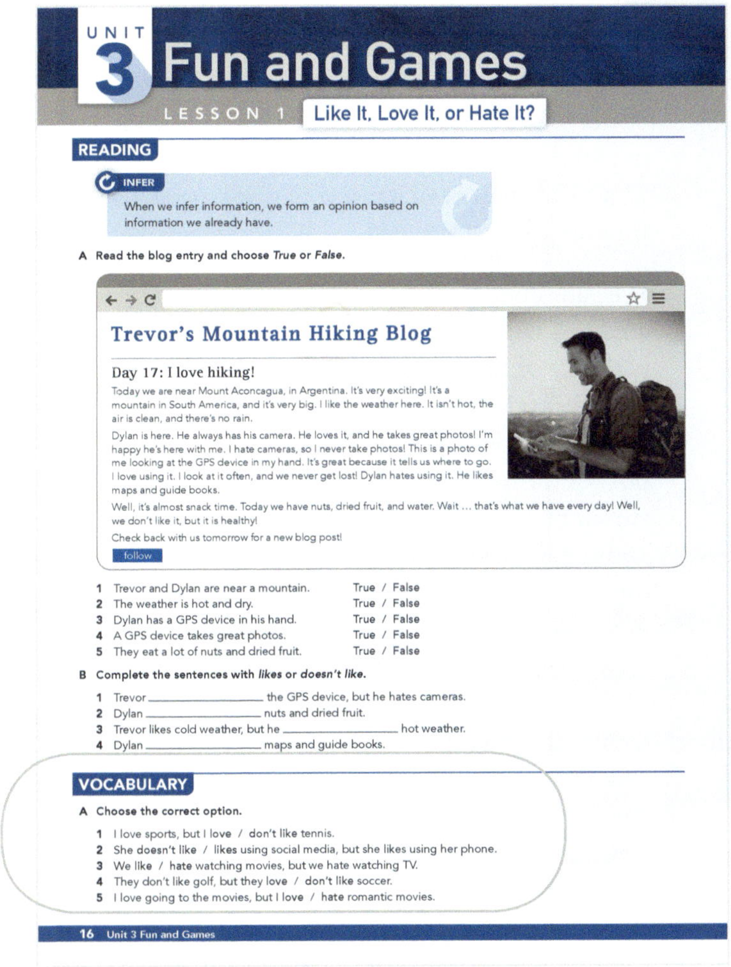
UNIT 3 Fun and Games

LESSON 1 Like It, Love It, or Hate It?

READING

INFER
When we infer information, we form an opinion based on information we already have.

A Read the blog entry and choose *True* or *False*.

Trevor's Mountain Hiking Blog

Day 17: I love hiking!

Today we are near Mount Aconcagua, in Argentina. It's very exciting! It's a mountain in South America, and it's very big. I like the weather here. It isn't hot, the air is clean, and there's no rain.

Dylan is here. He always has his camera. He loves it, and he takes great photos! I'm happy he's here with me. I hate cameras, so I never take photos! This is a photo of me looking at the GPS device in my hand. It's great because it tells us where to go. I love using it. I look at it often, and we never get lost! Dylan hates using it. He likes maps and guide books.

Well, it's almost snack time. Today we have nuts, dried fruit, and water. Wait … that's what we have every day! Well, we don't like it, but it is healthy!

Check back with us tomorrow for a new blog post!

follow

1 Trevor and Dylan are near a mountain. True / False
2 The weather is hot and dry. True / False
3 Dylan has a GPS device in his hand. True / False
4 A GPS device takes great photos. True / False
5 They eat a lot of nuts and dried fruit. True / False

B Complete the sentences with *likes* or *doesn't like*.

1 Trevor ________ the GPS device, but he hates cameras.
2 Dylan ________ nuts and dried fruit.
3 Trevor likes cold weather, but he ________ hot weather.
4 Dylan ________ maps and guide books.

VOCABULARY

A Choose the correct option.

1 I love sports, but I love / don't like tennis.
2 She doesn't like / likes using social media, but she likes using her phone.
3 We like / hate watching movies, but we hate watching TV.
4 They don't like golf, but they love / don't like soccer.
5 I love going to the movies, but I love / hate romantic movies.

16 Unit 3 Fun and Games

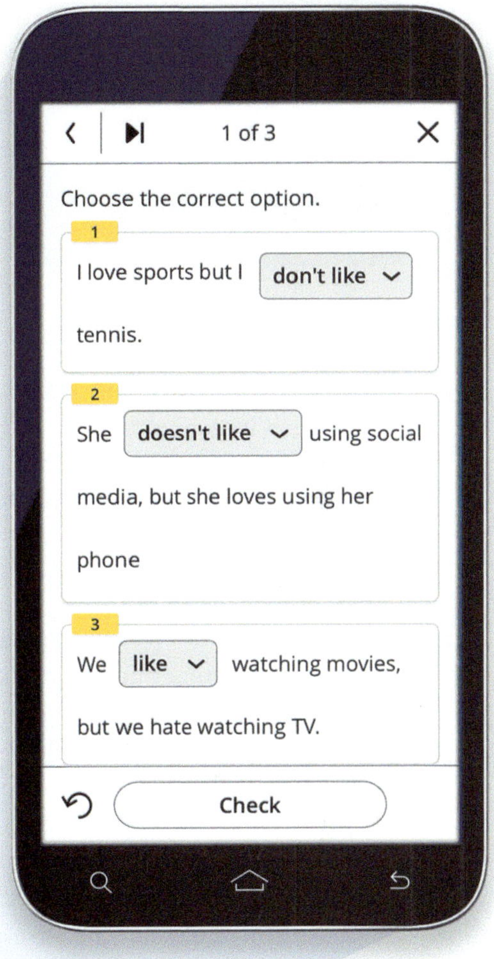

Thinking Skills

Dr. Spencer Kagan
Director, Kagan Publishing & Professional Development

Educators worldwide increasingly recognize that we must revise our educational objectives if we are to prepare students for life in the 21st century. One dimension of primary concern is thinking skills. Thinking skills are an essential, if not the single most important element of a good 21st century curriculum.

A century ago, most people lived in rural areas and were employed in agriculture. The teacher had a good idea of what information and skills students would need for a lifetime. The teacher could prepare the student for a life in a predictable and relatively constant world. Today, we as teachers have the unprecedented challenge of preparing students for a world we can only dimly imagine. The change rate itself accelerates exponentially as new technology produces even newer technology. We take for granted picture phones, television watches, personal digital assistants, video conferencing, and GPS tracking devices that keep us updated in real time on traffic conditions—all of which were things of science fiction but a few decades ago. Think for a moment of all the things we have today that were not invented just a decade ago. We can no longer imagine with confidence what our lives will include a decade from now, never mind the myriad changes that will occur over the entire course of the lives of our students.

Preparation for accelerating change must include development of a full range of thinking skills. Change means adapting, and adapting means problem solving, predicting, questioning, applying old skills to new situations, and analyzing and evaluating options. We don't know the situations to which our students will have to adapt, but we do know they will need a range of thinking skills if they are to be successful.

We can predict with certainty also that our students will need information skills. The majority of all scientists who have ever lived are alive today, busy making new discoveries. Advanced computers are answering questions not yet formulated by humans; the sum of stored human information doubles each year and the doubling rate itself is doubling so, during the lives of our students, the time it takes for human information to double will be measured in months, not years. In the face of the accelerating information explosion, having the student memorize one more fact is of little value compared to having the student learn how to categorize, analyze, synthesize, summarize, and apply information. Information memorized today will be outdated before our students graduate from high school; skills will be replaced many times over the course of a student's life. Improving the ability to generate new information is more important than trying to improve the human brain's capacity to store information—something even a handheld computer does far better.

The Information Processing Approach to Thinking

An increasing percentage of people are employed in the information segment of the economy, and it is the fastest growing segment. In the information age, we earn our living by generating, analyzing, categorizing, evaluating, and communicating information. An information processing approach to thinking skills aligns well with preparation of students for 21st century life. The approach to teaching thinking skills that I developed and that Kagan Professional Development teaches is based on an information processing approach to thinking. This approach divides thinking skills into three types: understanding information, manipulating information, and generating information. In each of the three categories are specific skills. For example, recall is related to understanding information; deduction is related to manipulating information; and brainstorming is related to generating information. This division of skills into three sets of five is not perfect (for example, questioning is related to understanding, manipulating, and generating); nevertheless, it is quite useful. See "The 15 Fundamental Types of Thinking" sidebar.

The Curricular Approach vs. the Instructional Approach to Developing Thinking Skills

To distinguish the curricular approach from the instructional approach, let's imagine we want to develop students' ability to summarize information. If we take a curricular approach, we would design some lessons on summarizing. We might spend some time developing summarizing worksheets. For example, the worksheet might include a paragraph and then, below, a place for the student to write a summary sentence. Or it might show a picture and have a place for the student to summarize what is going on in the picture using no more than 30 words.

In contrast, if we take the instructional approach, we would use our existing academic content, but teach that content using structures that foster summarizing skills. For example, as part of our lesson on the Great Depression, we might pair students up, one student role-playing the part of a business executive who is just learning about the stock market crash, and another student role-playing the part of a widow who is unable to make mortgage payments and, so, has just lost her farm. While students do this role-play, they use the Paraphrase Passport structure. When this structure is used, before a student may speak, he or she must first paraphrase the person who spoke before him or her. Paraphrasing is a form of summary, so students are acquiring summarizing skills without taking time away from the existing curriculum.

In the Kagan Structural Approach, we have identified 15 fundamental types of thinking, and many structures to develop each.

A teacher who regularly uses a range of structures develops in students a rich repertoire of thinking skills. Thinking in many ways is simply part of the ongoing process in a classroom that regularly uses Kagan Structures. The Kagan Structural Approach, along with many Kagan Structures.[1]

The 15 Fundamental Types of Thinking

Understanding Information	Manipulating Information	Generating Information
Recalling	Analyzing	Brainstorming
Summarizing	Applying	Synthesizing
Symbolizing	Inducing	Predicting
Categorizing	Deducing	Evaluating
Role-taking	Problem-solving	Questioning

The Kagan approach to thinking skills, and the 15 types of thinking have been described in detail.[2] Kagan Publishing has produced many resources to facilitate the use of Kagan Structures across the curriculum.[3]

Advantages to the Kagan Instructional Approach

There are a number of advantages to this instructional approach to thinking skills.

Not a Competing Curriculum. The instructional approach does not attempt to fit new lessons into an already overcrowded day; it is not something new to teach, but better way to teach. When thinking skills are a competing curriculum, they get dropped when there's pressure to cover existing curriculum and to prepare students for high-stakes tests. In contrast, with the instructional approach, students acquire the skills while covering content or preparing for the test. In effect, the instructional approach permits more learning from each valuable minute of class time. At the same time the teacher is covering academic content, the teacher is also fostering thinking skills. Thinking skills represent an embedded curriculum—a curriculum embedded into the way the teacher teaches.

Less Preparation. A curricular approach demands the teacher prepare special worksheets or lessons. In the worst case it demands the teacher spend the day teaching—and the night designing lessons. In contrast, the instructional approach demands no special preparation time. Once the structures are learned, they become part of how the teacher teaches on a daily basis.

Authentic Transfer. Special lessons on thinking skills create a transfer gap; the instructional approach sidesteps the transfer gap. In real life we do not fill in blanks on a worksheet. We do, though, interact with others, sometimes paraphrasing them. Because the instructional approach teaches the thinking skills in an authentic context, similar to how thinking is used in real life, it avoids the transfer gap. A transfer gap is created anytime the situation of acquisition is dissimilar to the situation of performance. The classic transfer gap was created in foreign language classes where students had to memorize lists of vocabulary and conjugations of verbs. Even students who did quite well on vocabulary and verb tests failed to become fluent in the language because the situation of acquisition was too dissimilar to the situation of performance. Thinking is not something we want students to do when faced with an inauthentic worksheet; it is something we want them to do in the full range of life's situations. Structures provide a broad range of authentic situations to promote thinking.

Rich in Redundancy. If we teach separate lessons on thinking skills, we are likely to teach each skill one time, then move on to the next. Learning, however, occurs via repetition. One worksheet on summarizing will never add up to enduring summarizing skills. If, however, students use Paraphrase Passport (and other summarizing structures) all school year, they will become better at the skill. The same holds true for each of the thinking skills: the redundancy created by repeated use of the structures ensures students don't just learn about the skill but rather acquire the skill. The curricular approach has students glimpse the skill; the instructional approach has students grasp the skill.

Conclusion

By making thinking skills an integral part of every lesson, we create thinking skills as habits of mind. Rather than learning about thinking skills, students acquire thinking skills while engaged in their regular academic lessons.

References

1. Kagan, Spencer & Kagan, Miguel. *Kagan Cooperative Learning.* San Clemente, CA: Kagan Publishing and Professional Developmen, 2009. **www.KaganOnline.com**

2. Kagan, Spencer. "Kagan Structures for Thinking Skills." ***Kagan Online Magazine***, Fall 2003. **www.KaganOnline.com**

3. Kagan, Spencer. *Cooperative Learning & Higher Level Thinking: The Q-Matrix with Question Manipulatives.* San Clemente, CA: Kagan Publishing and Professional Development. **www.KaganOnline.com**

Other Bibliography

Kagan, Spencer. *Cooperative Learning & Higher Level Thinking: The Q-Matrix w/Question Manipulatives (iBook).* San Clemente, CA: Kagan Publishing and Professional Development. **www.KaganOnline.com**

Kagan, Spencer. *Developing Character: Higher Level Thinking Questions (Grades 3–12) (PDF eBook).* San Clemente, CA: Kagan Publishing and Professional Development. **www.KaganOnline.com**

Kagan, Spencer. *Question Book: Chemistry (Grades 7–12).* San Clemente, CA: Kagan Publishing and Professional Development. **www.KaganOnline.com**

Kagan, Spencer. *Spin-N-Think Spinner.* San Clemente, CA: Kagan Publishing and Professional Development. **www.KaganOnline.com**

Student's Book Scope and Sequence

	Outcomes	Vocabulary	Grammar	Speaking
Unit 1 Who Are You? pp. 7–15	• Describe who you are and what you like in an online profile • Greet and introduce people in various settings • Complete registration information with numbers	• Forms • Greetings, introductions, and goodbyes • Ordinal numbers	• *Be* statements and *yes/no* questions • Information questions with *be* Grammar Reference pp. 142–143	• Describe people • Make introductions • Give personal information
	Language and Life—Communication: Make an Interesting Online Profile			
Unit 2 Work/Life Balance pp. 17–25	• Talk about various jobs • Talk about members of your family • Discuss your family members and their jobs	• Work life • Family • Jobs	• Articles *a*, *an*, and no article • Possessive adjectives and *'s/s'* Grammar Reference pp. 143–144	• Talk about a famous person • Talk about family • Describe a picture
	Language and Life—Self-awareness: Find the Right Job for Your Interests and Abilities			
Unit 3 Fun and Games pp. 27–35	• Express likes and dislikes • Talk about and recommend free-time activities • Plan and talk about an event	• Likes and dislikes • Free-time activities • Special events	• Simple present statements and *yes/no* questions • The imperative Grammar Reference pp. 145–146	• Talk about things you like to do • Recommend free-time activities • Describe an event
	Language and Life—Creativity: Create an Interest Group for a Website			
Unit 4 That's Life! pp. 37–45	• Talk about daily activities • Talk about how often you do activities • Describe your day off	• Daily activities • Frequency and time expressions • Routine activities	• Simple present information questions • Frequency adverbs Grammar Reference pp. 146–147	• Interview a partner about daily activities • Talk about routine activities • Discuss the perfect day off
	Language and Life—Adaptability: Give Advice about Keeping Life Interesting			
Unit 5 Finding Your Way pp. 47–55	• Talk about places to live • Describe your neighborhood • Give directions	• Where you live • Places in a neighborhood • Directions	• Adjectives • *There is / There are* Grammar Reference pp. 148–149	• Talk about where you live • Discuss a neighborhood • Give directions
	Language and Life—Problem-solving: Create a Guide to Your Neighborhood			
Unit 6 Going Viral pp. 57–65	• Talk about social media use • Talk about computer equipment and vlogging • Talk about buying and selling online	• Emotions • Technology equipment • Technology phrases	• Present progressive • Present progressive vs. simple present Grammar Reference pp. 149–150	• Talk about routines and feelings • Discuss vlogs • Discuss online activity
	Language and Life—Critical Thinking: Analyze the Pros and Cons of A Digital Detox			

Confident Communicator	Pronunciation	Listening/Reading	Thinking Skills	Writing
Repair It • Ask for repetition *Start Talking* • Add details *Start Talking* • Useful phrases	• Intonation in *yes/no* and information questions	Read a social media profile • Skill—Infer information Listen to short conversations of greetings • Skill—Listen for details Listen for personal details • Skill—Listen for numerical information	• Evaluate • Deduce	Write about a school calendar
Unit Review p. 16	**Study Skills** p. 127—Memory Strategies			
Keep Talking • Useful phrases *Repair It* • Check for understanding *Keep Talking* • Use notes	• *An* + vowel	Read an online article about a business owner • Skill—Scan Listen to a conversation about a family picture • Skill—Use visual clues Listen to a description of a family vacation picture • Skill—Predict	• Question • Analyze • Categorize	Write an online family profile
Unit Review p. 26	**Follow A Pro** p. 128—An IT Consultant ▶ An IT Professional			
Keep Talking • Emphasize preference *Keep Talking* • Give reasons *Keep Talking* • Express rules	• Third person *–s*	Read a magazine interview • Skill—Infer Listen to a phone conversation about an event • Skill—Take notes Listen to a recorded advertisement • Skill—Listen for gist	• Categorize • Understand • Recall	Create a poster to advertise a special event
Unit Review p. 36	**Study Skills** p. 129—Oral Presentations			
Start Talking • Give examples *Keep Talking* • Useful phrases *Keep Talking* • Express frequency	• Word stress in information questions	Read a blog post about a reporter's day • Skill—Scan Listen to an interview with an actress • Skill—Listen for specific information Listen to a radio show about daily routines • Skill—Listen for gist	• Analyze • Summarize • Recall	Write about the perfect day off
Unit Review p. 46	**Follow A Pro** p. 130—A Firefighter ▶ A Paramedic			
Keep Talking • Make guesses *Keep Talking* • Useful phrases *Start Talking* • Useful phrases	• Syllable stress in multi-syllable adjectives	Read an article about unusual places to live • Skill—Scan for specific information Listen to a radio show about neighborhoods • Skill—Listen for specific information Listen to conversations asking for directions • Skill—Listen for key words	• Apply • Evaluate • Analyze	Write an instant message
Unit Review p. 56	**Study Skills** p. 131—Research Skills			
Start Talking • Useful phrases *Keep Talking* • Show interest *Keep Talking* • Ask follow-up questions	• /ŋ/	Read an article about social media use and employment • Skill—Predict information Listen to vloggers describe their videos • Skill—Listen for fact and opinion Listen to an internet business owner • Skill—Listen for the main idea	• Analyze • Evaluate	Write a social media ad
Unit Review p. 66	**Follow A Pro** p. 132—A Chief Listening Officer ▶ A Social Media Manager			

	Outcomes	Vocabulary	Grammar	Speaking
Unit 7 Fit for Life pp. 67–75	• Talk about parts of the body and abilities • Talk about sports and athletes • Describe skills and abilities	• Parts of the body • Ball game action words • Exercise words	• *Can/can't* (ability) • Adverbs of manner Grammar Reference pp. 151–152	• Talk about abilities • Describe a famous athlete • Role-play a job interview
	Language and Life—Decision-making: Design an Outdoor Gym for Your City			
Unit 8 Foodie? pp. 77–85	• Talk about food and tastes • Talk about types of food and ingredients • Follow and write a recipe	• Food and tastes • Food groups • Cooking	• Countable and uncountable nouns • *This/that/these/those* Grammar Reference pp. 152–153	• Talk about food preference • Discuss and recommend healthy foods • Discuss recipes
	Language and Life—Communication: Design a Restaurant Guide			
Unit 9 Seeing the World pp. 87–95	• Talk about travel • Give advice and suggestions • Talk about clothes to wear on a trip	• Travel • Tourism collocations • Clothes	• Verb + infinitive or gerund • *Should/could* for advice and possibility Grammar Reference pp. 154–155	• Plan a virtual tour • Role-play a phone conversation • Discuss a planned trip
	Language and Life—Collaboration: Create an Advertisement to Attract Tourists			
Unit 10 Life Stories pp. 97–105	• Talk about life events • Talk about your social life • Describe a personal experience	• From the reading • Social life collocations • Collocations with *get, have,* and *make*	• Simple past (affirmative statements) • Simple past (negative statements and questions) Grammar Reference pp. 155–156	• Talk about milestones • Discuss events in the past • Talk about a specific experience from the past
	Language and Life—Empathy: Give Advice Based on Your Experience for an Advice Column			
Unit 11 Planning Ahead pp. 107–115	• Talk about plans and intentions • Give and receive advice for saving money • Talk about career goals	• To-do lists • Money • Career plans collocations	• *Going to* • Direct and indirect objects Grammar Reference pp. 157–158	• Talk about predictions and plans • Role-play a conversation about saving money • Discuss career plans
	Language and Life—Self-direction: Make a Career Plan Based On Your Interests			
Unit 12 The Great Outdoors pp. 117–125	• Discuss climate and weather • Talk about natural features in geography • Describe outdoor activities	• From the reading • Natural features • Adjectives to describe natural features	• Comparative adjectives • Review of tenses Grammar Reference pp. 158–159	• Discuss weather • Talk about a natural place • Talk about outdoor activities
	Language and Life—Problem-solving: Present Ideas for Developing a Natural Area			

Confident Communicator	Pronunciation	Listening/Reading	Thinking Skills	Writing
Start Talking • Useful phrases *Start Talking* • Buy time *Keep Talking* • Use imagination	• *Can/can't*	Read a magazine article about fitness gadgets • Skill—Read for gist Listen to people describe unusual sports • Skill—Listen for the main idea Listen to descriptions of exercises • Skill—Listen for specific information	• Analyze • Deduce • Evaluate	Write an email inquiring about a job
Unit Review p. 76 **Study Skills** p. 133—Effective Group Work				
Start Talking • Useful phrases *Keep Talking* • Useful phrases *Repair It* • Check for understanding	• Emphasis with *this/that/these/those*	Read posts from an online food forum • Skill—Read for the main idea Listen to an interview with street food vendors • Skill—Listen for specific information Listen to the steps of a recipe • Skill—Listen for specific information	• Apply • Analyze • Evaluate	Write a recipe
Unit Review p. 86 **Follow A Pro** p. 134—A Food Stylist ▶ A Baker				
Keep Talking • Take time to think *Keep Talking* • Useful phrases *Start Talking* • Follow-up questions	• *to*	Read an article about virtual travel • Skill—Scan Listen to a radio show about tourism • Skill—Listen for detail Listen to people talk about packing for a trip • Skill—Listen for gist	• Analyze • Recall • Deduce	Write advice for tourists
Unit Review p. 96 **Study Skills** p. 135—Formal vs. Informal Writing				
Start Talking • Useful phrases *Keep Talking* • Show interest *Start Talking* • Useful phrases	• the ending *–ed*	Read a biography on Malala Yousafzai • Skill—Scan for information Listen to a conversation about social life • Skill—Listen for main ideas Listen to personal stories • Skill—Listen for gist	• Summarize • Evaluate • Analyze	Write an email about a personal experience
Unit Review p. 106 **Follow A Pro** p. 136—An Event Organizer ▶ A Tour Guide				
Start Talking • Useful phrases *Keep Talking* • Suggest alternatives *Repair It* • Useful phrases	• *Going to*	Read an article about to-do lists • Skill—Read for the main idea Listen to a radio show about money • Skill—Listen for specific information Listen to a podcast about dream jobs • Skill—Listen for gist	• Apply • Calculate • Analyze	Write a journal entry about career plans
Unit Review p. 116 **Study Skills** p. 137—Personal Development				
Keep Talking • Useful phrases *Keep Talking* • Show interest *Keep Talking* • Useful phrases	• /ju/	Read a brochure about the Galapagos Islands • Skill—Scan for specific information Listen to a radio interview about waterfalls • Skill—Listen for specific information Listen to a conversation about visiting natural places in Mexico • Skill—Listen for detail	• Understand • Induce • Recall	Write a guidebook entry about a natural feature
Unit Review p. 126 **Follow A Pro** p. 138—A Forest Ranger ▶ A Botanist				

GO TO page xxi
for **GRAMMAR REVIEW** step-by-step instructions.

1 do not / don't know
2 want
3 travel
4 love
5 works
6 does not / doesn't make

1 's/is raining
2 are not / aren't listening
3 's/is working
4 'm/am cooking
5 is not / isn't doing
6 's/is wearing

Grammar Quiz: What Do You Already Know?

A Choose the correct option.

1 I'm am not / **I'm not** / I isn't Brazilian.
2 Am / **Is** / Are your teacher from Peru?
3 **It's** / It / It not nice to meet you.
4 Where be / is / **are** they from?
5 What **is** / are / does your last name?
6 We am / is / **are** not Spanish students.

B Complete the paragraph with the simple present form of the verbs in parentheses.

Many students **1** ___________ (not know) what they want to do after they finish college. But I do. I **2** ___________ (want) to be a flight attendant. Flight attendants **3** ___________ (travel) the world, and I **4** ___________ (love) to travel! My friend Beth **5** ___________ (work) as a flight attendant now. She **6** ___________ (not make) a lot of money, but she's happy.

C Complete the sentences with the present progressive form of the verbs in the box.

cook not do not listen rain wear work

1 It ___________ outside. Don't forget to take your umbrella.
2 The teacher is angry because the students ___________.
3 Harry has a great job. He ___________ at the office in Spain right now.
4 Sorry, I can't talk right now. I ___________ dinner.
5 Calvin ___________ the laundry now because he doesn't have any soap.
6 Dan ___________ shorts and a T-shirt because it's very hot today.

D Unscramble and write sentences.

1 listen / we / to / sometimes / music / .
We sometimes listen to music.
2 I / where / vegetables / buy / can / ?
Where can I buy vegetables?
3 never / is / our / teacher / late / .
Our teacher is never late.
4 hair / long / Sally / has / brown / .
Sally has long brown hair?
5 there / many / eggs / how / are / ?
How many eggs are there?
6 cook / does / Adam / how / often / ?
How often does Adam cook?

E Find one error in each sentence. Write the correct sentence.

1 My fathers' name is Antonio.
My father's name is Antonio.
2 Please take a umbrella with you.
Please take an umbrella with you.
3 Why do you have three cell phone?
Why do you have three cell phones?
4 Don't to forget to come to my party.
Don't forget to come to my party.
5 Jeff take the train to work.
Jeff takes the train to work. / Jeff took the train to work.
6 We have any tomatoes.
We have some tomatoes. / We don't have any tomatoes.

Go to the Grammar Review on pages 140–141.

GRAMMAR QUIZ

This quiz tests students' knowledge of language presented in **Student's Book** Starter level. For further review of the Starter level, have students do the Grammar Review on pages 141–142.

GO TO page vi
for **UNIT OPENER** step-by-step instructions.

UNIT 1 Who Are You?

WHAT DO YOU ALREADY KNOW?

1 Think of words you know that describe you. Write the words.

2 **IN PAIRS** Share and compare your words. If possible, add more words to the box.

STUDENTS MAY ALREADY KNOW:

- Numbers to 100.
- **Basic descriptions:** tall, short.
- How to say their age.
- Where they live.

VIDEO

DISCUSS & SHARE

3 **IN GROUPS** Watch the video and answer the question.

SYM Are you typical or different?

GO TO page xx
for **VIDEOS IN SYM** step-by-step instructions.

In this unit, you will ...

- describe yourself, introduce yourself and others, and give personal details about yourself.
- use thinking skills: evaluate and draw conclusions.
- read about a social media profile.
- use strategies to start talking and keep talking by asking for repetition or asking for details.
- use communication skills to create an interesting social media profile.
- learn strategies for memorization.

Unit 1 Who Are You? 7

WHAT DO YOU ALREADY KNOW?

If you notice students are struggling to understand what to do, you can provide one or two examples to help them get started:

- **Nationality:** Mexican, American, Peruvian
- **Gender:** girl, boy, woman, man
- **Age:** 16, 19, 22
- **Family:** There are five people in my family.
- **Description:** tall, short
- **Emotion:** happy, angry

VIDEO

Before viewing, ask:

How is Alex different? *rides a skateboard, has a parrot, plays the xylophone*
How is Sonya typical? *plays soccer, dresses like her coworkers*

After viewing, put the continuum on the board.

typical —— different

Students mark the continuum and explain how they are typical or different.

DISCUSS & SHARE

Encourage students to think about whether they feel like they are typical members of their group or different. Do they feel similar to everyone else, or do they strive to be different in their attitude, fashion, or career choice?

GO TO page x

for **READING** step-by-step instructions.

About You

READING

A Are you on any social media sites? Which ones? Discuss.

B 1.01 **READING SKILL—Infer information** Read the form. Then choose the correct answer.

International English Teachers

ABOUT YOU

I'm an English teacher in Germany. I'm from Berlin. I speak German, English, and Spanish. My hobbies are swimming, dancing, and yoga. My favorite music is rock and my favorite food is tacos (♥ Mexican food). My boyfriend is Juan. He isn't an English teacher. He's a yoga teacher.

Username:	Berliner100	Last name:	Steiner
Password:	DerSeestern!	Nickname:	Angie
Re-enter password:	DerSeestern!	Date of birth:	04/15/97
First name:	Angela	Country:	Germany

Your Profile

Edit Profile

1 Is this an English-language website? — **Yes, it is.** / No, it isn't.
2 Is Angie Steiner the name on her passport? — Yes, it is. / **No, it isn't.**
3 Is the number 04 a month? — **Yes, it is.** / No, it isn't.
4 Is she from Europe? — **Yes, she is.** / No, she isn't.
5 Is she a yoga teacher? — Yes, she is. / **No, she isn't.**
6 Is she married? — Yes, she is. / **No, she isn't.**

C **THINKING SKILL—Evaluate** Consider why some passwords are secure and others are not secure.

GO TO page vii

for **VOCABULARY** step-by-step instructions.

VOCABULARY

A Match the personal information (1–6) to a category (a–f). Write the letter.

1 11/18/90 __d__
2 Robert __e__
3 US __f__
4 Garcia __a__
5 playing video games __c__
6 Robbie __b__

a last name
b nickname
c hobby
d date of birth
e first name
f country

B Complete the profile for you. Then share with a partner.

First name ____________
Last name ____________
Nickname ____________
Date of birth ____________
Country ____________
Hobbies ____________

A: My first name is Amanda. And you?
B: My first name is Olivia. My last name is …

8 Unit 1 Who Are You?

READING OPTIONAL 1.01

READING SKILL—Infer information

Some examples of social media sites are Facebook, Instagram, and Twitter.

Ask students which sites they use, how and why they use them, and the advantages and disadvantages of each. Ask *What can you infer about someone based on the social media they use?*

THINKING SKILL—Evaluate

For further discussion of password safety, discuss the meaning of *lower case, upper case,* and *symbols.* Explain that many sites require passwords to include a combination of these to make accounts more difficult to hack.

- **hack:** (v) connect to another computer illegally in order to access or alter data

VOCABULARY

Elicit from students types of personal information that should never be shared on social media. They should not give out their home addresses, current location, when they will be somewhere, bank information, income details, or ID numbers. They should think about carefully guarding their information with safety in mind.

GRAMMAR *be* statements and *yes/no* questions

A IN PAIRS Complete the examples.

Affirmative	Negative
1 I ___am___ / I'm an English teacher.	**4** I am not / I'm ___not___ from Mexico.
2 We are / We'___re___ English students.	**5** They are not / They're not / They ___aren't___ German teachers.
3 He ___is___ / He's a yoga teacher.	**6** He is not / He's not / He ___isn't___ an English teacher.

Questions and Short Answers

7 Are you late? Yes, I am. / No, I'm ___not___.
8 Is she married? Yes, she ___is___. / No, she's not. / No, she isn't.
9 Are they from Berlin? Yes, they are. / No, ___they're___ not. / No, they aren't.

For more practice, go to page 142.

B Complete with the correct forms of *be*.

1 ________ you a student? No, I ________. I ________ a teacher.
2 ________ your parents from Mexico? No, they ________. They ________ from Brazil.
3 ________ your English teacher American? Yes, he ________.
4 ________ I in the correct classroom? No, you ________. This ________ English 5.

C Complete the answers for you.

1 Are you on social media?
Yes, I'm on two social media sites.
2 Is your favorite hobby playing video games?
____
3 Is your favorite food from your country?
____
4 Are your parents from this city?
____

MAKE IT REAL

Informal ways to say Yes: *Yeah, Uh-huh, Yep*
Informal ways to say No: *Uh-uh, Nope, No way*

D IN PAIRS Ask and answer the questions in C.

SPEAKING

A Complete the survey for you.

About me ...

From		Nickname		Favorite food	
Hobbies		Birth month		Favorite music	

B IN GROUPS Ask questions and try to guess your partner's answers. Use the Confident Communicator box to help you.

A: Are you from Brazil? *B: No, I'm not.*
C: Are you from Mexico? *B: Yes, I am.*

CONFIDENT COMMUNICATOR
REPAIR IT

When you don't understand or don't hear something, ask for repetition.
Excuse me?
Sorry, can you repeat that, please?

GO TO page viii
for GRAMMAR step-by-step instructions.

1 Are, 'm / am not, 'm / am
2 Are, aren't / are not, 're / are
3 Is, is
4 Am, aren't / are not, is

GO TO page xii
for SPEAKING step-by-step instructions.

GRAMMAR

Tell students that we usually use contractions (*I'm, you're, he's, she's, they're, aren't*) in speech and informal writing. It's OK to use contractions for texting and emailing friends, but the full form should be used for formal correspondence, like filling out forms and writing business emails.

SPEAKING

Before doing the survey, elicit the questions students will need to ask. Write examples on the board: *Are you from …? Is your nickname …? Is your favorite food …?*, and so on. For each category, elicit a couple of examples. Give students words for music genres to help with "Favorite music"—for example, *rock, pop,* and *classical*. Allow dictionary use.

Demonstrate how to do a survey before asking them to break into groups.

Extend the activity by having students form new groups and ask about previous partners using the third person. For example, *Is she from Mexico? Is her birthday in November?*

GO TO page xi
for **LISTENING** step-by-step instructions.

LESSON 2 Hello and Goodbye

LISTENING

A Look at the pictures (a–c). Match the pictures to the questions (1–4).

a 
b 
c 

1 How do you greet a good friend or a family member? _____
2 How do you greet a new classmate? _____
3 How do you greet an important person for the first time? _____
4 How do you greet someone you don't know well? _____

GO TO page 137
for **AUDIO SCRIPT**.

B 1.02 THINKING SKILL—Deduce Listen. Check (✓) if the people know each other.

1 ☑ Sandy and Jake
2 ☐ Janice Walters and Lynn Jefferson
3 ☐ Mr. Wilson and Sarah
4 ☐ Christine, Mark, and Jean Luc

4 Christine and Mark know each other, but Jean Luc and Mark don't.

C 1.02 LISTENING SKILL—Listen for details Listen again and choose the correct answer.

1 Where is Michelle?
a at work
b at home
c with Jake

2 Who is the office manager?
a Lynn
b Ms. Jefferson
c Janice

3 Why is Mr. Wilson at DT Bank?
a to work
b to talk about his account
c to get money

4 What country is Jean Luc from?
a France
b the US
c Canada

VOCABULARY greetings, introductions, and goodbyes

A Complete the table with phrases from the box.

Bye.	Good morning.	Hey!
~~Hi.~~	How's it going?	~~I'm John Smith.~~
Nice to meet you.	See you later.	How are you?
~~Take care.~~	This is Nicolle Martin.	It's nice to meet you.

MAKE IT YOURS
Can you think of situations when you have to introduce someone in English?

Greetings	Introductions	Goodbyes
Hi.	*I'm John Smith.*	*Take care.*
How's it going?	Nice to meet you.	Bye.
Hey!	This is Nicolle Martin.	See you later.
Good morning.	It's nice to meet you.	
How are you?		

LISTENING

THINKING SKILL—Deduce

In order to deduce, one must analyze the information given. Students will figure out the relationships between the speakers based on clues in the conversations. Students should listen for informal or formal greetings, words used for introductions, and use of full names or first names.

LISTENING SKILL—Listen for details

Play each conversation and stop after each one to allow students to answer each question individually, rather than trying to do it as they listen to all the conversations at once.

VOCABULARY

Remind students we often use *Take care* when we're not sure when we'll see someone again.

Before students practice the conversation in VOCABULARY **B** on their own, demonstrate it. Have them consider stress and intonation: *Hello/Hi/Hey*. *How's it going?*

B **Complete the conversation with words and phrases from A.**

Kara: **1** ____________, Josie. How's **2** ____________?

Josie: **3** ____________, Kara. I'm good. **4** ____________?

Kara: Fine, thanks. Josie, **5** ____________ my friend Michelle Kim.

Josie: Hi, Michelle. I'm Josie Grayson. It's **6** ____________.

Michelle: **7** ____________, too, Josie.

Kara: Well, it's good to see you, Josie. **8** ____________.

Josie: Nice to see you, too. **9** ____________.

MAKE IT REAL

In informal situations, people use very short and informal forms of greetings and goodbyes.

Greetings:	Goodbyes:
What's up?	*Later!*
How you doing?	*Catch you later.*
What's new?	*See ya!*

1 Hello/Hi/Hey
2 it going
3 Hello/Hi/Hey
4 How are you
5 this is
6 nice to meet you
7 (It's) Nice to meet you
8 Bye/Goodbye/ Take care
9 Bye/Goodbye/ Take care

C **IN GROUPS** **Practice the conversation in B using your own names.**

GRAMMAR information questions with *be*

A **Complete the table with** ***what, where, when,*** **or** ***how*****.**

Question Word + *be* + Word or Phrase	Answer
Who is your teacher?	Mr. Oliver is my teacher.
1 What is your name?	My name is Lisette.
2 Where is Mandy?	She's at the office in Chicago.
3 When is your birthday?	It's in May.
4 How are you?	I'm fine, thanks.

For more practice, go to page 142.

B **Complete the questions and answers for you.**

1 What's your name? It's ____________.
2 How old are you? I'm ____________.
3 Where are you from? I'm from ____________.
4 When is your birthday? It's in ____________. (month)
5 Who is your favorite singer? My favorite singer is ____________.

C **IN PAIRS** **Ask and answer the questions in B.**

SPEAKING

A **IN GROUPS** **Greet classmates you know. Introduce yourself to classmates you do not know. Ask questions to find out more information about each person.**

A: Hi. I'm Sal. How's it going?
B: Great. I'm Leslie. How are you, Sal?
A: Fine, thanks. Where are you from?
B: I'm from Port-au-Prince, Haiti. Where are you from?

B **Introduce someone to your class. The person you introduce then introduces someone else. Use the Confident Communicator box to help you.**

CONFIDENT COMMUNICATOR
START TALKING

When we introduce someone, it is common to give a little more information about the person.
This is Robert. He's my neighbor. He's from Chicago.

GRAMMAR

Check students' understanding of information words. Ask *Does "who" refer to a person or a place? Does "what" refer to a person or a thing? Does "where" refer to a time or a place? Does "when" refer to a time or a place?*

Additional Activity

Play Line Up. Have students line up in order of their birthday months, from January to December. They will have to ask each other the question *When's your birthday?*

SPEAKING

How to meet and greet someone properly is an important life skill. Explain that a brief, confident handshake while looking at someone will send a positive message. In pairs, have students greet each other with a handshake.

GO TO page 137 for AUDIO SCRIPT.

LESSON 3 Numbers

VOCABULARY ordinal numbers

A 1.03 **Write the ordinal numbers for the days of the month.**

APRIL						
SUNDAY	MONDAY	TUESDAY	WEDNESDAY	THURSDAY	FRIDAY	SATURDAY
	1 first	2 second	3 third	4 fourth	5 fifth	6 sixth
7 seventh	8 eighth	9 ninth	10 tenth	11 eleventh	12 twelfth	13 thirteenth
14 fourteenth	15 fifteenth	16 1 sixteenth	17 seventeenth	18 eighteenth	19 nineteenth	20 twentieth
21 2 twenty-first	22 3 twenty-second	23 twenty-third	24 twenty-fourth	25 twenty-fifth	26 twenty-sixth	27 4 twenty-seventh
28 5 twenty-eighth	29 twenty-ninth	30 thirtieth				

B **IN PAIRS Complete the sentences for you. Then discuss.**

1 My birthday is ______________.
2 Today is ______________.
3 New Year's Day is ______________.
4 My favorite holiday is ______________, on ______________.
5 In my family, I am the ______________ child.

LISTENING

A **IN PAIRS THINKING SKILL—Evaluate Make a list of dates that are important to you. Ask your partner why his/her dates are important.**

A: Why is August 2 important to you? Is it your birthday? *B: Yes, it is.*

GO TO page 137 for AUDIO SCRIPT.

B 1.04 **LISTENING SKILL—Listen for numerical information Listen to the conversation and answer the questions.**

MAKE IT REAL

Write dates with cardinal numbers: April 4.
Say dates with ordinal numbers: April fourth (4th).
US: write dates as month, day, year: 10/22/2019.
UK: write dates as day, month, year: 22/10/19.

1 What is Olivia's date of birth? 10/17/99
2 What is her address? 45 Third Avenue
3 Is her phone number 555-376-5832? No, it's 555-367-5823.
4 How much money is the registration? $25
5 When does Olivia's group start? 18–29
6 Is this her first marathon? No, it's her fourth marathon.

MAKE IT REAL

Remind students they will write dates with cardinal numbers (*March 23*) and say dates with ordinal numbers (*March 23rd*).

Let students know that the international format for writing the date is DD/MM/YY and that the American format is MM/DD/YY. Explain that this can result in misinterpretation, so they should be aware of the difference.

Have students review this information in the *Make It Real* box.

LISTENING

Tell students that in English, the house number comes before the street name. The apartment number or letter, if there is one, comes afterward (e.g., *22 Brown St. Apt., 26*). This is different from addresses in many countries where the street name often comes first (e.g., *Calle Grijalva 801, Dept. 6*).

PRONUNCIATION intonation in *yes/no* and information questions

A 1.04 Listen again. Draw an arrow pointing up if the speaker's voice goes up at the end of the question. Draw an arrow pointing down if the speaker's voice goes down at the end of the question.

What is your first name? ↘ *Is registration open?* ↗

1 What's your last name? ↘
2 And your phone number? ↗
3 What is your date of birth? ↘
4 Is this your first marathon? ↗

B IN PAIRS Ask and answer the questions from **A**. Use correct intonation for *yes/no* and information questions.

WRITING

A Read the rules for capital letters. Then correct the capitalization mistakes in the text.

Capitalize:
- names of people, pets, places: Daniel, San Francisco, my cat Coco
- countries, nationalities, languages: Ecuador, British, Chinese
- months, days, holidays: January, Monday, Independence Day
- the pronoun *I*
- the first letter of the first word in a sentence

Adams English Academy Academic Calendar

August 21–September 2	registration opens
September 2	fall semester begins
December 10	fall semester ends
December 15–January 5	school closed
January 6–10	registration opens
January 11	spring semester begins

i am a student at Adams english Academy. Registration is from August 21st to September 2nd. The first day of class is on September 2nd. The first semester is from September 2nd to December 10th. The school is closed from December 15th to January 5th for the new Year holiday. the next semester is from january 11th to May 3rd. I'm in the first level, and my teacher is Robert green. His nickname is rob.

(Corrections: I, English, New, The, January, Green, Rob)

B Write about your English class or school. Use the paragraph in **A** as a model. Remember to use capital letters.

SPEAKING

A IN PAIRS Read the questions out loud and answer them as quickly as you can. Use the Confident Communicator box to help you.

1 What is the eighth month of the year? 1 August
2 What is the fourteenth letter of the English alphabet? n
3 What is the day after the last day of the year? January 1st
4 What is two days after the second day of the weekend? Tuesday
5 What is the extra day in February? 29th
6 What is the 365th day of the year? December 31st
7 Write your own: ______

B IN GROUPS Check your answers. How many pairs got 100% correct?

CONFIDENT COMMUNICATOR START TALKING

To talk about numbers in math, say:
+ *plus* – *minus* × *times* ÷ *divided by* = *equals*
Five plus two equals seven, and five minus three equals two.

GO TO page ix for **PRONUNCIATION** step-by-step instructions.

GO TO page xiv for **WRITING** step-by-step instructions.

PRONUNCIATION

Provide students with more questions to extend their practice of rising and falling intonation: *What's your pet's name? Is this your favorite subject? What's your house number?*

Have them go back to the questions in previous lessons and check their intonation as they practice them again.

WRITING

Pair students and have them check that their partner caught all the mistakes in WRITING **A**. Then have them give feedback on each other's WRITING **B**. Tell students you expect them to be supportive in their peer feedback. They should acknowledge the effort before commenting on what can be improved.

SPEAKING

Have students write five new questions to quiz their classmates based on the questions in SPEAKING **A**.

Having groups working simultaneously increases the amount of speaking practice each student gets.

GO TO page xv for LANGUAGE AND LIFE step-by-step instructions.

Language and Life

Communication – Online Profiles

A 1.05 **Read the online article. Choose *True* or *False*.**

SOCIAL MEDIA PROFILE TIPS

Many social media websites have different parts in the personal profile section.

One part is often about specific preferences—movies, books, TV shows, and sports. Another part is for biographical information. When you create a social media profile, here are some things to consider:

- Are your preferences interesting?
- Is your personal information interesting? Write one or two interesting things about yourself!
- Is your information safe? Don't write your home address, phone number, or vacation dates.
- Are your grammar and spelling correct? Your language is part of your reputation!
- Finally, is your picture good? Use a clear picture of yourself.

1 This is a social media website. True / False
2 Many social media profiles have different sections. True / False
3 Your entertainment preferences are a part of your personality. True / False
4 It's a good idea to include your phone number and address in your profile. True / False
5 Grammar and spelling are not important in a social media profile. True / False

B IN PAIRS **Help Amanda improve her profile. Circle and correct five capitalization errors and one grammar error.**

SYM INSTITUTE

HOME | CALENDAR | FACULTY | STAFF | ORGANIZATION | STUDENT PROFILES

Basics
Name: Amanda herrero Herrero
Age: 20
Hometown: Recife
English level or class: 1B (Beginner)

Interests/Favorites
Music/Musicians: pop—Ed Sheeran, Camila Cabello; reggaeton
Games: *League of Legends*
People I like: Beyoncé, Bill and Melinda Gates, Neymar
Hobbies: dancing, going out to eat, beach parties
Other: my cats, my boyfriend julio Julio

More About Me
University
I'm a student in communications at the Federal university of Pernambuco, in Recife recife. My favorite Things is my pets and my car (an old Volkswagen Beetle!).
things are

OBJECTIVE

In this lesson, students learn how to identify interesting aspects of their own personalities and how to consider what information to include in an online profile. Explain that an online profile is a public document that is seen by many people, including prospective employers. They should carefully consider the information and photographs they make available online.

Personal safety is also a serious consideration when thinking about the creation of social media profiles.

PROCESS OPTIONAL 1.05

Students first analyze an article that discusses tips for how to write a successful profile. They then consider those tips and apply them to suggest information a character could add to her profile to make it more interesting. Finally, students create their own profile based on the tips they read in the article and the improvements they made to the model text.

C Circle two things for Amanda to add to the Basics section and three things for her to add to the Interests/Favorites section.

Basics	
Address	Email address
Birthday	Hair and eye color
Brothers and sisters	Phone number
Country	Social media sites

Interests/Favorites	
Actors	Movies
Animals	Places
Apps	Sports
Clothes	TV shows
Food/restaurants	

D Write questions Amanda can use as ideas for the More About Me section.

Who's your favorite person in the world?
What is your favorite animal?

1 ______
2 ______
3 ______
4 ______
5 ______

E Complete a profile for you.

HOME | CALENDAR | FACULTY | STAFF | ORGANIZATION | STUDENT PROFILES

Upload Photo

Basics
Name: ______
Age: ______
Hometown: ______
English level or class: ______

Interests/Favorites
Music/Musicians: ______
Games: ______
People: ______
Social activities: ______
Other: ______

More About Me

______

F **IN PAIRS** Read your partner's profile. Make suggestions to improve the profile. Does your partner ...

capitalize words correctly?	Yes / No
use *be* correctly?	Yes / No
describe herself/himself?	Yes / No

MAKE IT DIGITAL

Join an English-language social media site. Use some of the ideas in this lesson to create your profile.

CLASSROOM MANAGEMENT

Have students check each other's completed profiles for spelling and grammar mistakes. Explain that trusting others to read their work and point out problems takes courage but will make the quality of their writing much better. If they can have others check their work regularly, they could see big improvements.

CULTURE NOTE

Discuss how we judge and criticize what people post on their social media pages.

Discuss cyberbullying—sending threatening and intimidating messages to people online.

Discuss trolling—making offensive and rude comments in online posts to get a reaction from people. This is usually done to incite others to argue online.

MAKE IT DIGITAL

Tell students to be aware of privacy settings when they are creating a profile online. There are options for them to keep their information private on most sites.

GO TO page xvii
for UNIT REVIEW step-by-step instructions.

UNIT 1

VOCABULARY review

SCORE: / 10

A Complete the paragraph with words from the box.

favorite first food hello hobbies hometown meet nice nickname up

1 Hello! What's 2 up? My name is Manuel. My 3 nickname is Manny. I'm from El Salvador. My 4 hometown is Santa Ana. I'm 16 and a student. My 5 hobbies are swimming and playing soccer. My 6 favorite music is pop and my favorite 7 food is pizza. My birthday is August 8 first. It's 9 nice to 10 meet you!

GRAMMAR review

SCORE: / 10

A Unscramble the sentences. Use the correct form of *be*.

1 from Brazil / my parents / be / . My parents are from Brazil.
2 I / on social media / not / be / . I'm not on social media. / I am not on social media.
3 teachers / they / be / ? Are they teachers?
4 last name / your / Stevens / be / ? Is Stevens your last name? / Is your last name Stevens?
5 I / your English class / in / be / ? Am I in your English class?

B Complete the questions.

1 ______ your name? My name's Celia.
2 ______ it going? Great, thanks.
3 ______ you from? I'm from Medellin, Colombia.
4 ______ your birthday? It's July 3.
5 ______ your favorite singer? Ariana Grande.

1 What's / What is
2 How's / How is
3 Where are
4 When's / When is
5 Who's / Who is

16–20 correct: You can talk about greetings and ordinal numbers. You can use *be* statements and information questions.
0–15 correct: Look again at the Vocabulary and Grammar sections in the unit.

TOTAL SCORE: / 20

WHAT DO YOU KNOW NOW? Look back at page 7 and add the words you know now to the box.

GO TO page xviii
for STUDY SKILLS step-by-step instructions.

STUDY SKILLS MEMORY STRATEGIES

Take the quiz about memory strategies. Go to **Study Skills** on page 127 to find the answers. Then learn more about memory strategies.

1 Left-handed people have better memories.
a true b false

2 Which foods help your memory?
a chicken and potatoes b vegetables, fruit, and nuts c cheese and chocolate

3 What is a good way to help you remember things?
a Sleep after studying. b Exercise before studying. c Drink coffee when you study.

4 It is possible for students to learn … new words per hour of study.
a 1–5 b 5–10 c 10–20

CLASSROOM MANAGEMENT

For an added challenge, have students cover the words in the box in VOCABULARY **A** and see if they can figure out the answers based on context. This will help them hone their vocabulary skills. Then have them uncover the box and select the words to complete the paragraph.

ALTERNATIVE ACTIVITY

Ask each student to choose a celebrity. Give them time to research the answers to the questions in GRAMMAR **B**. Then have students answer interview questions in the role of their celebrity without saying the person's name. Others should guess. This can be done in groups or as a class.

FURTHER DISCUSSION

Put students in groups of three and ask the following questions for them to discuss:

- How many social media accounts do you have?
- How many times a day do you check your social media?
- Do you buy things you see advertised on social media pages?
- Are you worried about your privacy on social media?

GO TO page vi
for **UNIT OPENER** step-by-step instructions.

UNIT 2 Work/Life Balance

STUDENTS MAY ALREADY KNOW:

- **School or work:** books, teacher, class, university, college, exam, graduate, student, job, work, money, time.
- **Family:** mother, father, sister, brother.
- **Friends:** boyfriend, girlfriend, best friend.

WHAT DO YOU ALREADY KNOW?

1 Think about your day and the things you do at school or work, with family, and with friends. Write the activities and the percentage of time you do the activities each week.

2 **IN PAIRS** Share and compare your activities. Think of more words to add to each category.

School or work __%

Family __%

Friends __%

VIDEO

DISCUSS & SHARE

3 **IN GROUPS** Watch the video and answer the question.
SYM Is it possible to have a good work and life balance?

GO TO page xx
for **VIDEOS IN SYM** step-by-step instructions.

In this unit, you will ...

- talk about jobs, members of your family, and what jobs they do.
- use thinking skills: hypothesize, infer, and categorize.
- read about a young woman entrepreneur.
- use strategies to repair talking by checking for understanding.
- use notes when you speak in front of the class.
- use self-awareness skills to evaluate your interests and abilities for a job.
- follow an IT professional to learn about this job and the skills needed for this industry.

WHAT DO YOU ALREADY KNOW?

If you notice students are struggling to understand what to do, you can provide one or two examples to help them get started:

- **At school:** go to class, go to the library
- **Family:** eat a meal, talk about your day
- **Friends:** go to a movie, go to a restaurant
- **Home:** sleep, relax, listen to music

VIDEO

Before viewing, ask:

Who says it's difficult to balance work and life? *Amy*
Who says it's easy to balance work and life? *Max*

After viewing, put this continuum on the board.

work —— life

Students mark the continuum and explain their own work and life balance.

DISCUSS & SHARE

Ask students to think about how much time they or their parents spend at work and how much time they or their parents spend with friends and family. Are they spending too much time working and not enough with the people in their lives who are important?

GO TO page x

for **READING** step-by-step instructions.

LESSON 1 In Business

READING

A **Are you (or a member of your family) a business owner? What business is it? Discuss.**

B 2.01 **Read the article. Then discuss the questions.**

A Woman at Work Zinah Saleh, Iraq

Zinah Saleh is a **business owner** with a **successful** business. She is the owner of her **company**, Ishtar Handmade Soap. Her company makes eco-friendly soap and shampoo. The all-natural soap **products** are very popular. All of the products use olive oil from Iraq. They also use fruit from trees in Africa.

Female business owners are unusual in Iraq. Zinah has a degree in business administration, and she wants to help women find jobs. Zinah's **employees** are all women. There are female soap makers, **administrators**, and **marketers**. Zinah's parents are happy for her. Her father is an engineer and her mother is a homemaker. Zinah thinks working women are important for her country's economy.

Read more

1 Where is Zinah Saleh from? Iraq
2 What is her job? business owner
3 What is Zinah's business? Ishtar Handmade Soap
4 What is in the Ishtar products? olive oil, fruit
5 What is unusual about Zinah's company? All of the workers are women.

C **READING SKILL—Scan** **Read the article quickly and underline the jobs.**

D **THINKING SKILL—Question** **Why do you think eco-friendly products are popular? Are eco-friendly products important to you? Discuss.**

GO TO page vii

for **VOCABULARY** step-by-step instructions.

VOCABULARY

A **Find words from the article that match the definitions. Write the word.**

1 another word for business — company
2 people who advertise products — marketers
3 people who work for a business owner — employees
4 people who manage the paperwork of a business — administrators
5 a person who has a business — business owner
6 things that a business sells — products

B **List eight adjectives from the article.**

successful	all-natural	unusual	happy
eco-friendly	popular	female	important

READING OPTIONAL 2.01

Some examples of entrepreneurs are:

- Carlos Slim (businessman).
- Richard Branson (founder of Virgin Group).
- Oprah Winfrey (media mogul).
- Vera Wang (fashion designer).
- Sergey Brin and Larry Page (cofounders of Google).

Provide any names of entrepreneurs from your country.

CULTURE NOTE

For further discussion of culture and gender, explain that just 6.8% of Iraqi businesses are owned or co-owned by women. Ask students to think about why.

For more information about Zinah Saleh and her company, visit thestoryexchange.org or search online for Ishtar Handmade Soap.

GRAMMAR articles *a*, *an*, and no article

A Choose the correct option to complete the rules.

1. The words *a* and *an* come before **singular** / plural nouns.
2. *A* comes before a noun that starts with a vowel / **consonant**.
3. *An* comes before a noun that starts with a **vowel** / consonant.
4. In adjective + noun phrases, *a*/*an* comes before the **adjective** / noun.
5. If a noun is plural, use *a* / *an* / **no article**.

For more practice, go to page 143.

B Complete with *a*, *an*, or *X* (no article).

1. _A_ homemaker is an important job.
2. There are _x_ social media marketers at online companies.
3. I think business owners have _x_ exciting jobs.
4. A lot of women in my country are _x_ business owners.
5. I prefer _a_ creative job, like _an_ art teacher or _a_ music teacher.
6. Math is important to be _an_ engineer or _an_ architect.

MAKE IT YOURS

Make a list of local businesses in your area. What products or services do the businesses sell?

C IN PAIRS Read the sentences in B. Are they true, in your opinion?

PRONUNCIATION *an* + vowel

A 2.02 Listen and notice how phrases with *an* sound like /æ/ + a word beginning with *n*. Practice saying the words. Draw a line to connect *an* to the vowel of the next word.

an architect	an economist	an interior designer	an office manager
an art teacher	an engineer	an interpreter	an optometrist

SPEAKING

A Make a list of facts you know about a famous person in your notebook.

B IN GROUPS Ask questions and guess who the famous person is. Use the Confident Communicator box to help you.

A: Is it a man or a woman?	*B: A …*
A: How old is he/she?	*B: I think he/she's about …*
A: When is his/her birthday?	*B: I don't know.*
A: Where's he/she from?	*B: He/She's from …*
A: Is he/she married?	*B: I think so. / I don't know.*
A: What does he/she do?	*B: He's/She's a/an …*
A: Is it … ?	*B: Yes, it is! / No, it isn't!*

CONFIDENT COMMUNICATOR
KEEP TALKING

If you don't know the answer to a question, say:
I don't know.
If you think you know an answer, but you are not sure, say:
I (don't) think so. / I think it's/she's/he's …

GO TO page viii
for **GRAMMAR** step-by-step instructions.

GO TO page ix
for **PRONUNCIATION** step-by-step instructions.

GO TO page xii
for **SPEAKING** step-by-step instructions.

GRAMMAR

Articles in English are gender neutral. There are no masculine or feminine nouns. The indefinite articles *a/an* are used with singular countable nouns. No article is used with plural countable nouns and uncountable nouns. *Some* is often used instead of no article.

PRONUNCIATION

Have students think of more words they know that use *an* + vowel (or find them in the reading text) and have them practice pronouncing the words—for example, *an Iraqi woman, an eco-friendly product, an unusual company, an administrator.*

SPEAKING Alternative Activity

Put students into groups of four. Have each member write a celebrity's name on a piece of paper. Have members of the group ask questions to guess each celebrity. Make sure all group members participate in asking and answering questions.

LESSON 2 Family Connections

VOCABULARY family

A **Complete Sherry's family tree with words from the box.**

aunt brother cousin mother nephew niece son uncle

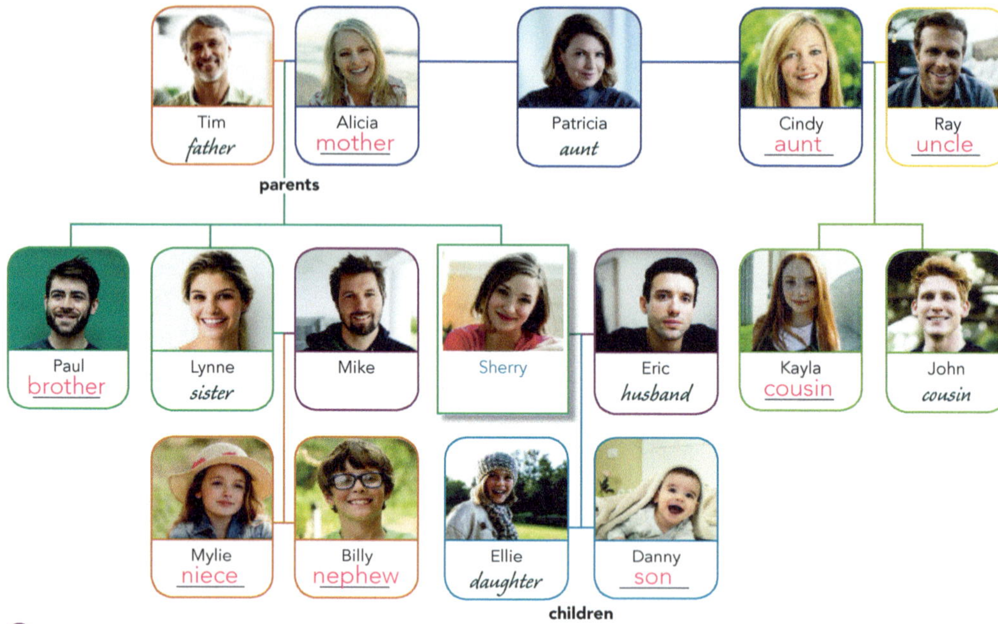

B **2.03 Listen and check your answers.**

GO TO page 138 for AUDIO SCRIPT.

MAKE IT REAL

People often use different words for immediate family members.

father: *dad, pa, pop, daddy* mother: *mom, mama, ma, mommy*
brother: *bro* sister: *sis*

GRAMMAR possessive adjectives and *'s/s'*

A **Read the examples. Then choose the correct option to complete the rules.**

Tim is **Sherry's** father.
Her children's names are Ellie and Danny.
Her **parents'** names are Tim and Alicia.
Whose sister is Sherry? She's Paul's and Lynne's sister.
Ellie and Danny are children. **Their** parents are Sherry and Eric.

Eric is married to **his** wife, Sherry.
Sherry has a sister. **Her** name is Lynne.

1 Show possession with *'s* for singular or irregular / plural nouns.
2 Show possession with *s'* for singular / plural nouns.
3 When you refer to a man, use the possessive adjective *his* / *her* / *their*.
4 When you refer to a woman, use the possessive adjective *his* / *her* / *their*.
5 When you refer to two or more people, use the possessive adjective *his* / *her* / *their*.
6 Use *Whose* / *Who* to ask how two people are connected in the family.

For more practice, go to page 144.

VOCABULARY

Some of your students may be members of blended families. They could have a stepsister or a half-brother. You might want to supply these words for blended families as they arise: *stepmom, stepdad, stepparent, stepsister, stepbrother, half-brother, half-sister, biological parent, adoptive parent, foster parent, guardian*.

GRAMMAR

Picking the right determiner can be tricky in some languages. Play a quick response game. Say a person's name and ask students to say the correct possessive determiner (e.g., *Maria's brother = her brother*). Go faster to reduce response time. Choose names that are easily identified as boys' or girls' names.

B Find and correct one error in each sentence.

Her ~~fathers~~ *father's* name is Tim.

1 ~~Sherrys'~~ Sherry's mother's name is Alicia.

2 Her ~~parent's~~ parents' hometown is Chicago.

3 ~~Who's~~ Whose children are Danny and Ellie? They're Sherry's children.

4 Ray is Cindy's husband. ~~Our~~ Their children are Kayla and John.

5 Sherry's children's ~~names'~~ names are Danny and Ellie.

C IN PAIRS Ask each other questions about Sherry's family tree.

A: Whose husband is Eric? *B: He's Sherry's husband.*

LISTENING

A IN PAIRS Look at the family picture. Guess how the people are connected to Alan.

B 2.04 LISTENING SKILL—Use visual clues Listen to Alan talk about the picture and complete.

1 Mary is Alan's __sister__.
2 Kaitlyn is Kevin's __wife__.
3 Kevin is Alan's __brother__. He's __married__ to Kaitlyn.
4 Linda is Alan's __mother__. Her __husband__ is Steve.
5 Mindy is Alan's niece. Her __aunt__ is Mary.
6 Robert isn't __married__. He's __17__ years old.

C IN PAIRS THINKING SKILL—Analyze Discuss the questions.

1 What is Sarah's relationship to Alan?
2 Does Sarah know Alan's family?
3 Why does Alan say, "Of course, Robert isn't married"?

GO TO page xi for LISTENING step-by-step instructions.

GO TO page 138 for AUDIO SCRIPT.

Suggested answers:
1 Sarah is Alan's (new) girlfriend. She is a little nervous, suggesting Alan's family might be important to her.
2 No. Alan has to explain who the family members are.
3 Robert is only 17.

SPEAKING

A Draw your family tree in your notebook. Fill in some of the names, but leave the others blank.

B IN PAIRS Ask questions to complete your partner's family tree. Then look at your family tree and correct errors. Use the Confident Communicator box to help you.

A: What's your aunt's name? *B: Her name is Anna. Her husband is Frank.*

CONFIDENT COMMUNICATOR
REPAIR IT

Names can be difficult to understand. Ask questions to check your understanding.
Can you repeat his/her name?
How do you spell that?

LISTENING

When listening to check answers, play the audio more than once. Before giving the answer, play the audio, pause when key information is given, and elicit answers.

THINKING SKILL—Analyze

To analyze something means to break information down into its parts to discover interrelationships. Have students listen carefully to analyze other relationships.

SPEAKING Extra Practice

Have students answer these questions:

- Is anyone in your family named after anyone else?
- What does your name mean?
- What girl's/boy's name do you like?
- What are popular boys' and girls' names at the moment?
- Do you have a favorite aunt or uncle? What is his or her name?

CONFIDENT COMMUNICATOR

To help students be assertive speakers and active listeners, highlight the use of visual cues to facilitate communication. Encourage students to use gestures with the questions they use to repair a conversation; a quizzical look and a hand signal might go with *Can you repeat his/her name?*

LESSON 3 Jobs

VOCABULARY jobs

A **IN GROUPS** Make a list of jobs you know in your notebook.

Suggested answers: business owner, engineer, soap maker, administrator, social media marketer, economist, architect, art teacher, interpreter, interior designer, optometrist, office manager

B Match the pictures to the jobs from the box. Write the words under each picture.

accountant	architect	computer technician	interpreter
journalist	nurse	pharmacist	pilot

1 
pilot

2 
architect

3 
journalist

4 
pharmacist

5 
interpreter

6 
accountant

7 
computer technician

8 
nurse

LISTENING

A **LISTENING SKILL—Predict** Look at the family picture. What do you think Molly will talk about?

Suggested answers: the names of the people, their relationships to Molly, their ages, where they are in the picture

MAKE IT YOURS

Make a list of the jobs your family members have. Include your job or the job you want to have in the future. Use your dictionary if necessary.

B 2.05 Listen and answer the questions.

1 Who's in the picture? *Molly's aunt,* uncle, cousins
2 Where are they? Italy
3 How old is Jeff? 24
4 What is Jeff's job? computer technician
5 What is Elsa's job? pharmacist
6 What is Pete's job? a pilot
7 How old is Laurie? 21

C **THINKING SKILL—Categorize** Discuss the questions.

1 What jobs in this lesson are associated with math ability, science ability, or creative ability?
2 What jobs require a university degree?

1 Math ability: economist, optometrist, architect, administrator, pilot
Science ability: architect, optometrist, pharmacist, nurse
Creative ability: (art, music) teacher, social media marketer, interior designer

2 University degree: economist, administrator, architect, teacher, interpreter, interior designer, optometrist, pharmacist, computer technician, nurse, pilot

VOCABULARY

Many occupations can be formed by adding the suffix *–er* to the action, such as *driver*. Occupation words can also be formed from other nouns with *–ian*, such as *electrician*. Another suffix for jobs is *–ist*, such as *scientist*.

Additional Activity

Write the headings *Similar in English* and *Different in English* on the board in two columns. Have students write a list of jobs that are similar in English and their own language, such as *architect* and *arquitecto* (Spanish). And have them write a list of jobs that are different in English and their own language.

LISTENING

Elicit some of the predictions from the class before listening. For more language review, have students compare predictions with a partner.

THINKING SKILL—Categorize

Have students add the jobs they brainstormed in the Make It Yours box to the categories here. Ask about other specific abilities related to certain jobs.

WRITING

A Complete the family profile using information from the table.

	Person 1	Person 2	Person 3	Person 4
Relationship to you	father	mother	uncle	sister
Age	65	58	60	25
Job	engineer	accountant	math teacher	manager
Place of work	retired	New Systems	Lincoln High School	a restaurant

MY PROFILE

MY FAMILY

The members of my family have interesting jobs. My dad is a/an **1** engineer, but he's **2** 65 and he's retired now. My **3** mom/mother is 58, and she's an accountant at **4** New Systems. It's an IT company. My Uncle Joe is a **5** math teacher at Lincoln High School. He's my dad's brother. My sister is only **6** 25, but she's the manager of a large restaurant.

B Complete the table for your family.

	Family Member 1: ______	Family Member 2: ______	Family Member 3: ______	Family Member 4: ______
Relationship to you				
Age				
Job				
Place of work				

C Write your family profile in your notebook.

D IN PAIRS Read and discuss your family profiles. Correct grammar, spelling, and punctuation.

SPEAKING

A Prepare to talk about your favorite family picture and make notes in your notebook. Use the Confident Communicator box to help you.

1. Who's in the picture and what is their relationship to you?
2. Where are the people in the picture?
3. What are their relationships to other family members (for example, *my mother's sister*)?
4. How old are they?
5. What do they do?

B IN GROUPS Share and discuss your picture.

My favorite picture is of me, my sister, and our cousins Ronny and Jenny. Ronny is a computer programmer. Jenny is …

CONFIDENT COMMUNICATOR

KEEP TALKING

When you use notes to help you talk about something, look quickly at your notes, but don't read them aloud.

Unit 2 Work/Life Balance 23

GO TO page xiv for **WRITING** step-by-step instructions.

WRITING

You may feel students need further demonstration before getting down to writing their own family profiles. If so, have the class agree on a famous cartoon or television character and elicit the information about that character to complete the table in WRITING **B** on the board. Then, as a class, write the character's family profile.

Alternatively, this could be done as an extension activity for fast finishers, working individually.

SPEAKING

Expect students to be supportive and encouraging of each other when sharing personal information during speaking activities. The listener can show support through nonverbal communication by making eye contact, smiling, nodding their head, and making encouraging sounds like *ah*, *huh*, and *mmm* as they listen. The speaker should raise his or her head to make eye contact with the listener and not look at the picture all the time.

GO TO page xv
for LANGUAGE AND LIFE step-by-step instructions.

Language and Life

Self-awareness – The Right Job

A 2.06 **Read the Careers Profile and the job ads, then answer the question in your notebook.**

Which two jobs fit David's interests and abilities?

Journalist for city newspaper, Marketer for small communications company

CAREERS PROFILE **Name:** David Monetti

For each category, choose two areas that describe your interests and abilities.

Personality	[ ] organized	[x] friendly	[ ] patient	[x] independent
Natural abilities	[x] verbal	[x] logical/ mathematical	[ ] creative	[ ] social
Academic skills	[ ] science and math	[x] language	[x] technology	[ ] arts

CAREERS PROFILE Results

High school English teacher

Job description: Teach grammar, writing, and literature. Patience, good communication skills, and IT/social media skills are necessary.

Journalist for city newspaper

Job description: Talk to people and write stories. Need good English and computer skills. We want a creative, independent person.

Computer technician for large company

Job description: Work with computers and help people with computer problems. Lots of travel. A science and engineering education is required.

Marketer for small communications company

Job description: Need a friendly, creative, social person. Good computer and social media skills are necessary. Art or design education is not necessary, but good writing is very important.

24 Unit 2 Work/Life Balance

OBJECTIVE

In this lesson, students learn how to identify their strengths in order to help them make good career choices. People often do not know what to consider when deciding which academic path to take or which job to pursue. Point out that employers no longer look only, or even primarily, at college majors and work experience. They also take into account a potential employee's natural abilities and personality type, so it is important to be honest with oneself about one's strengths and weaknesses, as well as personality, when choosing a field of study or a job.

PROCESS OPTIONAL 2.06

Students first analyze a fictional person's characteristics and how well they match several potential jobs. They then consider what characteristics are suitable for different types of work. Finally, they analyze their own skills and personality and decide what jobs might be good choices for them.

B **IN PAIRS** **Compare your ideas and discuss.**

A: I think the right jobs for David are English teacher and journalist. His verbal and language skills are good.
B: Maybe journalist, but not English teacher. He isn't patient.

C **IN GROUPS** **Complete with the kind of personality, abilities, and skills you need for each job.**

1. accountant: *organized* ______
2. nurse: ______
3. journalist: ______
4. engineer: ______
5. designer: ______

D **Complete a Careers Profile for you.**

CAREERS PROFILE	**Name:**			
For each category, choose two areas that describe your interests and abilities.				
Personality	☐ organized	☐ friendly	☐ patient	☐ independent
Natural abilities	☐ verbal	☐ logical/ mathematical	☐ creative	☐ social
Academic skills	☐ science and math	☐ language	☐ technology	☐ arts

E **Complete a list of jobs and skills for you.**

Possible jobs

Job:

Skills I have for the job:

Job:

Skills I have for the job:

Job:

Skills I have for the job:

F **IN GROUPS** **Share your lists of jobs and skills. Discuss and make suggestions.**

A: What about an architect? Your logic and math skills are good, and you're creative.
B: Or a math teacher. You're patient.

MAKE IT DIGITAL

Go online and look for job listings in your area. Think about which jobs are good for you, based on your interests and abilities.

CLASSROOM MANAGEMENT

When grouping students, you have the choice of homogeneous or heterogeneous combinations. For the sharing task in F, it would be beneficial to group students with similar interests. This way, they will hear words and language relevant to their fields that they can add to their repertoire.

CULTURE NOTE

Discuss gender equality in different jobs in students' countries. You could have a simple discussion at this level by asking for observations and impressions about which jobs have more women and which jobs have more men, if this is changing, and how students see it changing.

MAKE IT DIGITAL

Tell students that each job field has its own jargon—special words or expressions used by that profession. While students are online looking at job listings in their area, ask them to make a list of 5–10 words particular to the jobs that are good for them. Then ask them to share their words, with translations or definitions, with others.

GO TO page xvii
for **UNIT REVIEW** step-by-step instructions.

UNIT 2

VOCABULARY review

SCORE: / 10

A Choose the correct option to complete the sentences about Elena's family.

My **1** mother / father is very creative. She's an art **2** engineer / teacher. My mother's sister Ana is my **3** aunt / cousin. Her house is beautiful. She's an **4** accountant / interior designer. Nina is Ana's daughter. She's my **5** sister / cousin. When I have a laptop problem, I call her. She's a **6** computer technician / marketer. My **7** father / daughter works for a large company. His name is Ricardo. He speaks English and Portuguese. He's an **8** interpreter / office manager. My **9** grandfather / uncle is my father's father. He sells computers. He's a small business **10** owner / optometrist.

GRAMMAR review

SCORE: / 10

A Complete the job ad with *a*, *an*, or *X* (no article).

Do you want **1** _an_ interesting job? Think about a job as **2** _a_ social media manager. **3** _A_ social media manager writes **4** _x_ comments and connects with **5** _x_ customers. Contact us at our website to apply.

B Complete the sentences with words from the box.

's s' his her their

1 My parent _s'_ names are Mark and Cindy.
2 My sister is named Kathy, but _her_ nickname is Kat.
3 My brother _'s_ name is Jeff.
4 He's married to _his_ wife, Ann.
5 _Their_ daughter's name is Barbara.

16–20 correct: You can talk about family and jobs. You can use *a/an* and the verb *be*.
0–15 correct: Look again at the Vocabulary and Grammar sections in the unit.

TOTAL SCORE: / 20

WHAT DO YOU KNOW NOW? Look back at page 17 and add the words you know now to the boxes.

GO TO page xix
for **FOLLOW A PRO** step-by-step instructions.

FOLLOW A PRO INFORMATION TECHNOLOGY (IT)

Take the quiz about IT (information technology). Go to Follow A Pro on page 128 to find the answers. Then learn more about the IT industry.

1 Which country has the most internet users?
a China **b** the UK **c** the US

2 How many new viruses go into the internet every month?
a 360 **b** 6,000 **c** 10,000

3 Why is November 30 a special day? It's …
a clean your computer day. **b** internet safety day. **c** computer security day.

4 What percentage of internet traffic is web robots?
a 8% **b** 55% **c** 21%

26 Unit 2 Work/Life Balance

CLASSROOM MANAGEMENT

For an added challenge, have students do the review exercises while timed. Give them 5 minutes to complete each review exercise.

ALTERNATIVE ACTIVITY

Play Alphabet Jobs. The first student says a job beginning with the letter *A*. The next student repeats the job and adds a job starting with *B*, and so on. If they get to a letter and they can't think of a job, they have to do a funny task, such as singing a lyric from a song. Then, the next student continues with the following letter in the alphabet.

FURTHER DISCUSSION

Put students in groups of three and ask the following questions for them to discuss:

- How many gadgets do you have?
- How many times a day do you check your messages?
- Do you communicate by chat or by telephone?
- Do you use social media?
- Do you buy things online?

GO TO page vi
for **UNIT OPENER** step-by-step instructions.

UNIT 3 Fun and Games

WHAT DO YOU ALREADY KNOW?

1 Think of words you know about free-time activities. Write activities that you can do indoors and outdoors.

2 **IN PAIRS** Share and compare your activities. Add more words to your lists.

Outdoor activities
play tennis

Indoor activities
play music

STUDENTS MAY ALREADY KNOW:

- **Outdoor activities:** run, hike, walk, ride a bike, play sports, play soccer.
- **Indoor activities:** read, sleep, watch TV, play computer games.

DISCUSS & SHARE

VIDEO

3 **IN GROUPS** Watch the video and answer the question.
SYM How much time do you need alone or with other people?

GO TO page xx
for **VIDEOS IN SYM** step-by-step instructions.

In this unit, you will ...

- express likes and dislikes, recommend free-time activities, and talk about an event.
- use thinking skills: categorize, infer, and recall.
- read a magazine interview.
- use strategies to keep talking and emphasize preferences, giving reasons, and expressing rules.
- use creativity skills to work with others and create an interest group for a website.
- learn tips for a successful oral presentation.

Unit 3 Fun and Games 27

WHAT DO YOU ALREADY KNOW?

If you notice students are struggling to understand what to do, you can provide one or two examples to help them get started:

- **Outdoor activities:** go on a picnic, walk the dog, do yoga in the park
- **Indoor activities:** go to a coffee shop, check social media, play on a tablet, shop online

VIDEO

Before viewing, ask:

How do Alex and Sonya balance time alone and together? *Alex works alone and likes to be with people after work and Sonya vice versa.*

After viewing, put the continuum on the board.

time alone —— time together

Students mark the continuum and explain how they like to spend their time.

DISCUSS & SHARE

Have students consider how much of their free time they like to spend alone versus with friends or family. Ask what activities they prefer to do alone and what they prefer to do with others.

GO TO page x
for **READING** step-by-step instructions.

LESSON 1 Like It, Love It, or Hate It?

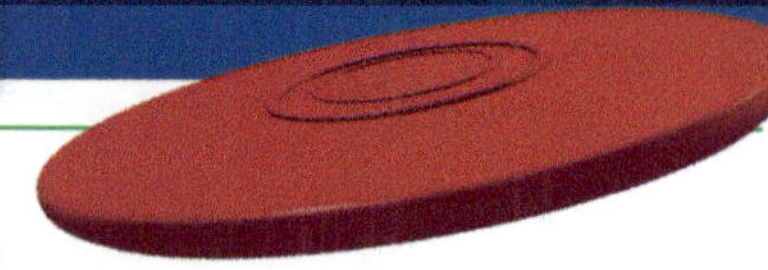

READING

A IN GROUPS Discuss free-time activities. What do you like doing in your free time? Which type of activity is the most popular in your group?

B 3.01 **READING SKILL—Infer** Read the magazine interview and answer the question. Who is Otto?

B a dog

NEW FRISBEE CHAMPIONS!

Here is an interview with Chris Watson, one half of the Chris-Otto Frisbee team. Chris and Otto are this year's winners.

Interviewer: Congratulations, Chris! You and Otto are the winners! Do you have time to talk to me?

Chris: Sure, thanks. Otto is a great Frisbee player! He runs really fast, and he always catches the Frisbee. Otto loves Frisbee, too. We practice together every day.

Interviewer: Does he like other outdoor activities?

Chris: Well, yes, he likes hiking, but he doesn't like hiking in cold weather.

Interviewer: Does he have any special likes or dislikes?

Chris: Yes, he does. He loves watching TV. He watches soccer and football with me a lot. I like golf, but Otto thinks it's boring. I don't watch it often. And … let's see. He likes eating—a lot! And he hates cats!

Interviewer: Thanks, Chris. Good luck to you and Otto next season.

Chris: Thanks.

Otto: Woof!

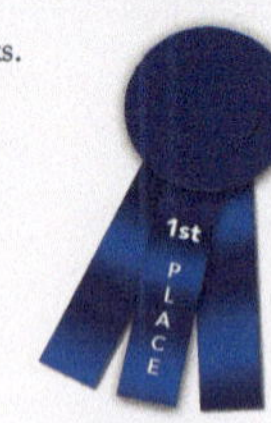

C THINKING SKILL—Categorize Read the interview again and write Otto's likes and dislikes in the table.

Otto likes …	Otto doesn't like …
Frisbee, hiking, watching sports on TV, eating	hiking in cold weather, golf, cats

GO TO page vii
for **VOCABULARY** step-by-step instructions.

VOCABULARY

A Read the verbs and complete the sentences for you. Discuss with a partner.

love — like — don't like — hate

1 I ______________ sports.
2 I ______________ romantic movies.
3 I ______________ hiking.
4 I ______________ playing video games.
5 I ______________ using social media.
6 I ______________ listening to music.

28 Unit 3 Fun and Games

READING OPTIONAL 3.01

Some popular free time activities for young people these days are:

- playing sports, running, and going to the gym.
- going to the beach, hiking, and going to the movies.
- playing video/computer games.
- playing games on the phone and texting (chatting with) friends.
- checking social media, posting on social media, and watching video clips online.

READING SKILL—Infer

When we infer something, we make guesses based on information given about something not directly stated. In the reading text, we read about things that both humans and dogs like to do. The fact that Chris speaks for him, that he hates cats, and the *Woof* all hint at Otto being a dog.

THINKING SKILL—Categorize

Categorizing information requires students to understand information and make decisions about it based on criteria.

Categorizing-type activities can vary in difficulty, and you will see them increase in complexity throughout the series.

GRAMMAR simple present statements and *yes/no* questions

A Read the examples from the interview. Then choose the correct option to complete the rules.

He loves watching sports on TV.
I like golf.
I don't watch it often.

He doesn't like hiking in cold weather.
Do you have time to talk to me? Yes, I do.
Does he have any special likes or dislikes? Yes, he does.

1 For statements with *I*, *you*, *we*, and *they*, add / don't add an –*s* to the verb.
2 For statements with *he*, *she*, and *it*, add / don't add an –*s* to the verb.
3 The correct word order for *yes/no* questions is *Do* or *Does* + subject + verb / Subject + *do* or *does* + verb.
4 Short answers to *yes/no* questions end in *do* or *does* / a verb.

For more practice, go to page 145.

B Choose the correct option.

1 Do / Does you like soccer? Yes, I like. / Yes, I do.
2 I love / loves tennis, but my brother isn't / doesn't like it.
3 Do / Does your dad like watching sports on TV? No, he don't / doesn't.
4 My sister and I love / loves video games, but my brother doesn't like / likes them.
5 He play / plays games on his phone, but I think / thinks games are boring.

MAKE IT REAL

Alternative phrases for short answers:
A: Do you like swimming?
B: Not really. / No, but I like ... / It's OK. / Sure. / Of course.

C IN PAIRS Discuss preferences.

A: Do you like basketball? *B: I like watching it, but I don't like playing it.*
A: Do you like playing soccer? *B: Yes, I do. I like watching it, too!*

PRONUNCIATION third person –*s*

A 3.02 Listen and notice the final sound of each word. Practice saying the words.

Sounds like /s/: likes, hates, walks, thinks
Sounds like /z/: loves, swims, plays, runs
Sounds like /iz/: watches, uses, practices, catches

B IN PAIRS Practice reading aloud. Pronounce the verbs correctly.

1 Otto runs fast, and he always catches the Frisbee.
2 My brother loves tennis. He practices every day.
3 My sister thinks hiking is boring, but she likes swimming.
4 My dad hates social media, but he uses it for his business.

SPEAKING

A Make a list of free-time activities that you like in your notebook.

B IN PAIRS Discuss what you like and don't like. Draw faces next to the activities on your list according to your partner's answers.

A: Do you like playing video games? *B: No, I hate it!*

C IN GROUPS Find another pair. Tell them about your partner's preferences. Use the Confident Communicator box to help you.

Mark hates playing video games, but he likes playing cards.

CONFIDENT COMMUNICATOR — KEEP TALKING

Add words to give more information about your preferences.
*I **really** like/hate swimming.*
*I don't like swimming **very much**.*
*I like swimming **a lot**.*

GO TO page viii for GRAMMAR step-by-step instructions.

GO TO page ix for PRONUNCIATION step-by-step instructions.

GO TO page xii for SPEAKING step-by-step instructions.

GRAMMAR

The tricky parts of this grammar for non-English speakers are the third person –*s* in the affirmative statements and the *do*/*does* auxiliary in the negative and question forms. Don't expect students to master it right away. It will take some time and practice.

PRONUNCIATION

Tell students the third person –*s* is hard to remember because it is hard to hear, and its use (or omission) doesn't actually interfere with understanding. Even harder to hear is when the third person –*s* meets an *s* sound in the following word—the extra *s* sound is omitted (e.g., *He loves sports.*).

SPEAKING

CONFIDENT COMMUNICATOR

Once students are comfortable expressing likes and dislikes, they can add intensifiers such as *really*, *very much*, or *a lot* to help their speech sound more natural.

LESSON 2 Preferences

VOCABULARY free-time activities

A Complete the table with words from the box.

audiobooks, dancing, ~~movies~~, music, online videos, parties, ~~podcasts~~, shopping, soccer, to eat, TV, video games, with friends, ~~the movies~~

listen to	watch	play	go	go to	go out
podcasts	*movies*	video games	dancing	*the movies*	to eat
music	TV	soccer	shopping	parties	with friends
audiobooks	online videos	music			dancing

B IN GROUPS Discuss whether you like or don't like the same things.

A: Do you like listening to music or to podcasts? I prefer music.
B: Music.
C: Music.
D: Podcasts.
A: OK, three for music and one for podcasts.

MAKE IT YOURS

List other free-time activities that you like to do or places that you like to go to.

GO TO page xi

for **LISTENING** step-by-step instructions.

LISTENING

A As a class, list some of your favorite games, movies, musicians, and TV shows.

games ______________________

movies ______________________

musicians ______________________

TV shows ______________________

B 3.03 Listen to the phone conversation and answer the question. What is the event?

GO TO page 139

for **AUDIO SCRIPT**.

B a concert

C 3.03 LISTENING SKILL—Take notes Listen again and complete the notes.

Event: a (Shawn Mendes) concert

Date: November 3

Time: 8:00 p.m.

Place: City Auditorium (Denver)

Ticket price: $45

D 3.03 THINKING SKILL—Understand Listen again and choose the correct option.

1 Who buys the tickets?
 a Rob **b** Sandy **c** Rob and Sandy

2 Who pays for the tickets?
 a Rob **b** Sandy **c** Rob and Sandy

VOCABULARY

Teach students the word *podcast*, a radio program or video that can be downloaded or streamed from the internet. Check understanding of the rest of the words in the box. Have those students who know the meanings act them out for everyone or have them use the words in sentences.

LISTENING

In LISTENING **A**, ask students to volunteer some of their favorite activities in each category. Then, ask who agrees with the choices.

In LISTENING **D**, ask students how they were able to choose the correct answers. Recall that Sandy says, "Please get me a ticket!" and Rob says the ticket is $45 and asks if that's OK. With that information we can understand that each person is going to pay for their own ticket.

GRAMMAR the imperative

A Read the examples from the conversation and choose the correct option to complete the rules.

Listen to this!
Please get me a ticket!
Don't forget to write down the information.
Tell me the date again, please.

1 We use the imperative to …
a give opinions. b give orders or instructions. c talk about likes and dislikes.
2 The verb form in imperative sentences is …
a base form. b *to* + verb. c verb + *–ing*.
3 To form a negative imperative, use …
a verb + *not*. b *doesn't* + verb. c *don't* + verb.
4 For a polite imperative, add *please* … of the sentence.
a at the beginning b at the end c at the beginning or end

For more practice, go to page 146.

B Complete the conversation with verbs from the box.

don't | buy forget listen tell turn use

Erika: 1 Listen to this new song by Logan Williams.
Laura: It's great! 2 Turn up the volume!
Erika: Here. 3 Use my headphones.
Laura: Excellent! What's the name of the song?
Erika: "Party Night." The song is great, but 4 don't buy the album. The other songs aren't very good.
Laura: OK. Hey, 5 don't forget to get that new app. It's really good.
Erika: Oh, yeah. 6 Tell me the name again, please.
Laura: It's called *Guess Who.*

C IN PAIRS Role-play the conversation in B with a singer, song, and app that you like.

SPEAKING

A Complete the table with things you like and don't like. Add two more things to the list of activities.

Activities	Like	Don't Like
Movies		
Apps		
Books		
TV shows		

B IN GROUPS Give recommendations. Use the Confident Communicator box to help you.

CONFIDENT COMMUNICATOR
KEEP TALKING

When you give a negative recommendation, try to give a reason.
OK, for movies, go see the new Spielberg movie. It's excellent.
Don't see Mystery on the Beach. It's terrible/boring/silly/violent.

GRAMMAR Additional Activity

Play an imperative game. Make a list of at least 10 affirmative and negative classroom instructions. For example, *Close your book. Don't raise your hand.* Tell everyone the rules of the game: *Follow the instructions. If you make a mistake, you are out of the game* (e.g., for *Don't raise your hand*, if you raise your hand, you're out). Choose a volunteer student to give the instructions.

SPEAKING

Demonstrate SPEAKING **A** by filling out the table with things you like and don't like. This helps students get to know you better, too.

CONFIDENT COMMUNICATOR

When giving negative recommendations, list specific evidence or reasons to support your opinion. Tell students they can use a thesaurus to help them find the appropiate words.

CLASSROOM MANAGEMENT

When grouping students, do so quickly. Use eye contact and clear physical gestures to show them how to arrange themselves. As time goes by, students will get used to working in groups and quickly get settled and get on with the activity at hand.

LESSON 3 **Special Events**

LISTENING

A Think about the words in the box and discuss the questions.

concerts festivals sports events other types of competitions

1 Which special events happen in your area?
2 What type of event is your favorite?

GO TO page 139 for AUDIO SCRIPT.

B 3.04 LISTENING SKILL—Listen for gist Listen and choose the correct option.

1 What type of recording is this?
a a TV program b an advertisement c a podcast
2 What is the speaker talking about?
a a festival b a concert c a race

C 3.04 Listen again and choose *True* or *False*.

1 This is a national festival. True / False
2 The festival includes two races. True / False
3 The soccer players are children. True / False
4 The festival is open eight hours every day. True / False
5 The festival doesn't welcome pets. True / False
6 Buy your tickets at the festival to get a discount. True / False

D THINKING SKILL—Recall Write and compare.

1 Make a list of the events from the advertisement. With a partner, compare your lists and add to them.

1 pet parade, 10-K race, dance contest, concert, bicycle race, kids' soccer game

VOCABULARY special events

A Write two words from the box in each column.

baseball motorcycle pop photography hip hop singing horse soccer

a … concert	a … game	a … race	a … competition
rock	football	10-km	cooking
classical	basketball	bicycle	dance
pop	soccer	motorcycle	singing
hip hop	baseball	horse	photography

B Complete the sentences for you.

1 I love __________ concerts.
2 I think __________ races are dangerous.
3 I don't like __________ competitions.
4 I love to watch __________ games.
5 I like going to __________ festivals.

MAKE IT YOURS

What types of local or special events are in your area? Add more events to the lists in **A**.

C IN GROUPS Discuss your opinions.

A: I love rock concerts.
B: Me, too.
C: I prefer pop concerts.

LISTENING

THINKING SKILL—Recall

Recalling is a powerful learning tool. It means bringing something you have just read, heard, or learned to mind and thinking about it again. After listening, have students make a list of things they remember and then compare lists with a partner. They will probably see that their partner remembered things they didn't and vice versa. Point out that when people work together, they will remember more.

VOCABULARY

Have volunteers write the answers from VOCABULARY **A** on the board, and then invite students to add more words to the categories they like.

Demonstrate VOCABULARY **B** with your own information and check that students understand. You may want to allow students to use other words that they look up on their own to express their personal likes and dislikes as the activity progresses.

WRITING

A Read the poster and label with words from the box.

date	description of event	name of event	place
a recommendation	ticket information	time	rules

1 name of event
2 place
3 date
4 description of event
5 ticket information
6 rules
7 time
8 a recommendation

B IN GROUPS Plan a poster for an event in your area.

EVENT PLANNING FORM

Name and/or type of event ____________
Specific information about the event ____________
Place ____________
Date ____________
Starting/Ending times ____________
Ticket information ____________
Rules ____________
Recommendation ____________
Other information ____________

C Create your poster. Emphasize important information and make your poster attractive.

SPEAKING

A IN GROUPS Describe the event from your poster. Use the Confident Communicator box to help you.

A: The event is … *B: The rules are …*
A: It's in/near … *B: My favorite thing is … / I don't recommend the …*

B Share with the class. Show your poster and describe the event.

C Take a class vote. What poster do you like best? What event do you want to go to?

CONFIDENT COMMUNICATOR
KEEP TALKING

Ways to express rules:
No dogs/food/backpacks *Children over 12 only*
Pets/food/drinks are OK *Drinks only; no food*

GO TO page xiv for **WRITING** step-by-step instructions.

WRITING

Explain to students that they do not have to include everything on the form or the poster in **C**. They should select the information they think their audience will need most. Additionally, they can use the last section to add any additional information they think necessary. Tell them to consider the colors and symbols that would work best on their posters based on the event. Tell students to be creative to make their posters attractive.

SPEAKING

If you did not do the writing section, have students first fill out the form in WRITING **B** so that they have an event to describe. Alternatively, have them find an advertised event in their area and bring it to class. They will use that information to practice describing an event to the class. They should assign different sections on the poster to different people so each student can speak.

GO TO page xv
for LANGUAGE AND LIFE step-by-step instructions.

Language and Life

Creativity – An Interest Group

A 3.05 **Read the social media web page. Then choose the correct option below.**

GET TOGETHER

Name of group: Music Lovers join

Do you love music? Do you sing or play an instrument? This is the group for you! We like to go to concerts together, but we LOVE to make our own music!

Name of group: Latinos Play join

We are a group of students from Latin American countries. We like eating food from our countries and meeting other Latin American students here in Los Angeles. If you speak Spanish and love good food, join our group!

Upcoming Meetings

Attend	Attend	Attend
15 SEP – Sat. Sep 15, 7... Music Lovers, Thompson Park	15 SEP – Sat. Sep 15, 9... Latinos Play Public library	16 SEP – Sun. Sep 16, 8... Biking Club, Riverside Park
15 going	8 going	12 going

How to join Get Together

Register for free. Then click on your interests and read about local groups. The members of the groups meet and do different activities. Join the groups that interest you.

How to create a Get Together group

You can start your own Get Together group. Click on "Create a Group." Enter your location. Click on your interest for the new group. Choose a title for the group. Write a short profile of the group. Click "Create Group."

CREATE A GROUP

1 People use this website to …
a take classes to learn new hobbies. **b** meet new friends with similar interests. **c** meet people to date.

2 The members of the first group like to …
a listen to music. **b** play music. **c** listen to and play music.

3 The members of the second group are all from …
a Latin America. **b** Los Angeles. **c** the same country.

B **IN PAIRS Read the social media post. Then discuss.**

1 What is Miguel's problem?
2 Are either of the two groups in **A** right for him?

Language Institute Blog

miguel Posted SEP 17 7:06 p.m.
My name is Miguel, and I'm from Ecuador. I study English in a language institute in Los Angeles. I want to meet new friends with similar interests and practice my English. I like hiking, concerts, and good food. My favorite foods are Italian and Chinese food. Please give me some ideas.

follow

1 He wants to meet new friends with similar interests, and needs some ideas.

2 No. Group 1: He says he likes going to concerts, but doesn't say if he plays an instrument. Group 2: He shares the Latin American culture, but he says he wants to practice English, and the group speaks in Spanish.

34 Unit 3 Fun and Games

OBJECTIVE

In this lesson, students learn how to identify interests and match interests to real-life activities organized through social media. Nowadays, we can socialize with people who share our interests, regardless of age or social status. These kinds of interest groups allow us to socialize outside of our immediate family or neighborhood. Point out that these groups meet in safe public places, and if anyone suggests they meet privately, students should avoid the situation.

PROCESS OPTIONAL 3.05

First, students read a model web page for interest groups that organize activities and complete the sentences. Then, they read a social media post and discuss the questions. After that, tell students to circle the topics that would probably be interesting to Miguel based on the information in his post. They then create an interest group for Miguel. Finally, they vote on the best one.

C IN PAIRS Choose Miguel's interests to help him create a new Get Together group.

GET TOGETHER

NEW GROUP

Location: Los Angeles, CA
Interests

watching sports ♡ | playing team sports ♡ | hiking ♡ | dancing ♡ | biking ♡ | dating ♡ | pets ♡ | food & restaurants ♡ | cooking ♡ | international students ♡ | concerts ♡ | musicians ♡ | movies ♡ | theater ♡ | gaming ♡

D Choose one of Miguel's interests from C and create a new group.

GET TOGETHER

NEW GROUP

Location: Los Angeles, CA
Interests

Interest area:

Name of group:

Description of group:

E Take a class vote. Read your description of Miguel's interest group and decide which new interest group is best for him.

F IN GROUPS Discuss.

1 Do you know of any websites like Get Together in your area?
2 Do you use a website like Get Together? If so, what groups do you belong to?
3 What are your interests? Do you want to join a website like Get Together?

MAKE IT DIGITAL

Start a network of interest groups in your school or institute to meet people with similar interests and practice your English.

Unit 3 Fun and Games 35

ALTERNATIVE ACTIVITY

In pairs, have students interview each other about their interests and create a new group on Get Together for their partner. They can show it to their partner to see if it would appeal to them and get instant feedback on how well they have understood their partner's interests.

FURTHER DISCUSSION

Ask students if they would want to participate in an interest group, and if so discuss the following questions:

- What kind?
- Would it be easy to join an online interest group?
- Would you feel comfortable going out alone to meet up with strangers?
- Would you go with someone? Who would you go with?

MAKE IT DIGITAL

Explain that images and color schemes are important to gain the attention of people they want to attract when making a post for an interest group. If they were to make a post for an interest group, what colors and images might be suitable to appeal to their desired audience?

GO TO page xvii
for UNIT REVIEW step-by-step instructions.

UNIT 3

VOCABULARY review

SCORE: / 10

A Match the sentence beginning (1–10) to the sentence end (a–j). Write the letter.

1. Dani likes to read books and listen to c
2. Sally loves to dance and go to d
3. Erik likes to watch e
4. Hannah loves to play a
5. Rich loves to go b
6. Pedro likes to go out j
7. Yumiko likes to run and play i
8. Marta likes to go for g
9. Isobel and her friends love to use h
10. My dog hates to take f

- **a** games on her phone.
- **b** shopping and spend money.
- **c** audiobooks.
- **d** parties with friends.
- **e** movies at home on his big TV.
- **f** a bath.
- **g** walks in the park.
- **h** social media.
- **i** tennis.
- **j** to eat in restaurants.

GRAMMAR review

SCORE: / 10

A Choose the correct option.

Berta: Hi, Frida! I'm in the online Music Interest Group with you. **1** Do you play / Do you plays more than one musical instrument?
Frida: Yes, I **2** am / do. Drums and piano! I **3** practice / practices every day. My parents **4** don't like / doesn't like the drums! I'm in the school band. **5** Does your school have / Do your school have a band?
Berta: No, it **6** doesn't / don't. But there's a music and dance club.
Frida: **7** Do you dance / Does you dance well?
Berta: No, I **8** don't / doesn't. Oh, I have to go to class!
Frida: OK. Please **9** Text / text again soon. **10** Not forget / Don't forget to post a picture! Here's a picture of me!

16–20 correct: You can talk about likes, dislikes, and free-time activities. You can use the simple present and *yes/no* questions.
0–15 correct: Look again at the Vocabulary and Grammar sections in the unit.

TOTAL SCORE: / 20

WHAT DO YOU KNOW NOW? Look back at page 27 and add the words you know now to the boxes.

GO TO page xviii
for STUDY SKILLS step-by-step instructions.

STUDY SKILLS ORAL PRESENTATIONS

Take the quiz about oral presentations. Go to **Study Skills** on page 129 to find the answers. Then learn more about oral presentations.

1 You need to spend 50% of your time writing your presentation.
a true **b** false

2 When people see pictures, they remember … of what they hear and see.
a 60% **b** 80% **c** 95%

3 You want to begin your talk. What do you say?
a "Please listen to me." **b** "Silence!" **c** "Hello. Today I'm talking about …"

4 You want to finish your talk. What do you say?
a "That's all." **b** "Thank you for listening. Any questions?" **c** "The end!"

CLASSROOM MANAGEMENT

For an added challenge, have students do the review activities while timed. Give them five minutes to complete each review activity. To support the class, have students read the columns in VOCABULARY **A** first and then match the sentences.

ALTERNATIVE ACTIVITY

VOCABULARY **A** could be an oral activity. Give each student a number and a letter. They should memorize the corresponding sentence part. Have them walk around while saying their text out loud until they find their match. Once they find their match, ask each pair to say their sentence aloud.

FURTHER DISCUSSION

Put students in groups of three and ask the following questions for them to discuss:

- How many hobbies do you have?
- How often do you participate in organized hobbies?
- Do you need special equipment?
- Do you use social media in your hobbies?
- Have you made new friends?

UNIT 4 That's Life!

GO TO page vi
for **UNIT OPENER** step-by-step instructions.

WHAT DO YOU ALREADY KNOW?

1 Think of words about the activities you do every day. Write the words for the activities.
2 **IN PAIRS** Share and compare your information. Add more words to your lists.

Planned Activities
eat breakfast

Unexpected Things
get sick

STUDENTS MAY ALREADY KNOW:

- **Planned activities:** get up, have breakfast, lunch, dinner, go to school, study, work.
- **Unexpected things:** get sick, arrive late, traffic, have an accident.
- Days of the week.
- Time.

VIDEO

DISCUSS & SHARE

3 **IN GROUPS** Watch the video and answer the question.
SYM Do you plan your day or decide what to do at the last minute?

GO TO page xx
for **VIDEOS IN SYM** step-by-step instructions.

In this unit, you will ...

- talk about daily activities and how often you do them. Describe a day off.
- use thinking skills: draw conclusions, summarize, and recall.
- read about a reporter's typical day.
- use strategies to start and keep talking by giving examples and expressing frequency.
- use adaptability skills to give advice about keeping life interesting.
- follow an emergency worker to learn about this job and the skills needed for this industry.

WHAT DO YOU ALREADY KNOW?

If you notice students are struggling to understand what to do, you can provide one or two examples to help them get started:

- **Activities:** walk the dog, make phone calls, work on my computer, go out for coffee, go to the movies

VIDEO

Before viewing, ask:

Who likes to plan? *Max*
Who likes to decide what to do at the last minute? *Amy*

After viewing, put the continuum on the board.

planner —— last-minute decider

Have students mark the continuum and explain what type of activities they plan or don't plan.

DISCUSS & SHARE

Have students consider how they manage their days. Do they use a planner, calendar, or organizer on their phones to plan their day? Do they prefer to keep their day mostly unplanned until the last minute?

GO TO page x
for **READING** step-by-step instructions.

LESSON 1 A Day in the Life

READING

A Take a class survey. How many people think their lives are boring, average, or exciting?

B 4.01 **THINKING SKILL—Analyze** Read the blog post. In your opinion, is Jerry's life boring, average, or exciting?

The Daily Blog

Jan 21 1:43 p.m.

A Day in the Life of a Reporter

I'm a reporter. I work for an entertainment magazine in New York City. My friends think my job is amazing because I meet famous people. But this is my typical day.

I get up at about 6:30 a.m., and then I **walk my dog**, **have coffee**, and **get ready for work**. I leave home at 7:15 a.m., and I **take the subway** to my office. I **start work** at 8:00 a.m. I don't eat breakfast at home because I don't have time. I buy something at the café in the subway station. At work, I go to meetings and write articles for the magazine. I also **make** a lot of **phone calls** to get interviews with people. The interviews are interesting, but sometimes the people I interview aren't very friendly or they don't have time to talk.

In the evening, I **go home** and walk my dog again. Then, I **have dinner** and watch TV for about two hours. I go to bed at about 10:00 p.m. On weekends, I go out with friends, go shopping, or go to a movie.

follow

1 6:30 a.m.
2 in New York City
3 because he meets a lot of famous people
4 He takes the subway.
5 with friends

C **IN PAIRS READING SKILL—Scan** Find the answers as quickly as possible.

1 What time does Jerry get up?
2 Where does he live?
3 Why do his friends think his job is amazing?
4 How does he get to work?
5 Who does he go out with on weekends?

GO TO page vii
for **VOCABULARY** step-by-step instructions.

VOCABULARY

A Find words from the blog post that match the definitions. Write the word.

1 begin your workday: start work
2 exercise with your dog: walk my dog
3 drink coffee: have coffee
4 prepare for work: get ready for work
5 travel by subway: take the subway
6 call people: make phone calls
7 return to your home: go home
8 eat dinner: have dinner

GO TO page viii
for **GRAMMAR** step-by-step instructions.

GRAMMAR simple present information questions

A Complete the questions with words from the box.

how what when where who why

Information Questions: Question Word + *Do/Does* + Subject + Verb / Verb Phrase	
1 What do your parents do?	They're teachers.
2 Where does your brother work?	He works at a bank.
3 When does he work?	He works from Monday to Friday.
4 Why do you like your job?	I like it because it's very interesting.
5 How do you get to work?	I take the bus.
6 Who do you see on weekends?	I see my best friend.

For more practice, go to page 146.

READING OPTIONAL 4.01

Before students scan, have them play a game using times and numbers—the kind of data students often have to find when reading for specific information. Divide the class into three or four teams and call out a time (e.g., 4:45 p.m.), a number (e.g., 13), or an ordinal number (e.g., 2nd). Have one student from each team run to the board and write what they hear. The first student to write the information correctly on the board wins a point for their team. The team members take turns running and writing. The first team to earn five points wins.

VOCABULARY

Stretch students' vocabulary by asking them to find other words that collocate with these verbs—for example, 1 start school, start the meeting; 2 walk to work, walk to school; 3 have lunch; 4 get ready for school, get ready to go out; 5 take the bus; 6 make appointments; 7 go to school, go to work, go to a meeting; 8 have breakfast.

B Unscramble the questions.

1. do / on weekends / you / what / do / ?
What do you do on weekends?
2. in your free time / who / you / do / see / ?
Who do you see in your free time?
3. go / you / where / on vacation / do / ?
Where do you go on vacation?
4. English / you / study / do / why / ?
Why do you study English?
5. do / when / you / your English homework / do / ?
When do you do your English homework?
6. to English class / you / do / get / how / ?
How do you get to English class?

C IN PAIRS Ask and answer the questions in B.

PRONUNCIATION word stress in information questions

A 4.02 Listen and underline the stressed words.

1. What do you do?
2. Where do you live?
3. Why do you like your job?
4. When do you go on vacation?
5. How do you get to class?

B 4.02 Listen again. Practice reading the questions with the correct word stress.

GO TO page ix for PRONUNCIATION step-by-step instructions.

SPEAKING

A Use the cues to write interview questions.

1. What / do?
What do you do?
2. Where / work or study?
Where do you work (study)?
3. When / have English class?
When do you have English class?
4. How / get to work?
How do you get to work?
5. What time / start work?
What time do you start work?
6. What / do in your free time?
What do you do in your free time?

B IN PAIRS Interview your partner. Write his/her answers in A.

C IN GROUPS Is your life boring, average, or exciting? Are your partners' lives exciting? Use the Confident Communicator box to help you.

CONFIDENT COMMUNICATOR — START TALKING

To describe your life, give examples to support your opinion using *because*.
My life is exciting because I travel a lot / meet a lot of interesting people / have a great social life.
My life is average because I like my job, but it isn't exciting / I just do normal things.
My life is boring because my job isn't interesting / I don't do many interesting things / I do the same things every day.

GO TO page xii for SPEAKING step-by-step instructions.

GRAMMAR Alternative Activity

Play Tic-Tac-Toe with *Wh–* question words. Draw a Tic-Tac-Toe grid on the board. Write a *Wh–* question word in each square. Divide the class into two teams. Each team can win a space by creating a correct *Wh–* question. The team that creates three grammatically correct questions in a row wins.

PRONUNCIATION

Point out that the stressed words in a sentence are the question words, main verbs, and nouns. Auxiliary verbs, subject pronouns, and function words are usually not stressed.

Students should listen to the intonation of the questions; information questions usually have falling intonation. They should practice this when saying the questions.

SPEAKING Extra Practice

Extend the speaking activity by asking students to choose a "secret" classmate. Tell them to answer the questions as that person without saying who they are. Their partner should guess which classmate they are based on their answers.

GO TO page xi
for **LISTENING** step-by-step instructions.

GO TO page 140
for **AUDIO SCRIPT**.

B Suggested answer: She doesn't think her job is very exciting because she works long hours, and in her free time she does normal things with her family.

LESSON 2 Always? Sometimes? Never?

LISTENING

A As a class, discuss jobs you think are exciting.

B 4.03 Listen to an interview with an actress. Does she think her life is exciting? Why or why not?

MAKE IT REAL

Really means *very*: *That's really early.*
Some Americans say *real* for *really*: *That's real early.*
Kind of means *a little*: *My job is kind of unusual.*
Americans often pronounce it as *kinda*.

C 4.03 **LISTENING SKILL—Listen for specific information** Listen again and choose the correct option.

1 Audrey often starts work …
 a at 6:00. b at 8:00. c at 10:00.
2 She frequently finishes work at …
 a six o'clock in the evening. b seven thirty in the evening. c eight or nine at night.
3 On weekends, Audrey almost always …
 a works. b spends time with her family. c goes to San Francisco.
4 Audrey and her family go to San Francisco to …
 a see her parents. b go to the zoo. c work.
5 Audrey thinks that her life is …
 a exciting. b normal. c boring.

D **IN PAIRS THINKING SKILL—Summarize** Describe Audrey's life.

A: She's married / an actress.
A: She works from … to …
A: She doesn't often …
B: She has children / an interesting life / a difficult job.
B: On weekdays / weekends / Saturdays / Sundays, she …

VOCABULARY frequency and time expressions

A Complete the table with the words in the box.

3:00 a day a week week
day Friday March year
March 20 month morning ~~2020~~
night once the evening
three times Tuesdays twice

in	on	at	every	several times	… a day / month / year
2020	Tuesdays	night	week, March,	a day	once
March	Friday	3:00	month, night,	a week	twice
the evening	March 20		morning, day,		three times
			Friday, year		

LISTENING

Before listening to the interview, elicit a list of jobs and write them on the board. Play Go to Work. Nominate a job for each corner of the room. Have students choose a job and go to that corner. Ask them to share why they chose that job. Rename the corners with different jobs and play again.

THINKING SKILL—Summarize

When asking students to summarize, you want them to express, in their own words, the main points of what they listen. Give them time to formulate their ideas.

VOCABULARY

Share the audio script from LISTENING **B** and have them underline examples of frequency and time expressions. For example, *We often start at about 6 a.m., Four times a year …*

Ask about the difference between *four times a year* and *every four years*. Ask *Which is more frequent: several times a day or once every several days?*

B **IN PAIRS** Ask and answer questions. Use frequency expressions.

1 How often do you eat at restaurants?
2 How often does your family go on vacation?
3 How often do you play video games?
4 How often do you have English class?
5 How often do you go shopping?

GRAMMAR frequency adverbs

A Look at the scale. Then complete the rules.

100%	75%	50%	25%	10%	0%
always	usually	often	sometimes	rarely	never

I'm always tired!
We usually work a lot of hours.
Sometimes we go to San Francisco to see my parents.
I rarely work on Saturdays.

1 Frequency adverbs come before / **after** the verb *be*.
2 Frequency adverbs come **before** / after other verbs.
3 Frequency or time expressions come at the end / **at the beginning or end** of a sentence.

For more practice, go to page 147.

B Look at the scale. Then complete the sentences.

100%	75%	50%	25%	10%	0%
eats breakfast	sees friends on the weekend	listens to podcasts	talks on the phone	is sad	is late to work

1 Robert sometimes talks on the phone. (25%)
2 He always eats breakfast.
3 He's almost never sad.
4 He usually sees friends on the weekend.
5 He often listens to podcasts.
6 He's never late to work.

SPEAKING

A Complete the survey for you.

How often do you ...	You				
go out to eat?					
go to a movie?					
take a vacation?					
use social media?					

B **IN GROUPS** Write each group member's name at the top of the table in A. Ask and answer the questions for each group member. Use the Confident Communicator box to help you. Then discuss. Do the people in your group have similar routines or very different routines?

CONFIDENT COMMUNICATOR
KEEP TALKING

When you don't know the exact frequency of an activity, use words like *about*, *around*, and *more or less*: *about once a month*, *around four times a year*, *more or less twice a day*.

GRAMMAR

The adverbs of frequency or adverbs of time describe how often something occurs. You may want to point out that an exception to Rules 1 and 2 is *sometimes*. It can come before the subject and verb as in *Sometimes I'm late to work* or *Sometimes I go out with friends*. Some other adverbs of frequency are: *annually, daily, constantly, frequently*.

SPEAKING

Have students make predictions about their group members before asking the survey questions. Encourage them to include adverbs of frequency, time expressions, and the recommendations in the Confident Communicator box.

Once they have finished the survey, they can play One of Us, Some of Us, All of Us. Have students work in groups of four and talk to each other about their routines. Then, they make sentences that are true for one, some, or all of the group members. For example, *One of us eats out every day. Some of us sleep late on Sundays. All of us like to eat Mexican food.*

1 hangs out at home, watches TV or plays video games

2 gets dressed, cooks breakfast, does housework, goes shopping, goes out with friends

3 goes to the gym, has lunch, plays soccer, hangs out and watches other soccer games, does housework, cooks dinner

4 reads or listens to podcasts, takes a nap, orders food, watches TV

GO TO page 140 for **AUDIO SCRIPT**.

LESSON 3 The Perfect Day

VOCABULARY routine activities

A Match the expressions from the box to the photos.

cook	do housework	get dressed	go to the gym
go out with friends	hang out at home	take a nap	take a shower

1 
take a shower

2 
get dressed

3 
cook

4 
go out with friends

5 
do housework

6 
go to the gym

7 
hang out at home

8 
take a nap

B IN PAIRS Discuss the activities using frequency expressions.

A: I often do housework. *B: I never take a nap.*
A: I rarely cook. *B: I usually go to the gym in the morning.*

LISTENING

A Look at the pictures. Which type of day off do you prefer?

a 

b 

B 4.04 LISTENING SKILL—Listen for gist Listen to a radio show. Write *C* (*crazy*) or *L* (*lazy*) for each caller.

1 Brendon: L
2 Carla: C
3 Ali: C
4 Melissa: L

C 4.04 IN PAIRS THINKING SKILL—Recall Listen again. List the activities each caller does on a day off.

1 Brendon: gets up late, ______
2 Carla: takes a shower, ______
3 Ali: goes to the gym, ______
4 Melissa: hangs out at home, ______

D IN PAIRS Compare your lists with another partner.

MAKE IT YOURS
Make a list of activities that you like doing on a day off.

VOCABULARY Extra Practice

Have students choose four activities from VOCABULARY **A** and write the activities in order for them. They can use different categories, such as earliest to latest, easiest to hardest, and so on. For example, *I get dressed at 6:00 a.m. I sometimes do housework at 7:00 a.m. I often go to the gym at 7:30 a.m.*

LISTENING

THINKING SKILL—Listen for gist

Tell students that when they listen for gist, they should listen for key words to give them an idea of what the information is about. They don't have to understand every word.

MAKE IT YOURS

More day-off activities might include *go to the movies, walk the dog, visit family, go to a yard sale, play on my phone, chat (text) with friends, shop online, help my neighbor, take a class, fix the car, and do yoga.*

WRITING

A **Read the blog post. In your opinion, is Olivia's day crazy or lazy? Discuss.**

THE PERFECT DAY OFF

March 2 3:32 p.m.

I love to write this blog, but I also love to have a day off! On my perfect day off, I usually get up late. I take a shower and get dressed. I go out and eat a big breakfast. After breakfast, I go for a walk. Then, I usually hang out with friends. We go to a café or go shopping. Sometimes we go to a movie. In the evening, I almost always order food, usually pizza. I don't like cooking! I never read blogs or use social media on my day off.

follow

B **Complete the table for you.**

	Activities on a Day Off
always	
usually	
often	
sometimes	
rarely	
never	

C **Write a paragraph about your perfect day off in your notebook.**

D **IN PAIRS Read your partner's paragraph. Answer the questions and make recommendations. Use your partner's comments to make any changes to your paragraph.**

1 Does your partner …

a capitalize words correctly? Yes / No
b use *be* correctly? Yes / No
c have any spelling errors? Yes / No
d have any grammar errors? Yes / No

SPEAKING

A **IN GROUPS Discuss your perfect day off. As you listen to each person, write *C* (*crazy*) or *L* (*lazy*), depending on the person's favorite type of day off.**

B **Take a class survey to see how many people enjoy lazy days and how many enjoy crazy days. Use the Confident Communicator box to help you.**

CONFIDENT COMMUNICATOR
KEEP TALKING

You can use negative verbs with *always*, *usually*, *often*, and *sometimes*. Notice the word order:
*I **don't always** eat breakfast.*
*I **don't usually** exercise on Saturdays.*
*I **don't often** get up late.*
*I **sometimes don't** check my email.*

GO TO page xiv
for **WRITING** step-by-step instructions.

WRITING

Before writing, have students underline the activities mentioned in the blog and circle time expressions. Ask them to review the time expressions in this lesson. Let them know that the chart in WRITING **B** is for brainstorming purposes and they should write down as many ideas as they can. The purpose is to generate their thoughts related to the topic. They don't have to use all the ideas they generate in WRITING **B** in the final version of their writing.

SPEAKING

Let students know that they can use the information they wrote about their perfect day off but that they should speak without looking at their writing. Invite them to add information spontaneously at the speaking stage. Have them read the Confident Communicator box to check the word order. Supporting their comments with reasons using *because* will add depth to their conversations.

GO TO page xv
for LANGUAGE AND LIFE step-by-step instructions.

Language and Life

Adaptability – An Interesting Life

A 4.05 **Read the social media web page. In your opinion, why is Andy bored? Discuss. Do your classmates agree?**

I Need Advice!

Andy6_24:

Q:

I'm 25, and I live in Tampa, Florida, with my two friends Joe and Mario. I have a good job. I'm a nurse, and I work at a big hospital. My work schedule is 9:00 to 5:00 Monday through Friday. I eat lunch in the hospital cafeteria at 1:00 p.m. every day. I always go to the gym after work. In the evening, my roommates and I cook dinner—usually pasta or burgers. We watch TV for about two hours, and I almost always go to bed at about 10:30 p.m. On Saturdays, I go to the gym in the morning and go shopping or do housework in the afternoon. On Saturday evenings, my roommates and I usually order pizza and watch movies. On Sundays, I always play soccer with my friends in the afternoon. I have a very good life—nice friends and a good job, but I'm kind of bored. What do you recommend?

OBJECTIVE

In this lesson, students learn how to determine habits a person could change in their life. Then, they figure out how to give advice to someone about how they can make good life choices and have a more interesting life. People often do not know what to consider when looking for a change in their lives. Point out that we all get into daily routines that we take for granted and, sometimes, when others shine a light on our patterns, we realize a change is needed. It is important to be honest but also sensitive when giving advice.

PROCESS OPTIONAL 4.05

Students first analyze a case study and plot when and for how long a person does habitual activities. They should make suggestions for alternative things to do and what a person might stop doing. Then, they make a case for ways to have a more exciting life. Finally, they analyze their own routines and give each other advice for more exciting lives.

B Complete the notes with information from the web page.

Weekdays:

9:00–5:00 *works at the hospital*
1:00 p.m. eats lunch in the hospital cafeteria
after work goes to the gym
in the evening cooks dinner (pasta or burgers)

Saturdays:
in the morning goes to the gym
in the afternoon goes shopping or does housework
in the evening orders pizza and watches movies

Sundays:
in the afternoon plays soccer

C **IN PAIRS** Write recommendations to Andy for making his life more interesting.

D **IN GROUPS** Think of more recommendations for Andy to make his life more interesting.

E **IN GROUPS** Discuss your routine. Give each other recommendations to make your lives more exciting.

MAKE IT DIGITAL

Post ideas for people to make their lives more interesting on your own social media site.

CAREER NOTE

To be successful at work, students will have to know how to organize the activities of their day. Ask them to think of jobs they know and brainstorm activities people do in the morning, in the afternoon, and in the evening for their jobs.

MAKE IT DIGITAL

Tell students that once they have posted on their social media some ideas for people to make their lives more interesting, they should open up the forum to their social media contacts. Have them get their friends to share ideas and tips. What has worked well? What hasn't worked?

Extra Activity

Have students go online and enter *8 ways to make your life more exciting* or *10 ways …* or *3 ways …* into their favorite search engine. Inserting a number into the search phrase will result in a list of articles with advice for making your life more exciting.

GO TO page xvii
for **UNIT REVIEW** step-by-step instructions.

UNIT 4

VOCABULARY review

SCORE: / 10

A Complete the sentences with verbs from the box.

exercise	go	get	get up	hang out
have	order	start	take	walk

I'm a dessert blogger, and I have a usual daily routine. I **1** get up at 9:00, **2** have coffee, and **3** walk the dog. Then, I **4** take a shower and **5** get ready for my workday. I **6** start work at 11:30. I eat lunch at a different restaurant every day. After lunch, I **7** order a dessert from the menu to eat. In the afternoon, I write my blog. Sunday is my day off. I don't just **8** hang out at home. After all those desserts, I **9** go to the gym and **10** exercise for an hour!

GRAMMAR review

SCORE: / 10

A Write the question that asks about the underlined information.

1 I talk to my friends several times a day. Who do you talk to several times a day?
2 We do housework on Sundays. What do you do on Sundays?
3 My sister works in a café on weekends. Where does your sister work on weekends?
4 I eat cake every afternoon. What do you eat every afternoon?
5 He studies English because it's fun! Why does he study English?

B Rewrite the sentences with the words in parentheses.

1 Meg takes a nap in the afternoon. (often) Meg often takes a nap in the afternoon.
2 Mr. Nelson is late for class. (never) Mr. Nelson is never late for class.
3 Kyle sees his parents. (twice a year) Kyle sees his parents twice a year. / Twice a year Kyle sees his parents.
4 Anita takes the train to work. (rarely) Anita rarely takes the train to work.
5 We're at the gym on Sundays. (always) We're always at the gym on Sundays.

16–20 correct: You can talk about daily activities and frequency. You can use simple present information questions and frequency adverbs.
0–15 correct: Look again at the Vocabulary and Grammar sections in the unit.

TOTAL SCORE: / 20

WHAT DO YOU KNOW NOW? Look back at page 37 and add the words you know now to the boxes.

GO TO page xix
for **FOLLOW A PRO** step-by-step instructions.

FOLLOW A PRO — EMERGENCY SERVICES

Take the quiz about emergency services. Go to Follow A Pro on page 130 to find the answers. Then learn more about the emergency services industry.

1 The oldest emergency telephone number is 999. How old is it?
a over 70 years old **b** over 80 years old **c** over 90 years old

2 How many hours of training do you need to become a paramedic?
a about 2,000 **b** about 1,000 **c** about 500

3 What US state has a festival every year to celebrate its emergency workers?
a Washington **b** California **c** Alabama

4 70% of emergency medical technicians in the US are male.
a true **b** false

46 Unit 4 That's Life!

ALTERNATIVE ACTIVITY

Play Vocabulary Auction. Give an amount of play money to pairs. Make paper strips with words from VOCABULARY **A**. Include some extra words that don't fit anywhere, like *study* and *eat*. Read the text. When you get to the blanks, students bid and pay for the word they want. "Sell" the words to the highest bidders as you go along. The pair that buys the most correct words wins.

CLASSROOM MANAGEMENT

Before doing open-class feedback to check answers, have students check their answers with a partner. The review stage is, after all, a chance for students to check that they have understood the concepts. Peer checking is empowering.

FURTHER DISCUSSION

Put students in groups of three and ask the following questions for them to discuss:

- What is your typical day like?
- What do you like to do on your days off?
- What activities do you always do?
- What activities do you never do?
- How different are your weekend days from your weekdays?

UNIT 5

Finding Your Way

GO TO page vi
for **UNIT OPENER** step-by-step instructions.

WHAT DO YOU ALREADY KNOW?

1 Think of places you usually go and places you sometimes go. Write the names of the places.

2 **IN PAIRS** Share and compare your information. Add more words to your list.

Places I usually go
school

Places I sometimes go
museum

STUDENTS MAY ALREADY KNOW:

- **Places I usually go:** school, friend's house, supermarket, store, restaurant, grandmother's house, aunt's house.
- **Places I sometimes go:** museum, library, theater.

VIDEO

DISCUSS & SHARE

3 **IN GROUPS** Watch the video and answer the question.
SYM Do you ask for directions or try to find your way?

GO TO page xx
for **VIDEOS IN SYM** step-by-step instructions.

In this unit, you will ...

- talk about places to live, your neighborhood, and directions.
- use thinking skills: apply, evaluate, and analyze.
- read about unusual places to live.
- use strategies to keep talking by making guesses.
- use problem-solving skills to create a guide to your neighborhood.
- learn research skills for school and work.

WHAT DO YOU ALREADY KNOW?

If you notice students are struggling to understand what to do, you can provide one or two examples to help them get started:

- I go to the gym every day.
- I usually go to a café on Fridays with my friends.
- I go to the cafeteria every day for lunch.

VIDEO

Before viewing, ask:

How does Jill try to find her way? *She uses GPS, a map, signs, and buildings, and asks another person.*

After viewing, put the continuum on the board.

ask directions —— find your way

Students mark the continuum and explain how they find their way.

DISCUSS & SHARE

Encourage students to talk about funny anecdotes about getting around, asking directions, or finding their own way. Ask them if they use any apps to get to their final destination.

GO TO page x

for **READING** step-by-step instructions.

LESSON 1 Where Do You Live?

READING

A Look at the pictures in **B** and discuss the questions. Do you want to live somewhere like this? Why or why not?

B 5.01 **READING SKILL—Scan for specific information** Read the article and answer the questions.

PLACES WE LIVE

For many young people, the idea of buying a **home** is important. But what happens when you don't have a lot of money to buy? Here are two interesting options for millennials.

Oscar Knight lives in a new apartment in an exciting **neighborhood** in London. "This is an **apartment building** designed for young people between the ages of 20 and 35," he says. "We live, work, and play all in one space. It's not boring at all! There are different spaces for us to use, such as a library, a community **garden**, a gym, an office, a popular restaurant, and a grocery store."

"London is expensive," says Layla, one of Oscar's neighbors. "But it's a fun **city**. I pay £330 per week here, but that includes Wi-Fi, electricity, water, and a gym. I never feel bored here. It's a great place to live, and the people are very friendly."

Eco-pod similar to Jay's eco-pod.

Jay Nilsson, from Sweden, lives in an unusual house. He has a one-room eco-pod. "This eco-pod is great," says Jay. "You can live wherever you want. My eco-pod is in my parents' **yard** on a quiet **street**, but I can move my eco-pod, too." Eco-pods are not cheap—Jay's eco-pod cost him almost $93,000. They are also very small—only 8 meters long. But there is a bed, a bathroom, and a tiny kitchen. It's good for one person only!

1. What city does Oscar live in? London
2. Does Layla think it is a good place for young people to live? Yes, she does. It's exciting.
3. Where does Jay live? in his parents' yard on a quiet street / in an eco-pod
4. How big is Jay's eco-pod? 8 meters long.

C **IN PAIRS THINKING SKILL—Apply** Discuss your preferences and explain. Do you want to live in an apartment building like Oscar or in an eco-pod like Jay?

GO TO page vii

for **VOCABULARY** step-by-step instructions.

VOCABULARY

A Complete the definitions with words from the article.

1. a place to live: house, apartment
2. an area around a house: garden, yard
3. the area around where you live: neighborhood
4. the people who live near you: neighbors
5. a very large town: city
6. a road: street

MAKE IT YOURS

Find more words that describe your neighborhood and the house, apartment, or street where you live.

READING OPTIONAL 5.01

Have students consider the needs of daily life and how our homes provide for those. Ask *What activities do you do at home?* Students should come up with different activities (e.g., *sleep, eat, shower,* etc.). Considering their own needs will help them answer READING **A**.

THINKING SKILL—Apply

Students must understand what they have read and use that information to support their preferences. Those who choose an apartment building might like having people around. Those who choose an eco-pod may enjoy privacy.

VOCABULARY

More words to describe *neighborhood* are *district, area, community, region, zone,* and the phrase *around here.* Some more words to describe *apartment* are *flat* (British) or *unit.* More words for *home* might be *residence, dwelling,* or *abode.*

GRAMMAR adjectives

A **Circle adjectives in READING B.**

B **Read the grammar rules. Complete the examples from READING B.**

1 Use adjectives to describe nouns. Adjectives often come before a noun. Write three examples from the text.
a new apartment, ______, ______, ______
2 Adjectives can also come after the verbs *be*, *look*, or *feel*. Write one example from the text.
London is expensive. ______
3 Some adjectives end in *–ing* and describe things or places. Write one example from the text.
an exciting neighborhood, ______
4 Some adjectives end in *–ed* and describe feelings. Write one example from the text.
excited, bored

For more practice, go to page 148.

C **Unscramble and write the sentences.**

1 expensive / this / café / an / is / .
This is an expensive café.

2 this / the / great / restaurant / at / popular / is / food / .
The food at this popular restaurant is great. / The food is great at this popular restaurant.

3 neighbors / very / noisy / my / are / .
My neighbors are very noisy.

4 class / boring / really / is / this / a / .
This is a really boring class.

D **IN PAIRS Discuss your neighborhoods using adjectives.**

A: What's your neighborhood like? *B: It's quiet. How about yours?*

GO TO page viii for GRAMMAR step-by-step instructions.

Suggested answers:
1 young people, interesting options, exciting neighborhood, a popular restaurant, an unusual house, a quiet street, a tiny kitchen
2 is important, is not boring, feel bored, are very friendly, is great, are not cheap
3 not boring at all, interesting options

PRONUNCIATION syllable stress in multi-syllable adjectives

A **5.02 Say the words. Underline the stressed syllable. Then listen and check.**

1 lively quiet busy
2 expensive exciting important

B **5.03 Listen and notice how the stressed syllable is louder and longer than the unstressed syllables. Practice stressing the syllables.**

1 expensive houses 2 an exciting city 3 busy neighborhood

GO TO page ix for PRONUNCIATION step-by-step instructions.

SPEAKING

A **Write two sentences that are true and one sentence that is not true about your home and neighborhood.**

B **IN GROUPS Read your sentences aloud. Ask your group members to guess which sentence is not true. Use the Confident Communicator box to help you.**

CONFIDENT COMMUNICATOR
KEEP TALKING

When you're not sure about something, you can make guesses:
It's just a guess, but …
It's difficult to say, but …
I bet it's …

GO TO page xii for SPEAKING step-by-step instructions.

GRAMMAR Extra Practice

In groups of five, give each student part of a sentence from the article in READING **B** on a strip of paper. Tell them not to show the piece of paper and only say their part. Ask them to arrange themselves in order to make the sentence. They must speak clearly and listen carefully. Students will practice a cooperative activity.

PRONUNCIATION

Have students emphasize the stressed syllable with a snap, a clap, or a tap of the foot. Some students have a hard time understanding English rhythm, word stress, and sentence stress. The physical manifestation of stress in words can be a revelation.

SPEAKING

Have students report back to the class things they learned about their group members. Increasing the level of accountability in speaking activities improves listening. When students know they'll be reporting back on what they hear, they become more active listeners.

LESSON 2 What's in Your Neighborhood?

VOCABULARY places in a neighborhood

A **Write the places under the pictures with words from the box. Compare your answers with a partner.**

apartment building	bus stop	coffee shop	grocery store
gym	high school	library	train station

1 
coffee shop

2 
apartment building

3 
bus stop

4 
gym

5 
library

6 
train station

7 
high school

8 
grocery store

B **Use words from A to complete the table.**

Places to ...

live/study	exercise	shop	travel to/from	hang out
apartment building	gym	grocery store	bus stop	coffee shop
library			train station	
high school				

MAKE IT REAL

Sometimes you hear different words for the same places in a neighborhood.

gym = fitness center, health club | *coffee shop = café*
grocery store = supermarket | *apartment (American English) = flat (British English)*

GO TO page xi
for **LISTENING** step-by-step instructions.

LISTENING

A **Look at the pictures. Would you like to live in these neighborhoods?**

MAKE IT REAL

Although British and American people speak the same language, there are differences between British and American English. Some differences are in spelling (e.g., *neighbourhood* in British English vs. *neighborhood* in American English) and vocabulary (e.g., *flat* in British English vs. *apartment* in American English).

LISTENING Alternative Activity

Play Categories. Write five categories on the board—for example, *places in a neighborhood, types of dwellings, vehicles, colors,* and *food.* Give students one minute to write a word in each category. Then, elicit answers students wrote. Each player gets a point for an original answer. If they have an answer someone else wrote down, they cross it out. If you have a large class, divide students into groups of five and have them compare answers and win points for original answers in the group. Have another round with five new categories.

B 5.04 **LISTENING SKILL—Listen for specific information** Listen to the radio show. Check (✓) the places Elsa and Ahmed mention.

	coffee shop	park	gym	bus stop	train station	grocery store	library	apartment building	high school
Elsa		✓	✓			✓	✓		
Ahmed	✓							✓	✓

GO TO page 141 for AUDIO SCRIPT.

C 5.04 **Listen again. Who likes their neighborhood? Discuss.**

C Ahmed

D IN PAIRS THINKING SKILL—Evaluate Compare and discuss where you want to live.

1. What are the differences between living outside of a town or city and living close to the city?
2. Where do you like to live?

GRAMMAR *there is / there are*

A Read the sentences. Complete the rules.

There is a grocery store and a park.
There's no gym and no library.
Are there things to do or places to hang out in your neighborhood?
There's a coffee shop where I hang out with my friends.

1. We use *There is* and *There are* to talk about **things that exist** / things that don't exist.
2. We use *There is no* and *There are no* to talk about things that exist / **things that don't exist.**
3. *Are there ...?* is the question form for one thing / **more than one thing.**
4. *There's* is the contraction of **there is** / *there are*.

For more practice, go to page 148.

B Find one mistake and write the correct sentences.

1. There ~~aren't~~ a train station near my house. There isn't a / There's no train station near my house.
2. ~~Are there~~ a gym in your neighborhood? Is there a gym in your neighborhood?
3. In my town, ~~there~~ a grocery store, but no library. In my town, there's a grocery store, but no library.
4. ~~There's not coffee~~ shop in my neighborhood. There's no / There isn't a coffee shop in my neighborhood.
5. ~~There are~~ a good restaurant near the bus stop. There is a good restaurant near the bus stop.

C Make notes about your neighborhood and what amenities you think it needs. Share with a partner.

D As a class, discuss your neighborhoods.

SPEAKING

A Draw a map of a neighborhood with at least six places on it in your notebook.

B IN PAIRS Discuss your maps. Use the Confident Communicator box to help you.

Do not look at your partner's map. When your partner asks about a place on your map, put a check (✓). When your partner asks about all the places on your map, say *Bingo!* The first pair to find all the places on both maps wins.

A: Is there a library? *B: No, there's no library. / Yes, there's a library.*

CONFIDENT COMMUNICATOR
KEEP TALKING

Visitors often need information about a place from a person who knows the area. To say you know or don't know an area, say:
I'm from (near) here. *I'm (not) a local.*
I'm (not) from around here. *I (don't) live close by.*

LISTENING

THINKING SKILL—Evaluate

To evaluate is to form an idea of the value of something. In order to compare living outside of a town or city to living close to the city, students must first understand the value of living in either place. Then, they can choose what suits them.

Extra Practice

In pairs, play Where Am I? Students describe a place using *there is* and *there are* and their partner guesses the place. For example, *A: There is coffee. There are customers. There are chairs and tables. Where am I? B: You're in a coffee shop!*

SPEAKING

After completing the Bingo game in SPEAKING **B**, have students from the same neighborhood work together to identify six things that their area doesn't have. For example, *There isn't a stadium in our neighborhood. There aren't any libraries. There aren't any coffee shops.* Then, from that list, ask them to identify the three things they need most. For example, *We need a stadium most. We need a stadium for soccer games and concerts.*

LESSON 3 Are You Lost?

VOCABULARY directions

A Match the directions to the pictures. Write the letters.

1. Take the first left. __b__
2. Turn around. __a__
3. Take the second left. __c__
4. Go straight ahead. __d__

B Look at the map. Write the answer.

1. It's next to the apartment building. __coffee shop__
2. It's between the apartment building and the gym. __coffee shop__
3. It's across from the grocery store. __bus stop__
4. It's on the corner of River Street and Third Avenue. __library__

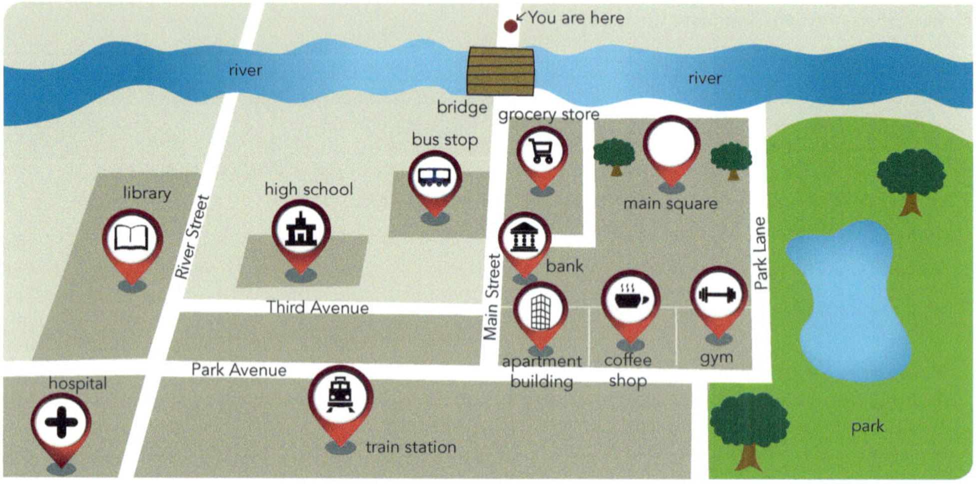

C Look at the map in B again. Then complete the directions.

1. A: Excuse me. How do I get to the high school? B: Go over the bridge. Then take the first __right__.
2. A: Can you tell me how to get to the train station? B: Yes. Go __straight ahead__ and then take the second right.
3. A: Is there a bus stop near here? B: It's over there, across from the __grocery store__.
4. A: How do I get to the library? B: Take the next __right__. Then take another right.
5. A: Hi. Do you know where the coffee shop is? B: Yes. It's __between__ the apartment building and the gym.

D IN PAIRS Discuss directions. Ask for and give directions to and from the places.

1. from the library to the bus stop
2. from the train station to the coffee shop
3. from the apartment building to the high school
4. from the park to the library

LISTENING

A IN PAIRS Check (✓) what you do if you get lost.

- ☐ call a friend or relative
- ☐ ask a person on the street for help
- ☐ keep walking or driving
- ☐ use a map on your phone

VOCABULARY

Before starting this section, ask students to close their eyes. Give them a minute to retrace their steps over the past two days in their minds. Ask them to open their eyes and write down all the places they have been.

After finishing the vocabulary exercises, have students review places from the unit and ask them to extend their vocabulary by brainstorming other places in their neighborhoods that might have come to mind. These might be *pharmacy, park, police station, hospital, restaurant, hair salon, department store, hotel,* and *government offices*. Allow students to use dictionaries to look up more words.

LISTENING

When listening to the conversations in LISTENING **B**, pause after each one for students to write their answers. Then play all of the conversations straight through for the second listening. Finally, play the conversations again and this time pause after each one as you elicit and check answers.

B 5.05 **LISTENING SKILL—Listen for key words** Listen to the conversations. Write the places the speakers want to go to.

1 Conversation 1: Jackson Street and Ninth Avenue
2 Conversation 2: bus stop
3 Conversation 3: Central Station
4 Conversation 4: grocery store
5 Conversation 5: the beach

C 5.05 **Listen again and write the directions in your notebook.**

D **IN PAIRS THINKING SKILL—Analyze** Discuss.

1 Where do you sometimes get lost?
2 What do you do?
3 Do you ask for help? Who do you ask?
4 How often do you get lost?

WRITING

A **Read the instant messages. Does Samantha know how to get to the coffee shop? Discuss.**

B **Match the words from the box to the abbreviations.**

Samantha:
Hi! How RU? Meet for coffee tomorrow?

Melissa:
Sure. Baker's? 4 p.m.?

Samantha:
OK. Send directions!

Melissa:
Main St. to 3 Ave. Cross the bridge. Turn left at Harry's. Take next right. Baker's bldg is on the corner. CU 2morrow!

building	tomorrow	are you
see you	avenue	street

1 Ave avenue
2 2morrow tomorrow
3 CU see you
4 RU are you
5 bldg building
6 St street

C **Rewrite the instant messages in complete sentences in your notebook. Don't use abbreviations.**

D **IN PAIRS** **Practice writing directions. Text or write directions to your partner using abbreviations and/or emojis. Then write your partner's directions in complete sentences.**

SPEAKING

A **IN PAIRS** **Practice the conversation. Use the Confident Communicator box to help you.**

A: Excuse me. Where is the bus stop?
B: It's straight ahead. Go one more block.

B **IN PAIRS** **Role-play asking for and giving directions. Then change roles and role-play again.**

Student A: You are lost. Ask how to get to places from your school.
Student B: Give directions to Student A.

CONFIDENT COMMUNICATOR
START TALKING

To ask for directions, say:
Excuse me. Where is/are …?
How do I get to …?
Can you tell me where the … is/are?
Is there a/an … nearby?

GO TO page 141 for AUDIO SCRIPT.

1 Take the second left.
2 It's across from the park.
3 Cross the bridge.
4 Turn around.
5 Follow signs for the airport.

GO TO page xiv for WRITING step-by-step instructions.

A No, she doesn't. She asks Melissa for directions.

Suggested answers:
Samantha: Hi! How are you? Do you want to meet for coffee tomorrow?
Melissa: Sure. Do you want to meet at Baker's? Is 4:00 p.m. OK?
Samantha: OK. Please send me directions!
Melissa: Take Main Street to Third Avenue. Cross the bridge. Turn left at Harry's. Take the next right. Baker's is the building on the corner. See you tomorrow!

WRITING

Once students have written down directions for each other to get to different places around town, have them consider how they would do the same thing using different modes of transportation. If they gave directions for driving, have them give directions for the same route but using public transportation, riding a bike, or walking.

SPEAKING

Invite students to use a map app on their phones to bring up their current location and get directions to another location. Ask them to describe the route the app gives them and also check the alternative routes the app suggests. Which route would they take? Would they take a different route altogether?

GO TO page xv for LANGUAGE AND LIFE step-by-step instructions.

Language and Life

Problem-solving – A Neighborhood Guide

A 5.06 **Read the magazine article. Is Katy happy in her new neighborhood? Discuss.**

A New Place to Call Home

Name: Katy Morgan
From: Austin, Texas

I'm Katy. I'm from the United States, but now I live in a small neighborhood outside Cusco, Peru. Cusco is an amazing city. Machu Picchu is very close by. I have my own business here. I organize eco-tours around the area.

Life in Peru is great. I speak Spanish, so communication isn't a problem. There are other differences. In the States, things happen fast and people run from place to place. Here, life is slow, and I like it that way!

My neighborhood is small, but there are stores, restaurants (amazing food!), and a beautiful main square (the Plaza de Armas) in the city center. I live in a one-bedroom apartment on a quiet street. There's a small coffee shop across from my house, so I hang out with my neighbors before work. People here like to get together and talk.

It's hard to find a place to live when you arrive in a new city. There's a great company called Home Abroad Rentals. They find apartments for people from other countries who are new to Cusco. They match people to the right home. I'm happy Cusco is the place I call home.

OBJECTIVE

In this lesson, students learn how to think critically about a part of a city or town. Students have to consider the features of a neighborhood. They will consider the needs of different groups of people. Point out that while one neighborhood may appeal to one person, it may not appeal to the next. These factors depend on people's varying needs at specific points in their lives because needs change at different stages of their lives.

PROCESS OPTIONAL 5.06

Students first analyze a magazine article written by a Texan living in Peru describing her new town. Then, they make suggestions for places to live in their city. They must understand the needs of the people in the profiles and consider what they know about their own city to evaluate where a suitable area would be for each person. Then, they write a guide for an area they know well. Finally, they discuss and analyze their guides with the class.

B Read the profiles of people who want to find a place to live in your city. Make notes about neighborhoods that are good for each person, and say why those places are good.

Profile 1
Name: James Quigley
Age: 28
From: Johannesburg, South Africa
Job: translator for a large tech company
Prefers: to live outside the town/city center; to live alone
Wants to find: a small house with a yard
Hobbies: swimming, cooking, going out to eat, seeing friends, biking

follow

Profile 2
Name: Christine Summers
Age: 23
From: Sydney, Australia
Job: English teacher
Prefers: to live in the town/city center; to have roommates
Wants to find: a one-bedroom apartment; a shared house
Hobbies: dancing, running, reading, traveling

follow

C **IN PAIRS** **Compare your ideas for the profiles.**

A: I think a good neighborhood for Christine is … because there's a park.

B: I think … is a good neighborhood for James because there are houses with yards.

D **IN PAIRS** **Complete a neighborhood guide for an area you know well.**

Neighborhood guide for: ______________________
Types of housing available: ______________________
Sports facilities: ______________________
Popular restaurants: ______________________
Good places to shop: ______________________
How to get around (bus/train): ______________________
Directions from housing to one or two other interesting places: ______________________

____

____

E **IN GROUPS** **Discuss your guides. Then share with the class.**

MAKE IT DIGITAL

Go online and look for more information about the neighborhood. Include any information you think is useful.

CLASSROOM MANAGEMENT

Giving feedback is a great life skill to master. Not everyone will be naturally able to give or receive feedback easily. Good feedback techniques require good active listening strategies. Tell students to approach feedback in three steps:

1 Listen carefully.

2 Say two or three positive things.

3 Suggest how it could be improved.

CULTURE NOTE

In Latin America, train travel is not as accessible as it is in Europe or Asia where it is a means of daily transportation for much of the population. Public transportation may vary from country to country.

MAKE IT DIGITAL

Two useful sites for finding information in English about a neighborhood are TripAdvisor (www.tripadvisor.com) and Yelp (www.yelp.com).

GO TO page xvii
for **UNIT REVIEW** step-by-step instructions.

UNIT 5

VOCABULARY review

SCORE: / 10

A Complete the sentences with words from the box.

across	boring	expensive	on	square
apartment	difficult	gym	popular	tiny

Jasper: I live near the university. There are many students here, so it's not an expensive part of town. I live in an old **1** [apartment] with only one room. It's **2** [tiny], but it's OK for me.

Kate: I live with my parents. It's a big house near the main **3** [square] in town, but there is nothing fun to do in the neighborhood. It's **4** [boring].

Ed: I have a new apartment **5** [on] the corner of Main and First. I like it, but I pay a lot—about $1,300 a month. It's a very **6** [expensive] neighborhood.

Kim: I love my neighborhood. There are fun coffee shops, great restaurants, and a new **7** [gym] to work out in. The neighborhood is **8** [popular] with students and families.

Neil: My new house is on Third Street. From here, cross the bridge and then turn left. It's **9** [across] from the park. It's not **10** [difficult] to find.

GRAMMAR review

SCORE: / 10

A Combine the two sentences into one.

1 Cusco is a city. Cusco is exciting.
Cusco is an exciting city.

2 It's a place. It's friendly.
It's a friendly place.

3 There are many neighborhoods. They're lively.
There are many lively neighborhoods.

4 There's a market. It's very interesting.
There's a very interesting market.

5 Cusco has some buildings. They're very old.
Cusco has some very old buildings.

B Match the sentence beginning (1–5) to the sentence end (a–e). Write the letter.

1 There are [c]
2 There is [e]
3 There's no [d]
4 Is there [b]
5 Are there [a]

a many Cuban restaurants?
b an airport near the city?
c people from all over the world.
d train to Everglades National Park.
e a zoo with lots of different animals.

16–20 correct: You can talk about places in a neighborhood and give directions. You can use adjectives and *there is*/*there are*.
0–15 correct: Look again at the Vocabulary and Grammar sections in the unit.

TOTAL SCORE: / 20

WHAT DO YOU KNOW NOW? Look back at page 47 and add the words you know now to the boxes.

GO TO page xviii
for **STUDY SKILLS** step-by-step instructions.

STUDY SKILLS RESEARCH SKILLS

Take the quiz about research skills. Go to **Study Skills** on page 131 to find the answers. Then learn more about research skills.

1 About ... people around the world work full-time as researchers.
a 5.3 million **b** 7.8 million **c** 10 million

2 It takes the average person ... to read one page.
a one minute **b** two minutes **c** three minutes

3 Only 12% of teachers say their students use books for research.
a true **b** false

4 About 95% of internet users believe that most or all of the information they find online is true.
a true **b** false

Correct answer: It's 52.8%.

CLASSROOM MANAGEMENT

Before starting the review section, give students some time to glance over the unit and review the vocabulary and grammar sections in each lesson. Once they have looked over the material, they will find the review section more relevant.

ALTERNATIVE ACTIVITY

For fast finishers, tell them to write sentences similar to those in GRAMMAR **A**. Have them exchange the sentences they wrote with a partner, then read and combine them into one.

FURTHER DISCUSSION

Put students in groups of three and ask the following questions for them to discuss:

- Do you find it easy to give directions?
- Do you get lost often?
- Can you think of a time you got lost? What did you do?
- What is the best map or a GPS app?

GO TO page vi
for UNIT OPENER step-by-step instructions.

UNIT 6 Going Viral

WHAT DO YOU ALREADY KNOW?

1 Think of words about social media and the internet. Write the words or draw the icons of apps you use.
2 **IN PAIRS** Share and compare your information. Add more words to your lists.

Social media

Internet

STUDENTS MAY ALREADY KNOW:

- **Social media:** Facebook, post, photos, friends, to friend someone, apps.
- **Internet:** upload, download, surf, search, Google.

VIDEO

DISCUSS & SHARE

3 **IN GROUPS** Watch the video and answer the question.
SYM How much time do you spend online?

GO TO page xx
for VIDEOS IN SYM step-by-step instructions.

In this unit, you will ...

- talk about media use, computer equipment, and online business.
- use thinking skills: analyze and evaluate.
- read about social media use and employment.
- use strategies to keep talking by showing interest and asking follow-up questions.
- use critical thinking skills to analyze the pros and cons of a digital detox.
- follow a social media marketing manager to learn about this job and the skills needed for this industry.

WHAT DO YOU ALREADY KNOW?

If you notice students are struggling to understand what to do, you can provide one or two examples to help them get started:

- **Gadgets:** smartphone, tablet, webcam
- **Popular apps:** WhatsApp, Facebook, Twitter, Instagram

VIDEO

Before viewing, ask:

How does Sonya like to stay connected? *online and on her phone*
How does Alex like to stay connected? *face-to-face*

After viewing, put the continuum on the board.

devices —— face-to-face

Have students mark the continuum and explain how they stay concted.

DISCUSS & SHARE

Take a poll of students' online activity time. Ask who spends less than an hour a day online, who spends one to three hours online, and who spends three or more hours online. Talk about the pros and cons of spending time online.

GO TO page x

for **READING** step-by-step instructions.

LESSON 1 You and Social Media

READING

A IN PAIRS Discuss the social media apps you use and how often you use them.

A: I use … every day. *B: I never use …*

B 6.01 READING SKILL—Predict information Read the article and guess the missing information. Then check your answers below.

Social Media Use and Employment

Do some things about social media make you **angry**? If your answer is "yes," read on …

Young adults are spending a lot of time on social media these days. According to Statista, about **1** ___2.5___ billion people use social media. Are you **surprised**? That's about one-third of the world's population! In the US, around **2** ___98___% of people aged 16 to 24 have social media accounts. On average, they spend **3** ___109___ minutes per day—almost two hours—on social media. **4** ___China___ has more social media users than any other country—596 million. That number is growing all the time.

Many people are **afraid** that employers are getting information about them from social media. This information can make them feel **embarrassed**.

A study by Statista from 2017 shows that **5** ___61___% of employers look at social media profiles before they hire someone. So, be very careful and check your settings. Keep your social media profiles for family and friends only.

Read more

Answer Key for Reading B:
1 2.5; **2** 98; **3** 109; **4** China; **5** 61

GO TO page vii

for **VOCABULARY** step-by-step instructions.

VOCABULARY

A Read the sentences (1–4) and match the words in bold to the emojis (a–d). Write the letter.

1. 2.5 billion people use social media! Really? I'm **surprised**! ___b___
2. I'm **embarrassed** when I tell people I don't use social media. ___c___
3. I'm **mad** when there are ads on social media sites all the time. ___a___
4. Don't be **afraid** to take a break from social media. ___d___

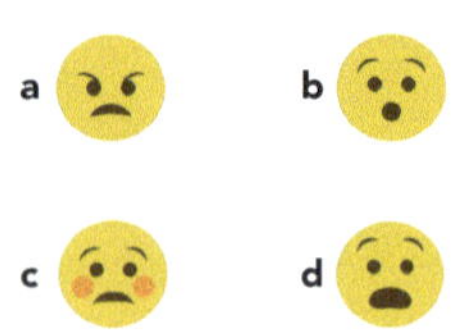

B THINKING SKILL—Analyze Which of these opinions do you agree with? Why?

1. Social media friends are not real friends.
2. Social media is a great way to share information.

MAKE IT YOURS

Which emojis do you use most often? Send an emoji to a classmate to say how you are feeling. Ask that person to say in English how you are feeling.

READING OPTIONAL 6.01

Some popular social media apps are:

- Facebook: for keeping up with friends.
- Instagram: for posting photos.
- Snapchat: for sending pictures and messages.
- Twitter: for posting short messages, photos, and videos.

Students should be aware of their settings on social media: they should activate privacy settings so only those they know will be able to see their information.

You may like to discuss other apps that students use every day.

VOCABULARY

Ask students what other emojis they use to communicate emotions. Additionally, ask them about shorthand. What shorthand do they use to communicate emotions—for example, *LOL* (laughing out loud)? Do they use shorthand in their own language, or have they adopted English shorthand in their everyday lives?

GRAMMAR present progressive

A Read the examples. Then choose the correct option to complete the rules.

Young adults are spending a lot of time on social media these days.
Employers are now using social media sites.
They're getting information about future employees.

1 Use the present progressive for things that are happening every day / now.
2 Form the present progressive with the verb *be* + *–ing* / infinitive.
3 When a verb ends in *–e*, remove *–e* and add *–ing*: *use* becomes *using*, *take* becomes *takeing* / *taking*.
4 When a verb ends in a vowel + consonant, double the last consonant and add *–ing*: *get* becomes *getting*, *stop* becomes *stopping* / *stoping*.
5 When a verb ends in *–ie*, change the *–ie* to *–y* and add *–ing*: *lie* becomes *lying*, *tie* becomes *tying* / *tieing*.

For more practice, go to page 149.

GO TO page viii for GRAMMAR step-by-step instructions.

B Complete the conversation with the present progressive.

Jenny: Hi, Gemma. **1** What ___are___ you ___doing___ (do)?
Gemma: **2** Oh, I___'m/am looking___ (look) at things online.
Jenny: **3** Why___aren't___ you ___studying___? (not study)
Gemma: **4** I ___'m/am taking___ (take) a break. So what's up?
Jenny: **5** I ___'m/am calling___ (call) because I need help.
Gemma: Are you worried about the exam tomorrow?
Jenny: **6** No, I___'m/am buying___ (buy) some new shoes online. Can you look at them?
Gemma: Sure!

C IN PAIRS Role-play a phone conversation. Talk about what you are doing now and how you are feeling.

SPEAKING

GO TO page xii for SPEAKING step-by-step instructions.

A Complete the table with the things you are usually doing at these times and days.

	Tuesday	Friday	Saturday
7 a.m.			
12 p.m.			
6 p.m.			
11 p.m.			

B IN PAIRS Ask and answer questions about what you are doing at these times. Use the Confident Communicator box to help you.

A: It's 7 a.m. on Sunday. What are you doing? *B: I'm sleeping.*
A: And how are you feeling? *B: I'm relaxed!*

CONFIDENT COMMUNICATOR
START TALKING

To ask about feelings, say: *Are you OK? Is everything all right? What's the matter?*
To describe how you are feeling, say: *I'm feeling … today. / I'm sad about … / I'm happy about … / I'm tired / I'm sleepy / I'm hungry.*

GRAMMAR Extra Practice

To practice the present progressive further, have students work in pairs and wonder out loud what people they know are doing right now. For example, *I know my mom is working. She's probably answering emails and talking on the phone. My dad is probably having lunch,* and so on. Have them look for coincidences. For example, *A: My dad is traveling to work. He's driving now. B: Mine, too!*

SPEAKING Alternative Activity

Play I'm Reading a Book. Ask everyone to stand in a large circle. Do an action (e.g., reading a book) but say you are doing something else (e.g., *I'm brushing my teeth.*). The person on your left should do the action (brushing teeth) but say a different action (e.g., *I'm watching TV.*). The following student acts out watching TV, but says another action, and so on. Have students go faster and faster around the circle.

LESSON 2 Vlogging

VOCABULARY technology equipment

A Match the words from the box to the pictures.

microphone	headphones	keyboard	screen
smartphone	mouse	tablet	webcam

1 
smartphone

2 
tablet

3 
webcam

4 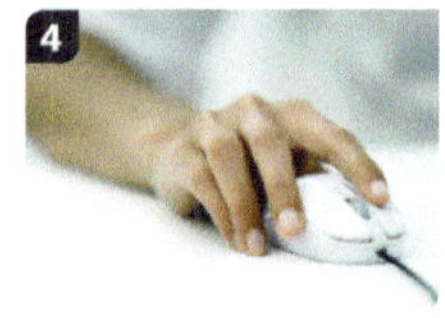
mouse

5 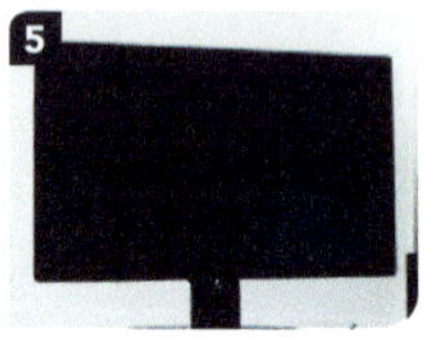
monitor

6 
keyboard

7 
headphones

8 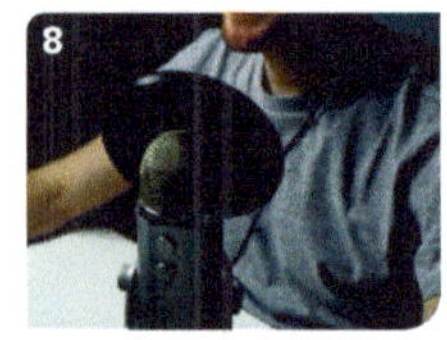
microphone

B Complete the information about vlogging with the words in the box.

microphone smartphone tablets webcam

So, you want to be a vlogger?

Here are some of the things you need.

To film your vlog, you need a video camera. If you are sitting at home with your computer, you can use the **1** webcam. Some vloggers use the camera on their **2** smartphone to make videos. The screens are very small, but they work fine. **3** Tablets are also OK to use, but a computer makes your vlog look more professional. When you speak, you use a **4** microphone. People need to hear what you are saying, so get a good one.

Happy vlogging!

MAKE IT YOURS

Compound words are two different words put together.

desk + *top* = ***desktop***

web + *camera* = ***webcam***

What other compound words do you know?

GO TO page xi

for **LISTENING** step-by-step instructions.

LISTENING

A IN PAIRS Match vlog types from the box to the pictures.

computer gaming food product reviews travel

1 
computer gaming

2 
product reviews

3 
travel

4 
food

VOCABULARY

You may want to define *vlogging* for the class. A *vlog* is a video blog that is posted online.

CULTURE NOTE

Vloggers are usually active on YouTube and they were on Vine, which was bought by Twitter. Some interesting, famous, or well-known vloggers are Shane Dawson, Emma Chamberlain, and Wengie. Latin American students will most likely know Yuya, a Mexican beauty vlogger with over 20 million subscribers.

MAKE IT YOURS

More technology compound words are: *headphones*, *website*, *online*, *offline*, *laptop*, *smartphone*, *voicemail*, *email*, and *filename*. Invite students to use an online dictionary if they have any questions.

B 6.02 Listen to the vloggers and match them to the vlog types in A.

1 Speaker 1: food Speaker
2 Speaker 2: travel Speaker
3 Speaker 3: computer gaming Speaker
4 Speaker 4: product reviews Speaker

C 6.03 LISTENING SKILL—Listen for fact and opinion Listen and choose *Fact* or *Opinion*.

1 Fact / Opinion
2 Fact / Opinion
3 Fact / Opinion
4 Fact / Opinion
5 Fact / Opinion

D THINKING SKILL—Evaluate Discuss the statement. Do you agree? What do you think makes a good vlogger?

A good vlogger is like the boy or girl next door—someone who feels like I do about things.

GRAMMAR present progressive vs. simple present

A Read the sentences. Underline the present progressive verbs. Circle the simple present verbs.

1 Right now, I'm using my laptop to upload videos …
2 I spend about six months of the year away from home …
3 I'm studying to be a computer programmer.
4 People always ask me for advice …

B Choose the correct option to complete the rules.

1 We use the simple present to talk about things that happen regularly / now or around now.
2 We use the present progressive to talk about things that are happening regularly / now or around now.

For more practice, go to page 150.

C Choose the correct option. Is the question in simple present or present progressive?

1 Where is your laptop?
 a simple present b present progressive
2 What are you watching on your laptop?
 a simple present b present progressive
3 What kind of camera do you use to make vlogs?
 a simple present b present progressive
4 What famous vloggers are you following?
 a simple present b present progressive

D IN PAIRS Ask and answer the questions from C.

SPEAKING

A Write complete questions in your notebook with the words given.

1 What / do / do?
2 What / do / generally / vlog / about?
3 How / usually / make / your vlog?
4 How / often / vlog?

B IN PAIRS Role-play. Use the Confident Communicator box to help you.

Student A: Imagine you are a well-known music vlogger.
Student B: Imagine you are a famous skateboarding vlogger. Ask and answer questions in A to find out more about your partner.

C IN GROUPS Discuss which vlogs you watch. Do you have your own vlog?

CONFIDENT COMMUNICATOR
KEEP TALKING

It's important to show interest when someone is talking to you:
Oh, right. *I see.* *Uh-huh.* *Really?*
When things are very interesting, your voice is usually higher and louder:
No way! *Wow, that's amazing!* *You're kidding!*

GO TO page 142 for AUDIO SCRIPT.

GO TO page 142 for AUDIO SCRIPT.

1 What do you do?
2 What are you vlogging about?
3 How do you usually make your vlog?
4 How often do you vlog?

LISTENING

LISTENING SKILL—Listen for fact and opinion

Have students listen for clues when listening for fact or opinion. People often use statistics to talk about facts, so numbers and percentages are good clues that facts are being stated. Opinions will often be preceded by *I think* … or *In my opinion* … Opinions are subjective. Facts are objective and can be verified.

GRAMMAR Extra Practice

Ask students to write five facts about themselves in the simple present and then add information in the present progressive. For example, *I'm a student. I'm studying engineering. I'm 21. I'm planning a big party next week.*

CULTURE NOTE

How do vloggers make money? Lilly Singh made $10.5 million dollars in 2017. YouTubers make money through views. Every 1,000 views pays two to four dollars according to www.lifehack.org.

Ask students if they know any other famous vloggers.

LESSON 3 Buying and Selling Online

LISTENING

A Check (✓) the things you like to buy and sell in online stores.

☐ books
☐ clothes
☐ electronics (smartphones, headphones)
☐ music, movies, video games
☐ sports equipment (soccer balls, athletic shoes, baseball bats)
☐ other: ______________________

GO TO page 142 for AUDIO SCRIPT.

B 6.04 LISTENING SKILL—Listen for the main idea Listen to an interview with an internet business owner. Then answer the question.

1 What does he buy and sell? (athletic) clothes

C 6.04 Listen again and answer the questions.

1 How old is Luca?
2 Where does he buy and sell things?
3 How much money does he make per item?
4 How often does Luca add new pictures to his website?
5 What is his day job?

1 20 (years old)
2 buys: online; sells: online (website), an app for buying and selling
3 $40–$50
4 every two or three days
5 He works in a restaurant.

D THINKING SKILL—Evaluate Consider some of the differences between shopping online and shopping in a store. What do you prefer? Why?

I like shopping in a store because I can see and touch what I'm buying.

VOCABULARY technology phrases

GO TO page 143 for AUDIO SCRIPT.

A 6.05 Listen and complete the phrases with words from the box.

go post send take update upload

1 ___send___ a text message
2 ___upload___ pictures
3 ___post___ comments
4 ___update___ my profile
5 ___go___ viral
6 ___take___ a selfie

B Match the phrases from A (1–6) to the definitions (a–f). Write the number.

a take a picture of yourself on a smartphone _6_
b write your opinion about something online _3_
c communicate by typing on your smartphone _1_
d become very popular on the internet _5_
e copy a picture to the internet _2_
f put new information about yourself on a social media site _4_

PRONUNCIATION /ŋ/

GO TO page ix for PRONUNCIATION step-by-step instructions.

A 6.06 Listen and notice the /ŋ/ sound for the letters *–ng*.

1 kin king
2 sin sing
3 thin thing

B 6.07 IN PAIRS Listen and practice saying the sentences. Is your partner using the /ŋ/ sound correctly?

1 Sing this song.
2 The teacher is talking.
3 I'm listening to music.

LISTENING

Discuss online purchasing disasters you and your students have had. Ask *Have you bought something that didn't fit and had trouble returning it? Have you bought something that arrived damaged? What about quality? Have you bought something that looked very different in real life from how it looked in the photo?*

LISTENING SKILL—Listen for the main idea

In English, the main idea usually comes early in the conversation, and then supporting details follow. This can be different in other languages. In Spanish, often the supporting details lead up to the main idea.

VOCABULARY

Have students practice saying the phrases with the correct intonation. Then have them use the phrases in *Wh–* questions. For example, *How many times a day do you send text messages?*

WRITING

A Check (✓) the details to include when you want to sell a product online.

- ☑ information about the product (name, type, color)
- ☑ what it does (takes pictures, plays music, etc.)
- ☐ where it is from
- ☑ condition (excellent, good, used, never used, etc.)
- ☐ why you're selling it
- ☑ the price

B Read and compare the two social media ads. Then discuss the questions.

1 Which ad do you like more?
2 Which ad makes you want to buy the headphones?

A

A pair of headphones for sale. They are good for listening to music. They are white. They are in good condition. They come from China. They cost $60. I am selling them for $45 because I want the money to buy new headphones.

follow

B

Hi! I'm selling my BodeA345 headphones. White. They're amazing! Fantastic sound. Very comfortable. Excellent condition. $40

follow

C Write *A* or *B*.

This ad ...

1 uses positive adjectives. __B__
2 doesn't use complete sentences. __B__
3 doesn't use the same phrases for every sentence. __B__
4 gives information that isn't important. __A__

D Write a social media ad for something you want to sell online in your notebook.

SPEAKING

A Write sentences in your notebook about how you use technology and how often you do it.

I upload pictures to my social media profile about once a week.
I don't take selfies on my smartphone very often.

B IN GROUPS Discuss your online activity and how you use technology. Use the Confident Communicator box to help you.

CONFIDENT COMMUNICATOR
KEEP TALKING

To keep a conversation going, it's a good idea to ask for more information. When someone gives you a *yes/no* answer, you can ask follow-up questions. They usually begin with *How, Where, When, What,* and *Who.*
Do you take selfies?
How often do you take them?
What social media sites do you use?

GO TO page xiv for WRITING step-by-step instructions.

WRITING

After completing the writing exercises, do a gallery walk. Ask students to post their social media ads around the room and have everyone circulate, reading them as if they were viewing exhibits in an art gallery. You may want to give students play money and they could bargain for the things they want to "buy."

SPEAKING

Before starting this section, encourage students to doodle, draw icons and charts, and write sentences about how they use technology and how often they use it. Encourage them to jot down as many ideas as they want to. Draw students' attention to the vocabulary on the previous page and let them know they can use the phrases they learned. Tell them they don't have to use all the ideas they wrote down—it will become clear to them which ideas are the best ones for the speaking activity.

GO TO page xv
for LANGUAGE AND LIFE step-by-step instructions.

Language and Life

Critical Thinking – A Digital Detox

A 6.08 **Read the article. Then answer the questions.**

Digital Detox

How to Do a Digital Detox

June 21 12:10

Are you spending too much time using your phone? Check the things that are true for you to find out:

- I check social media before I get out of bed. ☐
- I send messages while I have breakfast. ☐
- I often take my phone to the bathroom. ☐
- I never go out without my phone. ☐

Did you check three or four? Then, it may be time for a digital detox. Mandy Morgan, a social media expert, gives us this advice ...

"This isn't about tech devices," she explains. "It's about understanding what is healthy. People usually feel good when they don't use their smartphones all the time."

Morgan says that a seven-day detox helps with your sleep, your studies, and how you feel. She asks people to check their screen time and count how many times a day they pick up their phone.

When you do a digital detox, you don't have your phone all the time. For seven days, you practice when and where you use your smartphone. You learn to leave your phone at home sometimes.

Marcia Estefan (DJ Blade), 23, is a club DJ from Brasilia. She is also studying to be a doctor. "I use my phone all the time," she explains. "I never think about how often I look at my screen." These days Marcia doesn't use her phone often. She rarely takes it out with her in the evening. "It makes me think about how I use technology and that's a good thing."

Before the Digital Detox
Screen Time Per Day: 3 hours 20 minutes
Picks Up Her Phone: 56 times a day

After the Digital Detox
Screen Time Per Day: 1 hour 50 minutes
Picks Up Her Phone: 23 times a day

Read more

1 Mandy Morgan says tech devices are bad for your health. Yes / No
2 You do a digital detox for one month. Yes / No
3 A digital detox can help you in different areas of your life. Yes / No
4 Marcia thinks that doing a digital detox is a good idea. Yes / No

64 Unit 6 Going Viral

OBJECTIVE

In this lesson, students learn how to think critically about their use of digital devices. Students will consider their behavior related to their gadgets and think about the positive outcomes of not using them for a period of time. Point out to students that undertaking a digital detox is a serious commitment but that there are some proven benefits and they should consider trying it.

PROCESS OPTIONAL 6.08

Students first read an article about doing a digital detox. The writer outlines the process and reports on the results. Students consider the pros and cons of doing a digital detox themselves. There will be advantages and disadvantages of not using their phones, and there are rules that will need to be followed. Then, they do their own digital detox and make notes. Finally, students make a short video describing the experience.

B **IN PAIRS** **Discuss the questions.**

1 How much screen time do you have every day?
2 Do you think you use your phone too much? Be honest!

C **IN GROUPS** **Consider the pros (+) and cons (–) of doing a digital detox. Add other ideas of your own.**

Pros (+)
have time to think in class
have real conversations
your ideas: ______________________________

Cons (–)
the internet helps us study/learn
we know what our family/friends are doing
your ideas: ______________________________

D **Read the digital detox rules. As a class, decide if you want to have a digital detox for one class or one day.**

Digital detox rules
- Make your classroom a phone-free zone. No phones allowed!
- Put your phone in your pocket when you are talking or eating.
- Put your phone away on your way to/from school.
- Keep your phone on airplane mode in class, or leave it at home for a day.

E **Do the digital detox and make notes about how you feel.**

MAKE IT DIGITAL

Record a video on your smartphone about how you feel after a digital detox. Share your videos as a class. What did your classmates think?

CLASSROOM MANAGEMENT

Encourage students to reflect mindfully as they go about their days without their gadgets. Suggest that they keep a written diary along the way.

CULTURE NOTE

In Latin America, smartphones have proliferated. Some advantages to everyone carrying a phone in their pocket is that when crimes are spotted, often video evidence is taken. The downside of it is that there can be grave invasions of privacy. Trolling, fake news, and cyberbullying are the worst elements of the social media age.

MAKE IT DIGITAL

Remind students to think about lighting and sound when they are making their videos. They can make the video in a testimonial style, simply speaking into the camera. Tell students to record in a quiet, private place without the sounds of other voices or traffic to interrupt their recording.

GO TO page xvii
for UNIT REVIEW step-by-step instructions.

UNIT 6

VOCABULARY review

SCORE: / 10

A Choose the correct option.

1 Do you want to play / go / take a selfie with me?
2 I'm very afraid / mad / embarrassed. My new printer doesn't work.
3 Please post / download / take a comment after you read my blog.
4 I always use my smartphone to play / send / do a text message.
5 Please use my laptop to create / play / go an online profile.
6 It's easy to download an app with this headphones / tablet / webcam.
7 I sometimes use my desktop to go / read / upload a picture.
8 I'm surprised / afraid / embarrassed. She is giving away her new song.
9 I be / use / update my profile online once or twice a month.
10 Look into your mouse / webcam / keyboard to make a video.

GRAMMAR review

SCORE: / 10

Students can also use the full, uncontracted forms or alternative contractions for 2, 3, 6, 8, and 9.
2 am watching
3 am studying
6 am using
8 are talking
9 aren't / are not studying

A Complete the conversation with the correct simple present or present progressive form of the verb in parentheses.

Clare: Hey! What **1** ___are___ you ___doing___ (do)?
Matt: Not much. I **2** ___'m watching___ (watch) a movie. You?
Clare: I **3** ___'m studying___ (study) at the library.
Matt: Again?
Clare: You know I usually **4** ___come___ (come) here after class. Quick question: **5** ___Do___ you ___use___ (use) headphones with your laptop?
Matt: Sure. I **6** ___'m using___ (use) them right now.
Clare: What kind?
Matt: They're called AudioPlus. Electronics World **7** ___sells___ (sell) them.
Clare: Good to know. I need some. The people here are noisy! They **8** ___'re talking___ (talk) a lot. They **9** ___'re not studying___ (not study)!
Matt: Well, get these. They always **10** ___work___ (work) great!
Clare: Thanks! Gotta go—see you tomorrow.

16–20 correct: You can talk about emotions and technology. You can use the present progressive and simple present.
0–15 correct: Look again at the Vocabulary and Grammar sections in the unit.

TOTAL SCORE: / 20

WHAT DO YOU KNOW NOW? Look back at page 57 and add the words you know now to the box.

GO TO page xix
for FOLLOW A PRO step-by-step instructions.

FOLLOW A PRO MARKETING

Take the quiz about marketing. Go to Follow A Pro on page 132 to find the answers. Then learn more about the marketing field.

1 In New York, around … people work in marketing full-time.
a 17,000 b 31,000 c 52,000

2 More customers go to a website when the company has a regular blog.
a true b false

3 How do 90% of businesses respond when customers complain?
a by social media b by email c by phone

4 When customers have a bad experience with a company, about 4% complain. What do the other 96% do?
a They buy the product again. b They tell their friends. c They never buy from that company again.

CLASSROOM MANAGEMENT

Once students have completed the vocabulary and grammar review exercises, post the answers in small print in different places in the classroom. Tell students that as they finish, they are free to go and check the answers. Give students sticky notes and have them write down the numbers of the items they found difficult or confusing. Collect and check the sticky notes and address just the areas of difficulty during class feedback.

FURTHER DISCUSSION

Put students in groups of three and ask the following questions for them to discuss:

- Are you addicted to your gadgets?
- Do you have all your information backed up?
- What would you do if your phone was stolen?
- Do you follow any vloggers?
- What do you spend most of your online time doing?
- Are you concerned about the health effects of excessive screen time?

GO TO page vi
for **UNIT OPENER** step-by-step instructions.

UNIT 7 Fit for Life

WHAT DO YOU ALREADY KNOW?

1 Think of words you know about popular sports. Write a list of words for individual sports and team sports.

2 **IN PAIRS** Share and compare your information. Add more words to your lists.

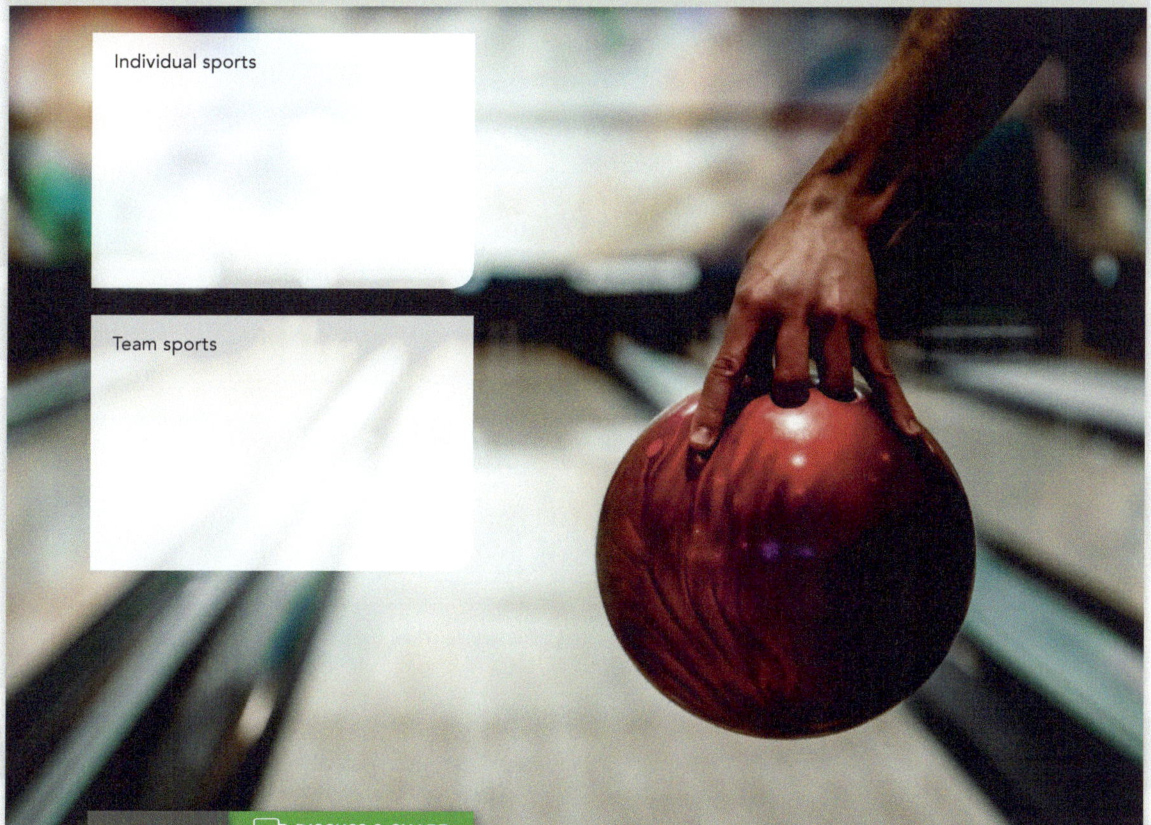

Individual sports

Team sports

STUDENTS MAY ALREADY KNOW

- **Individual sports:** swimming, archery, diving.
- **Team sports:** baseball, soccer, volleyball.

VIDEO

DISCUSS & SHARE

3 **IN GROUPS** Watch the video and answer the question.
SYM Do you prefer individual or team sports?

GO TO page xx
for **VIDEOS IN SYM** step-by-step instructions.

In this unit, you will ...

- talk about the body, abilities, sports, and exercise.
- use thinking skills: analyze, decide, and evaluate.
- read about fitness gadgets.
- use strategies to start and keep talking by buying time and using your imagination.
- use decision-making skills to design an outdoor gym for your city.
- learn tips for effective group work.

WHAT DO YOU ALREADY KNOW?

If you notice students are struggling to understand what to do, you can provide one or two examples to help them get started:

- **Individual sports:** cycling, surfing, running
- **Team sports:** football, synchronized swimming, basketball

VIDEO

Before viewing, ask:

What sports does Jill like?
individual sports
What sports does Marcus like?
team sports

After viewing, put the continuum on the board.

individual —— team

Students mark the continuum and explain which individual or team sports they like.

DISCUSS & SHARE

In small groups, have students talk about what sports they like and why they like them. Ask *Do you prefer individual sports? Do you prefer team sports? Which ones do you prefer and why?* Also, have them discuss what sports they don't like and why.

GO TO page vii

for **VOCABULARY** step-by-step instructions.

LESSON 1 Fitness Gadgets

VOCABULARY

A IN PAIRS Look at the picture. Use words in the box to label the parts of the body.

arm back foot head knee leg shoulder neck

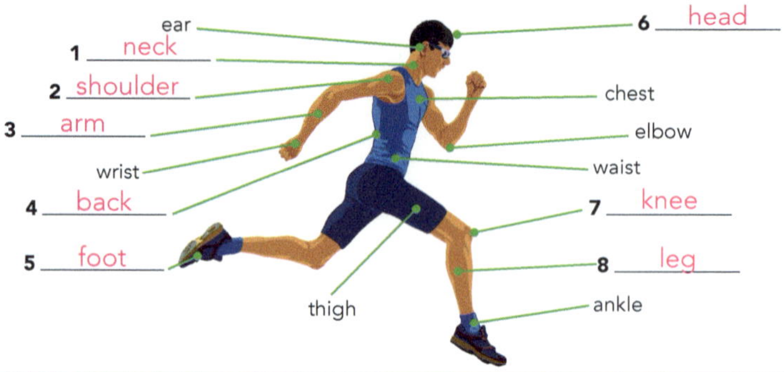

MAKE IT YOURS

Label any other parts of the body you know. Share your ideas in groups.

GO TO page x

for **READING** step-by-step instructions.

READING

A Match the words in the box to the pictures (1–4).

ankle sensor fitness tracker sports camera underwater headphones

1 
fitness tracker

2 
sports camera

3 
ankle sensor

4 
underwater headphones

1 fitness tracker
2 underwater headphones
3 sports camera
4 ankle sensor

B 7.01 READING SKILL—Read for gist Read the magazine article. Then complete with the gadget that matches the review.

New GADGET Reviews

Are you looking for a new fitness gadget? Four athletes give their opinion about these gadgets.

1 ____________ Daniella, Boston. This is great. You can wear it on your **arm** or your **ankle**. It records your steps, your calories, and your sleep. You can use it when you ride a bike, run, walk, play volleyball, do judo, and every kind of sport. $76 ★★★★½

2 ____________ Miguel, Puebla. I love swimming and listening to music at the same time. I can swim really fast when I listen to music. These go around your **neck** and fit in your **ears**. They're very comfortable. $200 ★★★½

3 ____________ Felix, Sagres. It can take videos when I'm surfing. But when I'm on my surfboard, I can't hold it in my **hand**. I put it on my surfboard instead. You can also wear it on your **head** or on your **shoulder**. It takes pictures, too. $152 ★★★★

4 ____________ Clare, Santa Fe. You wear it on your **foot** and it checks that you're running correctly. Can you wash it? No, you can't wash it, even when it's dirty. It's expensive, in my opinion, but it's useful for professional runners. $120 ★★½

C THINKING SKILL—Analyze Take a class survey. What gadgets do your classmates think are useful? Do you agree?

VOCABULARY

Practice the vocabulary by saying an action and asking students to name the part of the body used in the action (e.g., *eat: mouth, tongue, teeth, throat, stomach; run: arms, legs, thighs, knees, feet, lungs; scratch: fingers, fingernails; smile: mouth, face, eyes; sneeze: nose, eyes, lungs, throat*).

READING OPTIONAL 7.01

Before reading the magazine article, ask students what fitness gadgets they have and have them explain what they use them for.

After reading the magazine article, discuss how technology has changed sports. One example might be the challenge camera in tennis. Now players can have a close call checked on camera.

READING SKILL—Read for gist

Reading for gist is to find out what the story or article is about. The best way to approach reading for gist is to read the text quickly to see which topic is the most obvious.

GRAMMAR *can/can't* (ability)

A **Read the magazine article in READING B again. Underline the sentences with *can* and *can't*.**

B **Choose the correct option to complete the rules.**

1 Use *can/can't* to talk about ...	**a** habits.	**b** abilities.
2 After *can/can't*, use a ...	**a** verb.	**b** noun.
3 The contraction of *cannot* is ...	**a** cant.	**b** can't.

For more practice, go to page 151.

C **Rewrite the sentences correctly.**

1. I can to play cricket. I can play cricket.
2. She cans dance. She can dance.
3. Can not you swim? Can't you swim?
4. Yes, I can't. Yes, I can. / No, I can't.
5. He no can't play tennis. He can't play tennis. / He cannot play tennis.

D **IN PAIRS Ask and answer questions about the sports you can and can't do.**

GO TO page viii
for **GRAMMAR** step-by-step instructions.

PRONUNCIATION *can/can't*

A **7.02 Listen. Choose the words you hear.**

1. Can / Can't you swim?
2. I can / can't.
3. Can / Can't you come to a new water polo class with me?
4. Sorry, I can / can't. I play tennis then.

B **IN PAIRS Practice saying the conversation. Notice the /t/ sound in *can't*.**

GO TO page ix
for **PRONUNCIATION** step-by-step instructions.

SPEAKING

A **Check (✓) the things you can or can't do. Complete with your own ideas.**

	Can	Can't
1 play soccer	☐	☐
2 sing	☐	☐
3 cook Italian food	☐	☐
4 ____________	☐	☐
5 ____________	☐	☐

B **IN GROUPS Ask and answer questions about your abilities. Discuss information about what you like or dislike. Use the Confident Communicator box to help you.**

A: Can you surf? *B: Yes, I can, and I really enjoy it.*

CONFIDENT COMMUNICATOR
START TALKING

To ask about abilities and likes, use these phrases:
Can you ...?
Yes, I can ..., and I really enjoy it.
Yes, I can ..., but I don't really like it.
No, I can't ..., but I can ... Can you ...?

GO TO page xii
for **SPEAKING** step-by-step instructions.

GRAMMAR

For practice with *can* and *can't* for ability, play This Animal Can. Have students work in pairs or small groups. Describe what an animal can and can't do and have students guess the animal. For example, *This animal can't walk backward. It's a bird, but it can't fly. You can only find it in Australia. (an emu)*

PRONUNCIATION

It can be difficult to hear *can't* clearly. Let students know that there might be confusion with this pronunciation. That's normal. If they can't understand, they should ask for clarification. Have them listen a number of times to the sentences to distinguish the difference and have them practice saying the sentences.

SPEAKING Alternative Activity

Play Keep Talking. Have students work in pairs, ask each other follow-up questions about the topic, and keep talking with no pauses for 2 minutes. Each time there is a pause, a question should be asked: *Can you swim? Yes, I can. Do you like it? Yes, I love it.*

LESSON 2 Unusual Ball Games

VOCABULARY ball game action words

A IN PAIRS Match the verbs from the box to the pictures (1–8).

bounce	catch	hit	hold
kick	pass	throw	touch

1 
bounce

2 
catch

3 
kick

4 
pass

5 
throw

6 
hit

7 
touch

8 
hold

B Choose the correct option.

1 Basketball players can bounce / kick the ball during the game.
2 In soccer, the players use their feet to pass / hold the ball.
3 Lacrosse players hold / catch the ball in a net.
4 Football players throw / bounce the ball between them.
5 You kick / hit the ball with a bat in baseball.
6 Tennis players usually hold / kick the ball in their left hand when they serve.

C IN PAIRS Think about popular ball games in your country. Talk about what the players can and can't do with the ball.

In basketball, players can bounce the ball. They can't kick the ball.

GO TO page xi

for **LISTENING** step-by-step instructions.

LISTENING

A Look at the pictures and think about the questions.

1 What do you know about these sports?
2 Do they look like other sports you know?

Bossaball

360ball

footgolf

VOCABULARY

Have students practice the ballgame actions. Have students work in pairs; one student acts out the action while the other student guesses. Then they switch.

Name a sport and elicit the actions allowed. For example, *basketball—You can throw. You can bounce the ball. You can pass the ball to another player. You can catch the ball. You can't kick the ball. You win if you can score more points than the other team.*

LISTENING

Encourage students to research and describe unusual sports. One unusual sport might be curling. Heavy, round stones are pushed down the ice toward a mark to see who can get the closest. You can't touch the stones, but you can sweep in front of the stones with a small broom to keep them moving.

B 7.03 LISTENING SKILL—Listen for the main idea Listen and write the name of the ball games from A.

1 David: Bossaball. 2 Claudia: 360ball. 3 Marco: footgolf.

GO TO page 143 for AUDIO SCRIPT.

C IN PAIRS THINKING SKILL—Deduce Think about the three sports you learned about and discuss the question.

Which game do you think people your age want to play?

MAKE IT REAL

When people talk about the sports they do regularly, they often leave out the verb *go*.
I hike. = I go hiking.
I swim. = I go swimming.

GRAMMAR adverbs of manner

A Read the examples. Then complete the rules.

I can throw the ball hard.
You have to play fast.
My friend plays it well.
You have to kick the ball gently.
I can kick it easily.

1 Use adverbs of manner to describe an action / a thing.
2 Adverbs of manner go before / after the main verb.
3 To form an adverb of manner, add –ly to the adjective.
4 When a word ends in *–y*, add –ily.
5 Some irregular adverbs are the same word as the adjective: *fast–fast, hard–* hard.
6 One irregular adverb looks completely different from the adjective: *good–* well.

For more practice, go to page 151.

B Choose the correct form of the adverb or adjective.

1 Please drive careful / carefully.
2 Fernando is a slow / slowly swimmer.
3 Todd is a fast runner. He runs good / well.
4 This is a library. Please speak quiet / quietly.
5 Patti speaks angry / angrily to me sometimes.

C IN PAIRS Write activities from the unit in your notebook. Add adverbs to the things you can and can't do. Then ask and answer questions.

A: I can't cook Italian food well. Can you? *B: No, I can't, but I can run fast.*

SPEAKING

A IN PAIRS Make a list of famous athletes that you know and the sports that they play.

B IN PAIRS Play a game. Describe a famous athlete in one sentence. Your partner tries to guess who it is. Use the Confident Communicator box to help you.

CONFIDENT COMMUNICATOR START TALKING

Sometimes at the beginning of a conversation, you need time to organize your ideas. You can "buy time" by using these phrases:
Give me a minute to think about this …
Let me think about this for a second …

GRAMMAR

Elicit more adverbs of manner from the class and make a list for them to copy into their notebooks. Have students think of adverbs of manner in their first language and suggest cognates.

SPEAKING

Demonstrate activity **B** by giving students an example of a famous sportsperson in one sentence. For example, *This retired person who played for England can still play soccer very well and he probably plays with his sons and his famous, fashion-designer wife. (David Beckham)*

CONFIDENT COMMUNICATOR

Phrases like these give students more time to think and help them sound more natural. Have students watch TV in English and listen for fillers and phrases that give the speaker thinking time. More examples of these phrases are *That's a good question*, and *That's a really interesting question*.

LESSON 3 Exercising

VOCABULARY exercise words

A Match the words from the box to the exercises (1–8).

bend lift pull push stand stretch turn twist

1 
stretch

2 
pull

3 
lift

4 
bend

5 
push

6 
turn

7 
stand

8 
twist

B 7.04 Listen and complete the text.

One of the exercises that I do at the gym is very hard. It's called *the deadlift with an overhead press*. You **1** stand with your feet on the floor. Then, you **2** lift the weight (I use a 10 kilogram) up to your chest. You **3** hold it there for about five seconds. Then, you **4** bend your knees and **5** push the weight up above your head. It's not easy to **6** stretch your arms so they're straight. I can usually only hold it above my head for about 10 seconds. I'm amazed how weightlifters do this all the time!

LISTENING

GO TO page 144 for AUDIO SCRIPT.

A As a class, answer the question.

1 What do you think the word *deskercise* means?

B 7.05 LISTENING SKILL—Listen for specific information Listen and choose the word you hear for each exercise.

1 Exercise 1: shoulder / back
2 Exercise 2: legs / arms
3 Exercise 3: head / hand
4 Exercise 4: back / neck
5 Exercise 5: knee / foot

C 7.05 Listen again and do the exercises. How do they make you feel?

D THINKING SKILL—Evaluate Take a class survey. What parts of the body do you need to stretch when you work at a desk all day?

MAKE IT REAL

To "hit the gym" is a phrase people use when they decide to go to the gym regularly.
I need to get some exercise. I'm going to hit the gym.

VOCABULARY

Ask students to name as many exercises or exercise machines in the gym as they can. Then have them link the exercises or exercise machines to verbs. For example, *push-ups—Push your body straight up from the floor using your arms. Keep your body and your legs straight.*

LISTENING Extra Practice

Have students download a yoga app on their phones and listen to it on their own time. A nice, free meditation app is called Smiling Mind. Tell students to try it out at home or listen to it together as a class. It focuses on meditation, breathing, and connecting with your body.

MAKE IT REAL

Some more gym jargon is:

- set—a number of repetitions of the same exercise.
- superset—pairs of exercises done one immediately after the other that target muscles at different ends of the body.

Ask those who go to the gym to look up words they use in their routines.

WRITING

A Read the job ad. Which job are you interested in?

Are you free to work on weekends and holidays?

We are looking for people who can speak English to work at Our International Spa. We offer good pay, plus the use of our gym.

The jobs available are:

- teaching an adult volleyball class
- working in the café
- teaching swimming
- working in the beauty salon
- working at our reception desk

Please email *k.smith@ourspa.co* by Friday, June 21. Be sure to send a list of your abilities.

B Make a list of your abilities in your notebook. Then decide which jobs in the ad are right for you.

C Complete the email.

New Message

From: ____________

To: k.smith@ourspa.co Cc Bcc

Subject: Employment at Our International Spa

Dear Sir/Madam,

I'm writing about a job at Our International Spa. I am ____________ years old and I live in ____________.

I'm interested in the job of ____________.

I think I am a good person for this job because ____

____.

I look forward to hearing from you.

Regards,

____________.

Send

GO TO page xiv for **WRITING** step-by-step instructions.

SPEAKING

A IN PAIRS Role-play a job interview. Use the Confident Communicator box to help you.

Student A: You are K. Smith, the spa owner. Ask questions about why Student B wants the job.
Student B: Answer Student A's questions. Say why you are good for the job.

A: What job are you interested in? B: I'm interested in … because …

CONFIDENT COMMUNICATOR
KEEP TALKING

In speaking exercises in class, you don't need to say something that is true about yourself. The important thing is to say something. When you can't think of anything true to say, use your imagination.

WRITING

Some abilities students may want to mention, when applying for the job ad might be: *I can play volleyball. I can teach people how to play volleyball. I can teach people ball skills. I can motivate people. I can serve coffee. I can make coffee. I can prepare food. I can serve food. I have patience with customers. I can handle pressure well. I like working with people.*

SPEAKING

Ask students to record their interviews on their phones and watch them together. Ask them to comment on their performance. Remind them that positive feedback is constructive and that they should always say what they like about the performance before suggesting improvements in a tactful way.

GO TO page xv
for LANGUAGE AND LIFE step-by-step instructions.

Language and Life

Decision-making – Outdoor Gyms

A Look at the pictures and discuss the question as a class.

1 Where do you like to exercise?

B 7.06 Read the article. Then answer the questions below.

Outdoor Gyms Around the World

Many cities around the world have outdoor gyms. You see them on the beaches of Rio de Janeiro and in the parks in Shanghai or Spain. Here are some different outdoor gyms from around the world.

There is a famous outdoor gym called Muscle Beach in California, USA. Bodybuilders, weightlifters, athletes, and gymnasts train here. It's now a popular tourist attraction and you can buy a ticket to go see the place!

China has many outdoor gyms. This is the outdoor gym in the People's Park in Haikou. About 40% of China's 1.4 billion people use outdoor gyms regularly, according to Top.me. There are about 600,000 outdoor gyms in the country. They are all free!

A new outdoor gym in Sunnymead Park in Oxford, England, has some interesting technology. When people exercise on the machines, they create electricity. The electricity creates power for streetlights, smartphones, or tablets. Amazing!

Read more

1 Which gym can you pay money to visit? Muscle Beach
2 How many outdoor gyms are there in China? about 600,000
3 Where can you exercise to help the environment? Green Heart Park

74 Unit 7 Fit for Life

OBJECTIVE

In this lesson, students learn how to think critically about gym equipment that would be suitable for an outdoor gym. Students will have to consider the types of gym equipment available and the budget. Point out that these are the kinds of decisions that managers and leaders make for projects all the time.

PROCESS OPTIONAL 7.06

Students first read an article about three different outdoor gyms and answer questions. They analyze outdoor equipment to decide what part of the body it exercises. Then, they answer an email from the city to propose the best gym equipment for the new outdoor gym. The goal is to get the best equipment within the budget available, and so they should consider the pros and cons of each piece of equipment. Finally, they give a presentation to the class about their proposal. The presentation should include their reasons for choosing the equipment.

C IN PAIRS Look at the pictures and answer the question.

1 What parts of the body do you think the pieces of equipment are good for?

I think this equipment is good for the arms and the shoulders.

1 
skier, $1,100

2 
walker, $1,500

3 
arm and leg bike, $900

4 
waist twist, $1,080

5 
two-person leg push, $1,110

6 
two-person pull-down, $2,300

7 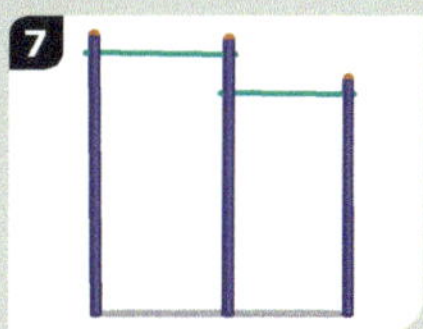
two-person pull-up, $2,300

D Read the email and answer the question.

1 What does the Director of Public Health want help with?

New Message

From: publichealth@gov.gov

To: citycouncil@gov.gov Cc Bcc

Subject: I need your ideas

Dear City Council Members,

We are looking at ways to help people be healthy in our city. We can have outdoor gyms in parks around the city. There is a budget of $8,000 for new gym equipment for one local park. People want equipment that is:

- for people of all ages
- easy to use
- good for different parts of the body

I look forward to hearing your ideas. Let me know what equipment is good for our park. Let's work together to create a great outdoor gym.

Regards,
The Director of Public Health

Send

E IN GROUPS Imagine your group works for the city council. Look at the equipment in C. Work together to decide what to buy.

A: I think we can get the … It's good for the …

B: I don't think we can get the … because it's expensive. How about we get the … instead?

F Share your choices with the Director of Public Health. Explain why you like this equipment.

MAKE IT DIGITAL

Go online and find your nearest outdoor gym. What equipment does it have?

CAREER NOTE

Sports coaching, sports therapy, sports psychology, personal training, high-impact exercise programs—these are all careers related to sports. Discuss the rise in sports-related jobs and ask if anyone plans to go into this field.

CULTURE NOTE

In many countries, there is mechanical gym equipment in public parks. Some of it falls into disrepair, but some is kept in good condition. Have students research outdoor gyms near them and visit one if they can. They should use each piece of equipment and take notes on the parts of the body that it exercises the best.

MAKE IT DIGITAL

Once they have done an online search for outdoor gyms in their area and have seen the equipment, tell students to look for home-gym equipment that is available. Tell them to compare prices between new and used equipment.

GO TO page xvii
for UNIT REVIEW step-by-step instructions.

UNIT 7

VOCABULARY review

SCORE: / 10

A Choose the correct option.

Almost New

Almost new fitness **1 pass** / **tracker**. Wear it on one **2 back** / **arm** while you **3 do** / **go** gymnastics, play **4 tennis** / **biking**, or any other sport. $55.

Used

Used exercise DVD. Do your daily **5 workout** / **kick** with trainer Danny Lee. Do **6 push-ups** / **baseball**, sit-ups, and other exercises to **7 get** / **cut** in shape fast. $10.

Almost New

Sports **8 fitness** / **camera**. Takes great pictures. I use it for water sports like **9 running** / **surfing** and swimming. Hold it in your **10 hand** / **shoulder** or wear it on your head. $150.

GRAMMAR review

SCORE: / 10

A Match the sentence beginning (1–5) to the sentence end (a–e). Write the letter.

1 She can't __b__
2 Can you explain __d__
3 Where can I __e__
4 I can play __a__
5 He can play soccer, __c__

a volleyball and tennis.
b sing or dance.
c but he can't play rugby.
d the rules of cricket?
e buy tickets to the game?

B Complete the sentences with the adverb form of the adjectives in parentheses.

1 Baseball players need to run __fast__ (fast) to first base after they hit the ball.
2 Good basketball players can score 20 to 30 points in a game __easily__ (easy).
3 It's important for a rugby player to pass the ball __carefully__ (careful) to another player.
4 Volleyball players near the net often hit the ball __hard__ (hard).
5 Soccer teams need to play __well__ (good) together to win.

16–20 correct: You can talk about parts of the body and exercise words. You can use *can/can't* and adverbs of manner.
0–15 correct: Look again at the Vocabulary and Grammar sections in the unit.

TOTAL SCORE: / 20

WHAT DO YOU KNOW NOW? Look back at page 67 and add the words you know now to the boxes.

GO TO page xviii
for STUDY SKILLS step-by-step instructions.

STUDY SKILLS EFFECTIVE GROUP WORK

Take the quiz on effective group work. Go to **Study Skills** on page 133 to find the answers. Then learn more about effective group work.

1 What kind of team performs best?
a a mixed-age team b a young-people-only team c a men-only team

2 You're in a meeting. Someone makes a suggestion you don't agree with. What do you say?
a "Really? Ha, ha!" b "That's interesting. Why do you think that?" c "You're wrong."

3 You're working in a group when you make a mistake. What do you say?
a "I'm sorry, my mistake." b "Excuse me?" c nothing

4 People who work alone get better results than small teams.
a true b false

76 Unit 7 Fit for Life

CLASSROOM MANAGEMENT

You can manage the review activities as competitive or collaborative activities. A collaborative way to approach VOCABULARY **A** might be to have students work in groups of three and assign one box to each student. Tell each student do their exercise and then share their part with the group. For GRAMMAR **A** and **B**, have two students do one activity each and give the third student the responsibility of checking their work.

FURTHER DISCUSSION

Put students in groups of three and ask the following questions for them to discuss:

- What do you think are the best sports for children?
- What sport is an emerging sport in your country?
- Are there any unusual sports in your country?
- Are you interested in a career in sports?
- What's your favorite exercise machine?
- How much exercise do you do each week?

UNIT 8 Foodie?

GO TO page vi
for **UNIT OPENER** step-by-step instructions.

WHAT DO YOU ALREADY KNOW?

1 Think of words for foods that are healthy and unhealthy. Write the words.
2 **IN PAIRS** Share and compare your information. Add more words to your lists.

Healthy

Unhealthy

STUDENTS MAY ALREADY KNOW

- **Healthy:** fruit, vegetables, apples, oranges, bananas, broccoli, meat.
- **Unhealthy:** hamburger, hot dog, sugar, soda.

DISCUSS & SHARE

VIDEO

3 **IN GROUPS** Watch the video and answer the question.
SYM Do you "eat to live" or "live to eat"?

GO TO page xx
for **VIDEOS IN SYM** step-by-step instructions.

In this unit, you will ...

- talk about food, tastes, ingredients, and recipes.
- use thinking skills: apply, analyze, and evaluate.
- read about international foods.
- use strategies to repair talking by checking for understanding.
- use communication skills to design a restaurant guide.
- follow a baker to learn about this job and the skills needed for this industry.

WHAT DO YOU ALREADY KNOW?

If you notice students are struggling to understand what to do, you can provide one or two examples to help them get started:

- **Food:** dairy, protein, bread, chili pepper
- **Fruit:** watermelon, pineapple, strawberry, coconut
- **Vegetables:** onion, carrot, lettuce, tomato

VIDEO

Before viewing, ask:

What does Amy like to eat? *food that tastes good*
What does Max like to eat? *simple, healthy food*

After viewing, put the continuum on the board.

eat to live —— live to eat

Students mark the continuum and explain how important food is to them.

DISCUSS & SHARE

Encourage students to consider their relationship to food. Ask *Do you really enjoy eating or cooking? Is eating an experience for you? Or do you eat only in order to keep yourself full and energized?*

GO TO page x

for **READING** step-by-step instructions.

LESSON 1 Are You a "Gastronaut"?

READING

A IN GROUPS **Look at the pictures. Do you know these foods? Do you want to try them? Discuss.**

hagelslag (the Netherlands)

bunny chow (South Africa)

empanadas (Venezuela)

cendol (Malaysia)

tom yum soup (Thailand)

B 8.01 READING SKILL—Read for the main idea **Read the posts from a world food forum and answer the questions.**

Wendy, Canada, 5:34 says ...
Hi, food fans! Do you know the word *gastronaut*? It's a person who travels and tries different foods. That's me! I love something **delicious** called *hagelslag*. It's from the Netherlands. It has small, sweet pieces of chocolate you put on bread for breakfast. My boyfriend thinks it's **disgusting**! Do you like foods from different countries? What kind? How many new dishes do you try each week?

Soraya, Bali, 9:45 says ...
I'm a gastronaut, too! I love to try different foods from all over the world. My favorite food is *tom yum soup*, from Thailand. It's a spicy soup with shrimp and vegetables. I often have it for lunch. It's a very **healthy** meal! I add chilies to mine to make it extra spicy.

Peter, South Africa, 9:54 says ...
Hi, Wendy! Do you know about *bunny chow*? It comes from South Africa. It's a loaf of bread, but you take the middle of the bread out and put **spicy** beef or chicken inside. How much meat do you need? It depends on how big the loaf is! We usually eat it for lunch or dinner.

Marlena, Venezuela, 11:32 says ...
My favorite food is *empanadas*. They are delicious. You can make them with corn flour, water, and salt. You can put cheese, meat, chicken—anything you like—inside. Then, you fry them. Some people eat them as a **snack**. My mom thinks they are **unhealthy** because you fry them.

Ben, Scotland, 12:54 says ...
I think I'm a gastronaut, too. Do you know a dessert called *cendol* from Malaysia? It's really unusual. It's green rice noodles, coconut milk, and sugar. You can also add fruit. It's very **sweet**. It looks like green spaghetti!

1 What kind of flour do you use for empanadas? corn flour
2 What food is from Thailand? tom yum soup
3 Is bunny chow a snack? no
4 What is cendol? a dessert from Malaysia
5 Are you a gastronaut? Why or why not? ______

C IN PAIRS THINKING SKILL—Apply **Think about a popular food in your country. What is it? When do you eat it? What is in it? Do you like it? Tell your partner.**

READING OPTIONAL 8.01

Before reading the forum, have students rate the unusual dishes from the one they would most like to try to the one they would least like to try. Have students look at the pictures and predict the ingredients that will be mentioned in the forum.

After reading and discussing a popular food in their country, you may like to extend the activity by asking students to discuss the most unusual dish they have ever eaten.

THINKING SKILL—Apply

When students apply information, it means they have understood that information and they can use it with their own experiences. Ask students to underline grammar and phrases in the forum that will help them talk about a typical popular dish in their country. For example, *My favorite food is … It's spicy. It has … I have it for … We usually eat it for … You can make it with …*

VOCABULARY

A Find and circle all the food items in READING B.

B Match the underlined words in READING B to the definitions (1–7).

1 has the hot taste of chilies (adjective) spicy
2 tastes very, very bad (adjective) disgusting
3 good for your body (adjective) healthy
4 has the taste of sugar (adjective) sweet
5 a small amount of food you eat between meals (noun) snack
6 not good for your body (adjective) unhealthy
7 has a very good taste (adjective) delicious

MAKE IT YOURS

Think about a food and a drink that you like. Use a dictionary to add the words to the vocabulary list for this lesson.

GO TO page vii for VOCABULARY step-by-step instructions.

GRAMMAR countable and uncountable nouns

A Complete the examples with the foods from READING B. Then complete the rules.

Countable nouns

Singular: *a vegetable*, a (spicy) soup, a snack, a dessert

Plural: *vegetables*, chilies (green), rice noodles

Uncountable nouns

chocolate, *bread*, ____, ____, ____, ____, ____

Questions

How many chilies ...? *How much* meat ...?

1 Countable nouns are people or things you **can** / can't count. Use numbers and the article *a*/*an* with countable nouns.
2 Countable nouns can be singular / plural / **both singular and plural.**
3 Uncountable nouns are not singular / **plural.**
4 We use *How many ...?* with **countable** / uncountable nouns.
5 We use *How much ...?* with countable / **uncountable** nouns.

For more practice, go to page 152.

GO TO page viii for GRAMMAR step-by-step instructions.

Suggested answers: water, chocolate, bread, soup, rice, beef, chicken, shrimp, flour, salt, coconut milk, sugar, fruit, spaghetti, meat

B Complete with the singular or plural form of the noun.

1 How much milk (milk) do you want in your coffee?
2 I like bananas (banana) and grapes (grape), but I don't like oranges (orange).
3 Can I have cheese (cheese) on my pizza, please?
4 How many eggs (egg) do you want for breakfast?
5 I don't eat fish (fish) or meat. I'm a vegetarian.

SPEAKING

A Make a list of foods you know from different countries in your notebook.

B IN PAIRS Ask and answer questions about the foods you like. Use the Confident Communicator box to help you.

C Take a class survey to see how many gastronauts are in your class. Discuss.

CONFIDENT COMMUNICATOR
START TALKING

There are different ways to ask about preferences.
Do you like Thai food? Yes, I do. / No, I don't.
Which do you prefer, chicken or fish?
I prefer chicken (to fish).
Do you prefer pasta or rice? I prefer pasta.

GO TO page xii for SPEAKING step-by-step instructions.

VOCABULARY

After finishing the exercise, have students choose five more food words and write their own definitions. Ask students to work in pairs to read the definitions and guess the food being defined.

GRAMMAR

Countable and uncountable nouns are difficult for some learners. Liquids and masses are often uncountable nouns. So, milk and sugar are uncountable until you divide them up into something like pounds, tablespoons, cups, or kilograms.

Other uncountable masses are divided up into their packaging, such as a jar, a packet, a bottle, or a carton.

SPEAKING

Elicit from different students the list of foods from different countries and write it on the board. As a class, compare the lists and have students repeat the foods out loud.

Tell students to go back to the reading and underline the definition of *gastronaut*. It is related to *gastronomy*, which is considered an art that refers to cooking and enjoying food.

LESSON 2 A Balanced Diet

VOCABULARY food groups

A Look at the food group diagram. Complete the diagram with words from the box.

apples	bananas	beans	bread	butter	cereal	cheese	chocolate	corn	eggs
fish	ice cream	milk	oil	pasta	potatoes	rice	soda	chicken	yogurt

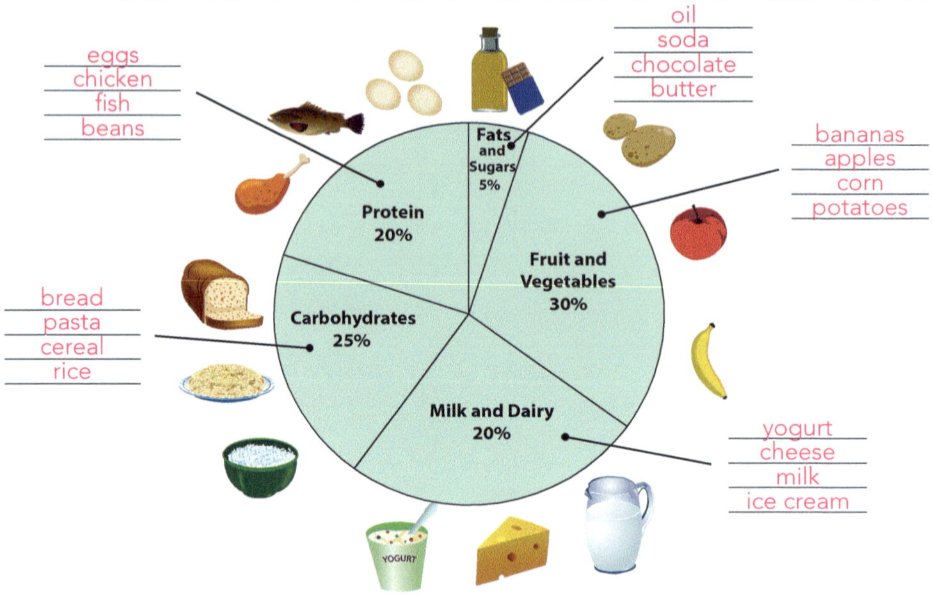

B IN PAIRS Discuss how much of each food group you eat.

I usually eat two kinds of protein a day, but I don't eat a lot of fruit and vegetables.

GO TO page xi for LISTENING step-by-step instructions.

GO TO page 144 for AUDIO SCRIPT.

LISTENING

A Discuss the questions.

1 Do you like going to food markets?
2 What foods do you eat there?

B 8.02 Listen to Conversations 1 and 2 and choose *True* or *False*.

1 The interviewer thinks falafel is spicy. **True** / False
2 The woman says that her falafel is unhealthy. True / **False**
3 The bibimbap has carbohydrates, vegetables, and protein. **True** / False
4 The man's bibimbap is vegan. True / **False**

C 8.02 LISTENING SKILL—Listen for specific information Listen again and write the words you hear.

1 Food markets like this sell cheap food, but is it ___healthy___?
2 This falafel is healthy because we grill it. Fried falafel has more ___fat___ and calories.
3 It looks like a/an ___balanced___ meal!
4 So, the food at this market is ___delicious___, and some of it is healthy, too.

D THINKING SKILL—Analyze Look up the words *vegan* and *vegetarian*. Do you think you can be vegan or vegetarian? Why or why not?

VOCABULARY

Consider defining the following words for students: *fruit*, *vegetables*, *carbohydrates*, *protein*, *milk*, *dairy*, *fat*, and *sugar*. A good source for definitions is the Macmillan English Dictionary (macmillandictionary.com). As an alternative, have students work together to come up with definitions before doing the exercise.

Extra Practice

Have students say a simple dish they can make and name all the ingredients in it.

LISTENING

Project pictures of local food markets on the board. Ask if they have been to food markets in other countries and if they remember the names of the food they ate there.

GRAMMAR *this/that/these/those*

A Read the conversation. Then complete the rules with *this/that* or *these/those*.

Shelly: Hi. Can I get a pound of apples, please?
Jon: Sure. Do you want those green ones?
Shelly: No, these apples, please. The red ones.
Jon: OK. Anything else?
Shelly: How big is that watermelon?
Jon: That one is small. It's 10 pounds.
Shelly: And this watermelon here?
Jon: This one is 15 pounds.
Shelly: OK, this one, please. Thanks.

1 Use ___this___ and ___that___ with singular nouns.
2 Use ___these___ and ___those___ with plural nouns.
3 Use ___this___ and ___these___ to talk about things near us.
4 Use ___that___ and ___those___ to talk about things not near us.

For more practice, go to page 153.

B Look at the pictures. Complete with *this, that, these,* or *those*.

1 Can we sit at ___that___ table, please?
2 Can I have ___those___ apples, please?
3 How much is ___this___?
4 I like ___these___. They're delicious.

PRONUNCIATION emphasis with *this/that/these/those*

A 8.03 Listen to the conversations. Underline the words the speakers stress.

Conversation 1
A: Is this my salad?
B: No, that's your salad.

Conversation 2
A: Are these your apples?
B: No, those are my apples.

Conversation 3
A: Do you want that snack?
B: No, I want this one.

B 8.03 Listen again and practice stressing the correct words.

GO TO page ix for **PRONUNCIATION** step-by-step instructions.

SPEAKING

A IN PAIRS Discuss the difference between healthy and unhealthy foods. Make a note of the healthy and unhealthy foods you eat every day.

B IN GROUPS Make a meal plan. Discuss and recommend healthy foods that your group can eat for every meal of the day. Use the Confident Communicator box to help you.

A: Hmm. How about donuts for breakfast?
B: Well, they're very sweet.
A: How about cereal with fruit instead?
B: Yes, that's healthy.

CONFIDENT COMMUNICATOR
KEEP TALKING

It's a good idea to recommend an alternative when you give advice. Use *instead* (in place of).
How about + noun + *instead*?
e.g., *How about a sandwich instead?*

GRAMMAR

Give a demonstration of *this, that, these,* and *those* with objects around the classroom. Then, ask volunteers to give examples of *this, that, these,* and *those* related to their position in the room. For example, *This is Raul's backpack. Whose are those books?* This will demonstrate the subjective nature of the terms.

PRONUNCIATION

This is a good example of how meaning changes stress. Tell students to listen carefully for the contrastive stress. When they say the sentences, tell students to put extra emphasis on the second demonstrative determiner in the conversations: *that's* in Conversation 1, *those* in Conversation 2, and *this* in Conversation 3.

SPEAKING

In groups, it is easy for one student to do all the work. Have students work in groups of three during the idea-generating stage and take turns giving ideas so you know everyone has contributed. Or assign roles; have them organize themselves by meals. One student is responsible for the breakfast ideas, one for lunch, and one for dinner.

LESSON 3 Cooking

VOCABULARY cooking

A Match the words from the box to the pictures (1–10).

baking dish bowl measuring cup fork knife spoon add bake mix slice

1  knife

2  slice

3  spoon

4  mix

5  bowl

6  fork

7  baking dish

8  bake

9  cup

10  add

B Read the recipe for ice cream banana bread. Match the instructions (1–7) to the pictures (a–g). Write the letter.

Ice Cream Banana Bread

EASY, DELICIOUS, AND ONLY FIVE INGREDIENTS!

a 

b 

c 

d 

e 

f 

g 

Oil
3 bananas
1 cup of flour
¼ cup of sugar
2 cups of chocolate ice cream

Oven: 175 degrees Celsius
Cooking time: 1 hour

1 Pour the mixture into the baking dish. f
2 Put oil on the baking dish. a
3 Bake for one hour. g
4 Slice the bananas. b
5 Add the flour and sugar. d
6 Mix again with a spoon. e
7 Put the bananas and ice cream together in a bowl and mix with a fork. c

C **IN PAIRS** Give instructions on making ice cream banana bread.

VOCABULARY

Have students extend their vocabulary by using a dictionary to look up more cooking verbs (e.g., *fry, boil, slice, chop*). Then, have them name a food for each verb (e.g., *bake vegetables, mix a cake, fry chicken, boil corn, slice a tomato, chop lettuce*). Tell students to circle the verbs in the Ice Cream Banana Bread recipe. Then, have students practice the actions by working in pairs to act them out and guess. Finally, you may want to have students link actions to utensils used to perform the action, such as *chop: knife, cutting board; slice: knife,* and so on.

CULTURE NOTE

Tell students that a healthier option for the Ice Cream Banana Bread recipe is to use stevia, a sugar substitute that comes from a plant and has no calories. And one way to enhance the flavor is to add some vanilla extract and use vanilla ice cream, too.

LISTENING

A **Do you cook? What do you make? Discuss as a class.**

B **8.04 LISTENING SKILL—Listen for specific information** **Listen and complete the ingredient list.**

Rainbow Pizza (a snack for 4–6 people)

Ingredients

- 2 ___cups___ of flour
- oil
- 1 cup of water
- 1 orange ___pepper___
- 1 cup of ___corn___
- 2 cups of ___yellow___ cheese
- 1 cup of red tomatoes
- 1 green pepper
- ___1/one___ purple onion
- salt and pepper

C **8.05** **Listen and complete the instructions.**

1. Put the flour in a/an ___bowl___. Add salt and pepper. Then add the water and oil.
2. ___Mix___ with a spoon or fork. Then use your hands to make a ball. Roll the ball into a circle.
3. Put the pizza dough on a ___baking dish___.
4. ___Slice___ all the vegetables into small pieces. Don't mix them together.
5. Put the ___cheese___ on the pizza dough first.
6. Make a row of ___tomatoes___, then orange peppers, then corn.
7. ___Next___, add green peppers. Then add purple onions.
8. ___Bake___ at 200°C for 20 minutes. Then slice.

MAKE IT REAL

I'm starving! = I am very hungry.
I'm stuffed! = I can't eat more food.

D **THINKING SKILL—Evaluate** **Think about the questions.**

1. Do you think it's important how food looks?
2. Does food that looks good usually taste good?

WRITING

A **Think about food you like from your country. Choose one dish that you know how to make.**

B **List the ingredients in your notebook.**

C **Read the recipe from LISTENING C and underline the imperatives.**

D **Write your recipe in your notebook using imperatives.**

SPEAKING

A **IN PAIRS** **Play a game. Student A: Read the recipe slowly. Don't say the name of the dish. Student B: Guess the dish. Then change roles. Use the Confident Communicator box to help you.**

CONFIDENT COMMUNICATOR
REPAIR IT

Sometimes you need to ask someone to say something again to check your understanding. There are polite ways to say this:
Can you say that again, please?
Can you repeat that?
Can you say that more slowly, please?

GO TO page 145 for AUDIO SCRIPT.

GO TO page 145 for AUDIO SCRIPT.

GO TO page xiv for WRITING step-by-step instructions.

LISTENING

Have students brainstorm more ways to measure food: *teaspoon, tablespoon, ¼ cup, ½ cup, a pinch of salt, a kilogram, half a kilogram,* and so on.

WRITING

Allow students to research their recipes online. Tell them to find two or three different versions of the same recipe and simplify them. They may need to use conversion charts on their phones. For example, changing ounces and grams to tablespoons and cups, or vice versa, might make a recipe easier to understand.

SPEAKING

Remind students that no one expects their English to be perfect immediately. There will be times when people will find it difficult to understand them and when they will find it difficult to understand others. Tell them to be patient with themselves and others.

GO TO page xv
for LANGUAGE AND LIFE step-by-step instructions.

Language and Life

Communication – A Restaurant Guide

A 8.06 **Read the reviews from a local restaurant guide. Do you want to try the restaurants? Why?**

Many people like to eat out in a neighborhood called Paradissos. There are a lot of bars and restaurants, and food from around the world, like Thai, Japanese, Greek, French—you name it! Some of the restaurants are great for snacks, but there are some expensive restaurants, too. It's hard to know what's good and what's not, so here is our guide to the places we like in Paradissos ...

Matilda's: vegetarian restaurant. Great for lunch. Healthy food.
We like: the mushroom burger and the delicious avocado salad
We don't like: the carrot cake, there are only five tables
$20 for lunch
★ ★ ★

Yu Garden: Chinese restaurant. Open evenings only.
We like: the chicken noodles and egg fried rice
We don't like: the noise, the open kitchen
$30 for 3 dishes
★ ★ ★ ★

Fred's Fish: fish and seafood restaurant. Lunch and dinner. Outdoor tables in the summer.
We like: spicy shrimp spaghetti with tomatoes
We don't like: the vegetable dishes, small portions
$40–$60
★ ★ ★ ½

Encore: French café and restaurant. Breakfast, lunch, and dinner.
We like: the steak and fries—so tasty!
We don't like: nothing—we love everything here!
$25 in the café, $70 in the restaurant
★ ★ ★ ★ ★

B Read the reviews again and complete.

Which restaurant ...

1 is expensive? Encore
2 is not open in the daytime? Yu Garden
3 is a good place for people who don't eat meat or fish? Matilda's
4 is a good place to eat outside? Fred's Fish

OBJECTIVE

In this lesson, students learn how to decide on the best information to include in a restaurant review, such as the kinds of comments to make and how to share information that is useful. Remind them that online reviews are public information and that a restaurant's livelihood often depends on reviews. They should be honest but diplomatic in their comments.

PROCESS OPTIONAL 8.06

Students first read reviews in an online restaurant guide and consider reviews posted about different places to eat. They examine different elements of a restaurant and the information that goes into a review. They respond to a post that invites the public to write reviews about restaurants for a new online restaurant guide.

Students work in groups to brainstorm ideas for different restaurants. They should agree on one restaurant as a group and write a review of it. Then, the groups share their reviews. Finally, they vote on a winning restaurant in their area to recommend to visitors.

C Read the article and make notes about a restaurant you know.

Write Restaurant Reviews

Do you like eating out? Do you have a favorite restaurant? We are making an exciting new food guide for the restaurants in your area. We are looking for people like you to write the restaurant reviews. We pay $100 for every review we use.

- What's the name of the restaurant?
- What type of food does it have? (for example, French / Spanish / Chinese / breakfast / snacks / etc.)
- What do you like / not like about the restaurant?
- How much is a meal for two people?
- How many stars (out of 5) do you give it?

1 Restaurant name: ______
2 Type of food: ______
3 What you like: ______
4 What you don't like: ______
5 How much is a meal for two people?: ______
6 How many stars (out of 5)?: ______

D **IN PAIRS** Discuss your ideas.

E **IN GROUPS** Choose one restaurant using the group's notes. Write a review.

F Take a class survey. Choose a restaurant to recommend to a visitor to your area.

MAKE IT DIGITAL

Go online to look for a new dish for the restaurant to serve. Include pictures, prices, and some information about the dish to make people want to try it!

CULTURE NOTE

Have students discuss the local restaurants that best represent their nation's typical food. Where are they? What's on the menu? What're their signature dishes?

Discuss celebrity chefs students may know and the chefs' influence nationally and internationally. What have they done to promote local cuisine around the world? Do they have restaurants? Have they been on TV? Have they published cookbooks?

MAKE IT DIGITAL

Have students investigate the best-rated restaurants in their city on TripAdvisor, Foursquare, Yelp, or another website or app that rates restaurants. Are there any surprises? Do they agree?

Have them search online for restaurants they know and read reviews that are in English.

GO TO page xvii
for **UNIT REVIEW** step-by-step instructions.

UNIT 8

VOCABULARY review

SCORE: / 10

A Choose the word that does NOT belong.

1. Proteins: steak / corn / beans
2. Fats/Sugars: oil / butter / eggs
3. Fruits/Vegetables: grapes / rice / carrots
4. Carbohydrates: beef / bread / cereal
5. Milk/Dairy: yogurt / raisins / cheese
6. Meals: dinner / snack / breakfast
7. Cooking utensils: spoon / knife / add
8. Cooking verbs: delicious / bake / mix
9. Words to describe food: sweet / tall / disgusting
10. Healthy foods: salad / apples / donut

GRAMMAR review

SCORE: / 10

A Find and correct one error in each sentence.

1. For this recipe, you need two banana and four eggs. two bananas
2. Use a fork to mash the bananas in bowl with the eggs. in a bowl
3. Pour into a pan with oils and cook on both sides. with oil
4. Cook on both sides and top with fruit or a chocolate. or chocolate
5. How much servings it makes is up to you! How many

B Choose the correct option.

1. Excuse me, but is that / these / those a vegetarian dish?
2. These / This / Those soup tastes delicious. Try it!
3. Waiter! These / Those / This vegetables don't taste good.
4. How much are these / those / that carrots over there?
5. Can you help me put this / that / these watermelon in my bag?

16–20 correct: You can talk about food and food groups. You can use countable/uncountable nouns and *this/that/these/those*.
0–15 correct: Look again at the Vocabulary and Grammar sections in the unit.

TOTAL SCORE: / 20

WHAT DO YOU KNOW NOW? Look back at page 77 and add the words you know now to the boxes.

GO TO page xix
for **FOLLOW A PRO** step-by-step instructions.

FOLLOW A PRO FOOD INDUSTRY

Take the quiz about food stylists. Go to Follow A Pro on page 134 to find the answers. Then learn more about the food industry.

1. **When food stylists take pictures of breakfast cereal, what do they use instead of milk?**
   a white glue b white toothpaste c cream
2. **Food stylists use hand soap for the top of a cappuccino.**
   a true b false
3. **What do food stylists do before they photograph a roast chicken?**
   a put newspaper inside it b paint it yellow c cover it with nail polish
4. **Food stylists use a special machine to add sesame seeds to hamburger buns.**
   a true b false

4 They add the seeds by hand.

86 Unit 8 Foodie?

CLASSROOM MANAGEMENT

Allow students time to look over the unit and ask questions before giving them time limits to complete the review activities.

FURTHER DISCUSSION

Put students in groups of three and ask the following questions for them to discuss:

- Do you cook?
- Who cooks at your house?
- Is it important for both men and women to know how to cook?
- Do you have any food allergies?
- Are you a vegan or a vegetarian?
- What food did you like and dislike as a child?

GO TO page vi
for **UNIT OPENER** step-by-step instructions.

UNIT 9 Seeing the World

WHAT DO YOU ALREADY KNOW?

1 Think about words you know about tourism and travel. Write the words.

2 IN PAIRS Share and compare your information. Add more words to your list.

Travel and Tourism

STUDENTS MAY ALREADY KNOW

- **Travel and tourism:** country, city, capital city, travel, fly, plane, airport, city center, hotel.

VIDEO

DISCUSS & SHARE

3 IN GROUPS Watch the video and answer the question.

SYM Is tourism good or bad?

GO TO page xx
for **VIDEOS IN SYM** step-by-step instructions.

In this unit, you will ...

- talk about travel, make travel recommendations, and give advice on packing.
- use thinking skills: analyze, recall, and infer.
- read about virtual travel.
- use strategies to start and keep talking by taking time to think and asking follow-up questions.
- use collaboration skills to work as a team and create an advertisement to attract tourists.
- learn tips for formal and informal writing.

WHAT DO YOU ALREADY KNOW?

If you notice students are struggling to understand what to do, you can provide one or two examples to help them get started:

- **Travel:** buy a souvenir, stay at a hotel, virtual travel
- **Tourism:** car rental, tourist guide, vacation

VIDEO

Before viewing, ask:

What's good about tourism? *Marcus says it's good for the economy.*
What's bad about tourism? *Jill says it's bad for the environment.*

After viewing, put the continuum on the board.

Tourism is good. — Tourism is bad.

Have students mark the continuum and explain how they view tourism.

DISCUSS & SHARE

Have students discuss in groups of three or four the pros and cons of tourism in general and in the areas where they live. Tell them to discuss why they would or wouldn't like to see tourism grow in their areas.

GO TO page x
for **READING** step-by-step instructions.

LESSON 1 Virtual Tours

READING

A You can go anywhere in the world. Where do you want to go? Discuss as a class.

B 9.01 Read the article and choose *True* or *False*.

There but Not There: Virtual Travel

Would you like to visit another **continent**—Europe, maybe? See Italy or Greece? Or how about a country in Africa, like Kenya? If you want to save time and money when you travel, here's a tip. You need to try virtual tourism! But what is virtual tourism? And how does it work?

When you plan to visit a new place, go online and take a virtual tour first. You can use a virtual reality headset and a computer to take a **tour**. You don't have to use a computer if you have an app on your smartphone.

A virtual tour gives you all the **sights** and **sounds** of a place. Take a tour of a street market in a city like Delhi or enjoy **tourist attractions** in Rio de Janeiro. You can decide what you like to do before you go.

Many people enjoy traveling more when they plan with virtual tours. They like spending time on things that interest them. With virtual tours, they can spend more time on the things they love when they finally get to their dream **vacation** destination!

1. Virtual tourism is only for people with a lot of money. True / **False**
2. On a virtual tour, you can see and hear a place. **True** / False
3. You need a computer to take a virtual tour. True / **False**
4. A virtual tour can help you decide where to go. **True** / False

C **READING SKILL—Scan** Scan the text and complete.

1. Continents: Europe, Africa
2. Countries: Italy, Greece, Kenya
3. Cities: Delhi, Rio de Janeiro

D **THINKING SKILL—Analyze** Answer the questions.

1. How does a virtual tour save you time and money?
2. Is taking a virtual tour a good idea? Why or why not?

GO TO page vii
for **VOCABULARY** step-by-step instructions.

VOCABULARY

A Match the words and phrases (1–6) to the definitions (a–f). Write the letter.

1. continent e
2. sights c
3. sounds f
4. tour b
5. tourist attractions a
6. vacation d

a. places tourists visit
b. a trip around a place to see interesting things
c. things you see
d. a trip to another place, usually to relax
e. large area of land, e.g., North America
f. things you hear

GO TO page viii
for **GRAMMAR** step-by-step instructions.

GRAMMAR verb + infinitive or gerund

A Complete with phrases from READING B.

1. Would you like to visit another continent—Europe, maybe?
2. If you want to save time and money, here's a tip.
3. You need to try virtual tourism!
4. You can decide what you like to do before you go.
5. Many people enjoy traveling more when they plan with virtual tours.
6. They like spending time on things that interest them.

READING OPTIONAL 9.01

Before reading and discussing places to travel, have students play a game to elicit country names. Tell students to take turns and name a country for each letter of the alphabet (e.g., *A* for *Australia*, *B* for *Barbados*, *C* for *Chile*, etc.). You could make it competitive by telling students if they hesitate too long, they are out, and the last remaining person is the winner. Alternatively, it could be a cooperative game where students help each other and see how far along in the alphabet they get in five minutes.

Discuss virtual reality in general. What experiences have the members of the class had with virtual reality? Did they like it?

VOCABULARY

If students have trouble matching the words to the definitions, tell them to go back to the text and reread the sentences in which the words appear. Reading words in context is a great way to learn them.

B Choose the correct option to complete the grammar rules.

to go = infinitive | *go* = base form | *going* = *–ing* form

1. After *want*, *would like*, *need*, *have*, and *plan*, use the infinitive / base form.
2. After *enjoy*, use the infinitive / *–ing* form of verb.
3. After *like*, we can use the infinitive / *–ing* form of the verb / both.

For more practice, go to page 154.

C Write sentences that are true for you.

1. want / don't want … visit Europe / visit Africa
   I want to visit Europe. I don't want to visit Africa.
2. would like / wouldn't like … visit a big city / visit a small village
3. like / don't like … travel by boat / travel by bus
4. enjoy / don't enjoy … visit new places / go to places I know

D **IN PAIRS** Ask and answer questions about your sentences.

A: Do you want to visit Europe?
B: Yes, I do. But I don't want to visit Africa.
A: I want to visit Europe and I want to visit Africa!

PRONUNCIATION *to*

A 9.02 Listen and notice how *to* sounds like /tə/.

I want **to** visit Europe.
Do you like **to** travel?
I don't have **to** work on Monday.

B 9.02 Listen again and practice saying the sentences.

SPEAKING

A Plan a virtual tour.

Where do you want to go? What do you want to see? Choose a place from the unit or use your own ideas.

B Write why you want to visit that place and see that sight in your notebook.
I want to go to Sydney, Australia, and see Bondi Beach because I like to swim.

C **IN PAIRS** Student A, ask Student B about his or her virtual tour choices. Use phrases and short questions to show you are interested. Then change roles. Use the Confident Communicator box to help you.

Where do you want to go on a virtual tour?
What do you want to do there?

CONFIDENT COMMUNICATOR
KEEP TALKING

Take time to think about what you want to say and how you want to say it. Use words and sounds like:
Um …
Uh …
Let me think …

GO TO page ix for PRONUNCIATION step-by-step instructions.

GO TO page xii for SPEAKING step-by-step instructions.

GRAMMAR

Depending on how well your class handles talking in pairs, you may want to write question starters on the board. For example, *Do you want to visit a big city or a small town? How do you like to travel? Do you enjoy visiting new places or going to places you know?*

PRONUNCIATION

The schwa is often a revelation to second-language learners. It explains why some grammar is difficult to learn—they can't learn what they don't hear. The schwa is the most relaxed sound in the English language. Have them listen carefully to the sentences to identify the strong and weak sounds.

SPEAKING

Have students talk to three different partners. They will become more and more confident as they repeat their information to new partners.

GO TO page xi
for **LISTENING** step-by-step instructions.

GO TO page 146
for **AUDIO SCRIPT**.

LESSON 2 Travel Advice

LISTENING

A IN PAIRS Discuss if you like to visit a place during high tourist season or low tourist season. Write advantages and disadvantages for each.

high season

1 Advantages: good weather, places are open, lots to do, meet new people

2 Disadvantages: lots of people, town is very busy, noisy, trash, more expensive

low season

3 Advantages: quiet, few people, low prices

4 Disadvantages: bad weather, poor weather, places are closed, nothing to do

B 9.03 Listen to part of a radio show. Decide whether each speaker prefers high season or low season.

	high season	low season
1 Manuel	☐	☑
2 Andra	☑	☐
3 Viktor	☑	☐

C 9.03 LISTENING SKILL—Listen for detail Listen again and write the words you hear.

1 Manuel: I like the winter, when it's quiet.

2 Andra: My favorite time of year is the middle of summer.

3 Viktor: We get tourists all year, but the high season is October to March.

D IN PAIRS THINKING SKILL—Recall Two of the speakers prefer the high season. Can you remember the two reasons?

VOCABULARY tourism collocations

A Check (✓) the things you like to do when you visit a place.

1 buy a souvenir

2 stay at a hotel

3 see the sights

4 take a taxi/bus

5 take a trip

6 take a guided tour

LISTENING

Tell an anecdote about a usual vacation choice—where you go, who you go with, how long you go for, and what time of the year you usually go on vacation. Mention things you like and don't like about your vacations. Then ask students to visualize their vacations. Do they go out of town? Do they go on trips to new places? Do they travel with friends or with family?

Explain that the *low season*, also known in American English as the *off-season*, is the time year when a place or a business is the least busy. The busiest time of year is *high season*.

VOCABULARY

Ask students what kind of typical sights or unusual places they like to see. What kind of transportation do they use? What's the most unusual type of transportation they know of? Do they like to take day trips? Do they like guided tours? What kind of souvenirs do they buy?

B **Complete the email with phrases from A.**

1 take a trip
2 stay at a hotel
3 take a guided tour
4 see the sights
5 take a taxi/bus
6 buy a souvenir

New Message

From: David Alegre, tour operator — Cc Bcc

To: Erin Rogers — Cc Bcc

Subject: Your trip to our city

Dear Erin,

Thanks for your email and the questions about our city. The high season is December to March. It's a good time to **1** ______________ to the area if you like lots of people. When you come, you can **2** ______________ on Copacabana Beach. There are lots of hotels on the beach. It's a good idea to **3** ______________ around the city with one of our tour guides. That way, you can **4** ______________, such as Sugar Loaf Mountain. If you prefer to explore on your own, **5** ______________ to Corcovado. From there, you can see the city, and of course you can **6** ______________ of your visit there. We look forward to seeing you in our city!

Best wishes,
David Alegre

Send

C **Discuss what tourists do when they visit your town or city. Use phrases from A.**

GRAMMAR *should/could* for advice and possibility

A **Read the sentences from the radio show. Then choose the correct option to complete the grammar rules.**

Manuel: Tourists are good for the economy. We should welcome them.
Lucia: We could get more tourists by opening more hotels.

1 Use *should* + base form of the verb / infinitive to talk about things that are *important* for people to do (advice).
2 Use *could* + base form of the verb / infinitive to talk about things that are *possible* for people to do (possibility).

For more practice, go to page 154.

B **Complete with *could* or *should* and the verb given.**

1 You ____could go____ to China! Or maybe India! They're both interesting. (go / possibility)
2 You ____should pack____ some warm clothes. It can be cold in Sweden! (pack / advice)
3 You need to rest. You ____should go____ on vacation. (go / advice)
4 Alex ____could take____ a taxi, or maybe a bus to get downtown. (take / possibility)

C **IN PAIRS Make a list of what a good tourist *should* or *could* do in your notebook.**

SPEAKING

A **IN PAIRS Role-play a conversation. Use the Confident Communicator box to help you.**

Student A: You want to take a vacation. Ask questions about your partner's country or city.
Student B: You are a tour operator. Sell a tour to your partner.

A: Hello. I'm going on vacation next summer and I want to visit your country. I want to take a trip, but I don't know where.
B: You could go to … because …

CONFIDENT COMMUNICATOR
KEEP TALKING

There are two ways to make suggestions:
*You **could** take a virtual tour.*
***Why don't you** take a virtual tour?*

GRAMMAR

Give examples of what a tourist should or could do in your country. For example, *Tourists shouldn't drink water from the faucet. They could buy bottled water. Tourists could peel fruit and vegetables before eating them. They should disinfect fruit and vegetables to make them safer.*

SPEAKING

If your class is made up of students from different regions of the same country, have them represent their own region for a vacation. If everyone is from the same area, assign or have students choose a country to research and represent for the speaking activity. They should research general information like the location, industry, and language, and then, more specifically, tell them to research tourist information for the place.

LESSON 3 What to Pack

VOCABULARY clothes

A Look at the pictures. Write the names of the clothing items using a dictionary.

1	jacket	6	coat	11	jeans	16	socks
2	shirt	7	scarf	12	sneakers	17	tie
3	skirt	8	gloves	13	shorts	18	suit
4	shoes	9	boots	14	hat	19	swimsuit/swim shorts
5	dress	10	sweatshirt	15	T-shirt	20	sandals/flip flops

GO TO page 146 for AUDIO SCRIPT.

LISTENING

A IN PAIRS Ask and answer questions about what you should pack for a short trip to a warm country and a short trip to a cold country.

B 9.04 LISTENING SKILL—Listen for gist Listen and choose the correct option.

1 José travels on vacation / **for work**.
2 Isabela enjoys **swimming** / hiking on vacation.
3 Mike likes swimming / **hiking** on vacation.
4 Amal likes to visit beaches / **cities**.

C 9.04 Listen again and complete. What do the speakers pack?

1 José: jacket, gloves
2 Isabela: swimsuit, sweater
3 Mike: boots, socks
4 Amal: blouses, jeans

D THINKING SKILL—Deduce Match the speakers (1–4) to another destination (a–d). Write the letter. Discuss why it's a good place for him/her.

1 José a
2 Isabela d
3 Mike c
4 Amal b

a Greenland
b New York
c Chile
d Spain

Suggested answers:
1 He likes cold countries.
2 She likes to go to the beach. Chile also has beaches.
3 He likes to go to the mountains. Spain and Greenland also have mountains.
4 She likes interesting cities.

MAKE IT YOURS

Use a dictionary to find words for clothes that you are wearing now or that you usually wear.

VOCABULARY Alternative Activity

Play Swap Meet with clothing items. Students exchange words they know for words they don't know with their classmates. Once they have exhausted all their known words and exchanged them for as many new words as possible, they can sit down with a dictionary and look up the rest of the words.

LISTENING

LISTENING SKILL—Listen for gist

Play the audio all the way through. But in LISTENING **C**, stop the audio after each person speaks to give students time to listen for gist and to write the correct answer.

THINKING SKILL—Deduce

When you deduce meaning, you reach a decision by thinking carefully and taking in consideration all the evidence. In LISTENING **D**, students will use the clothing that people take on trips and the activities they like to do as clues to guess the other countries the speakers would like to visit.

WRITING

A Read the tourism pamphlet. Then think about the climate in your area.

Before you book your trip to Thailand with Thai Tours, we'd like to share some information.

During the cool season (November to February), temperatures in the central region are about 21°C and 14°C in the north. You should pack some warm clothes, such as a sweater or a sweatshirt. During the hot season (March to June), temperatures are between 34°C and 40°C. You need summer clothes, such as shorts, T-shirts, and your swimsuit! The rainy season is from July to October. It's very wet! You should pack a hat and a raincoat.

We look forward to welcoming you to Thailand!

B Plan your writing. Complete the notes for your area.

My area: ______

High-season climate: ______

What to pack: ______

Low-season climate: ______

What to pack: ______

C Write information for tourists visiting your area. Give them advice on what to pack for different times of the year.

SPEAKING

A Look at the different vacations. Choose the one you like best.

1 
an adventure vacation

2 
a beach vacation

3 
a hiking vacation

4 
a sightseeing vacation

B You are going on that vacation! Where are you going? What is the climate like there? Write four things you need to pack for your trip in your notebook.

C IN PAIRS Discuss the trip you are planning. Say what you are taking with you and why. Use the Confident Communicator box to help you.

CONFIDENT COMMUNICATOR
START TALKING

Ask your partner these questions:
What kind of trip are you going on?
Why do you like that kind of trip?
What are you taking with you? Why are you taking that?

GO TO page xiv for WRITING step-by-step instructions.

WRITING

After reading the pamphlet and before you begin the WRITING section, review the months of the year. Then have an open-class discussion about temperatures in your area. Ask *When is it hot? When is it cold? When is rainy season? When is dry season? Do temperatures vary in the region? What activities do people do at particular times of the year? How do the seasons impact activities people like to do or that are available for people to do?*

SPEAKING

Do a brainstorming activity. Give the class 2 minutes to look at the different vacations. Divide the board into four sections (1, 2, 3, and 4) for the four vacations. Invite students to come to the board and write clothes and activities for the vacation destinations. This will serve as an idea bank for the speaking activity.

GO TO page xv
for LANGUAGE AND LIFE step-by-step instructions.

Language and Life

Collaboration – Detourism

1 A large number of people visit Venice every year. There are crowds and it's expensive to keep the city in good condition.

2 detourism—showing tourists other attractions in the city

A 9.05 **IN PAIRS** **Read the text and discuss the questions.**

DETOURISM

Love or hate it, Venice is a very popular tourist destination. Some people say it's too popular! Around 30 million people visit Venice, Italy, every year. The problem is, they all want to see the same things: the canals, St. Mark's Square, the Doge's Palace. The small city of Venice (population 50,000) attracts large crowds of visitors every year. Tourism is important for the economy of the city, but it's very expensive to keep Venice in good condition.

To deal with this problem, some people suggest detourism. A detour is a short trip in a different direction. Detourism shows tourists attractions that most people don't visit. That way, tourists aren't always in the same place at the same time. For example, when you move away from the canals, Venice also has interesting markets, restaurants, and shops. And there are unusual attractions, such as the multicolored houses on the island of Burano and the Lazzaretto Nuovo, home to the Vampire of Venice! It's a very different side of Venice.

Detourism can lead to many different kinds of vacations and new experiences. Have fun!

Read more

1 What problems does Venice have?

2 What do some people recommend?

B **Read the announcement and answer the questions.**

TOURISM COMPETITION

Win a weekend vacation for two!
Our area attracts many tourists every year. Most of the tourists are families, but we want to attract more English-speaking young adults to the area, too. We want them to visit our main attractions, but we need to tell them about the many interesting things in our area. Do you have any ideas how to do that? If so, enter the Tourism Competition. You could design a poster, or perhaps you could make a short video. You could also make a slideshow or design a special tour of our area. Choose anything that works for you!

Send your entry to the Local Tourist Office, 135 Main St.

1 What could you win in this competition? a weekend vacation for two people
2 Who does the Tourist Office want to attract? English-speaking young adults
3 What could you create? a poster / a video / a slideshow / a tour

OBJECTIVE

In this lesson, students create a tourism competition entry. They are encouraged to think of how to attract a new segment of tourists—to think broadly about what people of different age groups may find appealing about visiting their area. Remind them that people often visit places they have heard about, so marketing is a crucial part of tourism.

PROCESS OPTIONAL 9.05

Students first read a text about detourism and learn about how a city is trying to get visitors to do more than see just the typical sites. This practice disperses visitors more evenly throughout the city. Then, they read about a tourism competition, inviting people to make a poster or a video about their city to attract young tourists to alternative places and activities in the city.

Students work in groups to decide what kind of entry they want to create. They should include famous attractions, natural attractions, and other (detourism) attractions. Then, they read advice and create their competition entry. Finally, they share their competition entry with the class.

C **IN GROUPS** **Decide what you want to create. Choose or add your own ideas.**

a poster
a slideshow
a video
a tour

D **Make a list of tourist attractions in your area. Then choose attractions for your competition entry.**

famous attractions

natural attractions

other attractions (detourism!)

E **Choose three attractions and make notes.**

	Attraction 1	Attraction 2	Attraction 3
What is the attraction?			
What can you do there?			
Why do young adults like it?			

F **Read the advice and create your competition entry.**

TOURISM COMPETITION

Competition entries

A poster
Find some nice pictures of your area. Think about where you want to put the information on your poster. Use topics to interest people.

A slideshow
Find some nice pictures of your area. Use a different slide for each attraction. Include key information. Perhaps include a link to an online video.

A video
Decide who is doing what (such as filming and presenting). Write a short script. Film the tourism video on your smartphone. You can film the attractions!

A tour
Think about some unusual tourist attractions in your area. Think about what young people like to do and see. Write a description of each place on your tour. Find some nice pictures of your area to add to the tour.

G **Share your competition entry with the class.**

MAKE IT DIGITAL

Search online for a detourism tour of a city you are interested in. Tell your class about the tour.

MAKE IT DIGITAL

Have students research detourism tours online for five countries they are interested in visiting. Have them make notes to help them remember some of the interesting places they could go to and then share what they found with a partner.

CULTURE NOTE

Many nations depend heavily on tourism for a big part of their economy. How does this affect different regions? Can you think of any big resort destinations in your country? How many people do they employ? Do they employ locals, or do they recruit specialists from all over the country?

CAREER NOTE

Have students look up some major resorts in their country and see what kinds of employment are available and the skills and qualifications the resorts are looking for.

GO TO page xvii
for UNIT REVIEW step-by-step instructions.

UNIT 9

VOCABULARY review

SCORE: / 10

A Complete the definitions with the words in the box.

continent	guided	hotel	scarf	sights
gloves	hat	market	sneakers	souvenirs

1 gloves : you wear these on your hands
2 scarf : you wear this around your neck
3 sneakers : you wear these on your feet
4 hat : you wear this on your head
5 souvenirs : you buy these on a trip
6 hotel : you stay here on a trip
7 continent : Africa is an example of this
8 sights : you see these on a tour
9 market : a place to buy things
10 guided : a type of tour

GRAMMAR review

SCORE: / 10

A Choose the correct option.

Tom: I **1** want / enjoy to visit Ecuador this summer. I **2** enjoy / would hiking and shopping. I **3** have / would like to stay in Quito and visit some small towns as day tours. Is this a good idea?

Ana: I live in Quito, and summer here is very nice. You **4** like / have to visit Otavalo! There's great shopping there. **5** Plan / Want to go on Saturday—the market is very busy then.

B Complete the sentences with *could* or *should* and a word from the box.

eat	go	remember	take	visit

1 I think you ________ Korea in the autumn. It's the best time to visit.
2 There are different ways to get around. You ________ trains, buses, or even planes.
3 You ________ in a big hotel, but think about a small family-run restaurant.
4 Do you like hiking? You ________ to Seoraksan, or maybe Jirisan.
5 Korea can be cold in October. You ________ to pack a jacket.

1 should visit
2 could take
3 could eat
4 could go
5 should remember

16–20 correct: You can talk about travel, tourism, and clothes. You can use verb + infinite or gerund and *should/could*.
0–15 correct: Look again at the Vocabulary and Grammar sections in the unit.

TOTAL SCORE: / 20

WHAT DO YOU KNOW NOW? Look back at page 87 and add the words you know now to the box.

GO TO page xviii
for STUDY SKILLS step-by-step instructions.

STUDY SKILLS FORMAL AND INFORMAL WRITING

Take the quiz about writing skills. Go to **Study Skills** on page 135 to find the answers. Then learn more about formal and informal writing.

1 We often use slang expressions (e.g., *cool*, *kid*, *chill out*) in …
a formal writing. **b** informal writing.

2 Which of these sentences is from a formal piece of writing?
a Soccer is a popular sport in Brazil. **b** Soccer is awesome—I love it!

3 Contractions (*I'm*, *don't*, *who's*) are usually used in …
a formal writing. **b** informal writing.

4 How do you start a formal letter?
a Dear … **b** Hi …

ALTERNATIVE ACTIVITY

Do the VOCABULARY **A** as an oral activity before having students open their books. This will give them more input and illustrate how listening and reading are very different skills.

CLASSROOM MANAGEMENT

Do the GRAMMAR **A** and **B** as timed exercises. Give students 5 minutes to complete each activity. Then have them exchange books with a partner to check the answers. Have volunteers read the answers out loud.

FURTHER DISCUSSION

Put students in groups of three and ask the following questions for them to discuss:

- Where do you take all tourists in your town or city?
- Do you think your country needs more or fewer tourists?
- What is more important for you—the destination or the journey?
- What do you think about detourism?

UNIT 10 Life Stories

GO TO page vi
for **UNIT OPENER** step-by-step instructions.

WHAT DO YOU ALREADY KNOW?

1 Think about the last ten photos you took on your phone. Make a list of the photos.
2 **IN PAIRS** Share and compare your photos. Add more words to your list.

Last 10 photos on my phone

STUDENTS MAY ALREADY KNOW:

- **Events in your past:** birth, preschool, elementary school, graduation, vacation, birthday.

DISCUSS & SHARE

VIDEO

3 **IN GROUPS** Watch the video and answer the question.
SYM How much of your life do you put online?

GO TO page xx
for **VIDEOS IN SYM** step-by-step instructions.

In this unit, you will ...

- talk about life events, social life, and personal experiences.
- use thinking skills: summarize, evaluate, and analyze.
- read about a famous person.
- use strategies to keep talking by showing interest.
- use empathy skills to give advice based on your own experience.
- read about an event organizer to learn about this job and the skills needed for the tourism industry.

WHAT DO YOU ALREADY KNOW?

If you notice students are struggling to understand what to do, you can provide one or two examples to help them get started:

- **Important events:** education, career, social life

VIDEO

Before viewing, ask:

What does Sonya put online? *photos of her meals, soccer team, clothes, cat, friends*
What does Alex put online? *only important things – his graduation*

After viewing, put the continuum on the board.

post a little — post a lot

Have students mark the continuum and explain what they share online.

DISCUSS & SHARE

Have students work in pairs. Tell them to discuss how much of their private life they share online. Encourage them to answer what they are willing to share and what they are uncomfortable sharing. For more challenge, ask *Is it safe to share your private information, photos, and videos?*

GO TO page x
for **READING** step-by-step instructions.

LESSON 1 A Brave Life

READING

A Look at the picture. Do you know anything about this person? Why do you think she is famous?

B 10.01 Read the biography. Then complete the sentences.

An Inspiration For All

Malala Yousafzai was born in 1997 in the Swat Valley in Pakistan. Her father was an educator, and he wanted his daughter to get an education, but in 2007 and 2008, the schools for girls closed in her region of Pakistan, and Malala stopped going to school.

Malala wrote a **blog** for British TV about her life that year. She wanted all girls to have the opportunity to get an education. She became **well known** in Pakistan. Then in 2011, Malala's school finally opened again. Malala's blog made some powerful people angry. On October 9, 2012, Malala was shot on her way to school. She was only 14 years old.

Malala was lucky. She survived, and her family took her to England. When she was better, she started school there. She continued to talk about education for girls in Pakistan, and she went around the world to speak. In 2013, she started the Malala Fund. In 2014, she won the Nobel Peace Prize. The next year, a film of her life, called *He Named Me Malala*, told her story. In spring 2017, she went around the world on her Girl Power Trip and met world leaders. She asked them to support education for all girls. In autumn 2017, she started to study for a **degree** at Oxford University.

Malala continues to **inspire** young people around the world.

1 In 2008, Malala's ___school___ closed.
2 She wrote ___a blog___ about her life for British TV and became well known.
3 Malala was shot on her way to ___school___.
4 She met ___world leaders___ when she traveled around the world in 2017.

Suggested answer: Malala was born in 1997. Malala was shot in 2012. In 2013, she started the Malala Fund. After that, Malala won a prize in 2014. In 2017, she went around the world. Next, she started college.

C READING SKILL—Scan for information Put the milestones of Malala's life in the correct order. Write in your notebook.

D THINKING SKILL—Summarize Say what happened in Malala's life. Connect your ideas using *then*, *next*, and *after that*.

MAKE IT YOURS

Find the life story of a person who inspires you. Use a dictionary to find the vocabulary you need to tell his or her life story to the class.

GO TO page vii
for **VOCABULARY** step-by-step instructions.

VOCABULARY

A Match the words and phrases (1–4) to the definitions (a–d). Write the letter.

1 blog ___a___
2 well known ___d___
3 degree ___b___
4 inspire ___c___

a a website where people write their opinions
b what you get from a university, for example, Bachelor of Arts
c influence or motivate people
d famous or popular

GO TO page viii
for **GRAMMAR** step-by-step instructions.

GRAMMAR simple past (affirmative statements)

A Read the text in READING B again. Complete with the simple past form of the verbs.

Regular Verbs

1 start ___started___ **2** continue ___continued___ **3** stop ___stopped___ **4** open ___opened___

READING OPTIONAL 10.01

If students don't know who the person is, they should try to infer who she is by what they see in the pictures. For example, *She's a girl, young, about 20 years old, dressed in typical dress, speaking in pubic. She is happy, nice, determined, and strong.*

THINKING SKILL—Summarize

To summarize the biography, students recreate a condensed version that includes the main points and key details. Have them reread the biography and make some notes as they go. Note-taking can be a very helpful strategy for summarizing because we tend to focus on the main points for the notes.

VOCABULARY

Once students have matched the vocabulary words and phrases to their definitions, ask them to use the words in sentences. This will show they have understood the meanings.

B Complete the table.

Spelling Changes for the Simple Past		
Regular verbs Example: *ask*	Add **1** ___-ed___.	*asked*
Verbs ending in –*e* Example: *live*	Add **2** ___-d___.	*lived*
Verbs ending in vowel + consonant Example: *stop*	Double the last **3** ___letter___ and add *–ed*.	*stopped*
Verbs ending in consonant + –*y* Example: *cry*	Change *y* to **4** ___i___ and add *–ed*.	*cried*

For more practice, go to page 155.

C Read the text in READING B again. Write the simple past form of the irregular verbs.

1 have ___had___ **2** go ___went___ **3** become ___became___ **4** meet ___met___

D Complete the conversation with the past tense of the verbs.

Logan: Who's that in the picture?

Chase: Oh, that's my grandfather. He **1** ___was___ (be) born in 1940. He **2** ___died___ (die) a few years ago. He **3** ___had___ (have) an interesting life. He **4** ___became___ (become) an engineer. He **5** ___started___ (start) his own business and **6** ___went___ (go) around the world. He **7** ___met___ (meet) my grandmother in Spain and they **8** ___got married___ (marry) in 1970.

PRONUNCIATION the ending *–ed*

GO TO page ix for **PRONUNCIATION** step-by-step instructions.

A Read the pronunciation rules. How do you think the words are pronounced?

voiced consonant + *–ed* = /d/	unvoiced consonant + *–ed* = /t/	verb ends in *t* or *d* + *–ed* = /ɪd/
learned	stopped	decided

B 10.02 Listen and check. Practice saying the verbs.

SPEAKING

GO TO page xii for **SPEAKING** step-by-step instructions.

A Write sentences about milestones in your life in your notebook.

B IN PAIRS Discuss. Use the Confident Communicator box to help you.

Choose three milestones and tell your partner about them. Then find another pair and tell them what you learned about each other.

CONFIDENT COMMUNICATOR
START TALKING

To talk about milestones, use *when I was* and your age at the time: *I learned to walk* ***when I was*** *10 months old.* You can also say the year and then your age: *I graduated from elementary school in 2013, when I was 12.*

GRAMMAR

The simple past affirmative is useful as it enables students to express things in the past. Have students look up a list of five regular verbs and five irregular verbs that they think are the most common verbs in English. Have them test each other on the simple past forms of the verbs they wrote—for example, *eat (ate), sleep (slept), drive (drove), ride (rode), like (liked), love (loved)*, and so on.

PRONUNCIATION

Consonant clusters are hard for Spanish speakers to pronounce. An error they often commit in the simple past is to add a syllable before the final sound.

SPEAKING

Read the definition of *milestone* out loud—an event or achievement that marks an important stage in a process. Demonstrate **A** by telling students about three milestones in your life. Or choose three milestones in a famous person's life and describe them. Have pairs guess who they are.

Draw student's attention to the Confident Communicator box and let them know that time phrases are usually used with the simple past.

LESSON 2 Social Life

VOCABULARY social life collocations

A **Check (✓) things you did in the last month.**

- go out dancing ☐
- have a party ☐
- hang out with friends ☐
- see a movie ☐
- eat out at a restaurant ☐
- go to a concert ☐
- go on a date ☐
- visit family ☐

B **IN PAIRS Discuss your social life.**

I ate out at a restaurant.
I saw a movie.
I met up with friends and I visited family. And you?

GRAMMAR simple past (negative statements and questions)

A **Read the conversation. Underline a negative statement, a *yes/no* question, an information question, and a short answer. Then complete the rules.**

Caleb: What did you do last night?
Ryan: I went out with friends. Did you go out?
Caleb: No, I didn't. I didn't want to go out. I stayed home and watched TV.

1. For negative statements, use didn't/did not + the base form of the verb.
2. For *yes/no* questions, use ___did___ + subject + the base form of the verb.
3. For short answers, use *Yes* + subject + *did*, or *No* + subject + didn't/did not
4. For *wh*– questions, use a question word + ___did___ + subject + the base form of the verb.

For more practice, go to page 156.

B **Complete the conversation with an affirmative or negative form of the simple past.**

Ryan: What **1** ___did___ you watch on TV?
Caleb: I watched a movie. **2** ___Did___ you eat out at a restaurant?
Ryan: Yes, we **3** ___did___. We went to Luigi's.
Caleb: What **4** ___did___ you have?
Ryan: I **5** ___wasn't/was not___ hungry, so I **6** ___didn't/did not___ order a lot. I just had a small pizza.

C **IN PAIRS Ask your partner what he or she did last night.**

A: What did you do last night?
B: I watched TV.
A: What did you watch?

VOCABULARY Alternative Activity

Play Past Tense Bingo. Tell students to choose five of the verbs from the activity and write them on a piece of paper in the past tense. Call out verbs from the activity in the present tense in random order and tell students to check them as they hear them. The first person to check all five of their verbs and shouts *Past Tense Bingo!* is the winner.

Before beginning VOCABULARY **B**, write *What did you do last weekend?* on the board. After **B**, have students extend their vocabulary by looking up more activities to represent what they did last weekend.

GRAMMAR

The difficult part of using questions in the simple past and negative forms are the word order and use of the auxiliary *did*. Have students practice word order by writing five questions in scrambled format on a piece of paper. Tell them to exchange the questions with a partner and have their partner unscramble them.

LISTENING

A **Look at the pictures. What do you think the LISTENING is about?**

B **10.03 LISTENING SKILL—Listen for main ideas** **Listen to the conversation. Choose the things that the speakers talk about.**

order food	☑	have a party	☐
go on a date	☐	meet up with friends	☑
go out to eat	☑	see a movie	☐
go to a club	☐	visit family	☐

C **10.03** **Listen again, and write the reasons each person gives. Then check.**

1 Madison: I met up with friends because I didn't have any homework.
2 Madison: We went out to eat because we were hungry.
3 Luciana: I didn't go out because I had to study.
4 Luciana: I ordered a pizza because the restaurant is close to my house.

D **THINKING SKILL—Evaluate** **Is it important to you to have a lot of friends, or do you prefer one or two close friends? Why?**

SPEAKING

A **Choose a topic to ask your partner about.**

what you did last weekend	☐	what you did last summer	☐
the last time you had fun	☐	the last time you found something	☐
the last time you ate out	☐	the last time you forgot something	☐

B **IN PAIRS** **Ask each other about your topics. Ask questions to learn more. Use the Confident Communicator box to help you.**

C **Tell the class what you learned about your partner.**

CONFIDENT COMMUNICATOR
KEEP TALKING

To encourage someone to say more:
Really?
Tell me about it. *So, what did you do?*
Tell me more. *Then what happened?*

GO TO page xi for LISTENING step-by-step instructions.

GO TO page 147 for AUDIO SCRIPT.

LISTENING

Students may predict that the listening is about fun things and not-so-fun things to do on the weekend.

THINKING SKILL—Evaluate

Play a guessing game. Tell students to write on a piece of paper their best friend's name. Ask for a volunteer to go to the front of the classroom. Tell the volunteer to describe their best friend without saying the name. The student who guesses the name correctly goes at the front of the class to describe their best friend. Then introduce the thinking skill question.

SPEAKING

Read the topics aloud. Brainstorm questions around one of the topics. Some questions for what you did last weekend might be *What did you do last weekend? Did you do anything interesting last weekend?* Encourage follow-up questions (questions based on a person's answers). For example, *A: I went to see a movie. B: What movie did you see?*

LESSON 3 In My Experience

VOCABULARY collocations with *get, have,* and *make*

A Look at the pictures. Write which situations are positive experiences, which are negative experiences, and which can be positive *and* negative.

1
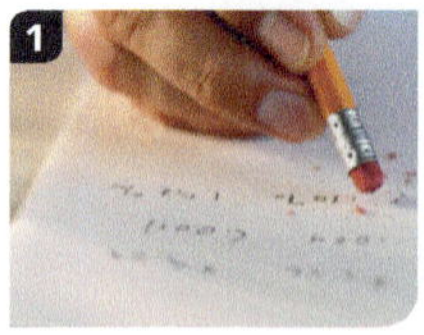
make a mistake
negative

2

get upset
negative

3

make a new friend
positive

4

have an argument
negative

5

make a decision
positive and negative

6

have fun
positive

7

get lost
negative

B Complete the conversation. Use phrases from A.

How was last night? Did you have **1** ___fun___ at the club?

Yes, we did. But at first Zac and I went to the wrong place! We got **2** ___lost___!

Oh, no! How did you make a **3** ___mistake___ like that?

I don't know! I thought Zac knew the location. But we didn't get **4** ___upset___ or have an **5** ___argument___. We asked a woman and finally found the club. It's a great place!

LISTENING

GO TO page 147 for AUDIO SCRIPT.

A 10.04 LISTENING SKILL—Listen for gist Listen and choose the correct option.

1 Kristina is talking about a time when she …
   a forgot something. **b** made a decision. **c** got upset.
2 Javier is talking about a time when he …
   a had an argument. **b** got lost. **c** made a new friend.
3 Lauren is talking about a time when she …
   a had an argument. **b** found something. **c** made a mistake.

B 10.04 Listen again and complete with the words you hear.

1 Kristina: I ___thought___ it was just a regular party, but it was her birthday, and I ___forgot___!
2 Javier: When I ___saw___ him, I ___showed___ him where to go.
3 Lauren: When we ___got___ there, they said they ___didn't have___ a table for us.

C THINKING SKILL—Analyze Compare the stories in the LISTENING to your life. Did anything like these experiences happen to you? Tell a partner.

VOCABULARY

Play a game to preview the vocabulary exercise. Tell students to close their books. Write *get, make,* and *have* on the board. Say a word and have students indicate the right verb by pointing to it while saying the phrase. For example, say *A mistake.* Students should point to *make* and say *Make a mistake.* Have them check their suggestions by opening their books.

LISTENING

LISTENING SKILL—Listen for gist

Tell students to listen to the tone of voice of the person speaking when they are listening to a conversation. This will help them predict mood and give them hints as to the situation. These contextual clues will help them understand the gist of a conversation.

WRITING

A Read the email. Choose *True* or *False*.

New Message

From: Juana@email.cc — Cc Bcc

To: avery@email.cc — Cc Bcc

Hi, Avery.

How are things?

The business trip to London was great, but I made a big mistake!

I went to a new restaurant with some friends. We had a good meal, but when we left, a car almost hit me outside the restaurant! I looked left, then right, before I crossed the street. But it's London! You have to look right, then left. Fortunately, the driver stopped in time, but we were both a little scared. He shouted at me to look both ways and drove away.

The next day, I went to the London office and guess what? I met the driver! He's one of my coworkers. In the end, we laughed about our "meeting" the day before. He's a really nice guy.

Write me soon with all your news!

Take care,

Juana

Send

1. Juana liked the restaurant. **True** / False
2. A car hit Juana. True / **False**
3. Juana had an argument with the driver. True / **False**
4. Juana met the driver again later. **True** / False
5. Juana and the driver are coworkers. **True** / False

MAKE IT YOURS

Business emails often include some personal experiences. When you describe some of your experiences, you connect with the people you work with.

B Write an email to a friend about a time you made a mistake, got lost, or had an argument. Use *first, next, later,* and *in the end*.

1. When did this happen? ______
2. What happened first? ______
3. What happened next / later / the next day? ______
4. What happened in the end? ______

GO TO page xiv for **WRITING** step-by-step instructions.

SPEAKING

A Choose one of the experiences and think about a time when it happened to you. What happened? Make notes to help you.

- a time when I got upset
- a time when I had fun
- a time when I lost something important
- a time when I made a new friend

B IN PAIRS Role play. Student A, tell your partner about your experience. Student B, listen carefully to your partner, and ask any questions you have. Then change roles. Use the Confident Communicator box to help you.

CONFIDENT COMMUNICATOR
START TALKING

To say when something happened, use *yesterday, the day before yesterday*, or *last Monday / week / month / year*, etc.
You can also use a period of time + *ago:*
This happened two years ago.

WRITING

After completing WRITING **A**, have students reread the email and underline all the time phrases, like *when we left* and *the next day*. Then ask them to circle the verbs in the simple past. Check answers as a class.

SPEAKING

Tell a personal anecdote to demonstrate the speaking activity. Draw students' attention to the Confident Communicator box. Tell students to make notes and rehearse what they want to say, but warn them not to look at their notes while they are talking to their partner. Instead, they should maintain eye contact as much as possible. The listener should lean forward, face the speaker, and nod as they are listening. They can use the short comments of encouragement to say more from the Confident Communicator box from the last lesson.

GO TO page xv
for LANGUAGE AND LIFE step-by-step instructions.

Language and Life

Empathy – Take My Advice

A 10.05 **Read the web page. Then answer the questions.**

THE WORLD ADVICE CORNER

The world's problem-solving web page

Got a problem? Got a solution? Here at the World Advice Corner, we want you to use your experience to help each other. Post your problem and then read the advice from people around the world. Or find a problem and give your advice. Here's a selection of problems on the World Advice Corner.

My problem is that I'm lonely. It's hard to make new friends. I went to a party recently and spent most of the night in the kitchen! I get nervous around people I don't know. Does anyone have any advice? –Adrian

Submit Advice

My parents try to control my life! When I go out with friends, they always want to know exactly where I am and what I'm doing. I have to text them every half an hour or they worry. How can I find a solution? I don't want to argue with them. –Maria

Submit Advice

I have a work problem. Last week, I made a mistake and my boss yelled at me. I got upset and didn't know what to do. Did this ever happen to you? What did you do? All advice is welcome! –Olivia

Submit Advice

1 What happens on the advice website? People ask about problems and other people give them advice.
2 What problem does Adrian have? He is nervous in social situations.
3 What problem does Maria have? Her parents try to control her life.
4 What problem does Olivia have? She doesn't know what to do when her boss shouts at her.

B IN GROUPS Discuss whether you have the same problem. Explain what happened.

I had the same problem as Olivia. I had an argument with my boss. She said …

C Read and choose the advice you think best fits each person.

1 What should Adrian do?
  a go to more parties **b** find a hobby **c** play a sport
2 What should Maria do?
  a explain how she feels **b** forget her parents and do what she wants **c** ask her parents to explain why they worry
3 What should Olivia do?
  a get another job **b** argue with her boss **c** explain to her boss how she feels

104 Unit 10 Life Stories

OBJECTIVE

In this lesson, students give advice on an advice web page. Students will think creatively about solutions to problems that people post online. They are encouraged to think carefully about the problems and possible solutions, using their own experiences, and responding with empathy. They should keep in mind that advice should be given with respect for the person's feelings.

PROCESS OPTIONAL 10.05

Students first read a web page forum with problems posted by three people and answer the questions. They analyze the problems and link the experiences to similar situations in their own lives. They consider various advice options and make notes on what they think the people should do. In pairs, students choose one of the problems and write a reply to the person, suggesting ways they could tackle their problem. Finally, students share their advice with the class, and the class votes on the best post.

D **Make notes on advice for Adrian, Maria, and Olivia.**

I think Adrian should find a hobby because he can meet people with the same hobby.

Adrian: ____

____

Maria: ____

____

Olivia: ____

____

E **IN PAIRS Choose one person from D and write a complete post with your advice.**

Hi, Adrian. It's often hard to make friends, but here's our advice. First, find a hobby you like …

Submit Advice

____

____

____

____

____

F **Share your advice with the class. Take a class vote for the best advice.**

MAKE IT DIGITAL

Find an advice website like the one in the text. Submit a problem you have or one of the problems from **A**. See what advice you receive.

FURTHER DISCUSSION

Put students in groups of three and ask them to discuss the following questions:

- Who do you go to for advice?
- Is mom usually the one people turn to for advice, or dad?
- Do you go to different people depending on what advice you are looking for?
- Do you have a trusted family member or friend who can give good advice?
- What do you do when you get bad advice?

MAKE IT DIGITAL

Some possible advice sites to submit a problem from **A** are Ask Amy at the *Washington Post* (https://www.washingtonpost.com/lifestyle/advice/ask-amy) and Ask Dr. M (http://www.askdrm.org/).

GO TO page xvii
for **UNIT REVIEW** step-by-step instructions.

UNIT 10

VOCABULARY review

SCORE: / 10

A **Match the sentence beginning (1–10) to the sentence end (a–j). Write the letter.**

1	Do you want to go on d	**a**	make a mistake?
2	Where do you usually meet up c	**b**	dancing?
3	How often do you go b	**c**	with friends?
4	At what age did you start e	**d**	a date?
5	When did you last a	**e**	school?
6	How do your friends like to have h	**f**	out at a restaurant?
7	What makes you get j	**g**	a movie?
8	Would you like to watch g	**h**	fun?
9	How often do you eat f	**i**	born?
10	In what year were you i	**j**	upset?

GRAMMAR review

SCORE: / 10

A **Complete the paragraph with the simple past form of the verbs in parentheses.**

3 didn't/did not see
5 didn't/did not look

In 2017, 16-year-old student Rayouf Alhumedhi **1** wrote (write) a text message to a friend. She **2** tried (try) to add an emoji, but she **3** ________ (do not see) any on her phone that she **4** liked (like). They **5** ________ (not look) like her. Alhumedhi, a Muslim from Saudi Arabia, **6** wanted (want) an emoji with a headscarf. So what **7** did she do (do)? She **8** asked (ask) Apple and the Unicode emoji committee to make one. "It's something important to my identity," she **9** told (tell) *Time Magazine*. Apple soon **10** had (have) the new emoji on all its phones.

16–20 correct: You can talk about social life with *get, have,* and *make*. You can use the simple past in affirmative and negative statements.
0–15 correct: Look again at the Vocabulary and Grammar sections in the unit.

TOTAL SCORE: / 20

WHAT DO YOU KNOW NOW? Look back at page 97 and add the words you know now to the box.

GO TO page xix
for **FOLLOW A PRO** step-by-step instructions.

FOLLOW A PRO EVENT PLANNING

Take the quiz about special events. Go to Follow A Pro on page 136 to find the answers. Then learn more about the event planning industry.

1 **Social media is the best way to tell people about an event.**
a true **b** false

2 **How many weddings are there in the US every year?**
a 1.2 million **b** 2.4 million **c** 158,000

3 **How many birthday cards do people send every year?**
a one million **b** one billion **c** two billion

4 **40% of couples spend ... hours per week planning their wedding.**
a 1–5 **b** 5–10 **c** 10–15

ALTERNATIVE ACTIVITY

You may want to do VOCABULARY **A** as a mingling activity. Copy and cut up the sentence parts and give a part to each student. They memorize their parts—either the beginning or the ending of a question. Then, they mingle around the room, saying their part in order to find their partner to make a complete question. Once students find their partners, ask them to answer their question.

FURTHER DISCUSSION

Put students in groups of three and ask the following questions for them to discuss:

- Where were you born?
- Where did you go to elementary school?
- What did you do last weekend?
- Did you go out with friends last week?
- Is there a person in history who inspires you? What did he or she do?

UNIT 11
Planning Ahead

GO TO page vi for UNIT OPENER step-by-step instructions.

WHAT DO YOU ALREADY KNOW?

1 Think of words you know about present and future goals. Write the words.

2 **IN PAIRS** Share and compare your information. Add more words to your lists.

Present

Future

STUDENTS MAY ALREADY KNOW:

- **Present goals:** school, college, friends.
- **Future goals:** job, study, family.

DISCUSS & SHARE

VIDEO

3 **IN GROUPS** Watch the video and answer the question.

SYM Do you think of your future or live for now?

GO TO page xx for VIDEOS IN SYM step-by-step instructions.

In this unit, you will ...

- talk about plans and intentions, ways to save money, and your career goals.
- use thinking skills: apply, calculate, and analyze.
- read about making to-do lists.
- use strategies to keep talking by suggesting alternatives.
- use self-direction skills to make a career plan based on your interests.
- learn tips about personal development.

Unit 11 Planning Ahead 107

WHAT DO YOU ALREADY KNOW?

If you notice students are struggling to understand what to do, you can provide one or two examples to help them get started:

- **Goals:** finish school, get a job, study for a master's degree

VIDEO

Before viewing, ask:

What is Amy's plan for her life? *own a business.*

What is Max doing with his life? *finding what he likes, taking classes*

After viewing, put the continuum on the board.

live for now — plan for future

Students mark the continuum and explain how they plan.

DISCUSS & SHARE

Students should consider how they approach life—do they live for today, or do they have their eye on the future? Have them discuss in groups the pros and cons of both ways of viewing life.

GO TO page x

for **READING** step-by-step instructions.

GO TO page 148

for **AUDIO SCRIPT**.

1 They list a lot of things and only do half.

LESSON 1 On Your To-Do List

READING

A Which statement is true for you? Check (✓) and explain.

I use to-do lists every day. I need them to organize my time! ☐
I sometimes use to-do lists when I have a lot of things to remember. ☐
I never use to-do lists. I keep it all in my head! ☐

B 11.01 Read the article and discuss the question.

1 What mistake do people make with to-do lists?

WHAT TO DO ABOUT TO-DO LISTS

What are you going to do today? Maybe you're going to write an important email, shop for a gift, or make a dentist **appointment**. We all have busy lives and it's easy to **forget** things we're supposed to do.

A list of things to do—or a "to-do list"—helps us **remember** what to do, but many people make a big mistake when they write their lists: they list a lot of things and then only do half of them. Here are some tips for writing a useful to-do list.

1. Write three things you are going to do in one day. Choose the things that are really important and write your list the night before. That way, you're **ready** to go in the morning!
2. When you have more than three things to do, write the top three and do them first. Then make a new list and write another three things. If you have one big job to do, break it into smaller jobs.
3. Write exactly what you need to do. Don't write "learn English." Write "learn eight new English words." People do things on their lists when it's **clear** what to do.
4. Be ready to change your list. Things are going to happen that you didn't **plan**. When they do, write a new list. Life is full of surprises!

C READING SKILL—Read for the main idea Choose the main idea of the text.

1 We should use to-do lists more.
2 To-do lists can be very helpful if you follow some basic tips.

D THINKING SKILL—Apply Write your to-do list for tomorrow. Follow the advice in the text. Compare lists with a partner.

GO TO page vii

for **VOCABULARY** step-by-step instructions.

VOCABULARY

A Complete with the words from the box.

appointment clear forget plan ready remember

1 I have my phone and my money. I'm ___ready___ to go!
2 Things on your list should be ___clear___ and easy to understand.
3 I have a/an ___appointment___ to see the doctor on Monday.
4 When you ___forget___ something on your list, you don't do it.
5 Did you ___remember___ to call your mom?
6 I ___plan___ to go shopping with friends on Saturday.

READING OPTIONAL 11.01

Show the class examples of to-do lists. You can access examples on the internet or write an example on the board. You may want to have students predict the answer to the question *What mistakes do people make with to-do lists?*

THINKING SKILL—Apply

Students are going to apply what they have understood to a new situation. They are going to personalize the information they have learned and apply it to something for their own lives. Have them underline what they consider to be the most effective tips in **B** and then use those tips when they write their own to-do lists.

VOCABULARY

If students struggle with the meaning of the words, encourage them to use an English dictionary. To check that students have understood the meanings of the words from the box, have them write their own sentences in their notebooks. Have them work in groups of three or four to share their sentences.

GRAMMAR *going to*

A **Underline the sentences with *going to* in the article from READING B.**

B **Read the sentences you underlined. Complete the rule.**

1 Before *going to*, we use the verb ________ in the correct form.
  a *be* b *have* c *do*
2 After *going to*, we use the ________ of the verb.
  a base form b *-ing* form c infinitive
3 We use *going to* to talk about plans and ________.
  a offers b requests c predictions

For more practice, go to page 157.

C **Read and complete the plans (1–2) and predictions (3–4).**

1 A: What are you going to do this weekend?
  B: Oh, I am / I'm going to see my cousins! (see my cousins)
2 A: Do you and your friend have any plans for tonight?
  B: Yes! We are / We're going to go dancing. (go dancing)
3 A: What do you think about your exams?
  B: I'm really worried. I think I am / I'm going to fail! (fail)
4 A: It's a beautiful day!
  B: Yeah … but it is / it's going to get cold later. (get cold later)

D **IN PAIRS Discuss the questions.**

1 What are you going to do tonight? What else is going to happen then?
2 What are you going to do this weekend? What else is going to happen then?

PRONUNCIATION *going to*

A **11.02 Listen and notice how the speakers say *going to*. *Going to* is often pronounced /gʌnə/. Practice saying the dialogues in GRAMMAR C.**

SPEAKING

A **Do you agree or disagree with the predictions? Then add your own prediction.**

	Strongly agree	Agree	Not sure	Disagree	Strongly disagree
1 More education is going to help me get a job.	☐	☐	☐	☐	☐
2 I'm going to own a successful business before I'm 30.	☐	☐	☐	☐	☐
3 My career is going to change a lot in the next five years.	☐	☐	☐	☐	☐
4 ________	☐	☐	☐	☐	☐

B **Choose a statement you agree with in A. Write a plan to help your prediction come true.**

I'm going to own a successful business before I'm 30. I'm going to start my own online business ...

C **IN PAIRS Talk about your predictions and plans. Use the Confident Communicator box to help you.**

CONFIDENT COMMUNICATOR
START TALKING

To ask about future plans, say: *What are you going to do?* To ask about future plans at a specific time in the future, say: *What are you going to do* + time expression, e.g., *What are you going to do tomorrow / next month / in December?*

GO TO page viii
for **GRAMMAR** step-by-step instructions.

GO TO page ix
for **PRONUNCIATION** step-by-step instructions.

GO TO page xii
for **SPEAKING** step-by-step instructions.

GRAMMAR

In GRAMMAR **D**, first have students predict what they each will say. Asking a question is a natural way to start a conversation about someone's plans. For example, *Are you going to work at your part-time job this evening?* The response elicited will be the actual plan: *No, I'm going to go shopping this evening.*

PRONUNCIATION

Tell students that if they want to listen to a good example of the natural pronunciation of *going to*, they should watch sitcoms. Elicit what sitcoms they watch in English.

SPEAKING

CONFIDENT COMMUNICATOR

People often ask each other what they're going to do for the summer, for spring break, or over the winter break. Common holidays and celebrations are a terrific talking point. You may want to suggest a number of breaks and holidays students have coming up that they can ask each other about.

LESSON 2 Saving for the Future

VOCABULARY money

A **Match the opposites. Write the number (1–6).**

1 

buy 3

2 

spend 5

3 

sell 1

4 

rich 6

5 

save 2

6 

poor 4

B **IN PAIRS Discuss the questions.**

1 Do you save money every month or do you spend all of it?
2 What was the last thing you bought? What was the last thing you sold?

GO TO page xi
for **LISTENING** step-by-step instructions.

GO TO page 148
for **AUDIO SCRIPT**.

LISTENING

A **Look at the picture. What do you think the person in the picture is doing? Why is he doing that?**

B **11.03 LISTENING SKILL—Listen for specific information**
Listen and match each person (1–2) to the reason why they want to save money (a–b). Write the letter.

1 David a — **a** to rent an apartment
2 Patricia b — **b** to go on vacation

C **11.03 Listen again and choose *True* or *False*.**

1 David earns a lot from his job. True / **False**
2 He spends a lot of money on rent. True / **False**
3 He is going to save money on food. **True** / False
4 Patricia wants to spend money on expensive gifts. True / **False**
5 She made a photo album for her mom. **True** / False
6 She wants her brother to make her a pizza. True / **False**

D **THINKING SKILL—Calculate** **Estimate how much you can save doing what David and Patricia are going to do.**

MAKE IT YOURS
Make a list of things you spent money on this month. Then make a list of ways you could save money next month.

VOCABULARY

More words related to money are: *sale, bargain, investment, put away, percentage, retirement, financial advisor, stocks, stock market, change, bills*, and *coins*. Ask students the meaning of these words and phrases. If they are not sure about the meaning of a word, use a dictionary.

LISTENING

THINKING SKILL—Calculate

Demonstrate a calculation. Tell students you want to save money by giving up your daily coffee bought from the coffee shop, by bringing in your own coffee maker to work. Show that the cost of every coffee multiplied by 5 is the weekly expenditure. That weekly expense multiplied by 40 weeks (because you're not always here or don't have time to buy coffee) minus the cost of your own coffee equals your savings. Let's say you currently buy one coffee a day at $2 dollars. 2 × 5 = $10, $10 × 40 = $400, and $400 – $20 (cost of 1kg of your own coffee) = $380. You save $380!

GRAMMAR direct and indirect objects

A Read and complete the rules.

David: This month, I'm going to make sandwiches for myself.
Patricia: I'm going to make him pizza!

1 In "make sandwiches for myself," *sandwiches* is the direct object. What is the indirect object? ___me___

2 In "make him pizza," *pizza* is the direct object. What is the indirect object? ___him___

Some verbs can take a direct object and an indirect object. Notice the word order.

3 subject + verb + direct object + preposition + indirect object
People give gifts ___to___ *each other.*

4 subject + verb + indirect object + direct object
People give each other ___gifts___.

5 Use the preposition ___to___ with the verbs *give, bring, sell, send, show,* and *tell.*

6 Use the preposition *for* with the verbs *buy, cook,* and *make.*

For more practice, go to page 157.

B Rewrite the underlined phrases. Do not use a preposition.

Money-saving tips

Why don't you make a gift for your friend for her birthday?

1 make your friend a gift

You could cook a meal for your family and save on eating out.

2 cook your family a meal

You could buy local food for a visitor as a souvenir of his visit.

3 buy a visitor local food

When your friends have a party, why not bring homemade cookies for them?

4 bring them homemade cookies

C IN PAIRS Write two more money-saving tips in your notebook. Use two of the verbs from A.

SPEAKING

A Make a list of reasons for saving money in your notebook.

B Role-play a conversation. Student A, you want to save money for a nice birthday gift for a family member. Tell your partner why you want to save money and ask him or her how to save money. Student B, suggest ways Student A could save money. Use the Confident Communicator box to help you.

CONFIDENT COMMUNICATOR
KEEP TALKING

To suggest alternatives, use *You could …* e.g., *You could make lunch at home.* You can also use negative questions with *Why don't you …?* e.g., *Why don't you make a gift?*

GRAMMAR

Some money-saving tips students may suggest are: *Don't buy a cake for a family member's birthday; make a cake. Buy a cheaper brand of coffee for the house. Cook dinner for friends instead of going out. Give people less expensive presents. Bring fruit and cheese from home for a morning snack in the office. Sell clothes you don't wear to people online.*

SPEAKING

Other reasons students may want to save money are: to buy a scooter, motorcycle, or car; to help a friend; to go on a trip; or to pay for a hobby.

Have students perform their role-plays for the class, or if you have a large class, divide students into groups of six to eight and have pairs perform their role-plays for the group. They should vote on the best reasons for saving money and the best suggestions.

LESSON 3 Career Plans

VOCABULARY career plans collocations

A Check (✓) the things you want to do in your future career.

1 
work outdoors

2 
manage people

3 
work in an office

4 

start a business

5 
work from home

6 
work overseas

B IN PAIRS Discuss your future career plans. Use phrases from A.

I want to work for a large company. I'm probably going to manage other people. I also want to work overseas …

LISTENING

A IN PAIRS What do you need to do to get your dream job? Discuss.

B 11.04 LISTENING SKILL—Listen for gist Listen and make notes on Jade's advice.

GO TO page 148 for AUDIO SCRIPT.

How to get your dream job:

First, start early.

Second, get information.

Finally, don't give up.

C THINKING SKILL—Analyze Decide what other advice is useful for getting your dream job.

- Talk to people with the job you want.
- Network with family and friends.
- Volunteer at places with similar jobs.
- Go to job fairs.
- other: ______

Answers will vary. Possible answers: start at the bottom, be realistic, measure your progress, speak to people in that job, etc.

VOCABULARY

To increase student's repertoire of words, write these collocations on the board: *work with others*, *work with children*, *manage businesses*, and *manage products*.

Tell students there are many factors about themselves they should consider when thinking about the job that is right for them. They may not know yet what they want, so they should pay attention to their preferences.

LISTENING

LISTENING SKILL—Listen for gist

Allow students to hear the entire interview first so they get a general understanding of the content to listen for gist. In order to accurately highlight the steps to get a dream job, play the recording again, but pause the recording to give students time to make notes.

THINKING SKILL—Analyze

When thinking about what other advice is important for getting your dream job, students may want to think about whether they agree with Jade's advice or not. Part of an analysis is seeing the pros and cons of a position.

WRITING

A Read the journal entry. Underline sentences with *so* and *because*.

Saturday, May 15

It's time to think about my career, so I need to set some goals and make a plan. In the next two years, I'm going to start my own business because I want to be the boss. I know a lot about cooking, so I want to open my own restaurant!

I need to learn more about cooking and food safety, so I'm going to study at a culinary college that teaches those things. Then, I'm going to take a business course. I have to understand money and business to run a restaurant.

And finally, I'm going to practice cooking because I need to improve my skills!

Well, that's my plan!

FOLLOW

B Choose the correct phrases to complete the rules.

1 Use *so* to talk about the result of / reason for something.
2 Use *because* to explain the result of / reason for something.

C Complete the career plan with your own goals.

In my future career, I'm going to ______

So, I'm going to ______

______

because ______

______

D Write a journal entry describing your career plans in your notebook.

SPEAKING

A Make notes to answer the questions.

1 What is your dream job? ______
2 What are you going to do to get that job?
learn a skill do an internship get a degree/certificate
______
3 Do you think you will use English in your dream job? How?
______

B IN PAIRS Discuss your career plans and if English is important for your dream job. Use the Confident Communicator box to help you.

CONFIDENT COMMUNICATOR
REPAIR IT

When you aren't sure about what you are saying, at the start of your sentence, say: *I guess* or *I suppose*.
I guess I'm going to use English with people on the phone.

GO TO page xiv for WRITING step-by-step instructions.

Suggested answers: It's time to think about my career, so I need to set myself some goals and make a plan. In the next two years, I'm going to start my own business because I want to be the boss. I need to learn more about cooking and food safety, so I'm going to study at a culinary college that teaches those things. And finally, I'm going to practice cooking because I need to improve my skills!

WRITING

Before writing the journal entry, have students check each other's planners and make suggestions about information to add. Tell them the guidelines for peer feedback are to make positive comments before identifying something that's missing. Remind students to be respectful when giving feedback.

SPEAKING Alternative Activity

Discuss *growing*, *popular*, and *declining* jobs as students see them. Write the sentence starters below on the board for an open-class discussion. The words in parentheses are suggestions in case students need some ideas.

- Jobs that are on the rise are … (solar panel installer, wind turbine technician, genetic counselor).
- Jobs that are popular with young adults are … (engineer, architect, doctor).
- Jobs that are declining are … (typist, file clerk, postman).

GO TO page xv
for LANGUAGE AND LIFE step-by-step instructions.

Language and Life

Self-direction – From Hobby to Career

A 11.05 **Read the article. Answer the questions.**

Follow Your Passion

15. Oct 11:24

Many of us have a hobby or a free-time activity we love, but is it possible to make that hobby a career? For some people, the answer is "yes." Love baking? Start a cake-making business. Exercise every day? Start a career as a personal trainer. Today, lots of people are finding that social media can help them turn their passion into a career.

Fiorella Pia has an interesting hobby. She takes photographs of food and shares them on a social networking website. She has a talent for making the food look nice. She has a lot of followers and her pictures are very popular. Now she wants to turn her hobby into a career. She wants to earn money from her photography. She's going to plan carefully. She needs to decide exactly what kind of business to start. She also needs to write a business plan. She's asking all her friends for their advice as she puts together her career plan.

Read more

1 Which hobbies can become careers, according to the article? cake-making, personal trainer
2 What is Fiorella's hobby? food photography
3 What does she want to do now? start a business

B IN GROUPS **Make a list of careers that involve photography. Then compare your lists as a class. Which group thought of the most careers?**

Suggested answers: food photographer, portrait photographer, forensic photographer, fashion photographer, photographer's assistant, photography store manager, scientific photographer, school photographer, sports photographer, etc.

wedding photographer

photojournalist

____

____

OBJECTIVE

In this lesson, students will make a career plan. Students will analyze ways to make a career out of a hobby. They are encouraged to think carefully about the opportunities and challenges involved in career planning and how to give themselves options and alternative choices along the way. Students analyze how to turn short-term and long-term goals into strategies for achieving the ultimate goal.

PROCESS OPTIONAL 11.05

First, students read an article about a person who wants to turn her passion for photography into a career but doesn't know how to do it. Students brainstorm a list of photography careers. They read advice for making career choices and apply it to Fiorella's predicament. Then, they make a list of goals for her to work on. Finally, in pairs, students apply what they have learned in Fiorella's case to their own lives.

C **Read the information. Then decide what Fiorella's A/B/Z choices should be.**

When you are making a career plan, it's a good idea to have "A/B/Z" choices. Reid Hoffman, founder of LinkedIn, created the A/B/Z plan. An "A" choice is your dream choice. This is the career you really want. You need a bit of luck to get it, but this is your dream career.

Your "B" choice is your alternative plan. This is the choice for when Plan A doesn't work out. It isn't your dream career, but it is close.

Your "Z" choice is an emergency choice. This is what you can do when Plan A and Plan B don't succeed. Perhaps you can do this for a short time and think about a new Plan A/B.

Fiorella Pia's Career Plan:

1 A choice: ______________________

2 B choice: ______________________

3 Z choice: ______________________

D **IN GROUPS** **Discuss the different goals Fiorella should have. Make a list of clear short-term, mid-term, and long-term goals.**

Short-term goals (up to 1 year):

do 3 or 4 weddings as a photographer and build a website

____

____

Mid-term goals (1–5 years):

employ one assistant and rent a studio

____

____

Long-term goals (5 years +):

employ photographers and open studios in three major cities

____

____

E **IN PAIRS** **Ask and answer questions about your choices and suggestions.**

1 Explain your A/B/Z choices for Fiorella.

2 Say what you think her short-, mid-, and long-term goals should be.

F **IN PAIRS** **Discuss the questions.**

1 Do you have a hobby that could become a career?

2 What could you do to make money from your hobby?

3 Is it always a good idea to make a career out of a hobby? Are there any possible problems?

MAKE IT DIGITAL

Go online and find careers related to your favorite hobby. Make a list of your A/B/Z choices.

MAKE IT DIGITAL

Here are some example hobbies that may become careers and the application of A/B/Z choices. Remember that A is the dream choice, B is the alternative plan, and Z is the emergency choice.

- Playing video games—The dream job could be video game designer. An alternative choice could be programmer, and the emergency choice could be giving coding classes in an afterschool program.
- Doing crafts—The dream choice could be jewelry maker/designer. Alternatively, they could make jewelry at home and sell it online. Or they could make it at home and sell it at the local craft market.

CULTURE NOTE

Jennifer Hyman and Jennifer Fleiss turned their interest in fashion into a dress rental company called Rent the Runway.

Michael Kittredge made his mother a scented candle for her birthday when he was young. His candle-making hobby is now Yankee Candle, a retail store in malls across the United States.

GO TO page xvii

for UNIT REVIEW step-by-step instructions.

UNIT 11

VOCABULARY review

SCORE: / 10

A Complete the conversation with words from the box.

appointment business luck manage overseas ready remember saved sell skills

Nate: Excuse me. Ms. King? I'm Nate West. We have a 2:30 **1** appointment.
Ms. King: Of course, I **2** remember. Have a seat. So, tell me about yourself, Nate.
Nate: Well, right now I work part-time in a café. I'm good with money and **3** manage people well. I think these are good **4** skills. I **5** saved some money from my job, so after I graduate, I plan to work **6** overseas for a year, maybe in Colombia.
Ms. King: Why is that?
Nate: You see, I'd like to start a **7** business someday. I want to **8** sell coffee to cafés. But I'm not **9** ready to do that now. First, I need to learn about growing coffee. I think with a little **10** luck, it can be a big success.

GRAMMAR review

SCORE: / 10

A Complete the sentences with the correct form of *be going to* and the verb in parentheses.

1 Greg and Lisa are going to get (get) married on Sunday.
2 My brother is sick, so he ________ (not go) to work today.
3 Are you going to visit (visit) me this weekend?
4 Where is your sister going to go (go) after work?
5 My mother and father are going to spend (spend) the weekend with me.

2 's not going/is not going/isn't going

B Choose the correct option.

1 Ken and Zoe's wedding is this weekend. Let's buy a special gift for him / it / **them**.
2 Mr. Green doesn't feel well. Why don't we make us / **him** / it some chicken soup?
3 Can you give it / **me** / you a campus tour? I'm new here.
4 Mrs. Ortega's company wants to send it / **her** / she to Moscow for three weeks.
5 Your parents are in town? Do you plan to cook dinner for him / her / **them**?

16–20 correct: You can talk about to-do lists, money, and career plans. You can use *going to*, direct and indirect objects.
0–15 correct: Look again at the Vocabulary and Grammar sections in the unit.

TOTAL SCORE: / 20

WHAT DO YOU KNOW NOW? Look back at page 107 and add the words you know now to the boxes.

GO TO page xviii

for STUDY SKILLS step-by-step instructions.

STUDY SKILLS PERSONAL DEVELOPMENT

Take the quiz about time management. Go to **Study Skills** on page 137 to find the answers. Then learn more about time management.

1 … of business and professional people regularly write to-do lists.
a 20% **b** 40% **c** **70%**

2 Around … of students feel stressed every day.
a **49%** **b** 68% **c** 99%

3 The average person uses … different methods to manage their time.
a 3 **b** 7 **c** **13**

4 Students who do their work at the last minute get … students who finish their work early.
a better grades than **b** **worse grades than** **c** the same grades as

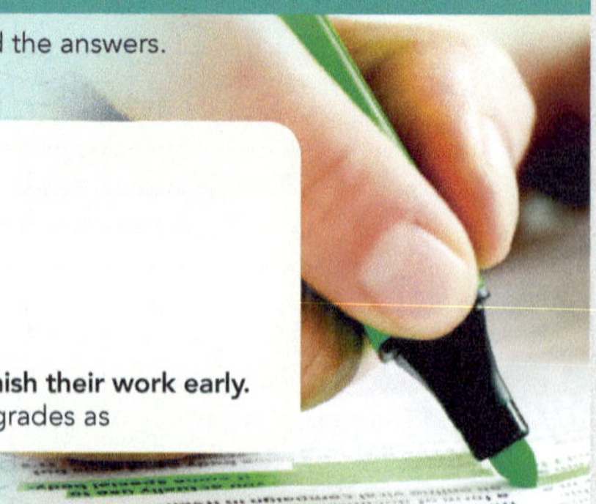

CLASSROOM MANAGEMENT

Have students look over the unit and then work individually to complete the review activities. Then have them check with a partner before checking the answers as a class. Ask students to identify an area they would like to review.

FURTHER DISCUSSION

Put students in groups of three and ask the following questions for them to discuss:

- Do you come from a family of planners?
- Are the people around you organized?
- How can you be more organized?
- What happens if you plan too far ahead?
- Do you like people who are spontaneous?
- What is the most spontaneous thing you have ever done?

GO TO page vi
for **UNIT OPENER** step-by-step instructions.

UNIT 12 The Great Outdoors

WHAT DO YOU ALREADY KNOW?

1 Think of words you know about the weather, climate, seasons, and natural features where you live. Write the words.

2 **IN PAIRS** Share and compare your words. Add more words to your lists.

Weather / Climate

Seasons

Natural features

STUDENTS MAY ALREADY KNOW:

- **Weather / Climate:** warm, cold, windy, rainy, snowy, tropical, desert.
- **Seasons:** spring, summer, fall, winter.
- **Natural features:** lake, mountain, volcano, trees.

VIDEO

DISCUSS & SHARE

3 **IN GROUPS** Watch the video and answer the question.

SYM Are you an adventurer?

GO TO page xx
for **VIDEOS IN SYM** step-by-step instructions.

In this unit, you will ...

- talk about climate, weather, natural features, and outdoor activities.
- use thinking skills: infer, hypothesize, and recall.
- read about the Galapagos Islands.
- use strategies to keep talking by showing interest.
- use problem-solving skills to decide how to develop a natural area.
- read about a forest ranger to learn about this job and the skills needed for the environmental field.

WHAT DO YOU ALREADY KNOW?

If you notice students are struggling to understand what to do, you can provide one or two examples to help them get started:

- **Weather / Climate:** storm, thunder, cloudy, weather forecast
- **Natural features:** island, river, waterfall, lake

VIDEO

Before viewing, ask:

What does Marcus like to do? *hiking, skiing, kayaking, swimming with sharks*
What does Jill like to do? *walking, easy kayaking, cross-country skiing*

After viewing, put the continuum on the board.

adventurer — not adventurer

Students mark the continuum and explain what they prefer.

DISCUSS & SHARE

Encourage students to think about how they feel about extremes—in sports, weather, or traveling. Do they like to seek out challenging destinations and activities, or do they like to play it more on the safe side? Take a poll of the class to see who enjoys the wilder side of life.

LESSON 1 Different Climates

GO TO page x
for READING step-by-step instructions.

READING

A Look at the pictures in the brochure in B. Answer the questions.

1 What are the people in the photographs doing?
2 Do you enjoy these kinds of activities?

In the first photograph, the people are diving. They are looking at fish. In the second photograph, the people are taking pictures to the animals on the beach.

B 12.01 Read the brochure. Answer the questions.

The Galapagos Islands

The Galapagos **Islands** are an amazing place for a tour. There are beautiful sandy beaches, awesome animals, and the people are friendly. Every year, new people learn what the Galapagos Islands have to offer. People can swim, dive, and see nature—the Galapagos have it all!

The islands are near the **equator**. They don't have seasons like some other places do, but there is a **cool** season from June to November. The water is colder at that time, and there's less rain, so it's drier. It's a great time for diving around the islands. It's also a good time to see whales, sea lions, and penguins. The **temperature** is around 21–27°C, and the water is around 18–24°C.

From December to May, the temperature is higher. It's called the warm season. It's more **tropical** during these months, and the skies are cloudier. It's also wetter than the rest of the year. The ocean is warmer and it's better for swimming. It's also a good time to see iguanas, flamingos, and other tropical birds. The temperature is around 27–32°C. The water is cooler than that, at around 21–26°C.

To get there, you need to go to Ecuador. From Ecuador, you can fly to Baltra Island or San Cristóbal Island, or go by boat. Of course, it's quicker to fly than go by boat. Flights are also cheaper, but then you have to pay for a hotel. A luxury cruise ship is more expensive than a trip on a small boat.

1 What time of year is better for diving in the Galapagos Islands?
2 What time of year is better for swimming?
3 How can you get to the Galapagos Islands?

1 June to November
2 December to May
3 You can fly or go by boat from Ecuador.

MAKE IT REAL

Most countries use the Celsius scale to measure temperature. For 27–32°C, we say "twenty-seven to thirty-two degrees Celsius." A few countries, including the United States, use Fahrenheit (F).

C READING SKILL—Scan for specific information Read and complete.

1 What is the air temperature in April? 21–27°C
2 Is it wet or dry in September? dry
3 When is the water temperature 18–24°C? June to November
4 When is a good time for seeing flamingos? December to May

D THINKING SKILL—Understand Answer the questions.

1 What time of year is there more rain in the Galapagos Islands?
2 Why don't the Galapagos Islands have spring, summer, fall, and winter?

1 Probably December to May because it's wetter than the rest of the year.
2 Because they are near the equator.

GO TO page vii
for VOCABULARY step-by-step instructions.

VOCABULARY

A Complete with words and phrases from READING B.

1 These are areas of land that have water around them. islands
2 This is an imaginary line around the center of the Earth. equator
3 This describes weather that is not very hot, or a little cold. cool
4 This tells you how hot or cold a place is. temperature
5 This describes weather that is very hot and wet. tropical

READING OPTIONAL 12.01

Have students look at the pictures to predict what the reading will be about.

Tell students that just like the Galapagos Islands, most places don't follow a strict pattern of four even seasons—spring, summer, fall, and winter. For example, Mexico City has about five distinct weather seasons: cool winter, hot dry, cool rainy, warm summer, and fall. Encourage students to analyze the weather in their region and redefine the seasons.

VOCABULARY

To increase student's repertoire of words regarding weather, explain the following vocabulary:

- **arid:** (adj) very dry; not enough rain
- **temperate:** (adj) a climate that is moderate; never extremely hot or extremely cold
- **subtropical:** (adj) around or bordering the tropics
- **inhospitable:** (adj) unwelcoming or difficult to live in or visit

For extra practice, encourage students to look up words that describe the weather in their region.

GRAMMAR comparative adjectives

A Read the text in READING B again. Underline the comparatives.

The water is colder and there is less rain, so it's drier.

B Complete the table with the examples.

Most one-syllable adjectives	Add *–er:* *long–longer, cold–* **1** colder, *quick–* **2** quicker
One-syllable adjectives ending in *–e*	Add *–r: nice–nicer, rare–rarer*
One-syllable adjectives ending in consonant–vowel–consonant	Double the final consonant and add *–er:* *hot–hotter, wet–* **3** wetter
One- or two-syllable adjectives ending in *–y*	Change the *y* to *i* and add *–er:* *dry–* **4** drier, *happy–happier*
Adjectives with two or more syllables	Use *more* or *less:* *interesting–more/less interesting, expensive–* **5** more/less expensive
Irregular adjectives	*bad–worse, good–* **6** better

When comparing two things directly in the same sentence, use *than*: *Today is hotter than yesterday.*

For more practice, go to page 158.

C Complete the text using the comparative form of the words given. Add *than* if needed.

Peru has three different regions: the coast, the Andes, and the rain forest. They all have different climates. The coast is **1** cooler than (cool) the other two regions, with average temperatures of 18°C in Lima in August. The weather is **2** warmer (warm) in February, with average temperatures of 27°C.

In the Andes, the weather is **3** wetter (wet) from September to May, and **4** drier (dry) from June to August. The Andes is **5** sunnier than (sunny) the coastal area.

The rain forest is **6** rainier than (rainy) the coast and the Andes. It is also **7** hotter (hot), with average temperatures of 30–32°C all year round.

SPEAKING

A Research the climate of a country or city you are interested in. Write down the temperature and weather at different times of the year.

B IN PAIRS Student A, you want to visit your friend. Ask about the weather in your friend's country or city at different times of the year. Student B, tell your friend about the weather in your country or city at different times of the year. Then change roles. Decide where you both would like to go on a trip, and when. Use your notes and the Confident Communicator box to help you.

CONFIDENT COMMUNICATOR
KEEP TALKING

To learn about a place, say: *What's it like?*
To ask about weather, say: *What's it like in summer?* or *What's it like in February?*

GO TO page viii for **GRAMMAR** step-by-step instructions.

GO TO page xii for **SPEAKING** step-by-step instructions.

GRAMMAR

The tricky parts of the comparative are the spelling changes and irregular adjectives. You may want to pay extra attention to these.

Dictate these sentences and have students write them down. Then write them on the board for the class to check their accuracy. *Australia is drier than New Zealand. The US is bigger than Mexico. Iceland is windier than Norway. Canada is snowier than the US.*

Have students practice spelling and irregular adjectives with a pair dictation activity. Ask them to create comparative sentences about weather and countries. Have them write what their partner dictates and then check.

SPEAKING

Allow students to research the climate of the countries they are interested in online.

Extra Practice

Have students work in pairs to name a city and predict the temperature and the weather of that city in real time. Then tell them to use the weather app on their phones to see if they were right.

LESSON 2 **Natural Features**

VOCABULARY natural features

A Check (✓) the natural features you can find less than 100 kilometers (60 miles) from where you live.

desert

forest

hill

lake

mountain

river

volcano

waterfall

B IN PAIRS Name examples of each natural feature in your country.

An example of a waterfall here in Chile is the Laja Falls.

Iguazu Falls, Argentina

GO TO page xi

for **LISTENING** step-by-step instructions.

LISTENING

A Look at the picture. Where do you think this place is?

MAKE IT YOURS

Can you think of more natural features in your country? Find out what they are called.

GO TO page 149

for **AUDIO SCRIPT**.

B 12.02 Listen and choose *True* or *False*.

1 Kerry is a student. **True** / False
2 The Iguazu River starts in Argentina. True / **False**
3 Niagara Falls is just one waterfall. True / **False**
4 The speaker went to Angel Falls last year. True / **False**

C 12.02 LISTENING SKILL—Listen for specific information Listen again and complete the table.

	Country	Height	Number of waterfalls	Good time to visit
Iguazu Falls	Argentina/Brazil	82 meters	300	July–October
Niagara Falls	Canada/US	50 meters	3	June–August
Angel Falls	Venezuela	979 meters	1	May–October

D THINKING SKILL—Induce Answer the questions.

1 Which of the waterfalls do you want to see? Why?
2 How do you think people feel when they visit places like Iguazu Falls?

VOCABULARY

Remind students that *desert* is with one *s* and the sweet things you order after your main meal are *desserts*, with two *s*'s. You may want to draw their attention to the change in stress in the words *desert* and *dessert*. Have students test each other in pairs on the words in VOCABULARY **A**.

LISTENING

In the interview, the speaker talks about three famous waterfalls. Have students choose a natural feature from VOCABULARY **A** and name three famous examples of it (e.g., Volcano: Mt. Etna, Popocatépetl, Mt. St. Helens; River: Mississippi, Amazon, Nile). You may want to play a competitive game between groups. Tell one group to name a natural feature. The other group gets a point for each famous example they can name. Then switch. If you have a large class, have everyone working simultaneously rather than everyone watching someone perform in front of the class.

GRAMMAR review of tenses

A Match the sentences. Write the letters.

1 I love waterfalls because **I'm studying** geology in college and waterfalls are great places to learn more. c
2 When it gets to the border with Argentina, **it falls** 82 meters. d
3 Last year, **I went** to the Iguazu Falls in Argentina and Brazil. a
4 **I'm going** to visit Angel Falls next May because the water is higher then. b

a This is a single action in the past.
b This is a future plan.
c This is true in the present.
d This is generally true.

For more practice, go to page 159.

B Complete with the correct form of the verbs from the box.

feel go (×2) have learn love stay

Two months ago, I **1** went to the White Mountain National Forest in Maine. The forest **2** has many hiking trails and lakes. I **3** stayed there for a week and camped. It **4** felt great to be outdoors, under the stars at night. I **5** ______ how to catch fish right now. Next time I go to Maine, I **6** ______ swimming in the lakes. Nature is very important to me. I **7** love the outdoors!

5 'm/am learning
6 'm/am going to go

C Play a game of *True or False?* Write two things that are true about you and one thing that is false. Use the time expressions. Ask your partner to guess if your statements are true or false. Take turns.

Last year, I ... *Right now, I ...* *Next month, I ...*

Last year, I flew on a plane. Right now, I'm learning the piano. Next month, I'm going to visit my cousin in the US.

SPEAKING

A Think of a natural place you enjoyed visiting. Make notes on what you know or what you want to find out about it.

Place: ______

Facts: ______

______

B Make notes on what happened when you went there. How did you feel there?

______

______

C IN PAIRS Discuss. Tell your partner about the place you visited. Use your notes from A and B. Use the Confident Communicator box to help you.

CONFIDENT COMMUNICATOR
KEEP TALKING

When someone tells a story, we can respond using the phrases:
That's very interesting!
That sounds really good/bad.
How interesting/wonderful/sad!

GRAMMAR

Practice simple past irregular verbs. Tell students to use the list of verbs at the back of their books and, in pairs, have them test each other.

SPEAKING

Before writing notes in SPEAKING **A**, do a visualization activity. Tell students to be silent, close their eyes, and listen to your voice. They shouldn't answer the questions but let their mind's eye see the answer. Use this script: *Think of a natural place you enjoyed visiting. You are there. Look around. What can you see? What does it look like? Listen. What can you hear? What does it sound like? Smell. What can you smell? What does it smell like? Hold out your hand and touch. What do you touch? What does it feel like?*

LESSON 3 Wonders of the Natural World

VOCABULARY adjectives to describe natural features

A **Circle the positive adjectives and underline the negative adjectives.**

amazing attractive awesome beautiful boring fantastic popular ugly

B **Choose three places. Say what you know and think about them. Explain.**

I think the Grand Canyon is awesome! It's beautiful and I want to see it one day.

THE SEVEN NATURAL WONDERS OF THE WORLD

Mount Everest, Himalayas, China/Nepal

Grand Canyon, Arizona, US

Great Barrier Reef, Australia

Parícutin Volcano, Mexico

Aurora Borealis, near the Arctic

Harbor of Rio de Janeiro, Brazil

Victoria Falls, Zambia/Zimbabwe

GO TO page ix for PRONUNCIATION step-by-step instructions.

PRONUNCIATION /ju/

A **12.03** **Listen and notice. The long *u* sound /u/ sometimes has a *y* sound /ju/.**

beautiful communicate cute document music popular

B **Practice saying the words with the correct pronunciation.**

GO TO page 149 for AUDIO SCRIPT.

LISTENING

A **12.04** **Look at the phrases and guess the natural wonder. Then listen to check.**

... it appeared in a corn field ...
... it grew very quickly ...
... local people take visitors ...
... on horseback ...

B **12.04 LISTENING SKILL—Listen for detail** **Listen and answer the questions.**

1. When did it appear? 1943
2. How can you get to the small town near the volcano? by plane or bus
3. How can you get to the volcano from the town? on horseback
4. How can you get to the top of the volcano? by walking
5. How long is the complete trip? 6 or 7 hours

C **THINKING SKILL—Recall** **Tell a partner what you learned about the volcano. Do you want to visit the volcano? Why or why not?**

VOCABULARY

Have students work in small groups. Tell them to choose one of the natural wonders to research. Ask *What is it? What's it like? Where is it? What threats is it under?* Then have them report back to their group. Do fast open-class feedback.

PRONUNCIATION

Have a pronunciation competition. Have two students at a time come to the front and say the words as clearly as possible. Tell the class to vote on the best pronunciation. Tell the winner to stay and invite a new competitor to come up.

LISTENING

LISTENING SKILL—Listen for detail

Tell students to listen once without writing anything down or trying to catch any details. Play the audio a number of times as students listen for details. Tell them it's easier to listen and not write the first couple of times. When they are more confident, they should write down details.

WRITING

GO TO page xiv for WRITING step-by-step instructions.

A Read the guidebook entry and check (✓) the information the writer mentions.

HAKONE, JAPAN, is a town with many hot springs. Hot springs are places with natural hot water that comes up from the ground. The Hakone hot springs are very popular with local people and tourists. You can relax in the hot water and enjoy the amazing natural views. Hakone is about 90 minutes from Tokyo by train. It is close to the famous Mount Fuji. You can take a train to Odawara Station and then take a bus. Hakone is 20 minutes by bus from the train station. There are many hotels in Hakone if you want to stay for a few days. You can also go on a tour of the area. Search "Hakone hot springs" online for more information.

who enjoys this place	✓	how much the train costs	☐
what you can do here	✓	where to stay	✓
where it is	✓	where to learn more	✓
how to get there	✓		

B Choose a local natural feature you know. Answer the questions.

1. What place are you going to write about? ______
2. Why is it interesting or attractive? ______
3. What can you do there? ______
4. Where is it? How can you get there? ______
5. Can you stay there? Where? ______
6. Is there a website with more information? ______

C Write a guidebook entry for young adults from other countries. Use your answers in B to create your entry.

SPEAKING

A Choose an outdoor activity to talk about. Make notes to answer the questions.

1. Where can you do this activity in your area?
______
2. What do you like about this activity?
______
3. Is there anything you dislike about this activity?
______

MAKE IT YOURS

Some guidebooks ask people to write about their local area for tourists. Do you know any examples of guidebooks like that? What do you think is interesting about guidebook writing?

B IN PAIRS Talk about the outdoor activities in A. Use the Confident Communicator box to help you.

CONFIDENT COMMUNICATOR — KEEP TALKING

When you are listing points (e.g., things you like about an activity), you can use *One thing I like about it is …* and *Another thing I like about it is …*

***One thing I like about camping** is that you sleep under the stars!*
***Another thing I like about it is** it's really quiet at night.*

WRITING

Students can use the elements in WRITING **A** and **B** to give them ideas about what kind of information to include in their guidebook. Additionally, they should use the guidebook entry in WRITING **A** as a model text. They can use a similar structure and style but adapt it to their own local natural feature.

SPEAKING Alternative Activity

Some outdoor activities might be hiking, bird watching, horseback riding, rock climbing, zip lining, butterfly viewing, camping, walking, jogging, bike riding, skydiving, hang gliding, flying light aircraft, and rappelling.

Draw students' attention to the Confident Communicator box to help them with their conversations.

MAKE IT YOURS

Examples of traditional guidebooks are *Lonely Planet*, *Fodor's*, Rick Steves's series, *Rough Guides*, and *Let's Go*. Crowdsourced online guides include TripAdvisor and Wikivoyage.

GO TO page xv
for LANGUAGE AND LIFE step-by-step instructions.

Language and Life

Problem-solving – Developing a Natural Area

A 12.05 **Read the newspaper article. Answer the questions.**

LOCAL COLLEGE ASKS FOR IDEAS by Janice Baskin

Meadowville College is a college near our city. There is a large lake and a forest on Meadowville's campus. Right now, not many people use the lake or the forest. Some people go swimming or camping there in the summer.

Recently, the college decided to use this area for its students. Dean Linda Collins says, "We want our students to learn about nature and learn new skills. Many of our students come from big cities and they don't know a lot about nature. They are more familiar with technology than they are with the natural world." The college wants students to be interested in nature. "They need activities to introduce them to outdoor life. Maybe something that uses technology can get them interested—something that connects nature to their studies," says Dean Collins.

The college is asking students for ideas and suggestions. They have money for the project and they are happy to spend it on the right ideas.

1. Where are the lake and the forest? on Meadowland's campus
2. What do people do there right now? Some people swim and some people go camping.
3. What does the college want students to learn? They want students to learn about nature and gain new skills.
4. Why don't some students know much about nature? They live in cities and spend time using technology.
5. What does the college want from students? ideas and suggestions

B IN GROUPS Read the statements from students. Talk about the ideas and check (✓) the ones you think are good suggestions.

1. What about an app with useful information about the natural features on campus? ☐
2. They should buy boats and tents and leave us to explore the area on our own. ☐
3. We need an information center where we can learn about the natural history. ☐
4. They should get instructors to teach courses on swimming and camping. ☐
5. Other: ______________________ ☐

OBJECTIVE

In this lesson, students create a proposal for the use of natural land. Students will identify strong and weak ideas for a proposal. They will identify criteria of a project and submit considered concepts. They are encouraged to think about a proposal from different angles. Students should keep in mind that they should be able to support their proposals with reasons.

PROCESS OPTIONAL 12.05

Students read an article written by the dean of a college asking for proposals for the use of some natural land that belongs to the university. After exploring the article and understanding the requirements of the university, students read some ideas that students of the university have put forward. Then, students choose an idea—relaxation, sports, technology, or nature—for the use of the land. They think of main points to support their idea, anticipate points against their idea, and prepare points to argue a case for their idea. They present their idea to the class, giving reasons. Finally, the class votes on the best proposal.

C IN PAIRS Choose one of the ideas. Answer the questions.

☐ **Relaxation**
They should make quiet, relaxing areas where students can chat and study on their own.

☐ **Sports**
They should build a sports center and have instructors offer classes for different outdoor sports or activities.

☐ **Technology**
They should create a mobile app that gives useful information to get people interested in exploring the area.

☐ **Nature**
They should build a center where students can learn about the wildlife and history of the area.

1 What are the main points that support your idea?

____

____

____

2 What is the main point against your idea?

____

____

____

3 What do you say to argue that point?

____

____

____

D Take turns. Explain your ideas to the class. Give reasons.

We think the college should build a nature center. It can even have art classes, so students can paint pictures of nature.
Also, …

E Take a vote with your class. Choose the idea you like best. Don't vote for your own idea.

MAKE IT DIGITAL

You are going to post your idea on the college website. What information should you give about your idea? What images should you use?

CLASSROOM MANAGEMENT

If you don't have time to do presentations in class, have students make videos with their smartphones and show them to each other. They could nominate the best ones to watch as a class. These could be the finalists and the winner selected from these.

CULTURE NOTE

You may want to define *crowdsource*: (v) to obtain things like ideas or services from a variety of people, usually online.

MAKE IT DIGITAL

Encourage students to find images online to support their proposal for the use of the university land. If you do this, encourage them to use darker-colored images, as they look sharper when projected. They can use images from images.google.com. Show them how to open the Tools tab, click on Usage Rights, and select "labeled for noncommercial reuse."

GO TO page xvii
for **UNIT REVIEW** step-by-step instructions.

UNIT 12

VOCABULARY review

SCORE: / 10

A Choose the correct option.

There are many boats on the **1** desert / river. Boat tours are very **2** ugly / popular.
People left cans and bottles at the top of the **3** mountain / forest. **4** It was ugly / awesome.
The **5** island / volcano looked red and orange at night. The colors were **6** beautiful / boring.
I walked in the **7** forest / waterfall all day. I had so much fun. It was **8** amazing / boring.
I swam in a lake under the **9** forest / waterfall. It was **10** fantastic / attractive!

GRAMMAR review

SCORE: / 10

A Read the information. Then complete the sentences with the comparative form of a word in the box. Add *than*.

expensive high long hot wet

The Mississippi River: 3,734 m / The Mekong River: 4,350 m
Yearly rainfall in Chicago: 93 cm / Yearly rainfall in Boston: 111 cm
Hotels in Istanbul: $120–$130 / Hotels in Panama City: $130–$140
Mt. Blanc: 4,808 m / Mt. Fuji: 3,776 m
Miami: 32°C / Montreal: 24°C

1 The Mekong River is longer than the Mississippi River.
2 Boston is wetter than Chicago.
3 Hotels in Panama City are more expensive than hotels in Istanbul.
4 Mt. Blanc is higher than Mt. Fuji.
5 Miami is hotter than Montreal.

B Complete the paragraph with the correct form of the verb in parentheses.

Every year my friend Wendy and I **1** take (take) a two-week vacation. We're in Belize right now. The sun **2** is/'s shining (shine) and we're on a beautiful beach. I **3** 'm/am learning (learn) how to scuba dive now. Tomorrow we **4** 're/are going to dive (dive) in the famous Blue Hole. I **5** learned (learn) about this in one of my classes last year.

16–20 correct: You can talk about natural features and adjectives to describe them. You can use comparative adjectives.
0–15 correct: Look again at the Vocabulary and Grammar sections in the unit.

TOTAL SCORE: / 20

WHAT DO YOU KNOW NOW? Look back at page 117 and add the words you know now to the boxes.

GO TO page xix
for **FOLLOW A PRO** step-by-step instructions.

FOLLOW A PRO NATURAL SCIENCE

Take the quiz about careers in natural science. Go to Follow A Pro on page 138 to find the answers. Then learn more about careers in natural science.

1 **How many gardeners and florists say they are happy in their job?**
a 52% **b** 79% **c** 87%

2 **Spending ... outside gives your brain as much energy as drinking one cup of coffee.**
a 10 minutes **b** 20 minutes **c** 1 hour

3 **Nearly half of all jobs need some kind of outdoor work.**
a true **b** false

4 **One park ranger, Roy Sullivan, lived through seven lightning strikes and ... bear encounters in his 40-year career.**
a 22 **b** 7 **c** 13

126 Unit 12 The Great Outdoors

ALTERNATIVE ACTIVITY

Have students work in groups of three to write a five-question quiz using comparative adjectives. Give each group the chance to give their quiz to the class.

FURTHER DISCUSSION

Put students in groups of three and ask the following questions for them to discuss:

- What is the worst weather you have ever experienced?
- Can you see a volcano from your house?
- What island would you like to visit?
- Do you like underwater activities?
- Do you like extreme sports?
- What's the highest mountain you have climbed?

UNIT 1

STUDY SKILLS

A **Read about memory strategies. People remember new information in different ways. Which way is best for you?**

MEMORY STRATEGIES

Ricardo I use different colors to take notes in my notebook because it helps me learn. Nouns are in red, verbs are in green, and adjectives are in yellow.

Maya I love art, and I make pictures with new words and phrases. After that, I don't forget them!

Sol I learn words that go together. So, I write down family words together, words for colors together, and words for jobs together.

Meera When I learn a new word, I write it down 10 times. That helps me to remember it!

Ana I make a sentence that's true for me with the new word. So, if I learn the word *swim*, then my sentence is "I swim every Saturday," because that's true for me.

Bob I talk about my learning with my friends and tell them the new words I know. I don't like learning things alone!

B **Match the example (1–6) to the memory strategy (a–f). Write the letter.**

a writing new words 10 times
b sharing learning with friends
c making sentences with new words
d using different colors
e making pictures to learn things
f learning words that go together

1 *player play playful* d

2 *hand* 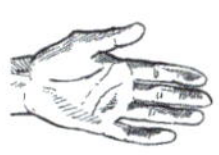 e

3 *mother, father, sister, brother, aunt, uncle* f

4 *beautiful, beautiful, beautiful, beautiful, beautiful, beautiful, beautiful, beautiful, beautiful, beautiful* a

5 *I study in the library. I don't study on Sundays.* c

6  b

C **Complete the sentences with the words from the box.**

laugh stories listen

1 I record my voice saying new words. Then, I listen.
2 I put new words together to make stories. That helps me remember.
3 I make a funny joke out of new words. If I laugh, I remember!

D **IN PAIRS** **Discuss the memory strategies you want to use. Use B and C to help you.**

A: I want to sing the new words I learn because I love music.
B: That's a good idea. I don't like singing, so I want to make stories from the new words I learn.

MAKE IT HAPPEN

Choose 10 new words you want to learn. Use three of the memory strategies to help you learn them. With a partner, talk about the three memory strategies. Use the phrases to help you.

A: I think that it's a good idea to study with friends.
B: I agree. And I want to use colors for my notes. It's easy to remember the new words that way.

E **THINKING SKILL—Remember** **Observe what kind of memory you have.**

1 Do you have a good memory for some things and not others?
2 What are some things that are difficult to memorize?
3 When do you need a good memory at your job?

Answers to the quiz on page 16
1 a 2 b 3 a 4 c

127

GO TO page xviii for STUDY SKILLS step-by-step instructions.

STUDY SKILLS TASK

Students work through **A**, **B**, and **C** individually. Each student will have their own learning-strategy preference. In **D**, they work in pairs and compare answers. Different strategies appeal to different students. Have students experiment with different techniques. They may use different strategies depending on the words they are learning.

THINKING SKILL—Remember

Here students are reflecting on whether they have a good memory or not. A good memory is a useful tool for language learning. The strategies above will help them exercise their memory.

MAKE IT HAPPEN

This exercise is designed to be open-ended in order to have students generate their own content while applying the study skills they learned.

GO TO page xix
for FOLLOW A PRO step-by-step instructions.

UNIT 2 FOLLOW A PRO

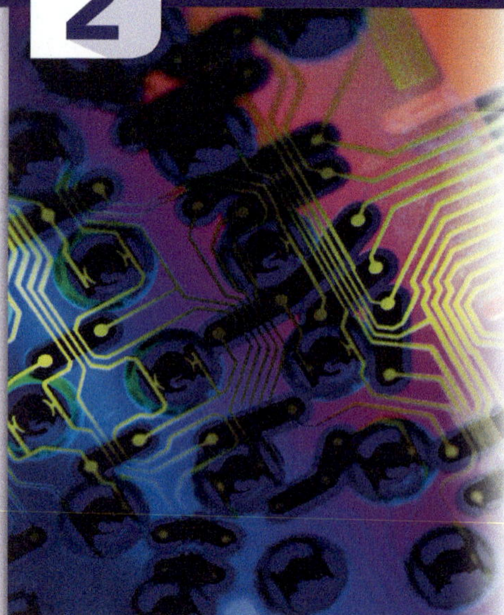

A Read about an IT consultant's job. Answer the questions below.

AN IT CONSULTANT

My name is Tim Watkins. I'm an IT consultant at my family's company, IT Computer Consultants. Our office is in the city center, not too far from my apartment. I help people with their computer problems. My sister is an accountant. She works with the company accounts. Her husband, Bob, is a computer technician. He has a degree in computer engineering. My mom is creative, and she likes to write. She's the social media marketing manager. She manages our website, writes our blog, and posts on social media. My dad is friendly and organized. He's the general manager. It's a good business and it does really well. I like working with my family.

1 Whose business is IT Computer Consultants? It is Tim's family's business.
2 What does Tim help people with? computer problems
3 Who is Bob? Bob is Tim's sister's husband.
4 Why is Tim's mom the social media marketing manager? She is creative and she likes to write.
5 What does Tim's dad do? He is the general manager.

B Discuss the questions as a class.

1 Is a family business a good idea? Why or why not?
2 Can you imagine your own family business?

Suggested answers:
1 Yes, because you can work well together; everyone knows each other. / No, because you can't leave your problems at work when you have a family business.

GO TO page xx
for VIDEOS IN SYM step-by-step instructions.

VIDEO

WATCH THE VIDEO AND FOLLOW AN IT PROFESSIONAL.

C IN GROUPS Answer the questions.

1 What job is the video about? IT Specialist
2 Who does the job? a person who is good with computers
3 What special skills or education does this person have? ______
4 Does this person like the job? Yes.
5 What are some of the good and bad things about the job? ______
6 How does this person use English at work? He speaks English to customers, coworkers, and technicians.

3 technical, people, organizational, and management skills
5 Good: He likes helping people. Bad: There is a lot of pressure when the network doesn't work.

D IN GROUPS Check your answers to the quiz on page 26 and discuss the questions.

1 Do you know people who work in IT?
2 What other IT jobs do you know?
3 Do you want this kind of job? Why or why not?
4 Is there an opportunity to have this kind of job where you live?
5 What skills does an IT professional need?

Answers to the quiz on page 26
1 a 2 b 3 c 4 c

128

ALTERNATIVE ACTIVITY

Before reading "An IT Consultant," write *family business* on the board and ask volunteers to explain what it means and give examples. Ask students if their family has a family business.

FURTHER DISCUSSION

- What family businesses are there in your area?
- What roles do people have in those businesses?
- How are family businesses and small businesses changing in your community?
- Do you support family businesses?
- In which family businesses do you shop?
- What do you buy there?

VIDEO

Watch with sound off. Look for: *computer, laptop, office, desk, cable, repair, watch, meeting.*

While viewing, listen for: *skills, computer, people, specialist, problems, help, go-to guy, cursor.*

After viewing, ask: *What did Carlos do with computers as a child that made him want to work in IT?* He took apart a computer to see how it worked.

UNIT 3

STUDY SKILLS

GO TO page xviii
for **STUDY SKILLS** step-by-step instructions.

A Read the oral presentations. Which presentation do you think is better and why?

ORAL PRESENTATIONS

1 Ella
The teacher says we have to do a talk, so … my talk is about photography. I do it every day and I like it. I don't know why. It's fun. I like it. My camera is good—it's a Lumix. And … um … I take pictures every day, and I also take pictures on weekends. My camera is black and it's not too big. And … this is my favorite picture. Um … yeah.

2 Vanessa
Hello, everyone. I want to talk to you today about my favorite hobby, swimming. I really enjoy swimming because it makes me feel good and it gives me energy. I swim every day at the swimming pool near my house. I also swim with the school swimming club: the Dolphins. There are 10 students in the club, and we swim in competitions with other schools. I love doing that! Our teacher is Mr. Skinner. He's a great swimming teacher. I like swimming because it's fun, it's good for me, and it doesn't cost a lot of money. Thank you for listening! Any questions?

B Write *Ella* or *Vanessa* next to the sentence each person said.

1 Vanessa says hello.
2 Ella, Vanessa talks about a favorite hobby.
3 Ella stops and starts when she gives her presentation.
4 Vanessa explains why she likes her hobby.
5 Vanessa organizes her presentation.
6 Ella isn't sure what she is talking about.
7 Ella doesn't finish in a clear way.

2 Make sure students understand that Ella and Vanessa both talk about a hobby, even though only Vanessa used the word *hobby*.

C Match the tips about oral presentations (1–6) to the explanations (a–f). Write the letter.

1 Smile and look at your listeners. d
2 Don't speak fast. Take your time. c
3 Plan your presentation. b
4 Organize your presentation. Use words like *First*, *Second*, and *Next*. f
5 Tell an interesting story. Don't just use facts and data. a
6 Answer questions at the end of your presentation. e

a People remember stories, but they forget facts and numbers.
b You feel nervous when you don't plan.
c Listeners need time to think as you speak.
d Your listeners feel comfortable when you are friendly.
e Your listeners can learn more when they ask questions.
f Present your ideas one at a time so your listeners can follow.

D Rewrite the first presentation in A as an interesting, clear presentation.

Hello, everyone. Welcome to my talk on photography …

E THINKING SKILL—Create Why is it a good idea to prepare and practice a presentation before you speak in public? In what jobs do you need oral presentation skills?

MAKE IT HAPPEN

Prepare an oral presentation on your favorite hobby. Organize your presentation with these questions.

When do you do your hobby?
Why do you like it?
Where do you do your hobby?
Who do you do your hobby with?

Answers to the quiz on page 36
1 b (You need to spend 70% of your time on writing.) 2 c 3 c 4 b

129

STUDY SKILLS TASK

Have students work alone or in pairs to complete the activities. They will explore two oral presentations and evaluate the elements of a good presentation and a bad presentation. They'll read tips for a good presentation and the explanations behind the tips. Students will then fix the bad example.

THINKING SKILL—Create

The ability to give good oral presentations is a beneficial skill. Students may be asked to give a presentation as part of a job interview. In many jobs (e.g., a salesperson, a training position, a teacher, or many jobs in the corporate world), this is a necessary skill.

MAKE IT HAPPEN

Students apply what they have learned in the lesson to prepare and give an oral presentation about a hobby. Tell them to use the questions to prepare thoroughly. Suggest they record themselves practicing and watch the recording to see what they need to improve.

GO TO page xix

for **FOLLOW A PRO** step-by-step instructions.

UNIT 4 FOLLOW A PRO

A Read about a firefighter's job. Answer the questions below.

A FIREFIGHTER

Sally Lane is a firefighter. She is at the fire station 24 hours a day for three days, and then she has three days off. On her workdays, Sally sleeps at the fire station. She gets up at 4:00 a.m., gets dressed, and eats breakfast with the other firefighters. She takes a shower in the evening, not in the morning. Sally usually works at least 15 hours on a workday. She fights fires, practices with the equipment, goes to the fire station gym, and takes online classes to learn new information about fighting fires. Sally's job is difficult, but she likes it. She says, "I love my job because the work is always exciting and interesting. I like to help people. It's not always easy. When we are busy, I don't have time to eat or sleep!"

1 Where does Sally sleep on workdays? at the fire station
2 When does she get up on workdays? at 4:00 a.m.
3 Who does she eat breakfast with? the other firefighters
4 How many hours does Sally usually work? at least 15
5 What different things does she do at work? fight fires, practice, exercise, take classes
6 Why does Sally like her job? It is exciting and interesting, and she likes to help people.

B Discuss the questions as a class.

1 Could you be a firefighter? Why or why not?
2 What are the good points and bad points about Sally's job?
3 There aren't many women firefighters. Why not?

Suggested answers:
1 Yes, because I like excitement and I am strong and in good shape. / No, because I don't like danger.
2 Good points: She can help people; it's interesting; no two days are the same. Bad points: it's dangerous, she has to get up early in the morning.
3 Maybe because they don't want to put themselves in dangerous situations when they have children; maybe because it is traditionally a man's job.

VIDEO WATCH THE VIDEO AND FOLLOW A PARAMEDIC.

GO TO page xx

for **VIDEOS IN SYM** step-by-step instructions.

C IN GROUPS Answer the questions.

1 What job is the video about? a paramedic
2 What skills does the person need for the job? medical skills, firefighting skills
3 Who does the person work with? people who need medical and emergency help
4 What's the most difficult part of the person's job? time (he needs to get to the emergency quickly)
5 Is the person happy in this job? Yes, he likes helping people and saving lives.
6 What is the person's work schedule? ______

6 He starts working at 8 a.m. He stays at the firehouse for 24 hours. Then he goes home for 48 hours.

D IN GROUPS Check your answers to the quiz on page 46 and discuss the questions.

1 Do you know any firefighters?
2 What other jobs in the emergency services do you know?
3 What are the good points and bad points of working in the emergency services?
4 What skills do you need to work in the emergency services?
5 What special physical abilities do you need to work in the emergency services?

Answers to the quiz on page 46
1 b 2 a 3 c 4 a

130

ALTERNATIVE ACTIVITY

Before reading "A Firefighter," write *women doing men's jobs* on the board and ask volunteers to give examples of women they know who do jobs that were traditionally seen as men's jobs and vice versa.

FURTHER DISCUSSION

- Do you know any firefighters?
- What daily routines do firefighters have?
- Are there jobs that are traditionally seen as men's and women's in your community?

VIDEO

Watch with sound off. Look for: *fire truck, ambulance, patient, kitchen, exercise room, medical equipment.*

While viewing, listen for: *emergency, patient, training, medical, firefighter, first line of response, fire pole.*

After viewing, ask: *What does it mean to be the "first line of response" to an emergency?* It means they are the first people who come to help in an emergency.

UNIT 5

STUDY SKILLS

GO TO page xviii for STUDY SKILLS step-by-step instructions.

A Read the texts. Who are the texts for?

RESEARCH SKILLS

Education at Morrison University

With an education major, you can study a subject you love and then teach others what you know! This major is a good choice for people who want to work with children or adults in school or college.

Courses include:
- Managing a class
- Health and well-being
- Art and creativity
- Teaching language

Good writing, math, and communication skills are necessary.

Students say:
"This major is fun! I loved it."
Prize for best education course in 1982.
99% of students at Morrison University get jobs after graduating.

Business at **Markston University**

Do you want to work in international business? With a business major, you can study how business, sales, and accounting work in different countries. Learn what you need to be successful.

Classes include:
- Marketing a product
- Growing a small business
- International business
- Social media today
- Accounting

You need math ability and a foreign language.

Students say: "This major prepares you for a life in business. I now have my own international hotel chain and it's doing very well."
—Sam Blackthorne, former student

95% of our graduates find jobs in business.

The university won "Best Business Major" in 2018.

B Write the letter *E* (Education) or *B* (Business) next to the sentences.

1. Students with this major find jobs in sales. B
2. A student says the courses are fun. E
3. You need to speak a foreign language to study this major. B
4. This is a good major if you want to be a teacher. E
5. You need good communication skills to study this major. E

C Match the tips about research (1–5) to the reasons to do them (a–e). Write the letter.

1. Always check the date on the texts you read. b
2. You don't always need to read every word. c
3. Make sure the text you read was written by an expert. a
4. Think critically about the information you find. e
5. Write questions before you start researching. d

a. You want the information to be correct.
b. You want to be sure that the information is up-to-date and not old.
c. Just look for the information you need—it's faster.
d. This helps you to focus on what to look for.
e. Don't believe everything you read. You have to use what you know to help you.

D Make a list of pros and cons about each of the majors in A. Share with your partner.

A: I think the education major looks good. Look! They won a prize, too.
B: Yes, but that was in 1982! I think the business major is better because …

E THINKING SKILL—Apply Do you often do research for your studies? Do you enjoy it? Why or why not? How do good research skills relate to jobs you know?

MAKE IT HAPPEN

Work with a partner. Look online and choose a major that interests you. Use the research tips in **C** to help you.

Answers to the quiz on page 56
1 a 2 b 3 b 4 b (It's 52.8%.)

131

STUDY SKILLS TASK

Ask students what research they did for this course. Write questions on the board and have them discuss: *Why did you choose this course? Did someone recommend it?*

Students answer questions about the ads and match tips about research with reasons why the tips are useful. Then, they analyze the ads.

THINKING SKILL—Apply

Applying knowledge gained is the key to learning. With application, students demonstrate mastery and put what they have learned to use. Application is a vital step in the learning process.

MAKE IT HAPPEN

Students apply what they have learned in the lesson by searching for courses online with a critical eye, putting into practice the research tips they have acquired.

GO TO page xix
for FOLLOW A PRO step-by-step instructions.

Suggested answers:
1 Yes, because he listens to other people's opinions and he can make a difference for his company's product. / No, because he needs to be on social media all the time.
2 He needs to have good social media skills and be a fast reader.
3 The company can use the information Dani gives them to make their drinks more popular. They can use Dani's information about the age, nationalities, and other details of their customers to target their advertising.

GO TO page xx
for VIDEOS IN SYM step-by-step instructions.

UNIT 6 FOLLOW A PRO

A **Read about a chief listening officer's job. Answer the questions below.**

A CHIEF LISTENING OFFICER

What does a chief listening officer do? Dani Chavez, 29, the chief listening officer (CLO) for a soft drink company in the US, tells us about his job.

"I'm working on an idea for a new soft drink, and it's important that my company knows who buys our drinks—their age, nationality, hobbies, and so on. How do we do this? We "listen to" social media and find out what people are saying about our soft drinks. This helps us decide what products to make. Social media is very important in my job. When I see a negative comment about my company, I send that information to our Customer Service Center. They then try to understand why our customers are not happy.

Being a CLO is a new job, but there are already a lot of us. As for skills, it's very important that I have good listening skills."

1 Dani works for a …
 a social media company.
 b soft drink company.
2 "Listen to" in the text means to …
 a read what people are saying online.
 b hear what people are saying on the street.
3 What does Dani do when he sees a negative comment about his company?
 a He contacts the person who wrote it.
 b He sends the comment to the Customer Service Center.
4 A good CLO needs …
 a listening skills. b creative skills.

B **Discuss the questions as a class.**

1 Do you think Dani's job is interesting? Why or why not?
2 What other skills (apart from listening skills) are important for this job?
3 How can Dani's work help his company to sell more soft drinks?

VIDEO — WATCH THE VIDEO AND FOLLOW A SOCIAL MEDIA MANAGER.

C **IN GROUPS Answer the questions.**

1 What job is the video about? a social media manager
2 Does the person like the job? yes
3 Where does the person work? her office, her clients' offices, and from anywhere on her phone
4 What is the person's favorite part of the job? She works with people from all over the world.
5 What is difficult about the job? Social media never ends. It's always going on.
6 What does this person do for the clients? She posts information on social media websites.

D **IN GROUPS Check your answers to the quiz on page 66 and discuss the questions.**

1 Do you know any people who work in marketing?
2 What other jobs in marketing do you know?
3 Do you need English for this job?
4 What skills do you need to work in marketing?
5 What personal qualities do you need to work in marketing?

Answers to the quiz on page 66
1 a 2 a 3 a 4 c

132

ALTERNATIVE ACTIVITY

Before reading the text, write *chief listening officer* on the board and have students work in pairs to guess the job. Then, students read to see if their prediction was accurate.

FURTHER DISCUSSION

- What social media sites are you on?
- Do you know about data collection?
- Do you answer online quizzes?
- Are you worried about your data being collected on the internet?
- How do you think brands get ideas for new products?
- What new products do you think are cool or are ridiculous?

VIDEO

Watch with sound off. Look for: *computer, dress, clothes, photos, calendar, media post, phone.*

While viewing, listen for: *client, posts, calendar, fashion designer, liked, commented, shared, clicked.*

After viewing, ask: *What is the goal of a social media manager's posts?* The goal is to get as many likes, comments, and clicks as you can and to reach as many people as possible.

UNIT 7

STUDY SKILLS

GO TO page xviii for STUDY SKILLS step-by-step instructions.

A Read the conversation. On a scale of 1–5, rate the group work (1 = no communication, 5 = excellent communication).

EFFECTIVE GROUP WORK

Amy So, we don't have very much time to get our presentation on Australian culture ready. Are you listening, Marco?
Marco Um, yes—I'm just reading about Australian art …
Amy What artists do you want to talk about?
Marco I don't know yet. Sorry—I didn't read the book.
Amy Well, let's …
Tammi Hey, guys! Sorry I'm late! The traffic is bad today.
Amy Oh, that's okay. So, Marco—you're reading about Australian art. Can you talk about that for about two minutes? And can you talk about music, Tammi?
Tammi I'm not sure … I don't know very much about …
Marco And what are *you* doing for the presentation, Amy?
Amy Um … well, I don't know yet. I'm still thinking …
Marco Can you talk about food?
Amy No, I don't want to do that …
Tammi The sports teams?
Amy No, that's a terrible idea. What are you doing, Roberto? You're very quiet!
Tammi So, am I doing food, then?

B Check (✓) the reasons the group is not working well together.

- [x] One student is late.
- [ ] One student wants to work alone.
- [x] One student isn't well prepared.
- [x] One student isn't saying anything.
- [x] One student is negative about the other students' ideas.
- [ ] One student is talking on the phone to a friend.
- [x] One student is giving jobs to other people but isn't doing any work.

C Match the tips about group work (1–5) to the expressions (a–e). Write the letter.

Tips	Expressions
1 Include all members of the group. _b_	**a** Why don't we find some old pictures?
2 Say when you agree with someone's idea. _d_	**b** Sara, what do you think?
3 Make suggestions. _a_	**c** I think that's a really good idea!
4 Be positive about other people's ideas. _c_	**d** Yes, I agree with you.
5 Share what you know. _e_	**e** I read an interesting blog post about that …

D Rewrite the conversation in A. Show how a group can work together well. Use the language in C to help you.

Amy: What are we doing for our presentation?
Marco: I'm reading a book on Australian art. Can I do something about that?

E THINKING SKILL—Understand Describe how teamwork is important in the workplace. What jobs need teamwork?

✓ MAKE IT HAPPEN

Prepare a group presentation on a famous English-speaking person. Decide what to present and how to do the work. Remember to work as a team!

A: Let's do a presentation on Abraham Lincoln. He's an interesting man.
B: I have a good book about Abraham Lincoln.

Answers to the quiz on page 76
1 a 2 b 3 a 4 b

STUDY SKILLS TASK

Have students role-play the conversation as it is using the script. They can work simultaneously as a class in groups of four (including Roberto, who doesn't speak). Tell them to really get into their roles to understand how poorly the group is working together. Then, have groups complete the exercises.

THINKING SKILL—Understand

Once students reach an understanding of how important teamwork is, they can better participate when they are part of a team.

✓ MAKE IT HAPPEN

This exercise is designed to be open-ended in order to have students generate their own content to figure out how to work together as a team using the tips they have just learned. Tell them to apply the teamwork skills they learned in **B**, **C**, and **D** to this task.

GO TO page xix
for **FOLLOW A PRO** step-by-step instructions.

Suggested answers:
1 It's important because it helps to sell more food, and it also helps to sell recipe books, food magazines, etc. / It's not important because food is for eating, not for looking at.
2 in magazines, on TV, in cookbooks; Food always looks really good (different from when I cook food at home).
3 Students' own answers

GO TO page xx
for **VIDEOS IN SYM** step-by-step instructions.

6 She has to taste everything, and sometimes she is tired of eating cake.

UNIT 8 FOLLOW A PRO

A Read about a food stylist's job. Answer the questions below.

A FOOD STYLIST

The photos of food in magazines, cookbooks, restaurant websites, and travel guides always look so good. Do you know why? It's because a food stylist works to make the food look amazing in pictures. And that's what I do. I'm Alfonso Garcia, and my job is to make food look real when it's not. For example, do you know that a bowl of strawberry ice cream isn't really ice cream? It's mashed potato! Ice cream melts very quickly in a hot studio, so we use pink mashed potato instead. And here's a disgusting idea—we put motor oil on meat to make it look delicious and hot! I love my job, but I can't eat the food I work with. It all goes in the trash can!

1 What does a food stylist do? They make food look amazing in pictures.
2 What do food stylists use instead of strawberry ice cream? Why? They use pink mashed potato, because ice cream melts very quickly in a hot studio.
3 Why do food stylists put motor oil on meat? to make it look delicious and hot
4 What happens to the food that Alfonso uses? The food goes in the trash can.

B Discuss the questions as a class.

1 How important is a food stylist's job?
2 Think about places where you see pictures of food. How does the food look?
3 Would you like to be a food stylist?

VIDEO

WATCH THE VIDEO AND FOLLOW A BAKER.

C IN GROUPS Answer the questions.

1 What job is the video about? a baker (a pastry chef)
2 Where does the person work? in a kitchen
3 Is the person's job difficult? Why or why not? Student's own answers
4 What skills does the person need for the job? organizational skills, creativity, math skills
5 Does the person work long hours? She works from 9 a.m. to 5 p.m.
6 What doesn't the person like about the job?

D IN GROUPS Check your answers to the quiz on page 86 and discuss the questions.

1 What different food industry jobs can you think of?
2 Which food industry job sounds most interesting to you?
3 What qualifications do you need to work in the food industry?
4 What skills and abilities do you need to work in the food industry?
5 What are the good and bad points about working in the food industry?

Answers to the quiz on page 86
1 a 2 a 3 a (to make it look fat)
4 b (They add the seeds by hand.)

134

ALTERNATIVE ACTIVITY

Have students work in pairs or small groups. Encourage them to discuss which is more important: the way food looks or the way it tastes. Tell students to give reasons to support their answer.

FURTHER DISCUSSION

- What food magazines do you read?
- Do you follow any food bloggers?
- Where do you get new recipes?
- Can you think of a food ad that you've seen on TV?
- Are there any billboards advertising food in your community?
- Do you photograph food for your social media posts?

VIDEO

Watch with sound off. Look for: *cake, milk, oven, mixing, cutting, photo book, cookies.*

While viewing, listen for: *chef, sweet, creative, baking, edible, decorating.*

After viewing, ask: *What does Lindsay do in a typical day?* She organizes her day, prepares the recipes, bakes and decorates the cakes.

UNIT 9

STUDY SKILLS

GO TO page xviii for STUDY SKILLS step-by-step instructions.

A **Read the two texts. Which one is formal and which one is informal? Why?**

A Text 1: formal; Text 2: informal

FORMAL VS. INFORMAL WRITING

Text 1

Corsica is an island on the south coast of France. The population is 330,000. The official language is French. Every year, more than three million people visit Corsica. Most people come in summer, when the weather is usually hot (the average temperature is 22°C, according to Météo France). It is warm and dry all year round.

In Corsica, you can swim in the sea and go to the beach. A lot of people go walking in the hills or visit the historical buildings. Sant'Antonino is a very old village in the northeast of Corsica. It goes back to the 9th century and is a popular place for tourists to visit.

Text 2

I love Corsica! I go to Corsica every year with my family and we always have a good time. It's a really cool place because it's so beautiful. The sea is very blue and the weather is always good—it never rains! The people are friendly, too, and there are lots of cafés and markets where you can find great fruit, cheese, and meat. Go there if you can! 🙂

B **Write *Text 1* or *Text 2* for each sentence.**

1. The writer uses sources with facts and data. Text 1
2. The writer doesn't give a personal opinion. Text 1
3. The writer says how he or she feels. Text 2
4. The writer uses contractions (e.g., "it's" instead of "it is"). Text 2
5. The writer groups ideas together in paragraphs. Text 1
6. The writer uses an emoji. Text 2

C **Write whether the sentences are *Formal* or *Informal*.**

1. Over 800 million people around the world do not have clean drinking water. Formal
2. I think that's so sad! Informal
3. It's a cool place to visit. Informal
4. First, we need to think about why this happens. Formal
5. I wanna try and answer that question. Informal
6. According to the *Daily Morning Times* news, hundreds of young people are going overseas to find work. Formal

D **Rewrite the informal sentences in C so that they are formal and rewrite the formal sentences so that they are informal.**

Suggested answers:
1. A lot of people don't have clean water to drink.
2. It is a sad situation.
3. It is an interesting place to visit.
4. Let's think about why this happens.
5. I want to try to answer that question.
6. I think lots of young people are looking for work abroad.

E **THINKING SKILL—Analyze** **Compare and contrast when you have to write formally and when you can write informally. What happens if you write formally in an informal situation?**

MAKE IT HAPPEN

Write a formal paragraph about a country. Do some research online to find out facts about that country.

Panama is a country between Central and South America. It has a population of around four million. It is famous for the Panama Canal, which connects the Atlantic and Pacific Oceans.

Answers to the quiz on page 96
1 b 2 a 3 b 4 a

STUDY SKILLS TASK

Ask students how they identify formal versus informal writing in their languages. Students read a formal and an informal text, then identify elements of each style. Students also identify sentences as being informal or formal writing. Finally, they should change formal examples to informal writing and informal examples to formal writing.

THINKING SKILL—Analyze

Comparing and contrasting is a useful technique for analyzing information. Here students compare and contrast when to use formal and informal language.

MAKE IT HAPPEN

Using Text 1 as a model and the practice in the lesson, students research and write a formal paragraph about a country of their choice. Have them check each other's work and comment on the language used.

GO TO page xix
for **FOLLOW A PRO** step-by-step instructions.

UNIT 10 FOLLOW A PRO

A **Read about an event organizer. Answer the questions below.**

AN EVENT ORGANIZER

Dale Langdon started Star Events, Inc. four years ago. He loves social events, and he likes to help people celebrate special times in their lives. It's not easy to organize a wedding for 300 people or an 80th birthday party for a large family, but Dale does that every day. Each event starts with a meeting. People tell Dale what kind of event they want and how many people they want to invite. Dale asks questions to find out more about the person's ideas. Dale then makes sure it all happens. He has to find a place for the event and make all preparations for the event—from the music to the parking. For some events, he has to find musicians, photographers, dancers, chefs, DJs, and servers. It's a lot of work, but Dale likes it.

1. Why did Dale start Star Events, Inc.? He loves social events and wants to help people celebrate.
2. What kind of events does Dale organize? large weddings and birthday parties
3. What does each event start with? a meeting
4. How does Dale find out what people want? He asks them questions.
5. What services does Dale need to find? everything—from the music to the parking

Suggested answers:
1 good salary / helping people / the feeling you have when an event is successful
2 long hours / difficult clients / the feeling you have when an event goes badly
3 Students' own answers

B **Discuss the questions as a class.**

1. What do you think is enjoyable about this career?
2. What do you think is not enjoyable about this career?
3. Imagine you are an event organizer. A young woman wants an unusual event for her 21st birthday. Money isn't a problem. What do you suggest?

VIDEO

WATCH THE VIDEO AND FOLLOW A TOUR GUIDE.

GO TO page xx
for **VIDEOS IN SYM** step-by-step instructions.

C **IN GROUPS Answer the questions.**

1. Where does the person work? in Miami Beach
2. What does the person do every day? shows tourists interesting, historical sites of the city
3. What does the person say is the best part of the job? ______
4. What skills does the person need? ______
5. Who does the person work with? visitors from Europe and Latin America

3 She gets to be a tourist every day (and sometimes she gets free food).
4 patience, people skills, love of learning, language skills (English/ Spanish)

D **IN GROUPS Check your answers to the quiz on page 106 and discuss the questions.**

1. What different events do people need help with planning?
2. Which events take the most time and money to plan?
3. What personal qualities do you need to work in the events industry?
4. Are there opportunities for this job where you live?
5. Do you need English for this job?

Answers to the quiz on page 106
1 a 2 b 3 c 4 c

136

ALTERNATIVE ACTIVITY

Ask students to work in pairs. Have them discuss events they have been to recently, such as weddings, graduation parties, birthday parties, and so on. Were they well organized? Who organized the event?

FURTHER DISCUSSION

- Do you know an event organizer?
- Have you used an event organizer?
- What's the nicest event you've attended?
- Is it expensive to use an event organizer?
- Have you ever organized your own event?
- What do you think is the hardest part of organizing an event?

VIDEO

Watch with sound off. Look for: *tourists, street, taxi, beach, ocean, welcome, café, coffee, selfie.*

While viewing, listen for: *tour, beach, people, tourist, vacation, bike tour company, guests, historically, architecture.*

After viewing, ask: *How did Carolina learn to be a tour guide?* She learned at a bike tour company, and followed a guide for two weeks to learn to do a tour.

GO TO page xviii
for **STUDY SKILLS** step-by-step instructions.

UNIT 11 STUDY SKILLS

A Read the conversation. Is Maria a good time manager?

PERSONAL DEVELOPMENT

Sally Hey, Maria! What are you doing?
Maria Hi, Sally! I'm writing a schedule.
Sally Why?
Maria Well, I have a lot of work to do, and it's important that I don't forget things. For example, I have a math test next month.
Sally But that's next month! You don't need to think about that now.
Maria I do! It's important to plan now so I don't rush at the last minute.
Sally Are you going to study for two hours every day? That's too much.
Maria Well, I don't know how long I need to study. So it's better to give it two hours in the schedule.
Sally What does it say here? "Relax"? Why are you writing that?
Maria It's important to have time for myself. If I work too hard, I can't focus.
Sally Oh, I see. And why are you coloring it in?
Maria I color the things that are really important red, like my math test, for example. If it's not so important, then it's green.
Sally "Sally's birthday." Ah, thank you, Maria. But hey ... why are you coloring that in green?

B Choose *True* or *False*.

1	Maria is making a schedule because she has a lot to remember.	**True** / False
2	Maria is writing her math test in her schedule at the last minute.	True / **False**
3	Maria is sure she needs to study math for two hours every day.	True / **False**
4	Maria doesn't want to relax because she wants to focus on her studies.	True / **False**
5	Maria colors in things so she doesn't forget them.	True / **False**

C Match the tips about managing your time (1–5) to the reasons (a–e). Write the letter.

1 Plan time to relax and do something you enjoy. b
2 Write down due dates in your calendar. d
3 Decide what is very important and not very important in your to-do list. a
4 Write down every important task you need to do. c

a Then you can do the important things first.
b If you feel better, you work better.
c That way you don't forget about it.
d Then you can see how long you have to complete the task.

D IN PAIRS Role-play. Student A: You are having problems managing your time. Student B: Give Student A advice about managing his or her time.

Ula: I'm so stressed! I have two exams this week, and I have no time to study!
Tony: Don't worry. Maybe I can help you ...

E THINKING SKILL—Predict What can happen if you don't manage your time well at school or work? Are you good at managing your time? Why or why not?

MAKE IT HAPPEN

Make a schedule for the next week. Talk with a partner about the ways you can manage your time.

Answers to the quiz on page 116
1 c 2 a 3 c 4 b

137

STUDY SKILLS TASK

Have students read the conversation in pairs and answer the opening question, then have them answer **B**. Have pairs match the tips to the reasons in **C**. Before starting **D**, have students underline ways to give advice from the conversation in **A** (*You don't need to ..., It's important to ...*).

THINKING SKILL—Predict

The ability to predict outcomes is a powerful thinking skill. Once students visualize possibilities for what may happen if they don't plan their time, they can predict what good outcomes will happen if they do manage their time well.

MAKE IT HAPPEN

In this activity, students put into practice everything they have learned in the lesson and make a schedule for next week. Give them a chance to show their schedules to a partner and do some peer counseling.

GO TO page xix

for **FOLLOW A PRO** step-by-step instructions.

UNIT 12

FOLLOW A PRO

A Read about a forest ranger's job. Answer the questions below.

A FOREST RANGER

Forest rangers usually work in national parks and areas of natural beauty. The job can be more dangerous than other jobs, but it's also more enjoyable than an office job for many people. Most rangers in the United States of America work for the Forest Service.

Forest rangers have many jobs. In the summer, when the weather is hotter, they need to prevent fires. They talk about the dangers of forest fires. They tell tourists and schoolchildren about fire safety. They sometimes cut down trees to stop fires. They help firefighters if there's a fire in the forest.

Forest rangers make sure people are safe outdoors. They give information about hiking trails. They teach people how to be safe when camping or hiking in the forest, and how to stay safe from bears and other wild animals. They also help rescue people if they get lost or if things go wrong.

1 Where do forest rangers usually work? in national parks and areas of natural beauty
2 What do they talk to tourists and children about? fire safety; how to stop fires from happening
3 Why do forest rangers cut down trees? to stop fires
4 What do forest rangers teach people to do? be safe in the forest, stay safe from wild animals

Suggested answers:
1 They have to deal with fires and sometimes with wild animals. They are outside in all kinds of weather.
2 Students' own answers
3 Be careful with campfires—don't burn them when it is too windy, and watch what you throw on them. Avoid smoking in the forest.

B Discuss the questions as a class.

1 Why is being a forest ranger sometimes a dangerous job?
2 Would you like to work outdoors all the time? Why or why not?
3 What can you do to prevent a fire?

GO TO page xx

for **VIDEOS IN SYM** step-by-step instructions.

VIDEO

WATCH THE VIDEO AND FOLLOW A BOTANIST.

C IN GROUPS Answer the questions.

1 What is the person's job? a botanist
2 Where does the person work? in a lab, in nature
3 What skills does the person need for the job? biology, math, computer technology, writing, fitness
4 Does the person like the job? Why or why not? Yes, because he works in beautiful places.
5 Who does the person work with? with other botanists and with students studying plants

D IN GROUPS Check your answers to the quiz on page 126 and discuss the questions.

1 Do you know anyone who works outdoors in nature?
2 What different outdoor jobs do you know?
3 What physical abilities do you need to work outdoors?
4 What are the challenges of working in nature?
5 What skills do you need to work in nature?

Answers to the quiz on page 126
1 c 2 b 3 a 4 a

138

ALTERNATIVE ACTIVITY

Write *forest ranger* on the board. Ask students to predict what a forest ranger does as part of their job. Ask them to read the article and check if their predictions were mentioned. After answering the questions, ask students to underline what they think a forest ranger's most important role is.

FURTHER DISCUSSION

- Are there any national parks in your area?
- Why are national parks important?
- Have you been to a national park recently?
- Have you been to a national park in another country?
- Have you met a park ranger?
- Would you like to work as a park ranger? Why? Why not?

VIDEO

Watch with sound off. Look for: *bird, flower, garden, fruits, waterfall, butterfly.*

While viewing, listen for: *plants, birds, nature, extinction, physically fit, species, ecosystem, outreach.*

After viewing, ask: *What are some of the challenges of being a botanist?* There aren't enough botanists in the world or enough people interested in protecting nature.

Student's Book Grammar Answer Key

Grammar Quiz Answer Key

A **1** I'm not **2** Is **3** It's **4** are **5** is **6** are

B **1** do not know / don't know **2** want **3** travel **4** love **5** works **6** does not make / doesn't make

C **1** 's raining / is raining **2** are not listening / aren't listening **3** 's working / is working **4** 'm cooking / am cooking **5** is not doing / isn't doing **6** 's wearing / is wearing

D **1** We sometimes listen to music. **2** Where can I buy vegetables? **3** Our teacher is never late. **4** Sally has long brown hair? **5** How many eggs are there? **6** How often does Adam cook?

E **1** My father's name is Antonio. **2** Please take an umbrella with you. **3** Why do you have three cell phones? **4** Don't forget to come to my party. **5** Jeff takes the train to work. / Jeff took the train to work. **6** We have some tomatoes. / We don't have any tomatoes.

Grammar Review Answer Key

A **1** f **2** d **3** a **4** h **5** b **6** g **7** c **8** e

B **1** is **2** aren't **3** isn't **4** are **5** a **6** any **7** an **8** some

C **1** works **2** don't work / do not work **3** take **4** don't live / do not live **5** has **6** doesn't go / does not go

D **1** Do you wear a uniform? **2** Where do they go after work? **3** Does your teacher drive to school? **4** Does that bookstore sell notebooks? **5** How do I get to the bus station? **6** Who does she study with on weekends?

E **1** They are often late for class. **2** I sometimes do laundry at night. **3** My sister hardly ever cleans the house. **4** Mr. Sanchez usually works on Saturday. **5** We are always at the office by 9:00. **6** They never go shopping on weekends.

F **1** can't dance **2** can speak **3** can I get **4** Can you play **5** can't drive **6** can you play

G **1** is reading / 's reading **2** are not feeling / aren't feeling **3** are playing **4** is raining / 's raining **5** are not listening / aren't listening **6** is checking / 's checking **7** is not snowing / 's not snowing / isn't snowing **8** are working / 're working

H **1** a **2** vegetables **3** some **4** an **5** any **6** many **7** much **8** any

Grammar Reference Answer Key

Unit 1

be statements and *yes*/*no* questions

A **1** b **2** d **3** e **4** c **5** a

B **1** are **2** isn't **3** Are **4** aren't **5** is **6** Is

information questions with *be*

A **1** How **2** Where **3** What **4** When **5** Who

B **1** Where **2** What **3** are your hobbies **4** Who **5** When **6** are they

Unit 2

articles *a*, *an*, and no article

A **1** a **2** an **3** a **4** an **5** an **6** A

B **1** an **2** a **3** X **4** a **5** X **6** X

possessive adjectives and *'s/s'*

A **1** his **2** your **3** Their **4** Her **5** Our **6** My

B **1** Tim and Marta are Susan's parents. **2** Max's new friend is from India. **3** Our grandparents' home is in Florida. **4** Their parents' names are Anna and Peter. **5** My brother's wife is an interior designer. **6** The children's teacher is married.

Unit 3

simple present statements and *yes*/*no* questions

A **1** Do you want **2** has **3** don't **4** don't like **5** prefer **6** doesn't start **7** Does your brother **8** does **9** loves

B **1** love **2** prefers **3** Do, know **4** don't like **5** Does, want **6** doesn't like

the imperative

A **1** Go **2** Don't forget **3** Read **4** turn up **5** Don't buy **6** don't be

Unit 4

simple present information questions

A **1** How do they get to work? **2** When does she talk to her parents? **3** Where does he eat lunch every day? **4** Who do they study with? **5** What does he do in his free time? **6** Why do you like your job?

B **1** Where does he work? **2** Who do you live with? **3** When does class start? **4** Why does she work there? **5** How do you feel? **6** What do they drink every morning?

frequency adverbs

A **1** is often **2** is always **3** usually runs **4** rarely eats **5** never has **6** sometimes has

B **1** never **2** rarely **3** usually **4** always

Student's Book Grammar Answer Key

Unit 5

adjectives

A **1** That is a dangerous city. **2** Those are friendly people. **3** This is a cheap apartment. **4** These are clear directions.

B **1** cafés are lively **2** quick stop **3** colorful paintings **4** Smart shoppers **5** people are friendly **6** fresh food

there is / there are

A **1** There are **2** Are there **3** There aren't **4** Is there **5** There **6** There's

Unit 6

present progressive

A **1** am chatting / 'm chatting **2** is not using / isn't using **3** is texting / 's texting **4** is listening / 's listening **5** are not watching / aren't watching **6** are playing **7** am not downloading / 'm not downloading **8** are waiting

B **1** Where are you going? **2** How is she feeling? / How's she feeling? **3** Why are they smiling? **4** Who am I speaking to? **5** What is he doing? / What's he doing? **6** Why are we stopping here?

present progressive vs. simple present

A **1** Are, using **2** need **3** Does, sell **4** do, cost **5** are, doing **6** are watching **7** do not like / don't like **8** prefer **9** Are, watching **10** plays **11** is not playing / isn't playing **12** is sitting / 's sitting

Unit 7

can/can't (ability)

A **1** can **2** can't **3** can **4** can **5** can't **6** can

B **1** can **2** can drive a car **3** can drive a car **4** can't **5** play tennis **6** can't drive a car **7** can speak Portuguese **8** play tennis

adverbs of manner

A **1** beautifully **2** well **3** slow **4** quiet **5** carefully **6** easily

B **1** slowly **2** fast **3** angrily **4** well **5** gently **6** hard

Unit 8

countable and uncountable nouns

A **1** C **2** U **3** U **4** C **5** C **6** C **7** U **8** U **9** C **10** U **11** C **12** U

B **1** much **2** Is **3** an **4** some **5** are **6** many

this/that/these/those

A **1** these **2** that **3** this **4** those

B **1** that **2** these **3** this **4** those

Unit 9

verb + infinitive or gerund

A **1** She wants <u>to get</u> a hotel near the city center. **2** Do you need <u>to get</u> a new backpack for your trip? **3** I don't enjoy <u>traveling</u> in a large group. **4** They plan <u>to spend</u> two weeks in Thailand. **5** He doesn't like to <u>eat</u> in hotel restaurants. / He doesn't like <u>eating</u> in hotel restaurants. **6** Would you like <u>to visit</u> Europe or Asia?

B **1** walking **2** to take **3** to try **4** to meet / meeting **5** to study **6** to buy **7** to get

should/could for advice and possibility

A **1** f **2** e **3** b **4** a **5** c **6** d

Unit 10

simple past (affirmative statements)

A **1** ate **2** learned **3** played **4** spoke **5** talked **6** became **7** did **8** had **9** cried **10** shopped **11** made **12** went

B **1** came **2** worked **3** met **4** got **5** started **6** had **7** moved **8** opened **9** bought

simple past (negative statements and questions)

A **1** didn't wake up / did not wake up **2** didn't feel / did not feel **3** didn't have / did not have **4** didn't seem / did not seem **5** didn't live / did not live **6** didn't give / did not give **7** didn't buy / did not buy **8** didn't read / did not read

B **1** Did, come **2** did **3** showed **4** did, go **5** didn't enjoy / did not enjoy **6** Did, take **7** didn't / did not **8** wanted **9** didn't mind / did not mind

Unit 11

going to

A **1** are, doing **2** 'm going to clean / am going to clean **3** Is, going to be **4** 's going to rain / is going to rain **5** isn't going to work / is not going to work **6** Is, going to help **7** are, going to visit **8** 're going to spend / are going to spend **9** Are, going to get **10** 're not going to have / aren't going to have / are not going to have

direct and indirect objects

A **1** Maggie your message **2** me their new car **3** us your new home **4** his wife a surprise gift **5** you a nice dinner **6** your mother flowers

B **1** I gave the letter to him. **2** I didn't buy a gift for her. **3** Let's cook dinner for your parents. **4** I want to show something to you. **5** She sold her used car to me. **6** I'm going to make some soup for you.

Unit 12

comparative adjectives

A **1** larger **2** hotter **3** happier **4** worse **5** more beautiful / less beautiful **6** easier **7** nearer **8** windier **9** bigger **10** more important / less important **11** thinner **12** better

B **1** Mt. Kilimanjaro is higher than Mt. Etna. **2** The Atacama Desert is drier than the Gobi Desert. **3** Iceland is cooler than Spain. **4** The Amazon River is wider than the Mekong River. **5** A plane ticket is more expensive than a bus ticket. / A bus ticket is less expensive than a plane ticket. **6** An A+ grade is better than a C– grade.

review of tenses

A **1** love **2** go **3** visited **4** flew **5** took **6** spent **7** am thinking / 'm thinking **8** going to go **9** want **10** going to drive **11** visit

Irregular Verbs

Infinitive	Simple past	Past participle
be	was/were	been
become	became	become
begin	began	begun
break	broke	broken
bring	brought	brought
build	built	built
buy	bought	bought
catch	caught	caught
choose	chose	chosen
come	came	come
cost	cost	cost
cut	cut	cut
do	did	done
draw	drew	drawn
drink	drank	drunk
drive	drove	driven
eat	ate	eaten
fall	fell	fallen
feed	fed	fed
feel	felt	felt
find	found	found
fly	flew	flown
get	got	gotten
give	gave	given
go	went	gone
grow	grew	grown
hang	hung	hung
have	had	had
hear	heard	heard
hit	hit	hit
hold	held	held
hurt	hurt	hurt
keep	kept	kept
know	knew	known
leave	left	left
let	let	let
lose	lost	lost
make	made	made
meet	met	met
pay	paid	paid
put	put	put
read	read	read
ride	rode	ridden
ring	rang	rung
rise	rose	risen
run	ran	run
say	said	said
see	saw	seen
sell	sold	sold
send	sent	sent
set	set	set
sing	sang	sung
sit	sat	sat
speak	spoke	spoken
stand	stood	stood
stick	stuck	stuck
take	took	taken
teach	taught	taught
tell	told	told
think	thought	thought
throw	threw	thrown
understand	understood	understood
wake	woke	woken
wear	wore	worn
win	won	won
write	wrote	written

Pronunciation Symbols

Vowels

ɪ	did
ɛ	bed
æ	bad
ʌ	cup
ʊ	book
ə	banana
i	feed
ɑ	father, box
ɔ	tall
u	student, food
ɝ	shirt, birthday
eɪ	date, table
aɪ	cry, eye
ɔɪ	boy
oʊ	comb, post
aʊ	about, how

Consonants

p	park, happy
b	back, hobby
t	tea
d	die
k	came, kitchen, quarter
g	game, go
f	face, photographer
V	vegetable
θ	thing, math
ð	then, that
s	city, summer
z	please, goes
ʃ	she, shop
ʒ	leisure
h	hot, who
tʃ	chicken, watch
dʒ	jacket, orange
m	men
n	sun, know
ŋ	sung, singer
w	week, white
r	rain, writer
l	light, long
j	yes, use, music

Unit 1

Track 01

International English Teachers

Your Profile

About You: I'm an English teacher in Germany. I'm from Berlin. I speak German, English, and Spanish. My hobbies are swimming, dancing, and yoga. My favorite music is rock and my favorite food is tacos (love Mexican food). My boyfriend is Juan. He isn't an English teacher. He's a yoga teacher.

Username: Berliner100
Password: DerSeestern!
Re-enter password: DerSeestern!
First name: Angela
Last name: Steiner
Nickname: Angie
Date of birth: 04/15/97
Country: Germany

Track 02

Conversation 1

Sandy: Hi, Jake!

Jake: Oh, hi, Sandy. What's up?

Sandy: Not much. Where's your wife, Michelle?

Jake: She's at work.

Sandy: Well, it's nice to see you.

Jake: Good to see you, too. Take care!

Sandy: You, too. Bye!

Conversation 2

Janice: Hello. I'm Janice Walters. I'm the office manager.

Lynn: It's nice to meet you, Ms. Walters. I'm Lynn Jefferson. I'm the new designer.

Janice: It's nice to meet you, too. Welcome to Design Associates. Please call me Janice.

Lynn: OK. Thanks, Janice.

Conversation 3

Sarah: Good morning, Mr. Wilson. Welcome to DT Bank. How are you?

Mr. Wilson: I'm fine, thank you. And you?

Sarah: I'm fine, thanks. How can I help you today?

Mr. Wilson: I have questions about my account.

Conversation 4

Christine: Hey, Mark.

Mark: Hey, Christine. How's it going?

Christine: Great. Mark, this is my friend Jean Luc. Jean Luc, Mark's in my English class.

Mark: Sorry. What's your name?

Jean Luc: Jean Luc. I'm from France.

Mark: Oh! Well, it's nice to meet you, Jean Luc.

Jean Luc: Nice to meet you, too, Mark.

Track 03

first, second, third, fourth, fifth, sixth, seventh, eighth, ninth, tenth, eleventh, twelfth, thirteenth, fourteenth, fifteenth, sixteenth, seventeenth, eighteenth, nineteenth, twentieth, twenty-first, twenty-second, twenty-third, twenty-fourth, twenty-fifth, twenty-sixth, twenty-seventh, twenty-eighth, twenty-ninth, thirtieth

Track 04

Olivia: Is registration open?

Registrar: Yes, it is.

Olivia: Great. I want to register for the marathon.

Registrar: What is your first name?

Olivia: Olivia.

Registrar: What's your last name?

Olivia: Lopez.

Registrar: What is your date of birth?

Olivia: October 17, 1999.

Registrar: What's your home address?

Olivia: 45 Third Avenue, Apartment 701.

Registrar: And your phone number?

Olivia: 555-367-5823.

Registrar: It's $25 to register for the marathon.

Olivia: OK. Here's 25.

Registrar: Thanks. OK, you're in group 3. Group 3 starts at 7:45.

Olivia: Thanks.

Registrar: Is this your first marathon?

Olivia: No, it's my fourth!

Registrar: Good luck!

Track 05

Social Media Profile Tips

Many social media websites have different parts in the personal profile section. One part is often about specific preferences—movies, books, TV shows, and sports. Another part is for biographical information. When you create a social media profile, here are some things to consider:

- Are your preferences interesting?
- Is your personal information interesting? Write one or two interesting things about yourself!
- Is your information safe? Don't write your home address, phone number, or vacation dates.
- Are your grammar and spelling correct? Your language is part of your reputation!
- Finally, is your picture good? Use a clear picture of yourself.

Unit 2

Track 01

A Woman at Work: Zinah Saleh, Iraq

Zinah Saleh is a business owner with a successful business. She is the owner of her company, Ishtar Handmade Soap. Her company makes eco-friendly soap and shampoo. The all-natural soap products are very popular. All of the products use olive oil from Iraq. They also use fruit from trees in Africa.

Female business owners are unusual in Iraq. Zinah has a degree in business administration, and she wants to help women find jobs. Zinah's employees are all women. There are female soap makers, administrators, and marketers. Zinah's parents are happy for her. Her father is an engineer and her mother is a homemaker. Zinah thinks working women are important for her country's economy.

Track 02

an architect	an interior designer
an art teacher	an interpreter
an economist	an office manager
an engineer	an optometrist

Track 03

This is Sherry's family. Alicia is Sherry's mother. Tim is her father. Eric is her husband. Her children are Ellie and Danny. Danny is her son and Ellie is her daughter. Her aunts are Cindy and Patricia. Ray is her uncle. John and Kayla are her cousins. Paul is her brother. Lynn is her sister. Mylie is her niece. Billy is her nephew.

Track 04

Sarah: Before we visit your family on Saturday, remind me of who's who.

Alan: OK. My parents' names are Linda and Steve. I have two brothers and a sister.

Sarah: Right. And what are their names?

Alan: Kevin, Robert, and Mary.

Sarah: How old are they?

Alan: Kevin is 28, Mary is 22, and Robert is 17.

Sarah: Are they married?

Alan: Kevin is. He and his wife, Kaitlyn, have a little daughter—my niece, Mindy. Mary isn't married, but she has a boyfriend. His name is Tommy. Of course, Robert isn't married.

Sarah: Well, I'm excited, but I'm a little nervous!

Alan: Don't worry, Sarah. They're all really nice people.

Track 05

Molly: Look at this picture.

Trevor: What a great picture! Who are they?

Molly: It's my Aunt Elsa, Uncle Pete, and my cousins Jeff and Laurie.

Trevor: Where are they?

Molly: They're on vacation in Italy.

Trevor: How cool! So, how old are your cousins?

Molly: Jeff and I are the same age. We're 24. Laurie's 21.

Trevor: What do your aunt and uncle do?

Molly: Aunt Elsa is a pharmacist, and Uncle Pete is a pilot.

Trevor: What do your cousins do?

Molly: Laurie's a student. She's in medical school. Jeff is a computer technician.

Trevor: They're a nice family.

Molly: Yes, they are.

Track 06

Careers Profile

Name: David Monetti

For each category, choose two areas that describe your interests and abilities.

Personality: organized, friendly, patient, independent

Natural abilities: verbal, logical/mathematical, creative, social

Academic skills: science and math, language, technology, arts

Careers Profile Results

High school English teacher

Job description: Teach grammar, writing, and literature. Patience, good communications skills, and IT/social media skills are necessary.

Journalist for city newspaper

Job description: Talk to people and write stories. Need good English and computer skills. We want a creative, independent person.

Computer technician for large company

Job description: Work with computers and help people with computer problems. Lots of travel. A science and engineering education is required.

Marketer for small communications company

Job description: Need a friendly, creative, social person. Good computer and social media skills are necessary. Art or design education is not necessary, but good writing is very important.

Unit 3

Track 01

New Frisbee Champions! Here is an interview with Chris Watson, one half of the Chris–Otto Frisbee team. Chris and Otto are this year's winners.

Interviewer: Congratulations, Chris! You and Otto are the winners! Do you have time to talk to me?

Chris: Sure, thanks. Otto is a great Frisbee player! He runs really fast, and he always catches the Frisbee. Otto loves Frisbee, too. We practice together every day.

Interviewer: Does he like other outdoor activities?

Chris: Well, yes, he likes hiking, but he doesn't like hiking in cold weather.

Interviewer: Does he have any special likes or dislikes?

Chris: Yes, he does. He loves watching TV. He watches soccer and football with me a lot. I like golf, but Otto thinks it's boring. I don't watch it often. And ... let's see. He likes eating—a lot! And he hates cats!

Interviewer: Thanks, Chris. Good luck to you and Otto next season.

Chris: Thanks.

Otto: Woof!

Track 02

sounds like /s/: likes, hates, walks, thinks
sounds like /z/: loves, swims, plays, runs
sounds like /iz/: watches, uses, practices, catches

Track 03

Rob: Hey, Sandy. Listen to this!

Sandy: What?

Rob: Shawn Mendes, in concert, here in Denver!

Sandy: When?

Rob: November third. It's a Friday.

Sandy: Cool! Where's the concert?

Rob: City Auditorium. It starts at eight. Do you want to go?

Sandy: Of course I want to go! Please get me a ticket!

Rob: OK. The tickets are $45. Is that OK?

Sandy: That's fine. I can pay you for it before you go.

Rob: OK. Don't forget to write down the information.

Sandy: Sure. Tell me the date again, please.

Rob: November 3, 8:00 p.m., City Auditorium. Got it?

Sandy: Yeah, thanks. Awesome!

Track 04

The City Festival is here! Some of the most popular events are the pet parade, the 10-kilometer race, the dance contest, and of course, the rock concert. Don't forget the bicycle race, the kids' soccer game, and many other fun events!

Festival activities are from 9:00 a.m. to 9:00 p.m. every day this week. Join us and support our festival! Bring your family! Pets are welcome. Buy your tickets online for a discount.

Track 05

Get Together

Name of group: Music Lovers
Do you love music? Do you sing or play an instrument? This is the group for you! We like to go to concerts together, but we LOVE to make our own music!

Name of group: Latinos Play
We are a group of students from Latin American countries. We like eating food from our countries and meeting other Latin American students here in Los Angeles. If you speak Spanish and love good food, join our group!

How to join Get Together
Register for free. Then click on your interests and read about local groups. The members of the groups meet and do different activities. Join the groups that interest you.

How to create a Get Together group
You can start your own Get Together group. Click on "Create a Group." Enter your location. Click on your interest for the new group. Choose a title for the group. Write a short profile of the group. Click "Create Group."

Unit 4

Track 01

The Daily Blog: A Day in the Life of a Reporter

I'm a reporter. I work for an entertainment magazine in New York City. My friends think my job is amazing because I meet famous people. But this is my typical day.

I get up at about 6:30 a.m., and then I walk my dog, have coffee, and get ready for work. I leave home at 7:15 a.m. and I take the subway to my office. I start work at 8:00 a.m. I don't eat breakfast at home because I don't have time. I buy something at the café in the subway station. At work, I go to meetings and write articles for the magazine. I also make a lot of phone calls to get interviews with people. The interviews are interesting, but sometimes the people I interview aren't very friendly or they don't have time to talk.

In the evening, I go home and walk my dog again. Then, I have dinner and watch TV for about two hours. I go to bed at about 10:00 p.m. On weekends I go out with friends, go shopping, or go to a movie.

Track 02

1 What do you do?
2 Where do you live?
3 Why do you like your job?
4 When do you go on vacation?
5 How do you get to class?

Track 03

Marco: This is a conversation with actress Audrey Lang. Audrey, people think that actors have very exciting lives. Is that true?

Audrey: Believe it or not, acting is hard work. We usually work a lot of hours, and most of us don't often go to parties or out with friends.

Marco: What time do you usually start work?

Audrey: Well, we often start at about 6:00 a.m., but sometimes we start later.

Marco: Six o'clock is really early! What time do you finish?

Audrey: We frequently finish at eight or nine at night. It's a long day, and I'm always tired!

Marco: Wow! When do you have days off?

Audrey: I almost always have weekends off. I rarely work on Saturdays, and I never work on Sundays.

Marco: So what do you do on the weekend?

Audrey: Oh, I do things with my family. We almost always go to the supermarket on Saturdays or Sundays. We take the kids to a movie, go to the zoo, or just hang out at home. Four times a year we go to San Francisco to see my parents.

Marco: That sounds like a very normal life.

Audrey: Yes, it is. I know that my job is kind of unusual, but my routine is normal. I get up, I go to work, I come home, we have dinner and talk, or watch TV, and then we go to bed.

Marco: OK. Audrey, thank you for your time.

Audrey: You're welcome.

Track 04

Justin: I'm Justin Watts, and this is *Tell Me About It*. Today our callers tell us if their perfect day off is crazy or lazy! Here's our first caller. Good morning. What's your name?

Brendon: Brendon Novak.

Justin: Thanks for calling, Brendon. What's your favorite type of day off?

Brendon: I get up really late. Then I usually just hang out at home and watch TV or play video games.

Justin: OK, so Brendon really likes relaxing on his days off. Thanks, Brendon. Our next caller is Carla DePalma. Hi, Carla. What kind of day off do you like?

Carla: Hi, Justin. I always do a lot of things on my days off. I take a shower, get dressed, and cook a big breakfast. I almost always do housework in the morning. I sometimes go shopping in the afternoon. I often go out with friends in the evening.

Justin: Carla really likes being active! Thanks, Carla. The next caller is Ali Demir. Hey, Ali. Tell us about your perfect day off.

Ali: I love sports and exercise. On a perfect day, I go to the gym in the morning. I have lunch around 12, and I play soccer with my friends in the afternoon. Then, we usually hang out and watch the other soccer games. In the evening, I do housework and cook dinner.

Justin: That's a busy day off! Thanks, Ali. Our last caller is Melissa Martinez. What's your perfect day off, Melissa?

Melissa: I usually hang out at home and read or listen to podcasts. I sometimes take a nap in the afternoon. I rarely go out, but sometimes friends come over and watch a movie on TV.

Justin: OK, it's a relaxing day for Melissa. That's it for our show until next week!

Track 05

I Need Advice!

I'm 25, and I live in Tampa, Florida, with my two friends Joe and Mario. I have a good job. I'm a nurse, and I work at a big hospital. My work schedule is 9:00 to 5:00 Monday through Friday. I eat lunch in the hospital cafeteria at 1:00 p.m. every day. I always go to the gym after work. In the evening, my roommates and I cook dinner—usually pasta or burgers. We watch TV for about two hours, and I almost always go to bed at about 10:30 p.m. On Saturdays, I go to the gym in the morning and go shopping or do housework in the afternoon. On Saturday evenings, my roommates and I usually order pizza and watch movies. On Sundays, I always play soccer with my friends in the afternoon. I have a very good life—nice friends and a good job, but I'm kind of bored. What do you recommend?

Unit 5

Track 01

Places We Live

For many young people, the idea of buying a home is important. But what happens when you don't have a lot of money to buy? Here are two interesting options for millennials.

Oscar Knight lives in a new apartment in an exciting neighborhood in London. "This is an apartment building designed for young people between the ages of 20 and 35," he says. "We live, work, and play all in one space. It's not boring at all! There are different spaces for us to use, such as a library, a community garden, a gym, an office, a popular restaurant, and a grocery store."

"London is expensive," says Layla, one of Oscar's neighbors. "But it's a fun city. I pay £330 per week here, but that includes Wi-Fi, electricity, water, and a gym. I never feel bored here. It's a great place to live. And the people are very friendly."

Jay Nilsson, from Sweden, lives in an unusual house. He has a one-room eco-pod. "This eco-pod is great," says Jay. "You can live wherever you want. My eco-pod is in my parents' yard on a quiet street. But I can move my eco-pod, too." Eco-pods are not cheap—Jay's eco-pod cost him almost $93,000 dollars. They are also very small—only 8 meters long. But there is a bed, a bathroom, and a tiny kitchen. It's good for one person only!

Track 02

1 lively, quiet, busy
2 expensive, exciting, important

Track 03

1 expensive houses
2 an exciting city
3 busy neighborhood

Track 04

Host: So, the question this morning is "Are there things to do or places to hang out in your neighborhood?" On the line we have … Elsa. Hi, Elsa. Tell us about where you live.

Elsa: Hi there. Well, I live in a neighborhood outside the city of Cartagena, Colombia. It's a boring place to live because it's very quiet and there are no places to hang out. There is a grocery store and a park where old people hang out, but there's no gym and no library. I go to downtown Cartagena to hang out with my friends. There are two areas I like—San Diego and Getsemani. They are popular with university students, and the area is very lively!

Host: Thank you, Elsa. Cartagena sounds like a fun place. Next, we have Ahmed. Ahmed, what is your neighborhood like for young people?

Ahmed: Hello. I'm from Cairo. I live near the city center in a big apartment building. My neighborhood—Zamalek—is an island. It's not busy. There's a high school, and there's a coffee shop where I hang out with my friends. Sometimes we meet in the main square, called Tahrir Square, and walk to the Nile River. It takes about 10 minutes. I like Zamalek a lot.

Host: Thank you, Ahmed. I love Cairo, too. It's a very noisy but interesting city.

Track 05

Conversation 1

A: Excuse me. I'm looking for my friend's apartment. He lives on the corner of Jackson Street and Ninth Avenue.

B: That's easy—just take the second left.

A: Great, thanks.

Conversation 2

A: Hi. Is there a bus stop near here?

B: Yes, there is. It's across from the park.

A: Oh, right. Thanks!

Conversation 3

A: I want to get to … uh … Central Station.

B: Cross the bridge and go straight.

A: Where do I get a ticket?

B: You can get it on the train.

A: OK. Thank you.

Conversation 4

A: I'm lost! Where is the grocery store?

B: It's on the left.

A: No, it's not. There's a restaurant on my left.

B: Oh. Well … turn around.

A: Oh, I see! Thanks!

Conversation 5

A: How do I get to the beach?

B: Follow signs for the airport.

A: The airport?

B: Yes, that's right. The beach is next to the airport. It's a noisy beach!

Track 06

A New Place to Call Home

Name: Katy Morgan
From: Austin, Texas

I'm Katy. I'm from the United States, but now I live in a small neighborhood outside Cusco, Peru. Cusco is an amazing city. Machu Picchu is very close by. I have my own business here. I organize eco-tours around the area.

Life in Peru is great. I speak Spanish, so communication isn't a problem. There are other differences. In the States, things happen fast and people run from place to place. Here, life is slow, and I like it that way!

My neighborhood is small, but there are stores, restaurants (amazing food!), and a beautiful main square (the Plaza de Armas) in the city center. I live in a one-bedroom apartment on a quiet street. There's a small coffee shop across from my house, so I hang out with my neighbors before work. People here like to get together and talk.

It's hard to find a place to live when you arrive in a new city. There's a great company called Home Abroad Rentals. They find apartments for people from other countries who are new to Cusco. They match people to the right home. I'm happy Cusco is the place I call home.

Unit 6

Track 01

Social Media Use and Employment

Do some things about social media make you angry? If your answer is "yes," read on …

Young adults are spending a lot of time on social media these days. According to Statista, about 2.5 billion people use social media. Are you surprised? That's about one-third of the world's population! In the US, around 98% of people aged 16 to 24 have social media accounts. On average, they spend 109 minutes per day—almost two hours—on social media. China has more social media users than any other country—596 million. That number is growing all the time.

Many people are afraid that employers are getting information about them from social media. This information can make them feel embarrassed.

A study by Statista from 2017 shows that 61% of employers look at social media profiles before they hire someone. So, be very careful and check your settings. Keep your social media profiles for family and friends only.

Track 02

Speaker 1

Yeah, I vlog every two or three days. Right now, I'm using my laptop to upload videos, but I usually use my smartphone. I think you get good pictures of the vegetables on it. My favorite? In my opinion, peppers. I love them!

Speaker 2

Well, it's my job and my hobby. I'm a travel writer for a magazine. I spend about six months of the year away from home. I'm staying in a very big hotel in Colorado now. It has 1,500 rooms! I love vlogging. I'm not just looking at a computer all day. I'm talking to people all over the world.

Speaker 3

I'm a college student. I'm studying to be a computer programmer. I make money by showing gamers how to play video games. In my opinion, all you need is a good desktop computer or a laptop, a webcam, and some headphones. I think vlogging is cool.

Speaker 4

I love shopping. The fact is people always ask me for advice on what to buy. I vlog about all the good and bad things I buy, like clothes, smartphones, beauty products—anything, really! In my view, helping people make decisions about what to buy is important.

Track 03

1 I think you get good pictures of the vegetables on it.
2 The fact is people always ask me for advice on what to buy.
3 In my opinion, all you need is a good desktop computer or a laptop, a webcam, and some headphones.
4 I'm staying in a very big hotel in Colorado now. It has 1,500 rooms!
5 In my view, helping people make decisions about what to buy is important.

Track 04

Host: Hello and welcome to *Digital Life*. With me today is Luca Morris, a 20-year-old entrepreneur from Toronto, Canada. Hi, Luca.

Luca: Hello.

Host: Now, tell us, what do you do?

Luca: Well, I sell athletic shoes.

Host: But not in a store, right?

Luca: No! I sell my athletic shoes online.

Host: So, how does it work? How do you make money?

Luca: Well, I go online and buy regular athletic shoes. Then I customize them. That means I make every pair look different. I add lots of colors and interesting designs on them.

Host: And then you sell them?

Luca: Yes. I usually add about $40 or $50 to my cost.

Host: Sounds easy! And how do actually sell your shoes?

Luca: I have a website. You can also download an app for buying and selling things online. I use that sometimes.

Host: I see.

Luca: I upload pictures of new shoes every two or three days. Sometimes I wear the shoes, take a selfie, and use that picture to update my profile. Or I take videos. People like that. I hope my videos go viral!

Host: OK.

Luca: When I add new shoes, I send a message to all my customers.

Host: And are your shoes popular?

Luca: I think so! People post comments about them online. They usually say good things.

Host: Is this an easy business?

Luca: Well, it takes a lot of my time. But I have a day job, too—I work in a restaurant.

Host: And what about the future?

Luca: Well, my business is growing. If I go viral, I can quit my day job.

Host: Good luck, Luca! Thanks for coming in.

Track 05

1 I send a message to all my customers.
2 I upload pictures of new shoes every two or three days.
3 People post comments about them online.
4 … update my profile …
5 If I go viral, I can quit my day job.
6 Sometimes I wear the shoes, take a selfie, and use that picture…

Track 06

1 kin, king 2 sin, sing 3 thin, thing

Track 07

1 Sing this song.
2 The teacher is talking.
3 I'm listening to music.

Track 08

How to Do a Digital Detox

Are you spending too much time using your phone? Check the things that are true for you to find out:

- I check social media before I get out of bed.
- I send messages while I have breakfast.
- I often take my phone to the bathroom.
- I never go out without my phone.

Did you check three or four? Then it may be time for a digital detox. Mandy Morgan, a social media expert, gives us this advice …

"This isn't about tech devices," she explains, "it's about understanding what is healthy. People usually feel good when they don't use their smartphones all the time."

Morgan says that a seven-day detox helps with your sleep, your studies and how you feel. She asks people to check their screen time and count how many times a day they pick up their phone.

When you do a digital detox, you don't have your phone all the time. For seven days, you practice when and where you use your smartphone. You learn to leave your phone at home sometimes.

Marcia Estefan (DJ Blade), 23, is a club DJ from Brasilia. She is also studying to be a doctor. "I use my phone all the time," she explains. "I never think about how often I look at my screen." These days Marcia doesn't use her phone often. She rarely takes it out with her in the evening. "It makes me think about how I use technology and that's a good thing."

Before the Digital Detox:
Screen Time Per Day: 3 hours 20 minutes
Picks Up Her Phone: 56 times a day
After the Digital Detox:
Screen Time Per Day: 1 hour 50 minutes
Picks Up Her Phone: 23 times a day

Unit 7

Track 01

New Gadget Reviews

Are you looking for a new fitness gadget? Four athletes give their opinion about these gadgets.

Fitness tracker. Daniella, Boston: This is great. You can wear it on your arm or your ankle. It records your steps, your calories, and your sleep. You can use it when you ride a bike, run, walk, play volleyball, do judo, or do any kind of sport. $76. Four and half stars

Underwater headphones. Miguel, Puebla: I love swimming and listening to music at the same time. I can swim really fast when I listen to music. These go around your neck and fit in your ears. They're very comfortable. $200. Three and a half stars.

Sports camera. Felix, Sagres: It can take videos when I'm surfing. But when I'm on my surfboard, I can't hold it in my hand. I put it on my surfboard instead. You can also wear it on your head or on your shoulder. It takes pictures, too. $152. Four stars.

Ankle sensor. Clare, Santa Fe: You wear it on your foot and it checks that you're running correctly. Can you wash it? No, you can't wash it, even when it's dirty. It's expensive, in my opinion, but it's useful for professional runners. $120. Two and a half stars.

Track 02

A: Can you swim?

B: I can.

A: Can you come to a new water polo class with me?

B: Sorry, I can't. I play tennis then.

Track 03

David

This is a ball game we play on the beach. It's a combination of volleyball, soccer, and gymnastics. Oh, and trampolining! And there's music—so young people like to do it. I can throw the ball hard, but I'm not very good at catching it. But my team usually wins!

Claudia

I can't play, but I like watching it. It's like tennis. Three or four players stand in a circle and bounce the ball to the middle. You have to play fast. My friend plays it well, so she usually wins.

Marco

It's an unusual ballgame, but I love it. It helps me stay in shape. It's like golf and soccer. I usually play it in the summer. You have to kick the ball gently. I can kick it easily, but I'm not good at getting the ball into the hole!

Track 04

One of the exercises that I do at the gym is very hard. It's called the deadlift with an overhead press. You stand with your feet on the floor. Then you lift the weight (I use a 10 kilogram) up to your chest. You hold it there for about five seconds. Then you bend your knees and push the weight up above your head. It's not easy to stretch your arms so they're straight. I can usually only hold it above my head for about 10 seconds. I'm amazed how weightlifters do this all the time!

Track 05

Do you work in an office? Do you get tired of sitting all day? Then how about deskercise—exercises you can do at your desk! The first exercise is for your neck. Sit up straight. Bend your neck to your right shoulder. Hold for a few seconds. Then repeat on the left side. The second exercise is good for your shoulders. Stretch your arms slowly above your head and hold for five seconds. Pull your shoulders back. The third exercise is called look around. Turn your head to the left and look over your shoulder. Twist your body and hold for five seconds. Then repeat it on the right side.

The next exercise is for your back. Stand up. Put your hands behind your back. Push your hands together and hold for five to 10 seconds. Pull your shoulders back. And the last exercise—exercise five. Lift one knee up and hold it to your body. Try to hold it for five to 10 seconds. Repeat it with the other leg. These are a few important warm-up deskercises. Try to do these deskercises for five minutes every day.

Track 06

Outdoor Gyms Around the World

Many cities around the world have outdoor gyms. You see them on the beaches of Rio and in the parks in Shanghai or Spain. Here are some different outdoor gyms from around the world.

There is a famous outdoor gym called Muscle Beach in California, USA. Bodybuilders, weightlifters, athletes, and gymnasts train here. It's now a popular tourist attraction and you can buy a ticket to go see the place!

China has many outdoor gyms. This is the outdoor gym in the People's Park in Haikou. About 40% of China's 1.4 billion people use outdoor gyms regularly, according to Top.me. There are about 600,000 outdoor gyms in the country. They are all free!

A new outdoor gym in Sunnymead Park in Oxford, England, has some interesting technology. When people exercise on the machines, they create electricity. The electricity creates power for streetlights, smartphones, or tablets. People who use the outdoor gym can download an app so their doctor can check their health online. Amazing!

Unit 8

Track 01

Wendy, Canada, says …

Hi, food fans! Do you know the word *gastronaut*? It's a person who travels and tries different foods. That's me! I love something delicious called *hagelslag*. It's from the Netherlands. It has small, sweet pieces of chocolate you put on bread for breakfast. My boyfriend thinks it's disgusting! Do you like foods from different countries, too? What kind? How many new dishes do you try each week?

Soraya, Bali, says …

I'm a gastronaut, too! I love to try different foods from all over the world. My favorite food is *tom yum soup*, from Thailand. It's a spicy soup with shrimp and vegetables. I often have it for lunch. It's a very healthy meal! I add chilies to mine to make it extra spicy.

Peter, South Africa, says …

Hi, Wendy! Do you know about *bunny chow*? It comes from South Africa. It's a loaf of bread, but you take the middle of the bread out and put spicy beef or chicken inside. How much meat do you need? It depends on how big the loaf is! We usually eat it for lunch or dinner.

Marlena, Venezuela, says …

My favorite food is *empanadas*. They are delicious. You can make them with corn flour, water, and salt. You can put cheese, meat, chicken—anything you like—inside. Then you fry them. Some people eat them as a snack. My mom thinks they are unhealthy because you fry them.

Ben, Scotland, says …

I think I'm a gastronaut, too. Do you know a dessert called *cendol* from Malaysia? It's really unusual. It's green rice noodles, coconut milk, and sugar. You can also add fruit. It's very sweet. It looks like green spaghetti!

Track 02

Conversation 1

Interviewer: Here we are at the Central Food Market. It's a Saturday morning and it's very busy now. Food markets like this sell cheap food, but is it healthy? Let's ask that woman selling food. This smells delicious! What are you making?

Woman: I'm making falafel. They're, a Middle Eastern snack food. Do you want to try one?

Interviewer: Yes, please!

Woman: OK, here you go. So, this is the falafel. There is salad here, and this is pita bread.

Interviewer: Oh, yum! It's delicious—spicy, too! What's in falafel?

Woman: They are balls made of chickpea flour.

Interviewer: Are they healthy?

Woman: This falafel is healthy because we grill it. Fried falafel has more fat and calories. Falafel is also vegan. There's no meat or dairy in it.

Interviewer: It's They are really delicious! Thank you.

Woman: No problem.

Conversation 2

Interviewer: OK, now let's ask this man what he's eating. Excuse me, what are you eating?

Man: Oh, this is bibimbap. It's Korean. It's a very healthy meal!

Interviewer: What's in it?

Man: Well, this one is a vegetarian dish. Um … there's an egg on top, and there are vegetables and rice. It's delicious!

Interviewer: So, the egg is protein, the rice is a carbohydrate, and there are vegetables—carrots, spinach, and mushrooms. It looks like a balanced meal!

Man: Yes, and it's only $5!

Interviewer: So, the food at this market is delicious, and some of it is healthy, too.

Track 03

Conversation 1

A: Is this my salad?

B: No, that's your salad.

Conversation 2

A: Are these your apples?

B: No, those are my apples.

Conversation 3

A: Do you want that snack?

B: No, I want this one.

Track 04

So, first, the ingredients you need are two cups of flour, one cup of water, and oil. You also need vegetables. Here, I have one cup of delicious red tomatoes, one orange pepper, one green pepper, one cup of corn, and one purple onion. You also need two cups of yellow cheese.

Track 05

To make the pizza dough, put the flour in a bowl. Add salt and pepper. Then add the water and oil. Mix with a spoon or fork. Then use your hands to make a ball. Roll the ball into a circle. Put the pizza dough on a baking dish. Next, slice all the vegetables into small pieces. Don't mix them together. Put the cheese on the pizza dough first. Make a row of tomatoes, then orange peppers, then corn. Next, add green peppers. Then add purple onions. Bake at 200°C for 20 minutes. Then slice. Eat this pizza for lunch. It's also great for a party!

Track 06

Eating Out in Paradissos

Many people like to eat out in a neighborhood called Paradissos. There are a lot of bars and restaurants, and food from around the world, like Thai, Japanese, Greek, French—you name it! Some of the restaurants are great for snacks, but there are some expensive restaurants, too. It's hard to know what's good and what's not, so here is our guide to the places we like in Paradissos …

Matilda's: Vegetarian restaurant. Great for lunch. Healthy food.
We like: the mushroom burger and the delicious avocado salad
We don't like: the carrot cake, there are only five tables
$20 for lunch
Three stars

Yu Garden: Chinese restaurant. Open evenings only.
We like: the chicken noodles and egg fried rice
We don't like: the noise, the open kitchen
$30 for 3 dishes
Four stars

Fred's Fish: Fish and seafood restaurant. Lunch and dinner.
Outdoor tables in the summer.
We like: spicy shrimp spaghetti with tomatoes
We don't like: the vegetable dishes, small portions
$40–$60
Three and a half stars

Encore: French café and restaurant. Breakfast, lunch, and dinner.
We like: the steak and fries—so tasty!
We don't like: Nothing—we love everything here!
$25 in the café, $70 in the restaurant
Five stars

Unit 9

Track 01

There but Not There: Virtual Travel

Would you like to visit another continent—Europe, maybe? See Italy or Greece? Or how about a country in Africa, like Kenya? If you want to save time and money when you travel, here's a tip. You need to try virtual tourism! But what is virtual tourism? And how does it work?

When you plan to visit a new place, go online and take a virtual tour first. You can use a virtual reality headset and a computer to take a tour. You don't have to use a computer if you have an app on your smartphone. A virtual tour gives you all the sights and sounds of a place. Take a tour of a street market in a city like Delhi or enjoy tourist attractions in Rio de Janeiro. You can decide what you like to do before you go.

Many people enjoy traveling more when they plan with virtual tours. They like spending time on things that interest them. With virtual tours, they can spend more time on the things they love when they finally get to their dream vacation destination!

Track 02

I want to visit Europe.
Do you like to travel?
I don't have to work on Monday.

Track 03

Host: Today, we're on the streets of cities around the world. We're asking people if they like high season or low season in their city. Excuse me. *Radio English Today*. Can I ask your name?

Manuel: Hello. Yes, it's Manuel.

Host: Think about tourism in your city. Do you like the high season or low season?

Manuel: Well, I live in Barcelona, Spain. We get a lot of tourists every year during the summer. Tourists are good for the economy, but it can be very busy and noisy. I like the winter, when it's quiet. You can always get a table at a restaurant!

Host: Thank you. Hello. What is your name?

Andra: Andra.

Host: Where are you from?

Andra: I'm from Reykjavik, the capital of Iceland.

Host: Do you like high season or low season in Reykjavik?

Andra: It's very dark in the middle of winter and we don't get many tourists then. My favorite time of year is the middle of summer. We have lots of visitors and all the cafés and restaurants are open. There's a lot to do.

Host: Thank you. Here's one more person. Can I ask your name?

Viktor: I'm Viktor.

Host: Viktor, do you like the high season or low season in your city?

Viktor: In Lima, Peru, we get tourists all year, but the high season is October to March. That's in the summer. I like it then because you meet lots of new people from other countries. It's my favorite time of year.

Host: Thank you, Viktor.

Track 04

José

I travel a lot! I like to go to cold countries, like Canada. I usually go for work. When I go there, I take a jacket and gloves. You have to stay warm!

Isabela

When I go on vacation, I like to go to the beach. I like swimming and I always pack a swimsuit. When you go to the beach, you should take something warm for the evening. I take a sweater.

Mike

I should travel more! I like to go to the mountains. I pack boots because I like to hike. I don't take swimsuits or shorts, but I always take lots of socks! You change your socks a lot when you're in the mountains!

Amal

You should look good on vacation! I like to go to interesting cities. When I go on a trip, I take nice blouses. I wear them when I go out to restaurants. I also pack jeans, of course. Those are the clothes I usually take.

Track 05

Detourism

Love or hate it, Venice is a very popular tourist destination. Some people say it's too popular! Around 30 million people visit Venice, Italy, every year. The problem is, they all want to see the same things: the canals, St. Mark's Square, the Doge's Palace. The small city of Venice (population 50,000) attracts large crowds of visitors every year. Tourism is important for the economy of the city, but it's very expensive to keep Venice in good condition.

To deal with this problem, some people suggest detourism. A detour is a short trip in a different direction. Detourism shows tourists attractions that most people don't visit. That way, tourists aren't always in the same place at the same time. For example, when you move away from the canals, Venice also has interesting markets, restaurants, and shops. And there are unusual attractions, such as the multicolored houses on the island of Burano and the Lazzaretto Nuovo, home to the Vampire of Venice! It's a very different side of Venice.

Detourism can lead to many different kinds of vacations and new experiences. Have fun!

Unit 10

Track 01

An Inspiration for All

Malala Yousafzai was born in 1997 in the Swat Valley in Pakistan. Her father was an educator, and he wanted his daughter to get an education. But in 2007 and 2008, the schools for girls closed in her region of Pakistan, and Malala stopped going to school.

Malala wrote a blog for British TV about her life that year. She wanted all girls to have the opportunity to get an education. She became well known in Pakistan. Then in 2011, Malala's school finally opened again. Malala's blog made some powerful people angry. On October 9, 2012, Malala was shot on her way to school. She was only 14 years old.

Malala was lucky. She survived, and her family took her to England. When she was better, she started school there. She continued to talk about education for girls in Pakistan, and she went around the world to speak. In 2013, she started the Malala Fund. In 2014, she won the Nobel Peace Prize. The next year, a film of her life, called *He Named Me Malala*, told her story. In spring 2017, she went around the world on her Girl Power Trip and met world leaders. She asked them to support education for all girls. In autumn 2017, she started to study at Oxford University.

Malala continues to inspire young people around the world.

Track 02

learned stopped decided

Track 03

Luciana: Hi, Madison! How are things in Los Angeles?

Madison: Great! But I'm really tired!

Luciana: Why?

Madison: Well, I met up with friends last night because I didn't have any homework.

Luciana: Where did you go?

Madison: We went out to eat because we were hungry. After that, we saw a movie. I went to bed after 1:00 a.m. because the movie finished late! What did you do last night?

Luciana: Oh, I didn't go out because I had to study. I ordered food online.

Madison: What did you get?

Luciana: I ordered a pizza because the restaurant is close to my house. Then I studied for a few hours until I felt tired and went to bed. That's my boring life! Oh, but I had a great time last weekend!

Madison: Really? What did you do?

Luciana: I went on a date!

Madison: Really? Tell me all about it!

Luciana: Well, it was someone from my English class …

Track 04

Kristina

This happened last year. I went to my cousin's party with some friends. I thought it was just a regular party, but it was her birthday, and I forgot! I didn't take a present or a card or anything. I felt bad, but I got her something the next day.

Javier

I met Isaac a year ago. He joined or soccer team, and he got lost on the way to practice. When I saw him, I showed him where to go. After practice, we went out to eat together. That's how we became good friends.

Lauren

I think this was about two months ago. I made a reservation at a restaurant for me and my friends. But when we got there, they said they didn't have a table for us. We waited for an hour! My friend said I forgot to reserve it, but I did reserve it! It was the restaurant's mistake. We argued, and I got a little upset, to be honest.

Track 05

The World Advice Corner

The world's problem-solving web page
Got a problem? Got a solution? Here at the World Advice Corner, we want you to use your experience to help each other. Post your problem and then read the advice from people around the world. Or find a problem and give your advice. Here's a selection of problems on the World Advice Corner.

My problem is that I'm lonely. It's hard to make new friends. I went to a party recently and spent most of the night in the kitchen! I get nervous around people I don't know. Does anyone have any advice? —Adrian

My parents try to control my life! When I go out with friends, they always want to know exactly where I am and what I'm doing. I have to text them every half an hour or they worry. How can I find a solution? I don't want to argue with them. —Maria

I have a work problem. Last week, I made a mistake and my boss yelled at me. I got upset and didn't know what to do. Did this ever happen to you? What did you do? All advice welcome! —Olivia

Unit 11

Track 01

What to Do about To-Do Lists

What are you going to do today? Maybe you're going to write an important email or take your car to the carwash. Or maybe you are going to shop for a gift, plan an evening with friends, or make a dentist appointment. We all have busy lives and it's easy to forget things we're supposed to do.

A list of things to do—or a "to-do list"—helps us remember what to do, but many people make a big mistake when they write their lists: they list a lot of things and then only do half of them. Here are some tips for writing a useful to-do list.

1 Write three things you are going to do in one day. Choose the things that are really important and write your list the night before. That way, you're ready to go in the morning!

2 When you have more than three things to do, write the top three and do them first. Then, make a new list and write another three things. If you have one big job to do, break it into smaller jobs.

3 Write exactly what you need to do. Don't write "learn English." Write "learn eight new English words." People do things on their lists when it's clear what to do.

4 Be ready to change your list. Things are going to happen that you didn't plan. When they do, write a new list. Life is full of surprises!

Track 02

1

A: What are you going to do this weekend?

B: Oh, I'm going to see my cousins.

2

A: Do you and your friend have any plans for tonight?

B: Yes! We're going to go dancing.

3

A: What do you think about your exams?

B: I'm really worried. I think I'm going to fail!

4

A: It's a beautiful day!

B: Yeah … but it's going to get cold later.

Track 03

Host: Welcome to *Money Talks*, the show about you and your money. Today, we're talking about planning for the future. How can you save money each month? We spoke to two people with different ideas. First, David.

David: I don't earn a lot from my job. I live with my parents, so I don't spend money on rent. I want to save money to rent my own apartment. Last month, I spent a lot of money on food. I bought my lunch. This month, I'm going to make sandwiches for myself. That way, I can save a little money every day.

Host: And this is Patricia.

Patricia: I have a large family, so I'm always giving people birthday gifts! It can be expensive, and I want to save for a vacation. This year, I'm going to make gifts for people. Last week, I made my mom a photo album with pictures of me at different ages. She loved it. Next week, it's my brother's birthday. I'm going to make him a pizza! It's his favorite!

Track 04

Host: Welcome to this week's podcast. Today, we're talking about how to get your dream job. With me is Jade Lewis from the website Careers Now. Jade, how do you get your dream job?

Jade: It isn't easy, but there are some things you can do to make your dreams come true. First, start early. Decide on your dream career now. That gives you time to make a career plan and work on that plan right away.

Host: So the first point is: start early. What else?

Jade: Second, get information. Learn what you can about your dream job. What skills do you need? What courses do you need to take? Information helps you plan.

Host: Great. So the second point is: get information. Anything else?

Jade: Finally, don't give up. It takes hard work to get that dream job, and it doesn't happen immediately. You need to be patient. Maybe you need to do another job first. But with a little luck, you might get there one day.

Host: So, don't give up. Jade, thank you very much for talking to us today. And good luck to all of you. I hope you get your dream job one day!

Track 05

Follow Your Passion

Many of us have a hobby or a free-time activity we love. But is it possible to make that hobby a career? For some people, the answer is "yes." Love baking? Start a cake-making business. Exercise every day? Start a career as a personal trainer. Today, lots of people are finding that social media can help them turn their passion into a career.

Fiorella Pia has an interesting hobby. She takes photographs of food and shares them on a social networking website. She has a talent for making the food look nice. She has a lot of followers and her pictures are very popular. Now she wants to turn her hobby into a career. She wants to earn money from her photography. She's going to plan carefully. She needs to decide exactly what kind of business to start. She also needs to write a business plan. She's asking all her friends for their advice as she puts together her career plan.

Unit 12

Track 01

The Galapagos Islands

The Galapagos Islands are an amazing place for a tour. There are beautiful sandy beaches, awesome animals, and the people are friendly. Every year, new people learn what the Galapagos Islands have to offer. People can swim, dive, and see nature—the Galapagos has it all! The islands are near the equator. They don't have seasons like some other places do, but there is a cool season from June to November. The water is colder at that time, and there's less rain, so it's drier. It's a great time for diving around the islands. It's also a good time to see whales, sea lions, and penguins. The temperature is around 21–27°C, and the water is around 18–24°C.

From December to May, the temperature is higher. It's called the warm season. It's more tropical during these months, and the skies are cloudier. It's also wetter than the rest of the year. The ocean is warmer and it's better for swimming. It's also a good time to see iguanas, flamingos, and other tropical birds. The temperature is around 27–32°C. The water is cooler than that, at around 21–26°C.

To get there, you need to go to Ecuador. From Ecuador, you can fly to Baltra Island or San Cristóbal Island, or go by boat. Of course, it's quicker to fly than go by boat. Flights are also cheaper, but then you have to pay for a hotel. A luxury cruise ship is more expensive than a trip on a small boat.

Track 02

Host: And now on *My Travels*, we're talking about waterfalls. My guest is Kerry Davis. Kerry, why do you love waterfalls?

Kerry: I love waterfalls because I'm studying geology at college and waterfalls are great places to learn. Last year, I went to the Iguazu Falls in Argentina and Brazil.

Host: They're beautiful!

Kerry: Yes, they are. The Iguazu River goes through Brazil. When it gets to the border with Argentina, it falls 82 meters. The Iguazu Falls are really interesting. There are many islands in the river, and they create about 300 different waterfalls!

Host: When is a good time to visit?

Kerry: There are fewer tourists at Iguazu between July and October, so that's a good time to visit.

Host: Do you plan to visit other waterfalls?

Kerry: This year, I'm going to visit Niagara Falls, on the border between Canada and the United States. Niagara Falls is 50 meters tall. It's really three waterfalls. A good time to visit is a little earlier than Iguazu, usually June to August. I'm going to go in July.

Host: And after that?

Kerry: Next year, I'm going to visit the Angel Falls in Venezuela. Angel Falls is just one waterfall, and it looks amazing. It's higher than the others, of course. It falls 979 meters. I'm going to visit Angel Falls next May because the water is higher then. It's going to be great!

Host: I hope you can come back and tell us all about your trips. Thank you, Kerry.

Track 03

beautiful	document
communicate	music
cute	popular

Track 04

Tourist: Hello. I'm going to visit Mexico this summer. I want to see an unusual natural place. Do you have any suggestions?

Travel Agent: Yes, of course. Mexico has many amazing natural places. One of them is the volcano called Paricutin. It appeared in a corn field in the state of Michoacán in 1943.

Tourist: What? It wasn't there before? It just … appeared?

Travel Agent: Yes! It grew very quickly. It was the first time scientists saw the birth of a volcano. It's popular with people from all over the world. You can get there by flying to Uruapan and then taking a bus to the village of Angahuan.

Tourist: Are there tours of the volcano?

Travel Agent: Local people take visitors to see the volcano on horseback. It's one to two hours from the town to the volcano. Then you can walk to the top of the volcano.

Tourist: Is it a long trip?

Travel Agent: It takes about six or seven hours. I can show you pictures of the area.

Tourist: Great!

Track 05

Local College Asks for Ideas

By Janice Baskin

Meadowville College is a college near our city. There is a large lake and a forest on Meadowville's campus. Right now, not many people use the lake or the forest. Some people go swimming or camping there in the summer.

Recently, the college decided to use this area for its students. Dean Linda Collins says, "We want our students to learn about nature and learn new skills. Many of our students come from big cities and they don't know a lot about nature. They are more familiar with technology than they are with the natural world." The college wants students to be interested in nature. "They need activities to introduce them to outdoor life. Maybe something that uses technology can get them interested—something that connects nature to their studies," says Dean Collins.

The college is asking students for ideas and suggestions. They have money for the project and they are happy to spend it on the right ideas.

Workbook Answer Key

Unit 1

Lesson 1

READING A **1** MChavez89 **2** Manny **3** Chavez **4** September 29, 1994 **5** Guadalajara, Mexico **6** mchavez@mail.com **7** cycling, traveling

READING B **1** b **2** a **3** a

VOCABULARY A **1** full name **2** password **3** nickname **4** birthday **5** country **6** city

VOCABULARY B **1** dancing **2** yoga **3** swimming **4** playing video games

GRAMMAR A **1** am **2** are **3** is **4** I'm not **5** are not **6** is not **7** Are **8** Is **9** I'm not **10** are **11** isn't

GRAMMAR B **1** am, is **2** Are, they are **3** is, isn't **4** Are, they are **5** Is, it's not, It's

GRAMMAR C **1** Elisa is from Berlin. **2** He's my math teacher. **3** Are they from Germany? **4** Yes, they are. **5** Is she your English teacher? **6** No, she's not.

Lesson 2

LISTENING A **1** Yes, she is. **2** No, he isn't. **3** No, they aren't. **4** Yes, it is. **5** Yes, he is. **6** No, she isn't.

LISTENING B **1** b **2** b **3** a **4** a **5** a

VOCABULARY A **1** morning **2** you **3** going **4** Nicole **5** meet you **6** care **7** later **8** Good

VOCABULARY B **1** going **2** I'm good. **3** How **4** Good morning! **5** Nice to meet you. **6** See you later. **7** take care

GRAMMAR A **1** person **2** thing **3** place **4** time **5** way

GRAMMAR B **1** What **2** When **3** Who **4** Where **5** How

GRAMMAR C **1** Who **2** David **3** How **4** Where **5** Chicago **6** When **7** October 19th

GRAMMAR D **1** How **2** Where **3** Who **4** What **5** When

Lesson 3

VOCABULARY A **1** fourth **2** twelfth **3** fifteenth **4** twenty-first **5** twenty-fifth **6** twenty-ninth **7** thirtieth

VOCABULARY B **1** third **2** sixth **3** eleventh **4** seventeenth **5** twenty-eighth **6** thirty-first

LISTENING A **1** b **2** a **3** b **4** b

LISTENING B **1** September 23, 1998 **2** 2513 Cedar Road **3** J8b7213 **4** 555-697-4398 **5** 555-697-2105

WRITING A **1** peru **2** english **3** march **4** american **5** day **6** i **7** york **8** thursday

WRITING B **1** L **2** S **3** O **4** t **5** J **6** C **7** N **8** Y **9** E **10** h **11** d

Unit 2

Lesson 1

READING A **1** the owner **2** computers **3** medical school **4** four

READING B successful, tech company, trains, computers, computer programmers, jobs, industry, business, owner, online store, work

VOCABULARY A **1** business owner **2** eco-friendly **3** parents **4** female **5** company **6** employees **7** successful

VOCABULARY B **1** parents **2** employees **3** marketers **4** business **5** an administrator

GRAMMAR A **1** an **2** a **3** a **4** an **5** a

GRAMMAR B **1** a **2** an **3** an **4** an, a **5** X, X **6** an, X

GRAMMAR C **1** an exciting **2** a successful **3** a necessary **4** a happy **5** an unusual

GRAMMAR D **1** It's important to know languages to be an interpreter. **2** I enjoy creative jobs in art and design. **3** Paula is a successful architect, and she designs great buildings. **4** Women own many businesses in my country. **5** Hard work is a necessary part of most jobs. **6** My mother's company sells products for children.

Lesson 2

LISTENING A **1** d **2** e **3** b **4** f **5** a

LISTENING B **1** b **2** a **3** c

VOCABULARY A **1** father **2** mother **3** son **4** daughter **5** brother **6** sister **7** uncle **8** aunt

VOCABULARY B **1** husband **2** grandfather **3** cousin **4** children **5** wife **6** grandmother

GRAMMAR A **1** Her **2** My **3** Our **4** Their **5** His

GRAMMAR B **1** Maria's **2** Their **3** his **4** parents' **5** husband's **6** niece's **7** children's **8** Whose

GRAMMAR C **1** Their **2** his **3** her **4** His **5** his **6** her **7** their

GRAMMAR D **1** Rebecca's **2** children's **3** parents' **4** cousins' **5** Victor's **6** Danny's and Cindy's

Lesson 3

LISTENING A **1** a **2** a **3** a **4** b **5** b **6** b

LISTENING B **1** mom **2** Spanish and English **3** journalist **4** pilot

VOCABULARY A **1** False **2** c **3** d **4** h **5** b **6** e **7** g **8** a

VOCABULARY B **1** interior designer **2** math teacher **3** office manager **4** nurse **5** technician **6** ?

WRITING A **1** d **2** b **3** c **4** e **5** a

WRITING B **errors:** a economist, acountant, moms', technician computer, an journalist **correct:** an economist, accountant, mom's, computer technician, a journalist

Unit 3

Lesson 1

READING A **1** False **2** False **3** False **4** False **5** True

READING B **1** likes **2** doesn't like **3** doesn't like **4** likes

VOCABULARY A **1** don't like **2** doesn't like **3** like **4** love **5** hate

VOCABULARY B **1** hates **2** love **3** like **4** likes **5** hate

GRAMMAR A **1** False **2** True **3** True **4** False **5** False **6** True

GRAMMAR B **1** loves, don't like **2** Do your parents like, do **3** don't like, hates **4** Does Marcus like, doesn't **5** practices, watch **6** Do you think, don't

GRAMMAR C **1** hates **2** likes **3** doesn't like **4** loves **5** love **6** swims

GRAMMAR D **1** Do, Does **2** thinks, think **3** play, do **4** catches, catch **5** do, does **6** use, uses

Lesson 2

VOCABULARY A **1** going **2** going out **3** going to **4** go to **5** plays **6** go out **7** play **8** go

VOCABULARY B **1** listens to **2** watch **3** listen to **4** watch **5** watches **6** listen to

LISTENING A **1** video games **2** music **3** audiobooks **4** podcasts

LISTENING B **1** like **2** great **3** lot **4** books

GRAMMAR A **1** give orders or instructions **2** the base form **3** don't + verb **4** add *please*

GRAMMAR B **1** watch **2** Don't **3** use **4** Don't **5** please tell **6** Don't turn

GRAMMAR C turn, play, download, tell

GRAMMAR D **1** go see the new *Lord of the Rings* movie **2** don't watch videos all day **3** listen to me **4** buy the tickets online **5** use my headphones **6** don't tell Thomas about the party

Lesson 3

LISTENING A **1** sports event **2** information

LISTENING B **1** c **2** b **3** b **4** a **5** c **6** c

VOCABULARY A **1** race **2** games **3** concerts **4** competitions **5** race **6** game

VOCABULARY B **1** cooking **2** soccer **3** singing **4** basketball **5** rock **6** dancing

WRITING A **1** a **2** b **3** a **4** b

WRITING B **1** Park **2** April **3** shows **4** singing **5** drinks **6** welcome **7** tickets

Unit 4

Lesson 1

READING A **1** False **2** False **3** True **4** True

READING B **1** at a zoo in Santiago, Chile **2** an hour from the zoo **3** her cats **4** have a meeting with colleagues **5** at 11 a.m. and in the afternoon **6** She gives short tours.

VOCABULARY A **1** b **2** b **3** a **4** b

VOCABULARY B **1** walk **2** have **3** get **4** make **5** take **6** go

GRAMMAR A **1** question word **2** *do*/*does* **3** subject **4** verb / verb phrase

GRAMMAR B **1** Where **2** How **3** What **4** Where **5** Why **6** When

GRAMMAR C **1** When do you get up? **2** Where do you have coffee? **3** How does Alice get to work? **4** Who do you talk to at work? **5** What do you have for dinner? **6** Why do your brothers watch a lot of TV?

GRAMMAR D **1** do **2** Why **3** you **4** Who **5** does

Lesson 2

LISTENING A **1** b **2** a **3** a

LISTENING B **1** photographer **2** 10 **3** 9 a.m. **4** often **5** boring **6** goes online

VOCABULARY A **1** in **2** a **3** on **4** at **5** on **6** every **7** three **8** in

VOCABULARY B **1** a **2** b **3** a **4** b **5** b

GRAMMAR A always, usually, often, sometimes, rarely, never **1** after the verb be **2** before the verb **3** at the beginning or end

GRAMMAR B **1** rarely takes **2** is always **3** usually see **4** are never **5** often go out **6** sometimes uses

GRAMMAR C talk rarely–rarely talk, always isn't–isn't always, play sometimes–sometimes play, finish usually–usually finish, watch often–often watch

GRAMMAR D **1** always has coffee **2** is rarely **3** often goes on **4** is never **5** sometimes sleep well

Lesson 3

VOCABULARY A **1** take **2** do **3** take **4** get **5** hang **6** go **7** out **8** cook

VOCABULARY B **1** to **2** housework **3** at **4** shower **5** get **6** go

LISTENING A **1** business owner **2** actor **3** student **4** dog walker

LISTENING B **1** True **2** True **3** False **4** True

WRITING A **1** wake up **2** have breakfast **3** check social media **4** have meetings **5** go home **6** have English class **7** sleep **8** go out **9** go to bed

Unit 5

Lesson 1

READING A **1** False **2** True **3** False **4** False **5** True

READING B **1** Stanley doesn't have neighbors. **2** I don't like the life in noisy cities. **3** the bathrooms are not like tiny airplane bathrooms **4** I think I pay $350 a month for everything. It's a good deal. **5** it's worth around $1,000,000

VOCABULARY A **1** house **2** neighborhood **3** apartment **4** city **5** street **6** neighbors **7** garden **8** yard

VOCABULARY B **1** neighbors, street **2** neighborhood, house **3** yard, garden **4** city, apartment building

GRAMMAR A **1** a **2** b **3** b **4** b

GRAMMAR B **1** big **2** friendly **3** expensive **4** bored **5** interesting

GRAMMAR C **1** small apartment **2** big house **3** young people **4** interesting places

GRAMMAR D **1** is beautiful **2** am excited **3** has, tiny **4** is boring **5** have, unusual **6** has many

GRAMMAR E **1** exciting **2** bored **3** interesting **4** excited **5** boring **6** interested

Lesson 2

VOCABULARY A **1** stop **2** school **3** store **4** building **5** station **6** shop

VOCABULARY B **1** train station **2** library **3** coffee shop **4** high school **5** gym **6** apartment building **7** grocery store **8** bus stop

LISTENING A **1** False **2** True **3** False

LISTENING B **1** b **2** a **3** b **4** a

GRAMMAR A **1** True **2** True **3** False **4** True **5** False

GRAMMAR B **1** is **2** are **3** Is **4** There are **5** There's no **6** Are

GRAMMAR C **1** There's **2** There's no **3** There are **4** There are no **5** Are there **6** There's **7** Are there **8** there are

GRAMMAR D **1** are **2** Is **3** is **4** Are **5** there **6** are

Lesson 3

VOCABULARY A **1** a **2** b **3** b **4** b

VOCABULARY B Students check: Go straight ahead on 1st Street. Go past the grocery store and the restaurant. Turn left on 2nd Street. My place is across from the hospital.

LISTENING A Possible key words: train station, 5th Avenue, bank, Marty's Restaurant, Main Street, Park Avenue, bus stop, lost, map, helpful **1** park **2** turn right **3** Main **4** John **5** asks people **6** phones

LISTENING B **1** False **2** True **3** False **4** True **5** True **6** False

WRITING A **1** Street St **2** Second 2nd **3** Avenue Ave **4** building bldg. **5** See you CU

WRITING B Take Jones Street to Fourth Avenue and turn left. Go straight for five blocks to Martin Street and turn right. Go past the big yellow building. My house is at 313 Martin Street. See you at 6!

Unit 6

Lesson 1

READING A **1** c **2** b **3** b **4** c

VOCABULARY A **1** b **2** a **3** b **4** b

VOCABULARY B **1** embarrassed **2** afraid **3** surprised **4** mad

GRAMMAR A **1** True **2** False **3** False **4** True **5** True

GRAMMAR B **1** writing **2** is **3** are they **4** isn't **5** are **6** is talking

GRAMMAR C **1** look **2** buy **3** read **4** have **5** write **6** not check

GRAMMAR D **1** is waiting **2** am not lying **3** are studying **4** am getting **5** are you looking **6** is not using

Lesson 2

VOCABULARY A **1** keyboard **2** webcam **3** microphone **4** headphones **5** smartphone **6** mouse

VOCABULARY B **1** webcam **2** smartphone **3** tablet **4** microphone **5** keyboard

LISTENING A **1** smartphones **2** headphones **3** tablets

LISTENING B **1** Opinion **2** Opinion **3** Opinion **4** Fact **5** Fact **6** Opinion

GRAMMAR A **1** a **2** b **3** b **4** b

GRAMMAR B **1** is speaking **2** uses **3** listen **4** are filming **5** Are you uploading **6** watch

GRAMMAR C **1** are you doing **2** am filming **3** Do you make **4** spend **5** do you upload **6** have **7** am using

GRAMMAR D **1** b **2** a **3** a **4** b **5** a **6** b

Lesson 3

LISTENING A **1** b **2** b **3** a

LISTENING B **1** give honest opinions, say how they feel **2** the product doesn't work, they're mad **3** look at other sites

VOCABULARY A **1** upload **2** send **3** update **4** a comment **5** a selfie **6** viral

VOCABULARY B **1** b **2** b **3** b **4** a **5** a **6** b

WRITING A **1** TechCam R620 **2** webcam **3** films vlogs, takes pictures **4** excellent **5** black **6** works for any computer system **7** $60

WRITING B Students check: It's good condition, It's about three years old. It has a DVD player and a wide screen. I'm selling it for $150.

Unit 7

Lesson 1

VOCABULARY A **1** foot **2** chest **3** elbow **4** head **5** knee **6** waist **7** ankle

VOCABULARY B **1** neck **2** wrist **3** thigh **4** back **5** ankle **6** arm

READING A **1** b **2** a

READING B **1** hard **2** new **3** head **4** not good **5** a lot of

GRAMMAR A **1** abilities **2** possible **3** can't **4** verbs **5** cannot

GRAMMAR B **1** can **2** can't **3** Can **4** can't **5** can't **6** can

GRAMMAR C **1** can **2** can't **3** can't **4** can't **5** can **6** can

GRAMMAR D **1** to get, get **2** can, can't **3** comes, come **4** cans, can **5** cant, can't **6** drives, drive

Lesson 2

VOCABULARY A **1** hit **2** throw **3** kick **4** bounce **5** pass **6** catch **7** hold **8** touch

VOCABULARY B **1** bounce **2** hits **3** touch **4** catch **5** hold **6** throws

LISTENING A **1** Santi **2** tennis **3** not frequently **4** baseball **5** doesn't go to work

LISTENING B **1** c **2** b **3** b **4** c

GRAMMAR A **1** b **2** a **3** b **4** b **5** a **6** a

GRAMMAR B **1** fast **2** carefully **3** kicks the ball hard **4** gently **5** quickly **6** angrily **7** easily **8** well

GRAMMAR C **1** well **2** fast **3** hard **4** quietly **5** easily

GRAMMAR D **1** easily **2** carefully **3** angrily **4** gently **5** well **6** fast

Lesson 3

VOCABULARY A **1** bend **2** stretches **3** lift **4** pushes **5** Twist **6** pull

VOCABULARY B **1** stretch **2** stand **3** push **4** Bend **5** twist **6** lift

LISTENING A **1** exercise **2** instructions

LISTENING B **1** a **2** b **3** a **4** b **5** b **6** a

WRITING A **1** athletes train **2** do exercises **3** how to stretch **4** twist your body **5** hit the ball hard

WRITING B **1** good, well **2** bad, badly **3** hit, kick **4** can't, can **5** ancle, ankle

Unit 8

Lesson 1

READING A **1** b **2** a **3** c **4** a **5** b

READING B **1** Som Tum, Yam Plah Duk Foo **2** salty, spicy **3** chili, fish **4** lemon, lime **5** unhealthy, healthy

VOCABULARY A **1** Spicy **2** breakfast **3** disgusting **4** a snack **5** unhealthy

VOCABULARY B **1** sweet **2** dinner **3** snack **4** healthy **5** spicy

GRAMMAR A **1** both singular and plural **2** Uncountable **3** countable **4** How many **5** How much

GRAMMAR B **1** some **2** many **3** is **4** much **5** a

GRAMMAR C **1** eight people **2** some eggs **3** much **4** a cup **5** about a cup **6** 45 minutes

GRAMMAR D **1** egg, eggs **2** much, many **3** a, some **4** an, a **5** apple, apples **6** a, some

Lesson 2

VOCABULARY A **1** carbohydrates **2** chocolate **3** eggs **4** fat **5** yogurt **6** fruit **7** fish **8** rice

VOCABULARY B **1** fish **2** beans **3** cheese **4** potatoes **5** cereal **6** vegetables

LISTENING A **1** bread **2** pasta **3** chicken **4** fries

LISTENING B **1** a **2** b **3** b **4** b

GRAMMAR A **1** c **2** c **3** a **4** a **5** b **6** b

GRAMMAR B **1** This **2** this **3** that **4** These **5** those **6** That **7** this **8** these

GRAMMAR C **1** this **2** those **3** these **4** this **5** that **6** that **7** That

GRAMMAR D **1** those **2** This **3** these **4** that **5** that **6** these

Lesson 3

VOCABULARY A **1** knife **2** fork **3** baking dish **4** Add **5** cup **6** bowl

VOCABULARY B **1** baking dish **2** bake **3** fork **4** cup **5** slice **6** add

LISTENING A **1** a **2** b **3** a **4** b **5** a

LISTENING B **1** a cake **2** an apple pie **3** on the apples **4** around the pie crust **5** an hour

WRITING A **1** vegetables **2** baking dish **3** add **4** oven **5** mix

WRITING B **1** Beats, Beat **2** ad, add **3** Moving, Move **4** to add, add **5** Mixes, Mix

Unit 9

Lesson 1

READING A **1** Shanghai **2** sights **3** 24 **4** river **5** London

READING B **1** can't visit **2** all of **3** helicopter **4** tourist attraction **5** a lot of **6** loves

VOCABULARY A **1** a **2** b **3** c **4** b **5** a

VOCABULARY B **1** vacation **2** sights **3** sounds **4** tour **5** continent **6** tourist attractions

GRAMMAR A **1** b **2** c **3** a **4** a **5** a

GRAMMAR B **1** to go **2** visiting **3** planning / to plan **4** to travel **5** taking

GRAMMAR C **1** to buy **2** to go **3** going **4** being **5** having

Lesson 2

LISTENING A **1** place **2** love **3** high season **4** families **5** low season

LISTENING B **1** a **2** a **3** b **4** a **5** b

VOCABULARY A **1** take a trip **2** stay at a hotel **3** take a guided tour **4** see the sights **5** take a taxi **6** buy a souvenir

VOCABULARY B **1** see the sights **2** take a guided tour **3** take a trip **4** take a taxi **5** buy a souvenir **6** stay at a hotel

GRAMMAR A **1** should **2** are possible **3** infinitive **4** base form

GRAMMAR B **1** I think we should take a taxi. **2** Could we buy some souvenirs today? **3** You should go on a guided tour tomorrow. **4** Should I stay at a hotel tonight? **5** We could go to a museum this afternoon. **6** You should take lots of photos of the Taj Mahal.

GRAMMAR C **1** could **2** could **3** shouldn't **4** could **5** could **6** could **7** should

GRAMMAR D **1** should visit **2** could go **3** could finish **4** should wear **5** should go **6** could pay

Lesson 3

VOCABULARY A **1** blouse **2** hat **3** dress **4** sandals **5** sneakers **6** jacket

VOCABULARY B **1** suit **2** boots **3** sweatshirt **4** tie **5** gloves **6** jeans

LISTENING A **1** packing for **2** hot and cold

LISTENING B **1** a **2** b **3** a **4** a **5** a **6** b

WRITING A **1** could **2** should **3** T-shirts **4** hat **5** coat **6** guided tour

Unit 10

Lesson 1

READING A **1** was **2** made **3** decided **4** graduated **5** trained **6** wrote

READING B 2, 4, 6, 1, 3, 5

VOCABULARY A **1** opportunity **2** degree **3** angry **4** lucky **5** support

VOCABULARY B **1** opportunity **2** angry **3** well-known **4** support **5** degree **6** lucky

GRAMMAR A **1** ed **2** e **3** vowel **4** consonant **6** irregular

GRAMMAR B **1** wanted **2** cried **3** dropped **4** received **5** studied

GRAMMAR C **1** lived **2** moved **3** went **4** got **5** studied **6** said **7** became **8** died

Lesson 2

VOCABULARY A **1** hang out with friends **2** go on a date **3** go out dancing **4** have a party **5** see a movie **6** eat out at a restaurant

VOCABULARY B **1** see a movie **2** go out dancing **3** eat out at a restaurant **4** go on a date **5** hang out with friends **6** have a party

GRAMMAR A **1** a **2** a **3** a **4** b

GRAMMAR B **1** did you do **2** went **3** see **4** didn't **5** Were you **6** was

GRAMMAR C **1** speaks, speak **2** does, did **3** he did, did he **4** went, go **5** did no, didn't **6** doesn't, didn't

GRAMMAR D **1** did he start **2** did not have / didn't have **3** did not win / didn't win **4** Did he make **5** he did **6** Did people help **7** Did he stop **8** he did not / he didn't

LISTENING A **1** didn't go out **2** Gabriel **3** didn't go out a lot

LISTENING B **1** b **2** a **3** b **4** a **5** a

Lesson 3

VOCABULARY A **1** a **2** a **3** b **4** b **5** b **6** b

VOCABULARY B **1** have an argument **2** make a decision **3** get lost **4** make a new friend **5** have fun **6** get upset **7** make a mistake

LISTENING A **1** False **2** True **3** True **4** True

LISTENING B **1** bad **2** working **3** do things differently **4** is

WRITING A **1** In the end **2** Later **3** First **4** Next

WRITING B 4, 2, 3, 1

Unit 11

Lesson 1

READING A **1** False **2** False **3** True **4** True **5** True **6** True

READING B **1** b **2** c **3** b **4** c **5** c

VOCABULARY A **1** ready **2** clear **3** forget **4** plan **5** appointment **6** remember

VOCABULARY B **1** remember, remember **2** an appointment, plan

GRAMMAR A **1** be **2** plans **3** base form **4** subject

GRAMMAR B **1** I am going to plan my day. **2** Miriam is going to meet me later. **3** Are you going to go on vacation next week?

GRAMMAR C **1** b **2** a **3** c **4** c **5** a **6** c

Lesson 2

VOCABULARY A **1** poor **2** save **3** buy **4** sell **5** rich **6** spend

VOCABULARY B **1** poor **2** sell **3** spend **4** rich **5** save **6** buy

LISTENING A **1** False **2** True **3** True **4** True **5** False

LISTENING B **1** b **2** a **3** b **4** a **5** b

GRAMMAR A **1** b **2** c **3** c **4** a

GRAMMAR B **1** Make an apple pie for me! **2** Horatio cooked dinner for me. **3** Are they going to buy a ticket for you? **4** I am going to sell some clothes to my friends. **5** We can make gifts for each other.

GRAMMAR C **1** for **2** him **3** to **4** buy **5** them **6** him

GRAMMAR D **1** show that email to my boss **2** make gifts for our friends **3** buy those shoes for me **4** sell the car to our neighbors **5** Give that cell phone to me

Lesson 3

VOCABULARY A **1** outdoors **2** in an office **3** start a business **4** working from home **5** overseas **6** managing people

VOCABULARY B **1** work overseas **2** work from home **3** working in an office **4** manage people **5** start a business **6** work outdoors

LISTENING A **1** plans for the future **2** overseas

LISTENING B **1** create a new company **2** doesn't like **3** boss **4** some **5** never

WRITING A **1** because **2** because **3** so **4** because **5** because **6** so **7** so

WRITING B **1** for me, me **2** to people, people **3** going, am going **4** oversea, overseas **5** because, so

Unit 12

Lesson 1

READING A — **1** True **2** False **3** True **4** False **5** True

READING B — **1** Aparados da Serra National Park **2** about 20°C **3** about 37°C **4** the Grand Canyon **5** Aparados da Serra National Park

VOCABULARY A — **1** a **2** b **3** b **4** a **5** a

VOCABULARY B — **1** temperature **2** cool **3** tropical **4** flight **5** equator

GRAMMAR A — **1** False **2** True **3** False **4** True **5** True **6** True **7** False

GRAMMAR B — **1** a **2** a **3** b **4** b **5** b **6** b **7** a

Lesson 2

VOCABULARY A — **1** volcano **2** river **3** hills **4** waterfall **5** mountains **6** lake **7** desert **8** forest

VOCABULARY B — **1** mountain **2** lakes **3** river **4** volcano **5** waterfalls **6** hills **7** forest **8** desert

LISTENING A — **1** b **2** a **3** b

LISTENING B — **1** a **2** b **3** b **4** a **5** a

GRAMMAR A — **1** a future plan **2** a general truth **3** a single action in the past **4** true in the present

GRAMMAR B — **1** saw **2** am going **3** love **4** are going to fly **5** studied **6** Are you working

GRAMMAR C — **1** c **2** b **3** a **4** a **5** c

GRAMMAR D — **1** arrived **2** went **3** feel **4** moves **5** am watching **6** makes **7** are going to fly

Lesson 3

VOCABULARY A — **1** b **2** b **3** a **4** a **5** b **6** a **7** a **8** a

VOCABULARY B — **1** amazing **2** awesome **3** beautiful **4** popular **5** attractive **6** boring **7** fantastic **8** ugly

LISTENING A — **1** go on vacation **2** different from

LISTENING B — **1** c **2** b **3** a **4** b **5** c

WRITING A — **1** Who Enjoys This Place **2** What to Do Here **3** How to Get Here **4** Where to Stay **5** Where to Learn More

Exam Training

Reading

SHORT MESSAGES WITH MULTIPLE-CHOICE QUESTIONS — **1** c **2** c **3** b **4** a **5** a **6** b

ONE TEXT WITH MULTIPLE-CHOICE QUESTIONS — **1** a **2** b **3** c **4** c **5** b

Listening

COMPLETE THE INFORMATION — **1** time **2** April 10th **3** 9 a.m. **4** 6 p.m. **5** April 13th

ONE LONGER TEXT, MULTIPLE-CHOICE QUESTIONS — **1** a **2** c **3** b **4** b **5** b **6** c

MATCHING TO PICTURES — **1** c **2** b **3** b **4** b **5** a

Writing

WRITING A — **1** True **2** False **3** True **4** False **5** True

WRITING B — third

WRITING C — **1** What **do** you think **2** ~~sport great~~ **great sport** **3** ~~fun really~~ **really fun** **4** There ~~are~~ **is** **5** ~~Has~~ **Have**

Unit 1

Track 01

Sam: Hi, I'm Sam.
Liz: Hello, Sam. I'm Liz. Nice to meet you.
Sam: It's nice to meet you, too. Are you a new student?
Liz: Yes, I am. Today is my first day.
Sam: Oh, great. Welcome to our school!
Liz: Thank you! My first class is Spanish. Are you in that class?
Sam: No, I'm not. My first class is French. I have Spanish at 3 p.m.
Liz: I see. Is that your French teacher?
Sam: No, that's Mr. Sanchez. He's your Spanish teacher!
Liz: Oh, really? He looks like a very nice teacher.
Sam: He is. The French teacher is very nice, too. That's Ms. Martin.
Liz: Oh, good. I want to take French next year.
Sam: Well, have a great first day at school.
Liz: Thanks, Sam. Bye!
Sam: See you later!

Track 02

Fran: Thank you for calling First Bank. My name is Fran. How can I help you?
Jane: Hello, I have a problem with my online account.
Fran: I can help you with that. What is your full name?
Jane: It's Jane Hansen. My last name is spelled H-A-N-S-E-N.
Fran: Thank you. I have your account here. What is your date of birth?
Jane: It's September 23, 1998.
Fran: OK. And what is your address?
Jane: It's 2513 Cedar Road.
Fran: Great, thank you very much. And what is the problem?
Jane: My password for my online banking doesn't work.
Fran: OK. I can fix that for you. There, all done. This is your new password. It's capital J, 8, lower case b, 7-2-1-3. You can change that online if you like.
Jane: Thank you.
Fran: You're welcome. I see your phone number is 555-697-4398. Is that correct?
Jane: No, it isn't. My new number is 555-697-2105.
Fran: OK. I have your new number now. Is there anything else?
Jane: No, that's all. Thank you very much.
Fran: You're welcome. Have a nice day!

Unit 2

Track 01

1 My sister has an exciting job as an interior designer.
2 I want to be a successful business owner someday.
3 A marketer is a necessary job for most companies.
4 My mother is a happy employee and she loves her job!
5 My father has an unusual job because he works at night!

Track 02

Mark: This is a nice photo, Alicia.
Alicia: Thank you, Mark. It's my family.
Mark: Is that Stephen on the right?
Alicia: Yes, that's my husband, Stephen. You know each other.
Mark: Yes, we do! And are those your children?
Alicia: Yes, that's my son, Daniel. He's seven. And my daughter, Julie, is next to him. She's five.
Mark: And are those your parents in the middle?
Alicia: Yes, that's my dad, George, and my mom, Vicky.
Mark: And who's taking the photo?
Alicia: My brother, Ryan. I have other photos of him, too, with my sister, Diane.

Track 03

Mark: ... and where are you in the photo?
Alicia: Oh, we're at my parent's house. We're in their backyard.
Mark: What a great day to take a photo.
Alicia: Yes, sunny and warm is my favorite weather.
Mark: Well, I need to get back to work. What a nice family you have!
Alicia: Thank you very much. See you later!

Track 04

This is a photo of my dad, Jorge. In the photo, he's at his job at the pharmacy where he works as a pharmacist. He's 55 years old, he's married to my mom, Camila, and he has three children: me, my sister Daniela, and my brother Raúl. He really loves his job and he's very good at it. He knows a lot about science. It's an important skill! He knows many things about medicine, too. His degree is from a medical school, and he uses his knowledge to help people every day. I want to be a pharmacist, too, just like my dad.

Track 05

My other family members have interesting jobs, too. My mom is an interpreter. She knows English and Spanish very well. My sister is a journalist. She works for a newspaper and she writes about travel. My brother is 17 years old, so he's still a student in high school. He wants to be a pilot. He loves planes and he loves to travel.

Unit 3

Track 01

Nate: Hey Susie, do you like sports?

Susie: I like some sports, Nate. I love tennis, but I hate soccer.

Nate: Oh, really? I like soccer. I think it's exciting. Do you like basketball?

Susie: I like watching it, but I don't like playing it. My brother thinks it's great. He plays basketball a lot and he watches it on TV all the time.

Nate: I see. I like basketball, but I love swimming.

Susie: Yeah, swimming is a great sport. I enjoy it a lot, and it's my sister's favorite sport. She swims every day.

Nate: Wow! She really loves it!

Track 02

Joe: Hey, Juan, do you like listening to music in your free time?

Juan: No, I don't. I prefer video games. What about you, Joe?

Joe: I love listening to music. I think it's great. How about you, Becca? Do you like video games?

Becca: No. I really like listening to audiobooks. I listen to them a lot. I don't like reading books.

Joe: Yeah. I like listening to books, too. Cindy, do you listen to audiobooks, or do you read books?

Cindy: I don't like books or audiobooks. I love listening to podcasts. That's really fun.

Joe: Podcasts? That's interesting!

Track 03

Do you like to ride bikes for fun or for sport? Then don't forget to come to this weekend's bike festival. We have many cycling events on both Saturday and Sunday. It's fun for the whole family! We also have bike races, awards for the best bikes, and food and drink. All ages are welcome to come. Tickets are on sale at the festival. It's 10 dollars for adults and 6 dollars for children 12 and under. The festival starts at 10 a.m. on both weekend days. The races take place in and around town for cyclists 14 years old and up. Visit our website for more details. Join us at Central Park for some cycling fun!

Unit 4

Track 01

Katy: We have a lot of English homework this week, Bill!

Bill: I agree, Katy! Where do you do your English homework?

Katy: I often do it in my bedroom.

Bill: Why do you study in your bedroom?

Katy: It's very quiet, and I have a nice desk. When do you do your homework?

Bill: I do it after dinner. So, I usually do it around 8 p.m.

Katy: Who do you study with?

Bill: I sometimes study with my brother. He's very smart and helpful.

Katy: What does your brother study?

Bill: He studies math and science.

Katy: Ah, that sounds interesting!

Track 02

Mike: Hey, Darren, how's work?

Darren: Work is very busy, Mike. I sometimes finish at 8 or 9 o'clock at night.

Mike: Really? That's a lot of hours.

Darren: I know. I am often tired when I go home. I have a difficult project at work right now. It's interesting, but it's hard work.

Mike: Is graphic design always this hard?

Darren: It's usually not very difficult. But two or three times a year, I work a lot of hours.

Mike: Do you work on weekends?

Darren: Sometimes. But I make a lot of money when I'm busy, so it's OK.

Track 03

Darren: How about you? How's your job?

Mike: It's great. I have a new job. I work as a photographer for a travel magazine.

Darren: That sounds great. Do you work a lot of hours?

Mike: Well, I usually work 8 hours a day, but I sometimes work 10. I start work in the office at 9 a.m.

Darren: What do you do in the office?

Mike: I look at photos and meet with colleagues. I often leave the office to do my work, which is good. I hate being in the office all day.

Darren: Yes, I know the feeling!

Mike: So, things are really exciting at work. But my home life is boring. I go home around 6 p.m. I go online for a while, then I have dinner and watch TV. I go to bed at 11 p.m. I need to go out more.

Darren: Well, you're out with me right now.

Mike: Yes, you're right!

Track 04

Cassandra

I'm a very busy person. I run my own business, and I work six days a week. I never do housework. I rarely have time to do the things I love, like cooking. My perfect day is to make a nice dinner for my family. It's Sunday, so that's what I'm doing today!

Sebastian

I'm not home very often. I work five nights a week in the theater. I'm often very busy, so I don't get to fix things around my house. My perfect day is to spend time at home and make it look nice.

Charlotte

I like going to the gym, but I rarely go there. I have lots of time. I don't have a job, so I don't have a lot of work to keep me busy. I just study, watch TV or go online, and go out with friends. I want to make a change, so my perfect day is to go to the gym and exercise. I need it!

Leonardo

I love dogs. I spend lots of time with them, and I get money for it, too. I usually walk the dogs in my neighborhood, but we don't have a park nearby. So my perfect day is to take the dogs to the city park and spend the afternoon there.

Unit 5

Track 01

1 This neighborhood is beautiful.
2 I am excited to move today.
3 She has a tiny kitchen, so she doesn't cook.
4 Paul thinks the library is boring.
5 Jason and Diana have an unusual house.
6 This building has many rooms for us to use.

Track 02

Claudia: Do you like life in the city, Diego?

Diego: It's OK, Claudia. I like the coffee shops and restaurants near my house. It's easy to get around, too. But I prefer life in the country.

Claudia: Oh, really?

Diego: Yes. There are a lot of parks in the city, but I don't live near one. I miss trees, and peace and quiet.

Claudia: I like living in the city. There are a lot of things to do and places to hang out with friends.

Diego: I don't have many friends. I'm new here, so I spend a lot of time alone.

Track 03

Claudia: Do you want to join me and my friends tomorrow? We study in the library downtown every Thursday afternoon. The library's a long way from my house, but I really enjoy being there.

Diego: Sure. When do you meet?

Claudia: I finish my classes at 4 p.m., so we meet at 4:30. We stay for about an hour or two, then we go home to have dinner.

Diego: Where is the library?

Claudia: It's two blocks from the train station. Do you know where the train station is?

Diego: Yes, I do.

Claudia: OK. Let's meet at the train station at 4:20. Then, we can walk to the library together.

Diego: Thanks so much! Well, maybe life in the city isn't so bad after all.

Track 04

Conversation 1

María: Excuse me, how do I get to the train station?

José: There are two train stations, the downtown station and the park station. Which station do you want?

María: The station by the park.

José: OK. Go straight ahead on this street. This is Baker Street. Then turn right on 5th Avenue. The train station is on the left. It's after the bank.

María: Thank you very much.

José: You're welcome.

Conversation 2

Henry: I think we're lost, Beth. Do you have the map?

Beth: Yes, Henry. I think it's in my bag. Here is it. Let's see, we're on Bridge Street. We want to go to Marty's Restaurant. That's on Main Street.

Henry: No, the restaurant is on Park Avenue. Let me look at the text from John. Yes, it's Park Avenue.

Beth: Oh, no. That's a long way from here. Maybe there's a bus stop.

Henry: Yes, I see one. Let's go there.

Conversation 3

Jack: I'm not sure which way to go now. Is it this way?

Raquel: I don't think so, Jack. I think it's this way, but I'm not sure.

Jack: What do you usually do when you are lost, Raquel?

Raquel: I use the map on my phone. What about you?

Jack: I don't usually have my phone with me. I ask a person on the street for help.

Raquel: Yes, that's a good idea. But people don't always know the way. A map on your phone is always helpful. And I don't see any people here now.

Jack: Maybe you're right. Let's look at your phone.

Unit 6

Track 01

1 I use social media every day. I'm looking at my profile right now.
2 I spend an hour online every day. I'm buying shoes at the moment.
3 She is reading an employee's profile. That way she can get information from it.
4 I'm having coffee with Lisa. She works in my office.
5 Gary is writing in his blog. He posts something every day.
6 No, I'm not checking my social media! I don't do that at work.

Track 02

Sandra

I work in an electronics store, and people ask me for advice on smartphones. They want to know which one has a good camera. I show them some of the phones in our store, and then they see the price. Some people think the price is very high. I don't know about that, but it's important to have a good phone.

Oliver

For great music, you need a great pair of headphones. But good headphones cost a lot of money. Some people don't want to pay $200 dollars for headphones. I understand that. There are cheap headphones, but music doesn't sound good on them.

Magdalena

With a laptop, you usually have to sit down. I hate that! So, I use a tablet. It's easy to carry in your bag. It does the same things a laptop does. It also takes great photos, and it looks cool, too.

Track 03

I really enjoy buying things online. It's where I go when I want a good deal on products. But how do you know if the product is good? Well, I think I can help. There are some things you can do to help with online shopping. First, look for a photo of the product. You can learn a lot from a photo. Do you like the way it looks? Is it a nice color? Does it look like it is right for you? Great!

Track 04

Then you need to read product reviews. This is very important. People usually give their honest opinions online. They don't lie about how they feel. People often write online reviews when something doesn't work right. They want other people to know. They're mad and want to say something about it! So read these things carefully.

Finally, look at the price of the product. Is it a good price? Maybe it is, but you can look at other online stores and check if there are better prices. So, before you buy that product, check these three things: the photo, the reviews, and the price. Happy shopping!

Unit 7

Track 01

Ian: Julia, can you surf?

Julia: Yes, Ian, I can! I love surfing! Can you?

Ian: No, I can't! The problem is, I can't swim!

Julia: Really? Well, I'm sure you can run. My father can't go running with me this weekend because he's busy at work. Can you come with me?

Ian: Yes, I can, Julia. And I love running!

Julia: Great! Well, can you meet me at the beach on Sunday morning? That's where we usually go running.

Ian: Yes, I can. I'll see you there!

Track 02

Chris: Hey, Santi, what's all this? Is it all yours? You play so many different sports!

Santi: Yes, Chris! Well, I play sports a lot. When I'm not working all weekend!

Chris: When do you have time to do all of this? I mean, I know we play tennis together on Mondays, but what about the other sports? There are some sports I don't know here.

Santi: Well, the black and white ball is for soccer—I play soccer on Wednesday evenings after work.

Chris: And what about the orange ball?

Santi: That ball is for basketball—I can't play basketball very often because the club opens on Thursdays, but I usually work then.

Chris: So is the red and white ball for baseball?

Santi: Yes, it is! That is my favorite sport, and I play every Sunday morning with my team—our team's name is *The Baseball Kings!* We're very good!

Chris: And do you play American football, too? When do you have time for that?

Santi: Usually on Friday afternoons—sometimes I don't go to work just so I can play football! And then I go home. Don't tell anyone!

Track 03

Chris: So why do you play sports so much?

Santi: Well, I have a lot of work to do, which sometimes makes me feel bad, and it also makes me tired. Playing sports makes me feel relaxed.

Chris: Do you want to try a new sport with me?

Santi: Really? Well, OK! I like team sports like football and soccer, but lacrosse is one I really want to try—and it makes you very fit!

Chris: Great, let's do that! I am very busy with work, too, but we can do it on a Sunday afternoon after lunch if you want.

Santi: OK, let's do it! Where do we meet?

Chris: Let's meet at the sports center at 3 p.m., OK?

Santi: Four is better for me. What do you think?

Chris: Yes, that's perfect. See you then!

Track 04

Hello, everyone! Welcome to Fitness Fun! Before we do the class, we need to warm up. Stand still and just breathe in slowly. That's right. In … out … in … out. Perfect! Now twist your body so that you can touch your left foot with your right hand. That's great! And now your right foot with your left hand! Great! Now do that 10 times on each side! Now turn to the left and lift your arms up over your head with the 2-kilogram weights. Push your hands up as far as you can for about 15 seconds. That's it! And now relax! Good job, everyone! I think we're ready to start our class!

Unit 8

Track 01

Hi guys, it's Georgina the cook here! So today, we're looking at how to make a cake for eight people. This is one of my favorite recipes. First, you need some eggs. Many people use three eggs, but for this cake, two is fine. Then, you need to get some flour—you don't need much—I'm adding about two cups. After the flour, we need to add some sugar. People always say to me, "I can't use sugar, it's so unhealthy!" But for this cake, we only use a cup of sugar, not two, as many people do—and it is delicious! Now you need to add some butter into the mix. It's important not to add too much butter. About a cup is fine. Finally, don't leave it in the oven for too long—it needs 45 minutes. Some people leave it in the oven for over 60 minutes, but that's too long. When it's ready, remember to let it cool before you eat it.

Track 02

Marta: Really, Pablo? Are you ordering pizza again?

Pablo: What's wrong with pizza? It has bread! I love bread! Bread has fiber! Bread is healthy!

Ray: Yes, Pablo, but pizza also has a lot of oil, which is fat—and that's not healthy!

Pablo: What are you having, Ray?

Ray: I'm ordering pasta. Lots of healthy carbohydrates for me!

Pablo: What about you, Marta? Are you ordering fish?

Marta: No, I rarely eat fish. But I like meat that has very little fat and a lot of protein, so, I'm ordering chicken. And you, Jen?

Jen: I think I want some fries. Fries are potatoes—they are healthy!

Pablo: That's not healthy! Those fries have a lot of oil in them—like that pizza!

Track 03

Jamie: So, how exactly do we make this, Dad? I have no idea. Grandpa knows, but I can't remember.

Dad: Oh, come on Jamie, it's so easy! We make this evening meal so often!

Jamie: OK. How do we prepare the vegetables?

Dad: You need to slice them with a knife.

Jamie: Then what?

Dad: Well, you have to mix the chicken and the vegetables together ... then put them in the oven, and ... that's it!

Jamie: How long for? About 60 minutes, right?

Dad: No, about half an hour is fine.

Track 04

Jamie: OK, Dad. What do you want to make now?

Dad: Good question. I know! Let's make a cake!

Jamie: Hmm ... I want to make an apple pie.

Dad: OK. I don't mind. I like both of them!

Jamie: So, after I slice the apples and put them in the pie crust, what do we do?

Dad: Well, you just need to put a little sugar and cinnamon on the apples before you put the pie in the oven.

Jamie: Like this?

Dad: Wait! Before you do that, put a little flour around the baking dish so that it doesn't stick. OK?

Jamie: Right, got it. And how long do we bake it for? An hour?

Dad: Exactly! You're getting good at this!

Unit 9

Track 01

Luke: Molly, I'm looking at a website with lots of information on vacations. I want to go to Florida this year. It looks like a really interesting place.

Molly: Oh, yes. Good idea. I love the idea of going to Florida. When is a good time to go? What about in the winter?

Luke: Winter is high season in Florida. A lot of people go there because it's warm. Hotels are busy and the rooms are expensive. Restaurants are very busy, too. I like it when it's quiet. Some people think it's exciting to be with a lot of people, but I think it's hard work.

Molly: I agree. Perhaps summer is a good time to visit.

Luke: In summer, families visit. That's when the schools are closed. The tourist attractions are busy. And it gets very hot in the summer.

Molly: OK. So when is low season in Florida?

Luke: There are fewer tourists in the fall. But there's a good reason for that. The weather is sometimes bad! And I want to spend time on the beach on this vacation. In the fall, you sometimes have to stay in the hotel. Maybe spring is a good time.

Molly: Let me see what the website says. The weather is good in May. And places are quiet. Children are in school, so families don't go. And hotel rooms are cheap. It sounds good.

Luke: I agree. Let's search for hotels.

Track 02

Yes, it's that time of year again, vacation time, when you ask yourself, "How should I get all my clothes into my suitcase?" Well, you don't need to ask yourself anymore, because I have some great ideas for you! The first idea is that you need to think about what you *should* pack, not what you *could* pack! What do I mean by this? Well, if you are visiting a hot country, you should pack a T-shirt, shorts, and, of course, a hat. Why a hat? Well, you should take a hat to make sure you don't get a sunburn on your face! Now, if you are going on vacation in a cold country, you should pack a coat, a scarf, and gloves to stay warm. But you should pack a hat for cold weather, too! Why? Because if your head is warm, you could be much more comfortable, even if it is very cold! The main idea is, don't pack any more than you need!

Unit 10

Track 01

Victoria: Wow, Gabriel! I can't believe we finish this project tomorrow! It's good because we have no social life at the moment. Did you go out last weekend?

Gabriel: No, Victoria, I didn't. The last time was about two weeks ago. I went out to eat at that new Thai restaurant downtown.

Victoria: Ah, the restaurant on Bridge Street? Did you like the food?

Gabriel: Yes, I did! The food was great. But it was next to this club—the music was very loud. We couldn't talk.

Victoria: Oh, I hate that! And we are all working so hard at the moment, we need to relax! Did you stay late again at the office last night?

Gabriel: No, I didn't. But last Wednesday I stayed here until very late. I was so tired the next morning. When was the last time you went out?

Victoria: Well, I didn't go out last weekend, either! But I went to see that new movie, *A Brave Life*, last week, I think that was the last time. Oh, yes, and I went to a concert with some friends about two weeks ago.

Gabriel: You went out a lot, then!

Victoria: Not really. But when this project is over, we can all go out together to celebrate!

Track 02

John

I had a horrible day at work last week! I decided that it would be a good idea to spend some extra money on pens and paper for the office, because we have a big presentation for a client next week. Anyway, my boss called me in for a meeting and said, "Why did you do that? We needed that money for other things!" I felt so stupid!

Nuria

I was at home last night, and I watched TV to try and relax after a very busy day. I got a text message on my cell phone from my boyfriend. He's on a business trip to Thailand, and he sent me a message—he said, "Sorry, Nuria, but I can't come back for three weeks!" Well, I got so upset! So I went out dancing with some friends.

Pete

I really didn't know what to do. Julian is a good employee, but he is always late to the office, and not just a little late—on Wednesday he was late by over an hour! I had to make a decision whether to ask him to change, or just tell him that he didn't have a job. In the end we talked and everything was OK, but it wasn't an easy choice to make.

Ruby

Rebecca and I were at her apartment just chatting about life and watching TV, when she told me that she was going to go on a date with my brother, Irian. I was like, no way, you can't do that! She told me that Irian and she talked for a long time and they have a good relationship. Then we had an argument—she started shouting at me! I couldn't believe it!

Unit 11

Track 01

Karina: Oh no … Miguel! Did you see how much this food is going to cost?! Maybe we should put some things back.

Miguel: You're right, Karina. It's expensive, but we're going to need all this for dinner with Ben and James tonight!

Karina: We're having dinner with Matt and Isobel, not Ben and James! They're coming over at 7:30. I'll make us some pasta.

Miguel: OK. We're trying to save money, and you're right, we spend money all the time! I guess we could sell one of the cars. Then we can save that money for our vacation in Florida next month!

Karina: Wait a minute! We need the cars! OK, look, this week, I'm going to make salad for lunch. We'll save money by not going out!

Miguel: We don't need a car each, Karina! Let's sell one of them! And we can get a box to save money in and add to it every day. What do you think?

Karina: OK, fine. That's a good idea … and we can make gifts for each other for our birthdays next week.

Miguel: Ah, well, the thing is … I really wanted you to buy me a new cell phone …

Track 02

Juan: So, what's next, Will? Do you think it's time to move on and start a business?

Will: You know, Juan, I'd love to do that, but I really don't like the idea of working in an office! I hate being in one place all day. I would really prefer to work outdoors or something like that.

Juan: Would you like to work in construction, for example? But not as someone's employee, right? With your experience in this industry, you could manage people yourself!

Will: Yeah, maybe something like that. But I also like the idea of what you do. Working from home is great! You're in your own space all the time!

Juan: It looks good, but it's hard work. I'm not sure I like it, really. I mean, it's very easy to just stop working and watch TV! And before you know it, you lose an hour! You know, I'd love to work overseas for a year or so—just like you're doing here!

Will: Yes, well, I love it, but take my advice, Juan. You can plan to work overseas for a year or so—but then you'll stay in that country for ten years, just like me!

Unit 12

Track 01

Clara: We are thinking of going on vacation somewhere a bit warmer than where we went last year, not like a desert or anything, obviously. Oh, and we want to be close to some water too, like a lake or river, don't we, Marcos?

Marcos: Exactly!

Agent: Well that's no problem at all—what about a waterfall? Victoria Falls in southern Africa is amazing! But, it would be better to go between April and June, when it's 25–30°C. It can be about 40°C there in October!

Clara: Wow! That's a bit hot for you, isn't it, Marcos?

Marcos: Sure is!

Agent: OK, well, what about something a little cooler, like Bariloche in Argentina? There's a lot of water there—it's on the shore of a lake. The surrounding area also has green forests, rivers, glaciers, and beautiful mountains to explore. The city gets around 800,000 visitors a year. The city is about 770 meters high, and the mountains reach to over 3,500 meters! They look amazing.

Clara: Marcos doesn't like mountains, do you, Marcos? We went to see a volcano a few years ago in Hawaii, Mauna Kea, which is over 4,000 meters.

Marcos: No, I didn't like the volcano. I don't like danger. I like more relaxing vacations.

Agent: I see. Well, what about the Everglades in Florida? There are rivers and lakes! And a lot of animals and plants to see. There are no volcanoes or mountains, and it's about 25°C in the dry season. You can hike and go camping. It's a very beautiful area.

Clara: Well, that sounds great, doesn't it, Marcos?

Marcos: It certainly does!

Track 02

Zoe: So, where are we going to go this year, guys? I think that Mount Everest looks awesome! It's so big! But I think it's going to be quite difficult to organize the trip there. What about you, Nora?

Nora: You're right, Zoe. To be honest, I prefer the idea of the Great Barrier Reef—we all love diving. Sarah, do you remember when we went diving in Greece a few years ago, after Josie's wedding?

Sarah: Yeah, Nora! That was amazing! But what about the harbor of Rio de Janeiro—you can go diving there, too! And the city's really beautiful!

Zoe: I'm more interested in going somewhere more out of town, like Patagonia! So beautiful! Look, I know Rio is popular, but there are so many tourists!

Nora: What, like us, you mean? Come on, Zoe! Don't be boring! Rio is a party city! And it has lots of art galleries to explore.

Zoe: I don't want to look at ugly modern art all week!

Sarah: I have an idea. Let's go see the Aurora Borealis in Norway! That would be fantastic, wouldn't it? And we've never been to northern Europe. And it's very different from last year, when we went to the Victoria Falls in Zimbabwe.

Nora: OK, Sarah, let's do it!

Zoe: Great idea!

Exam Training

Track 01

A lot of people want to do better at work. Our professional development course can help you! We show you how you can manage your time. We also show you how to speak to people in an interview, and lots of other useful things!

It's a very interesting course and you learn a lot. It starts on April 10th. We do the course at our office in the downtown area. You need to be there before 9 a.m. each day. That's when we start work. We work all morning, break for lunch, and then work again in the afternoon. We finish at 6 p.m. It's a three-day course, so it finishes on April 13th. So, does anyone have any questions for now?

Track 02

Mateo: Hi, Emma. How was your weekend?

Emma: Oh, hi, Mateo. I had a good weekend, thanks. I went out to eat on Saturday. It was my sister's birthday, so my family and I went to a new restaurant downtown after work.

Mateo: What restaurant did you go to?

Emma: It was the new Italian restaurant near the train station. We weren't sure exactly where it was, so we got a taxi. The driver knew where it was.

Mateo: And what was the restaurant like?

Emma: It's a nice place, but they made a mistake with our reservation. I reserved a table for six people at seven o'clock under my name. They thought I wanted a table at eight o'clock. But it wasn't a problem. They found a table for us.

Mateo: Do you like Italian food?

Emma: Yes, I do. I know some people find it boring, but I don't. I don't like unusual food. With Italian food, I know what all the dishes are. And the food at this place was really good. Very tasty.

Mateo: What did you have?

Emma: I had pasta with tomato sauce. My sister had pizza with spicy peppers. Too hot for me! And the others all had dessert, but I don't really like sweet things. And it's unhealthy. I like to eat things that are good for me.

Mateo: What did you do after the restaurant?

Emma: We went home. We finished eating at about ten o'clock. We had to wait half an hour for a taxi. And then it took us half an hour to get home. I was tired by that time. How was your weekend?

Track 03

1

Carla: Hi, Pedro. Are you free later?

Pedro: Hi, Carla. Yes. I have a lot of work to do now, but I'm free this afternoon. What are your plans?

Carla: I'm going to meet some friends at the movie theater. There's a new movie we want to see. Do you want to come? It's at three o'clock.

Pedro: That sounds great. See you later!

2

Claire: Tim, are you going out?

Tim: Yes. I'm going to go to the gym.

Claire: Don't forget to wear a coat. It's windy and not very warm outside.

Tim: OK. Do I need my umbrella?

Claire: I don't think so. It's dry, but you need a scarf and gloves.

Tim: OK. Thanks.

3

Owen: Excuse me. Is this Platform 3? I'm looking for the train to Pittsburgh.

Guard: Yes, this is Platform 3, but you need Platform 2 for the train to Pittsburgh. And you need to hurry. You only have five minutes to catch it.

Owen: Oh dear. I don't have a ticket. Can I get one on the train?

Guard: I'm sorry, but no, you can't. You need to go to the ticket office on Platform 1.

Owen: Platform 1. OK. Thanks for your help.

4

Ellie: I'd like to buy this hat but I can't see a price on it. How much is it?

Clerk: That hat is usually $30 dollars, but we have a special offer this week. All the hats are $10 dollars off.

Ellie: So that makes it $20 dollars. OK. Where do I pay?

Clerk: Over there, at the end of the store.

Ellie: Thanks.

5

Lily: Elena, do you play any sports? I'm going to start having tennis lessons on the weekend. Do you want to come?

Elena: That sounds like a good idea, Lily, but I can't. I have a lot of work to do at school, and I don't have much time for sports. I stopped playing basketball because I didn't have time. The only time I have is Friday evening, and I play volleyball then.

Lily: OK. No problem.